JOHN CONSTANTINE, HELLBLAZER: STARING AT THE WALL

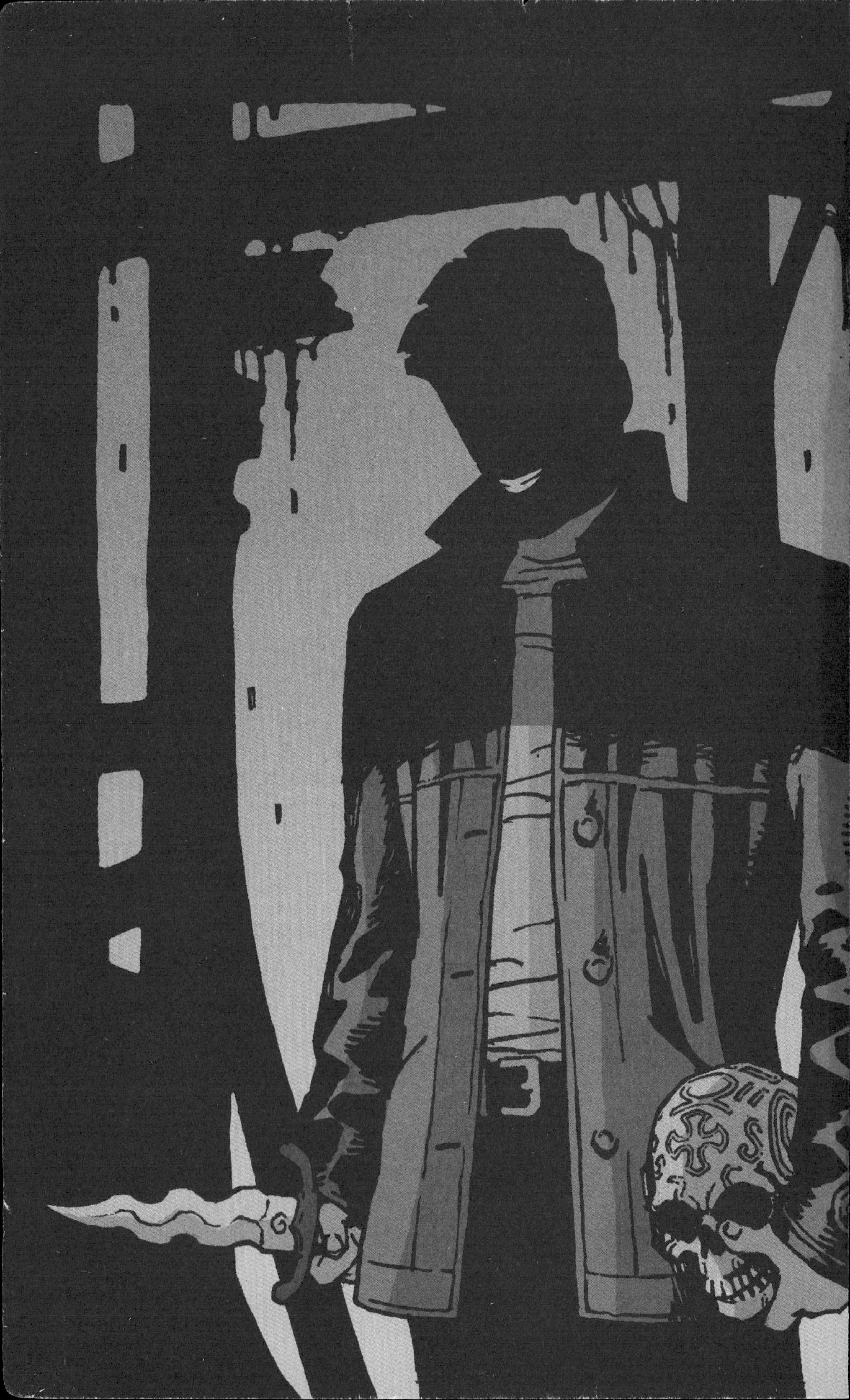

JOHN CONSTANTINE, HELLBLAZER:
STARING AT THE WALL

Mike Carey
Writer

"Bred in the Bone"
Doug Alexander Gregory
Artist

"Staring at the Wall"
Marcelo Frusin
Artist

Lee Loughridge
Colorist

Clem Robins
Letterer

Tim Bradstreet
Original Series Covers

JOHN CONSTANTINE, HELLBLAZER: STARING AT THE WALL

DC Comics, 1700 Broadway, New York, NY 10019
A Warner Bros. Entertainment Company
Printed in Canada. First Printing.

ISBN: 1-4012-0929-7
ISBN 13: 978-1-4012-0929-2

Cover illustration by Tim Bradstreet.

Publication design by Peter Hamboussi.

Logo design by Nessim Higson.

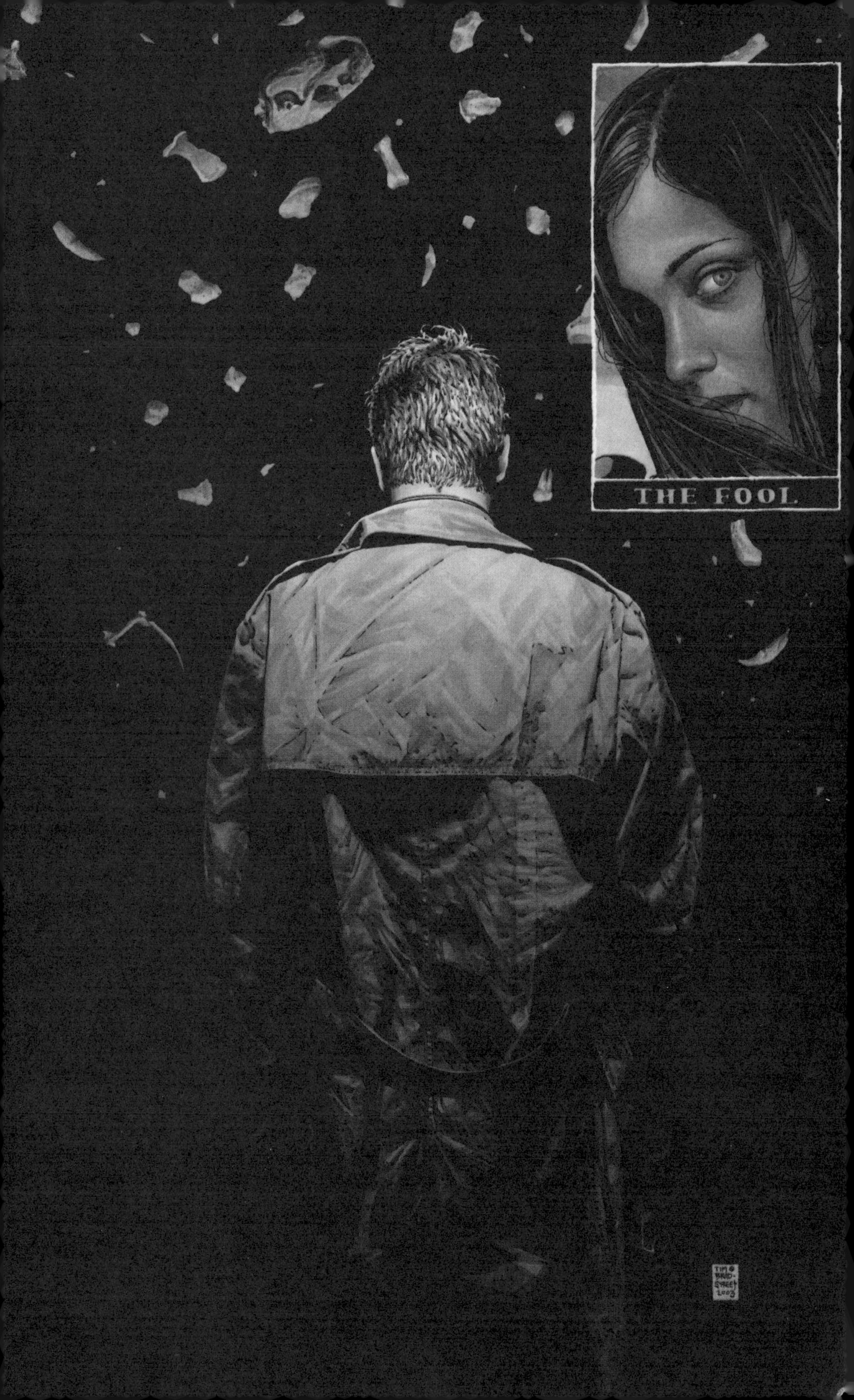
THE FOOL

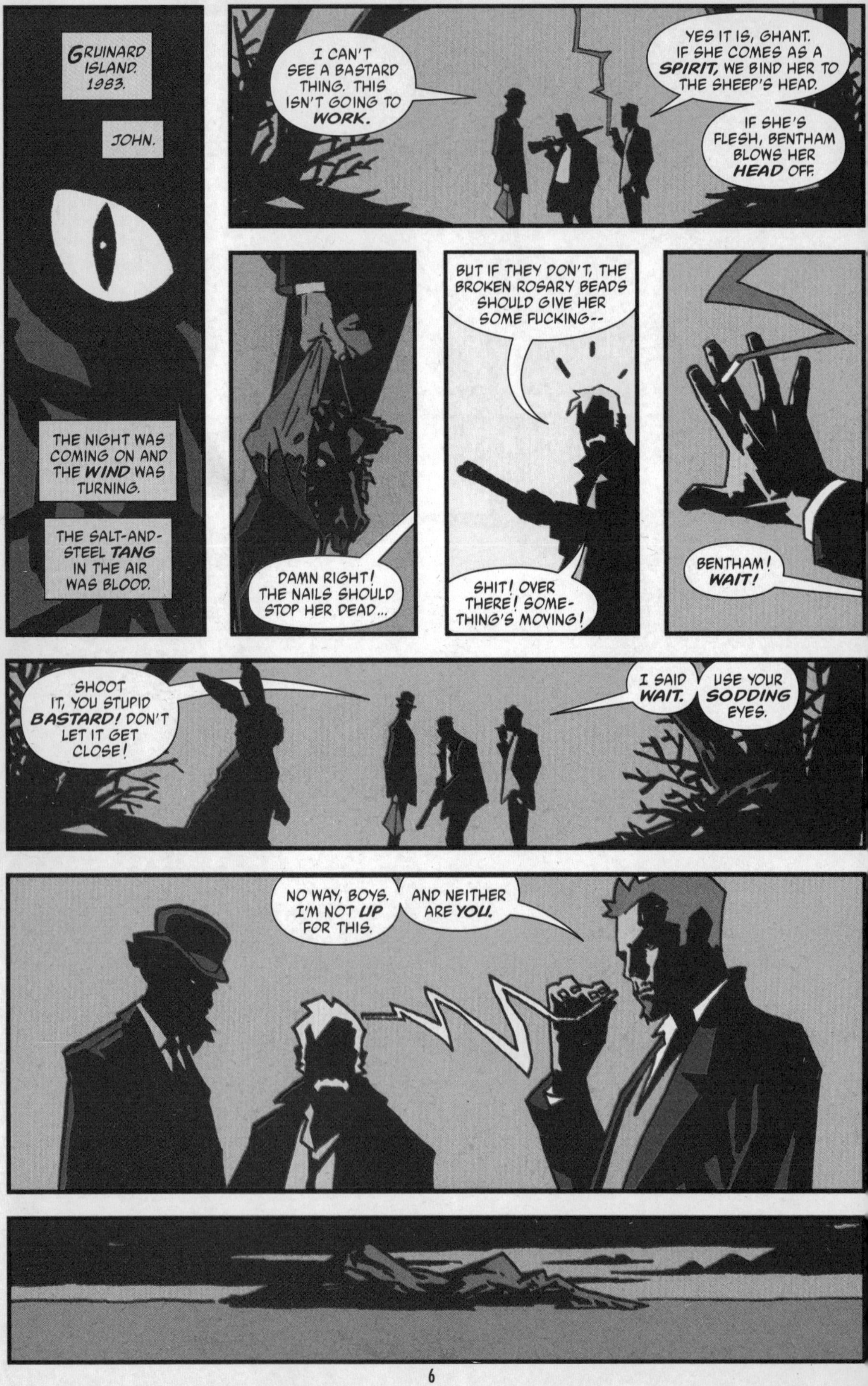
GRUINARD ISLAND. 1983.
JOHN.
I CAN'T SEE A BASTARD THING. THIS ISN'T GOING TO WORK.
YES IT IS, GHANT. IF SHE COMES AS A SPIRIT, WE BIND HER TO THE SHEEP'S HEAD.
IF SHE'S FLESH, BENTHAM BLOWS HER HEAD OFF.
THE NIGHT WAS COMING ON AND THE WIND WAS TURNING.
THE SALT-AND-STEEL TANG IN THE AIR WAS BLOOD.
DAMN RIGHT! THE NAILS SHOULD STOP HER DEAD...
BUT IF THEY DON'T, THE BROKEN ROSARY BEADS SHOULD GIVE HER SOME FUCKING--
SHIT! OVER THERE! SOMETHING'S MOVING!
BENTHAM! WAIT!
SHOOT IT, YOU STUPID BASTARD! DON'T LET IT GET CLOSE!
I SAID WAIT.
USE YOUR SODDING EYES.
NO WAY, BOYS. I'M NOT UP FOR THIS.
AND NEITHER ARE YOU.

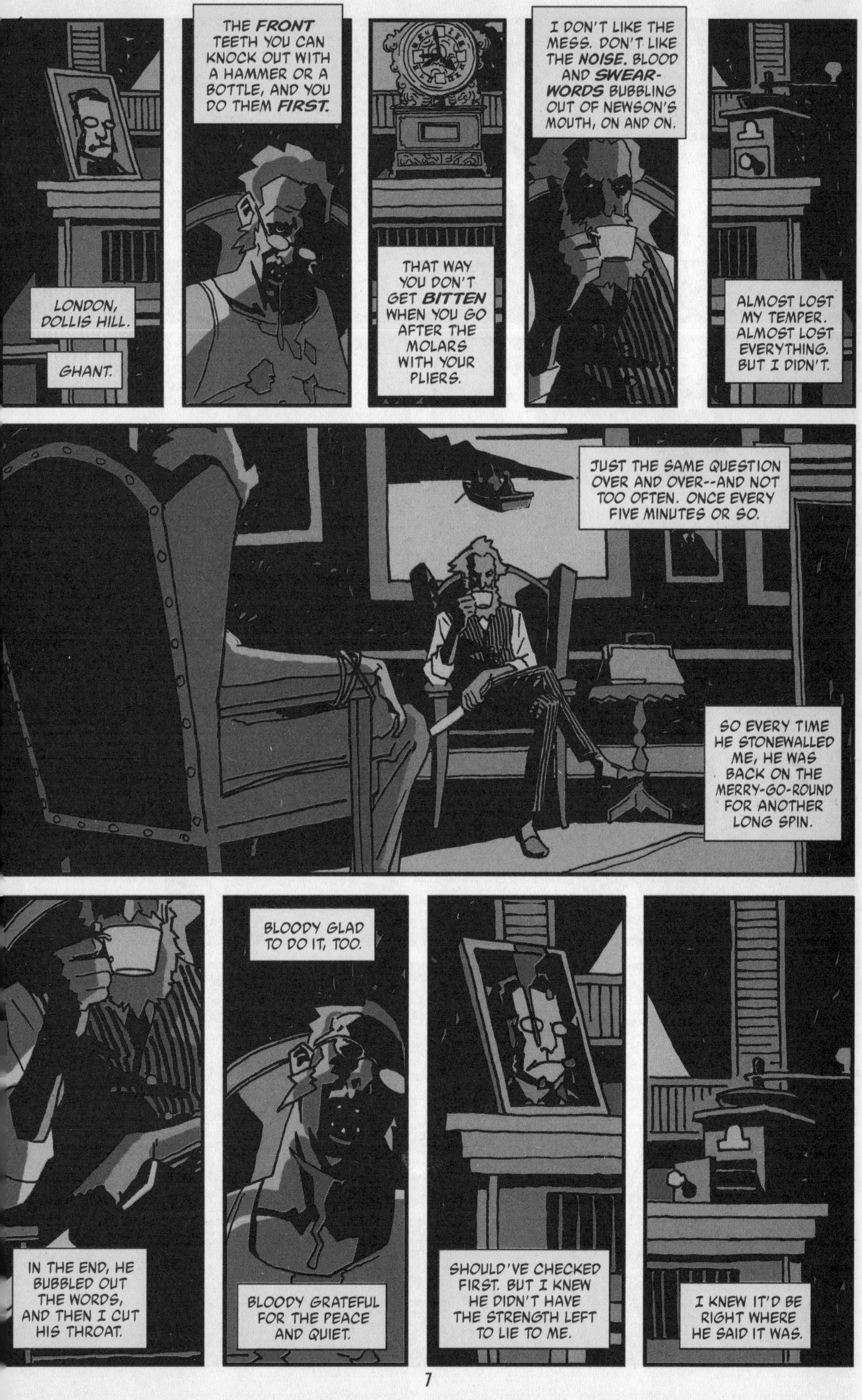
LONDON, DOLLIS HILL.
GHANT.
THE FRONT TEETH YOU CAN KNOCK OUT WITH A HAMMER OR A BOTTLE, AND YOU DO THEM FIRST.
THAT WAY YOU DON'T GET BITTEN WHEN YOU GO AFTER THE MOLARS WITH YOUR PLIERS.
I DON'T LIKE THE MESS. DON'T LIKE THE NOISE. BLOOD AND SWEAR-WORDS BUBBLING OUT OF NEWSON'S MOUTH, ON AND ON.
ALMOST LOST MY TEMPER. ALMOST LOST EVERYTHING. BUT I DIDN'T.
JUST THE SAME QUESTION OVER AND OVER--AND NOT TOO OFTEN. ONCE EVERY FIVE MINUTES OR SO.
SO EVERY TIME HE STONEWALLED ME, HE WAS BACK ON THE MERRY-GO-ROUND FOR ANOTHER LONG SPIN.
IN THE END, HE BUBBLED OUT THE WORDS, AND THEN I CUT HIS THROAT.
BLOODY GLAD TO DO IT, TOO.
BLOODY GRATEFUL FOR THE PEACE AND QUIET.
SHOULD'VE CHECKED FIRST. BUT I KNEW HE DIDN'T HAVE THE STRENGTH LEFT TO LIE TO ME.
I KNEW IT'D BE RIGHT WHERE HE SAID IT WAS.

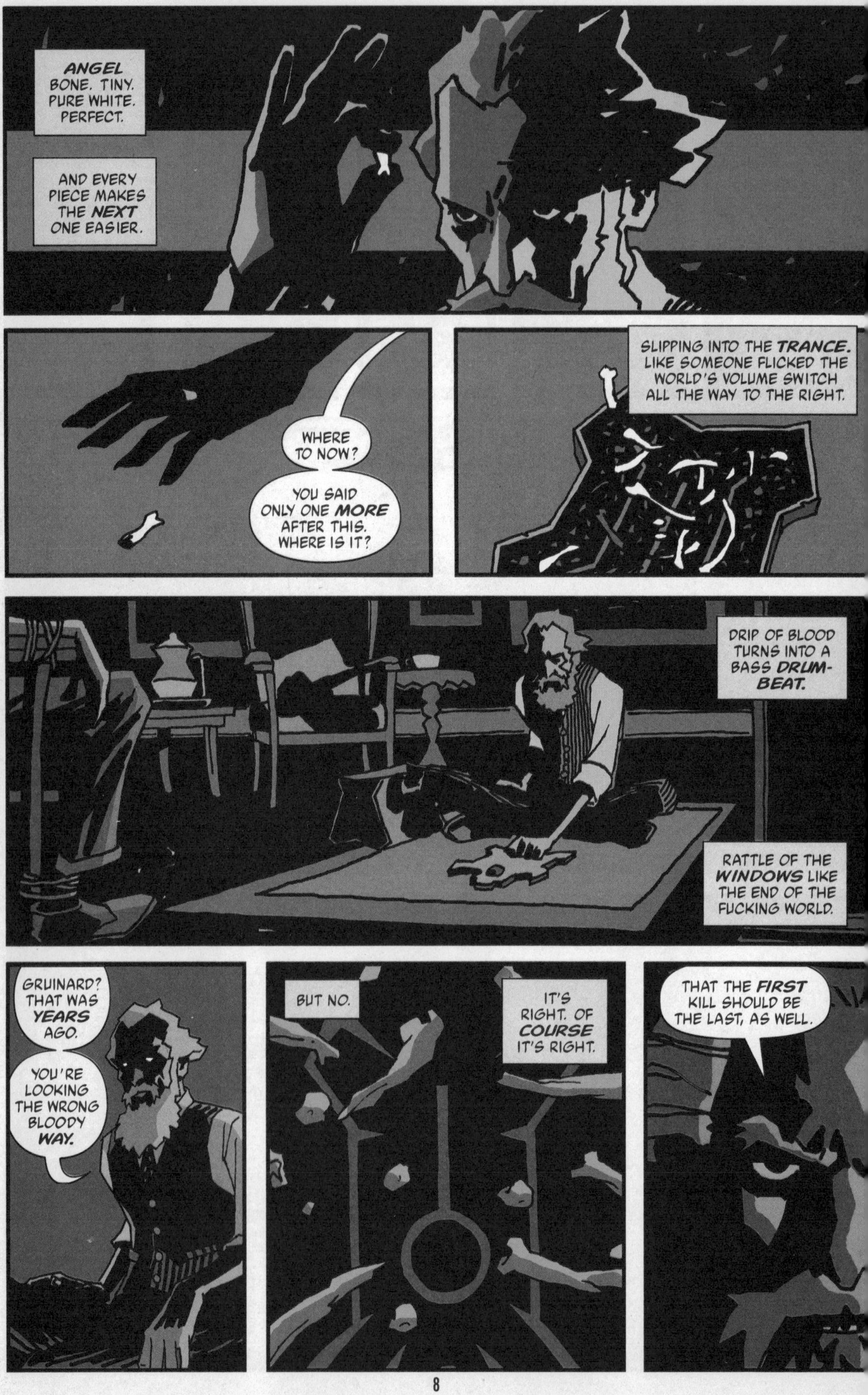
ANGEL BONE. TINY. PURE WHITE. PERFECT.
AND EVERY PIECE MAKES THE NEXT ONE EASIER.
WHERE TO NOW?
YOU SAID ONLY ONE MORE AFTER THIS. WHERE IS IT?
SLIPPING INTO THE TRANCE. LIKE SOMEONE FLICKED THE WORLD'S VOLUME SWITCH ALL THE WAY TO THE RIGHT.
DRIP OF BLOOD TURNS INTO A BASS DRUM-BEAT.
RATTLE OF THE WINDOWS LIKE THE END OF THE FUCKING WORLD.
GRUINARD? THAT WAS YEARS AGO.
YOU'RE LOOKING THE WRONG BLOODY WAY.
BUT NO.
IT'S RIGHT. OF COURSE IT'S RIGHT.
THAT THE FIRST KILL SHOULD BE THE LAST, AS WELL.

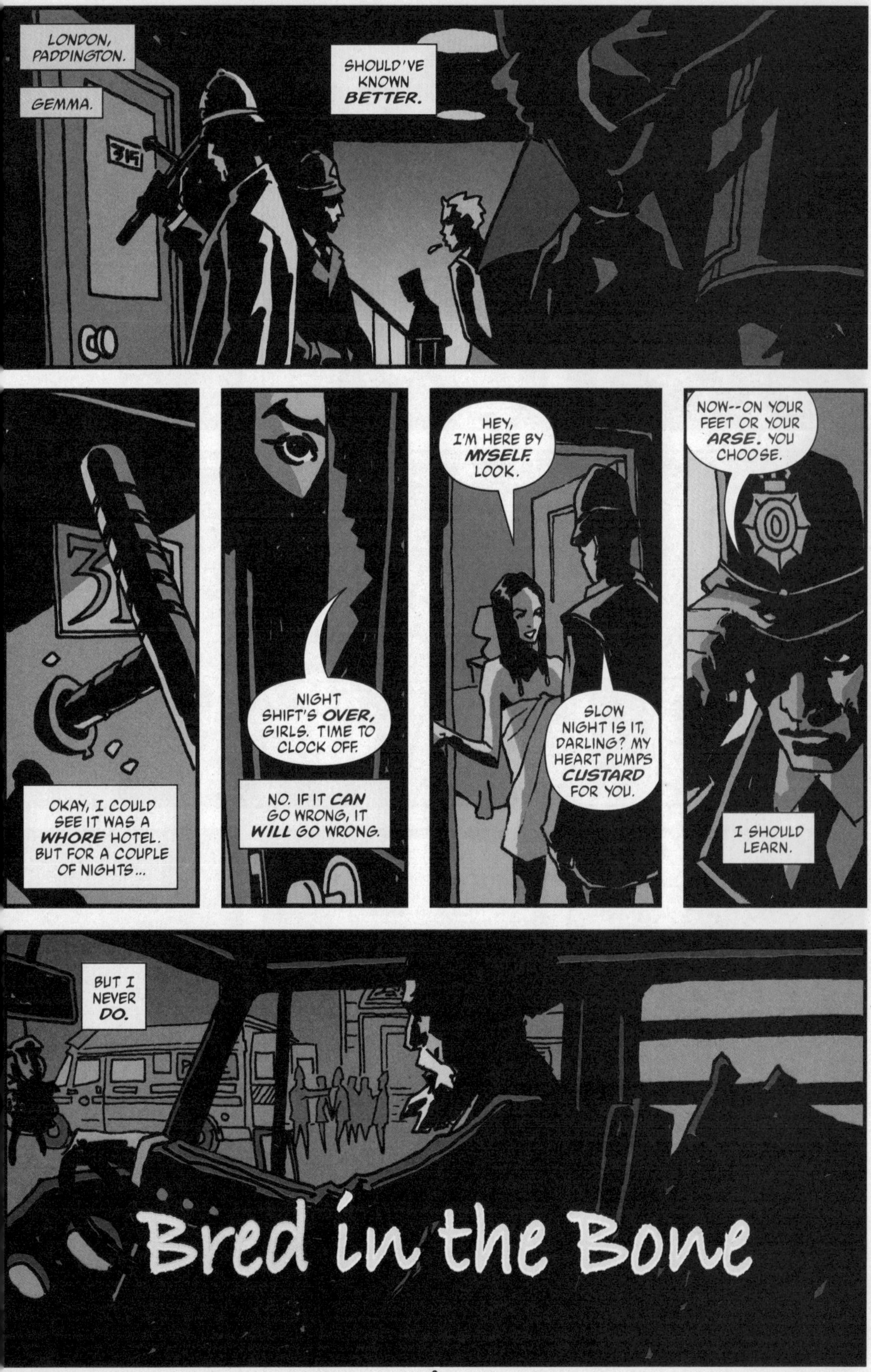
LONDON, PADDINGTON.
GEMMA.
SHOULD'VE KNOWN BETTER.
OKAY, I COULD SEE IT WAS A WHORE HOTEL. BUT FOR A COUPLE OF NIGHTS...
NO. IF IT CAN GO WRONG, IT WILL GO WRONG.
NIGHT SHIFT'S OVER, GIRLS. TIME TO CLOCK OFF.
HEY, I'M HERE BY MYSELF. LOOK.
SLOW NIGHT IS IT, DARLING? MY HEART PUMPS CUSTARD FOR YOU.
NOW--ON YOUR FEET OR YOUR ARSE. YOU CHOOSE.
I SHOULD LEARN.
BUT I NEVER DO.
Bred in the Bone

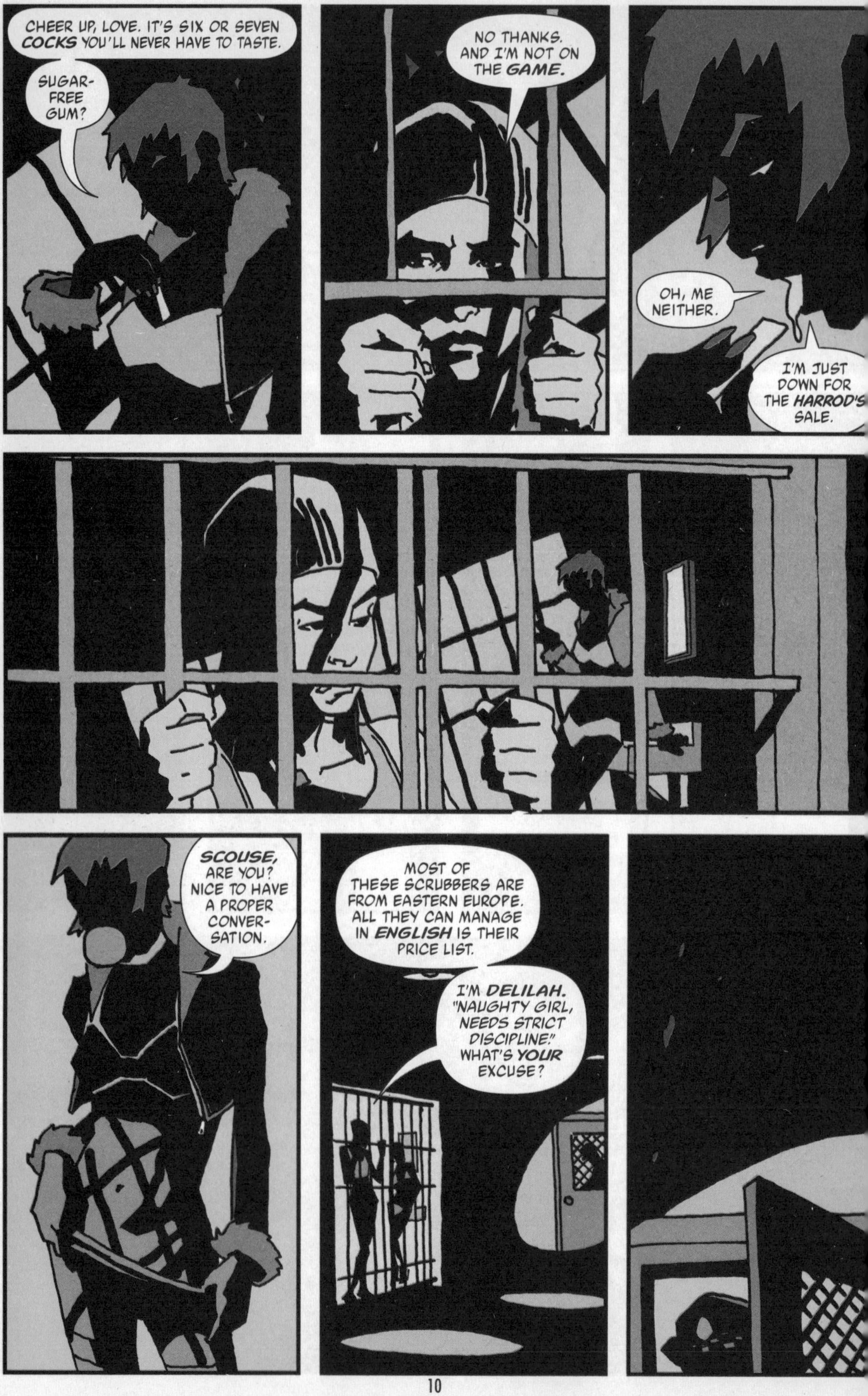
CHEER UP, LOVE. IT'S SIX OR SEVEN COCKS YOU'LL NEVER HAVE TO TASTE.
SUGAR-FREE GUM?
NO THANKS. AND I'M NOT ON THE GAME.
OH, ME NEITHER.
I'M JUST DOWN FOR THE HARROD'S SALE.
SCOUSE, ARE YOU? NICE TO HAVE A PROPER CONVERSATION.
MOST OF THESE SCRUBBERS ARE FROM EASTERN EUROPE. ALL THEY CAN MANAGE IN ENGLISH IS THEIR PRICE LIST.
I'M DELILAH. "NAUGHTY GIRL, NEEDS STRICT DISCIPLINE." WHAT'S YOUR EXCUSE?

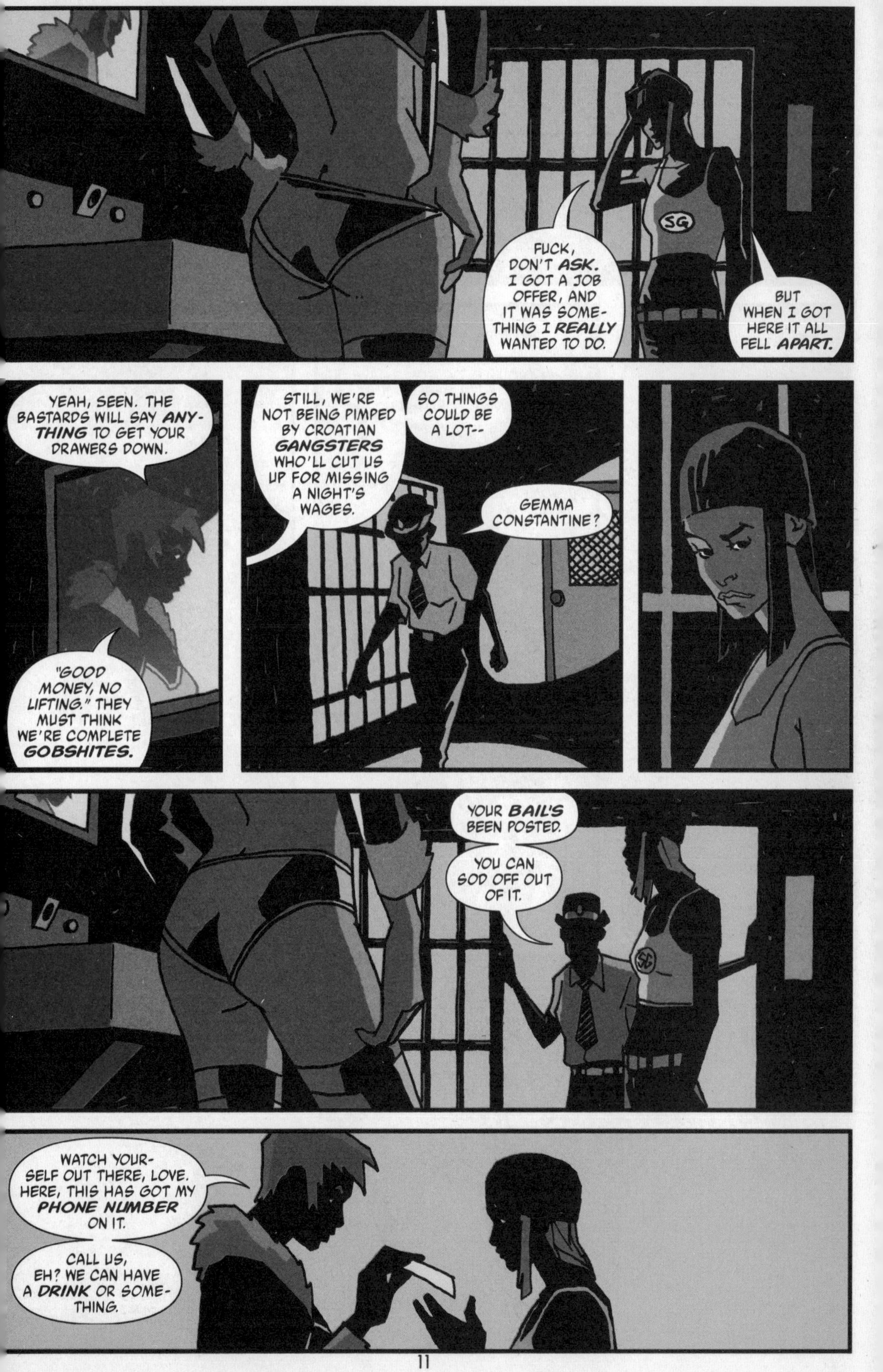
FUCK, DON'T ASK. I GOT A JOB OFFER, AND IT WAS SOME-THING I REALLY WANTED TO DO.
BUT WHEN I GOT HERE IT ALL FELL APART.
YEAH, SEEN. THE BASTARDS WILL SAY ANY-THING TO GET YOUR DRAWERS DOWN.
"GOOD MONEY, NO LIFTING." THEY MUST THINK WE'RE COMPLETE GOBSHITES.
STILL, WE'RE NOT BEING PIMPED BY CROATIAN GANGSTERS WHO'LL CUT US UP FOR MISSING A NIGHT'S WAGES.
SO THINGS COULD BE A LOT--
GEMMA CONSTANTINE?
YOUR BAIL'S BEEN POSTED.
YOU CAN SOD OFF OUT OF IT.
WATCH YOUR-SELF OUT THERE, LOVE. HERE, THIS HAS GOT MY PHONE NUMBER ON IT.
CALL US, EH? WE CAN HAVE A DRINK OR SOME-THING.

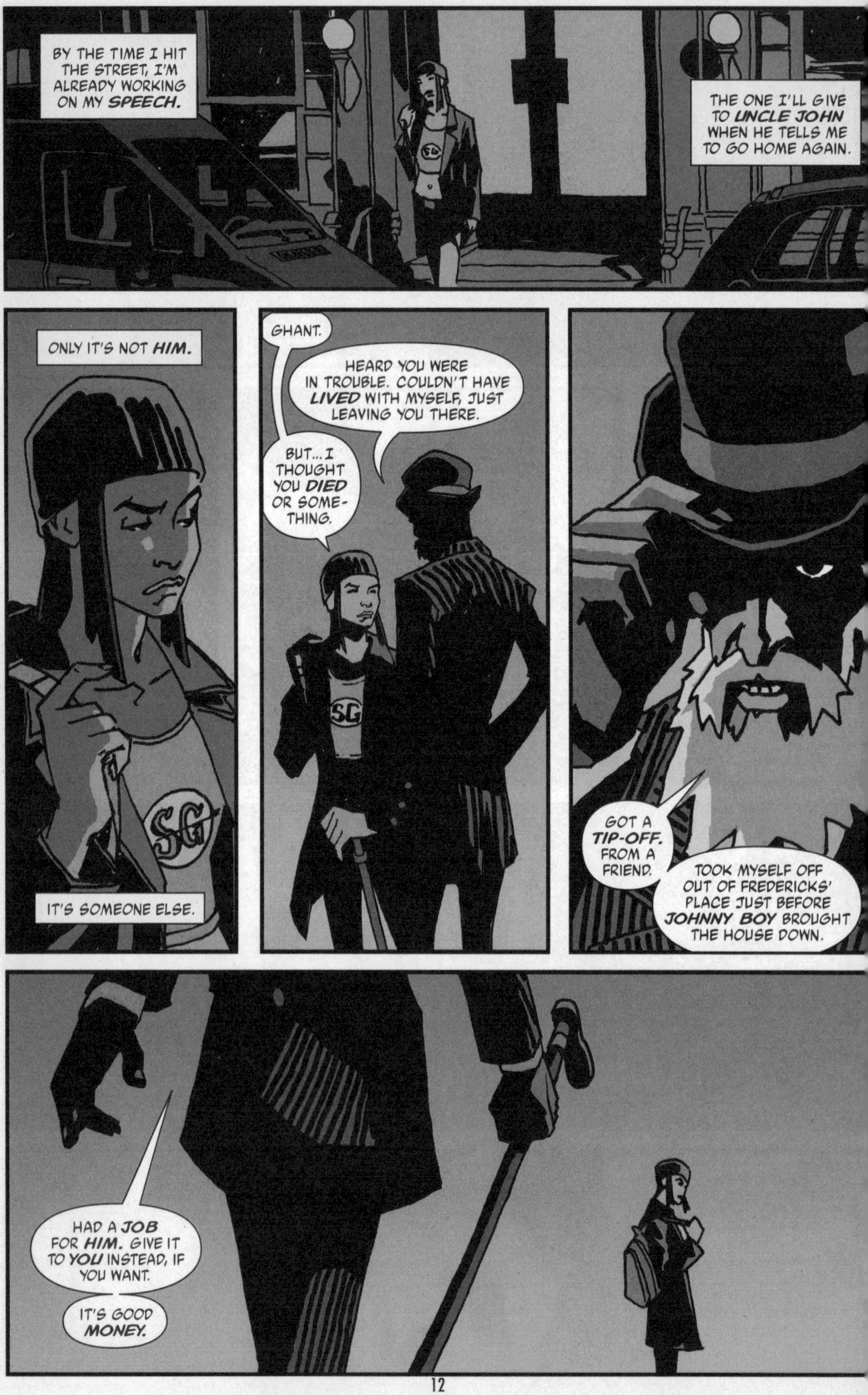
BY THE TIME I HIT THE STREET, I'M ALREADY WORKING ON MY SPEECH.
THE ONE I'LL GIVE TO UNCLE JOHN WHEN HE TELLS ME TO GO HOME AGAIN.
ONLY IT'S NOT HIM.
IT'S SOMEONE ELSE.
GHANT.
HEARD YOU WERE IN TROUBLE. COULDN'T HAVE LIVED WITH MYSELF, JUST LEAVING YOU THERE.
BUT... I THOUGHT YOU DIED OR SOME-THING.
GOT A TIP-OFF. FROM A FRIEND.
TOOK MYSELF OFF OUT OF FREDERICKS' PLACE JUST BEFORE JOHNNY BOY BROUGHT THE HOUSE DOWN.
HAD A JOB FOR HIM. GIVE IT TO YOU INSTEAD, IF YOU WANT.
IT'S GOOD MONEY.

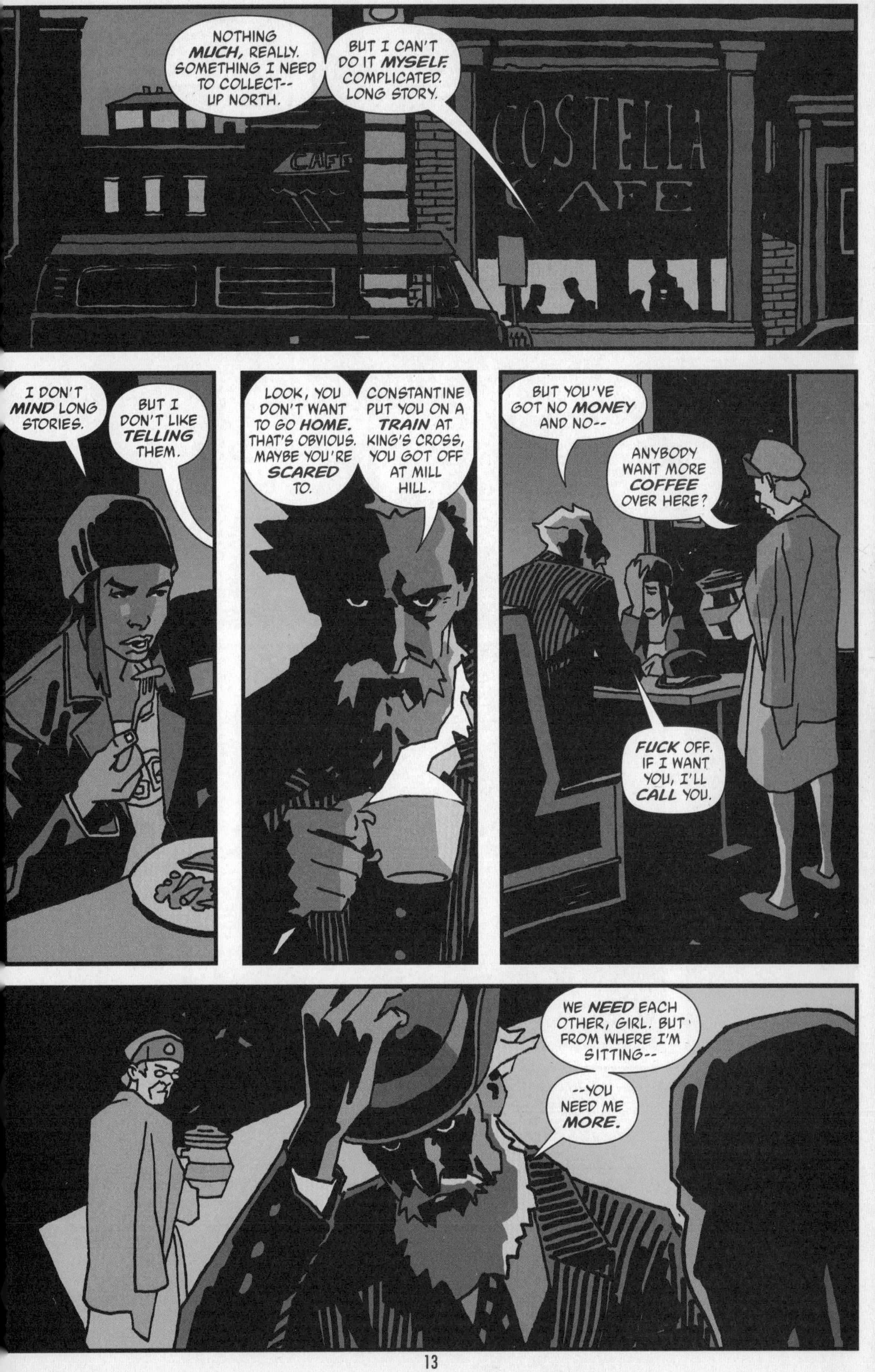

NOTHING MUCH, REALLY. SOMETHING I NEED TO COLLECT-- UP NORTH.
BUT I CAN'T DO IT MYSELF. COMPLICATED. LONG STORY.
COSTELLA CAFE
I DON'T MIND LONG STORIES.
BUT I DON'T LIKE TELLING THEM.
LOOK, YOU DON'T WANT TO GO HOME. THAT'S OBVIOUS. MAYBE YOU'RE SCARED TO.
CONSTANTINE PUT YOU ON A TRAIN AT KING'S CROSS, YOU GOT OFF AT MILL HILL.
BUT YOU'VE GOT NO MONEY AND NO--
ANYBODY WANT MORE COFFEE OVER HERE?
FUCK OFF. IF I WANT YOU, I'LL CALL YOU.
WE NEED EACH OTHER, GIRL. BUT FROM WHERE I'M SITTING--
--YOU NEED ME MORE.

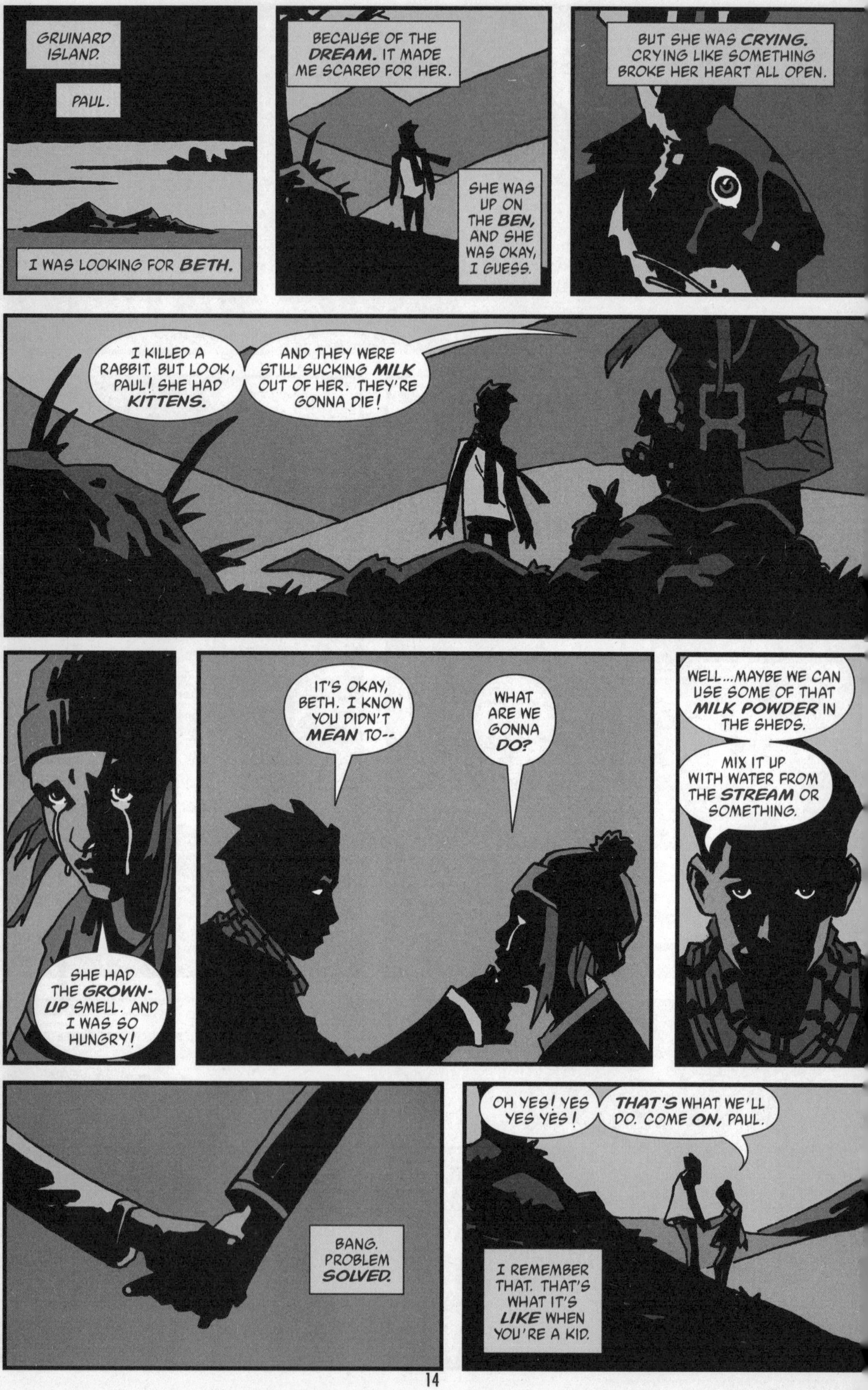
GRUINARD ISLAND.
PAUL.
I WAS LOOKING FOR BETH.
BECAUSE OF THE DREAM. IT MADE ME SCARED FOR HER.
SHE WAS UP ON THE BEN, AND SHE WAS OKAY, I GUESS.
BUT SHE WAS CRYING. CRYING LIKE SOMETHING BROKE HER HEART ALL OPEN.
I KILLED A RABBIT. BUT LOOK, PAUL! SHE HAD KITTENS.
AND THEY WERE STILL SUCKING MILK OUT OF HER. THEY'RE GONNA DIE!
SHE HAD THE GROWN-UP SMELL. AND I WAS SO HUNGRY!
IT'S OKAY, BETH. I KNOW YOU DIDN'T MEAN TO--
WHAT ARE WE GONNA DO?
WELL...MAYBE WE CAN USE SOME OF THAT MILK POWDER IN THE SHEDS.
MIX IT UP WITH WATER FROM THE STREAM OR SOMETHING.
BANG. PROBLEM SOLVED.
OH YES! YES YES YES!
THAT'S WHAT WE'LL DO. COME ON, PAUL.
I REMEMBER THAT. THAT'S WHAT IT'S LIKE WHEN YOU'RE A KID.

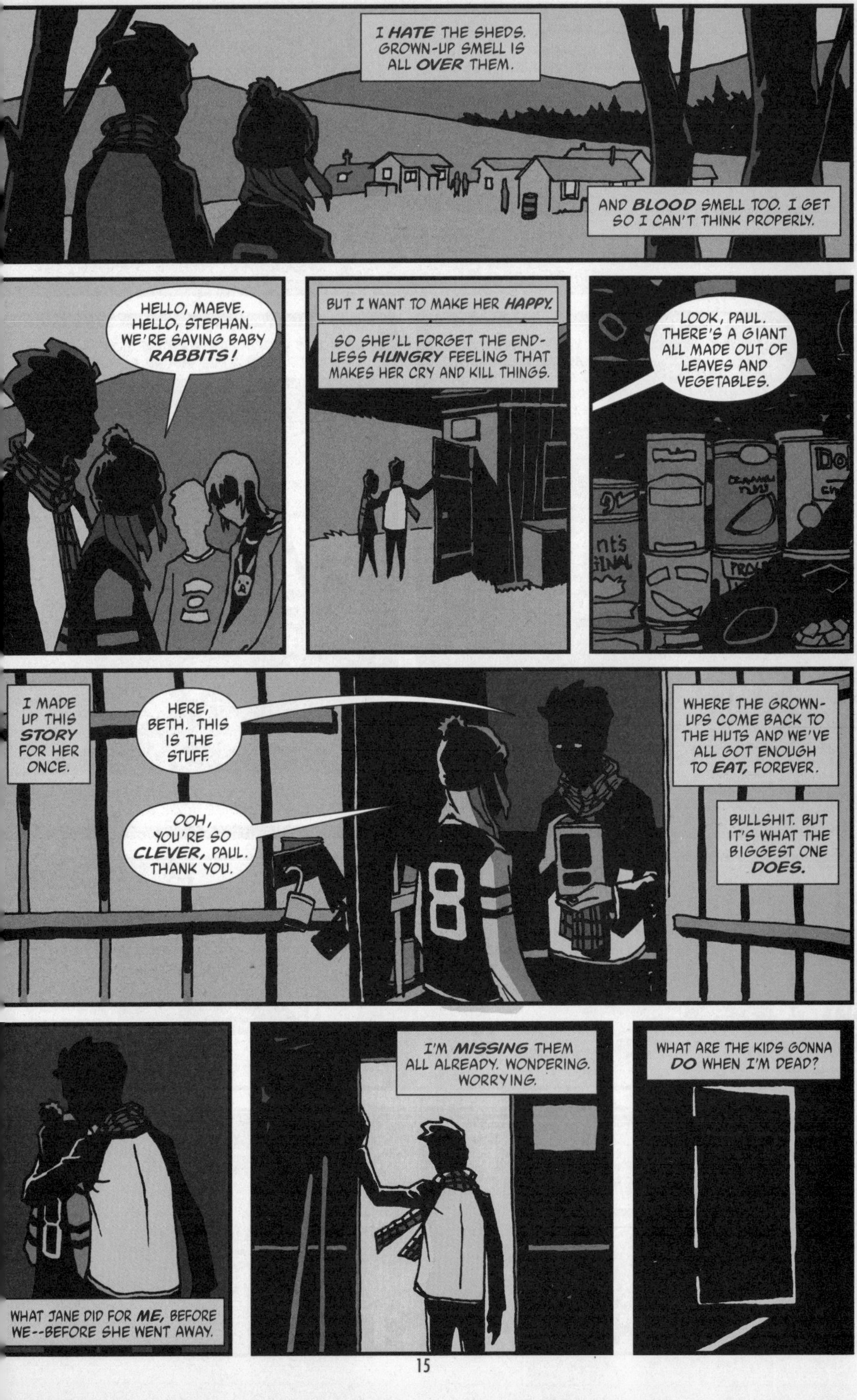
I HATE THE SHEDS. GROWN-UP SMELL IS ALL OVER THEM.
AND BLOOD SMELL TOO. I GET SO I CAN'T THINK PROPERLY.
HELLO, MAEVE. HELLO, STEPHAN. WE'RE SAVING BABY RABBITS!
BUT I WANT TO MAKE HER HAPPY.
SO SHE'LL FORGET THE END-LESS HUNGRY FEELING THAT MAKES HER CRY AND KILL THINGS.
LOOK, PAUL. THERE'S A GIANT ALL MADE OUT OF LEAVES AND VEGETABLES.
I MADE UP THIS STORY FOR HER ONCE.
HERE, BETH. THIS IS THE STUFF.
OOH, YOU'RE SO CLEVER, PAUL. THANK YOU.
WHERE THE GROWN-UPS COME BACK TO THE HUTS AND WE'VE ALL GOT ENOUGH TO EAT, FOREVER.
BULLSHIT. BUT IT'S WHAT THE BIGGEST ONE DOES.
WHAT JANE DID FOR ME, BEFORE WE--BEFORE SHE WENT AWAY.
I'M MISSING THEM ALL ALREADY. WONDERING. WORRYING.
WHAT ARE THE KIDS GONNA DO WHEN I'M DEAD?

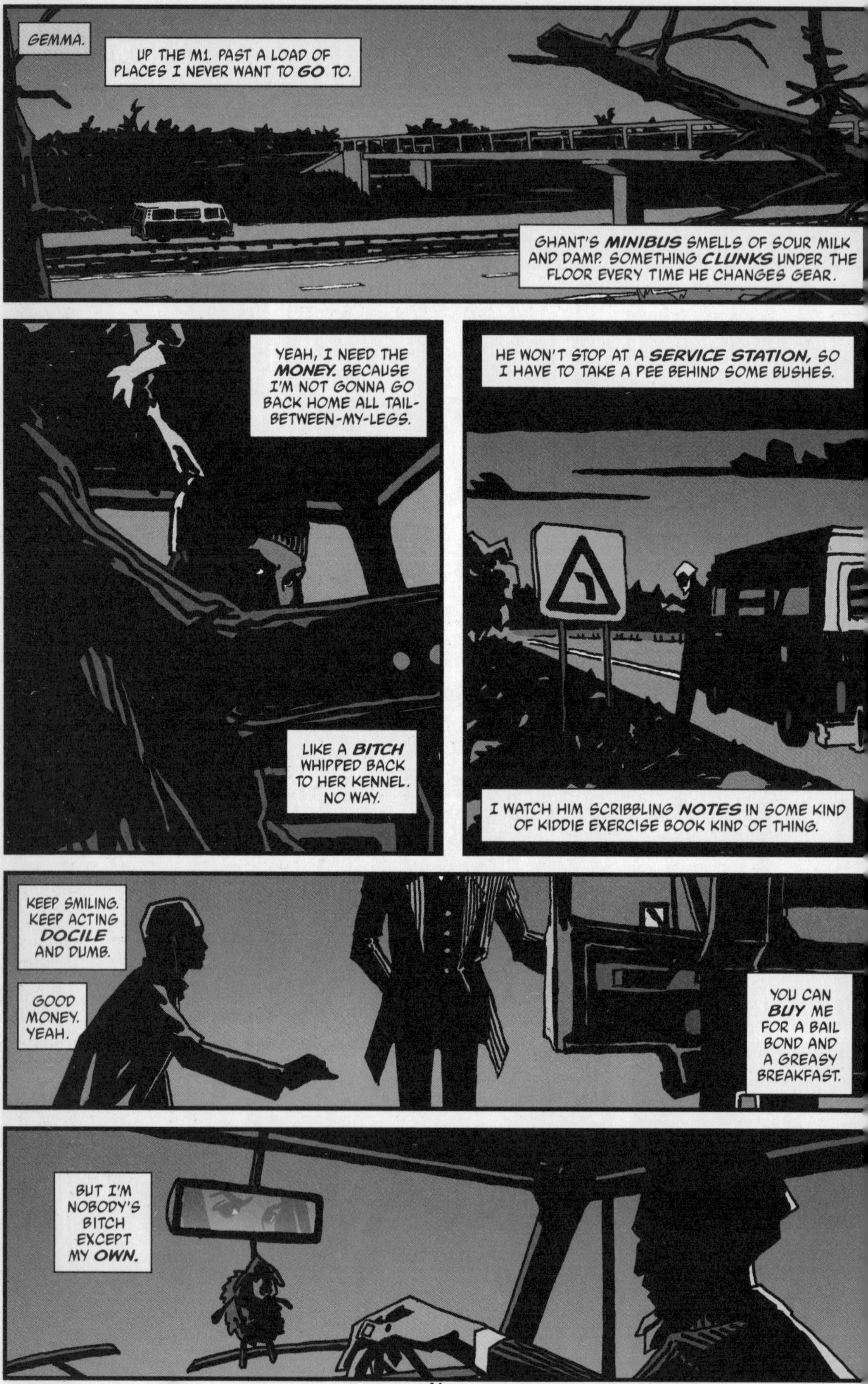
GEMMA.
UP THE M1. PAST A LOAD OF PLACES I NEVER WANT TO GO TO.
GHANT'S MINIBUS SMELLS OF SOUR MILK AND DAMP. SOMETHING CLUNKS UNDER THE FLOOR EVERY TIME HE CHANGES GEAR.
YEAH, I NEED THE MONEY. BECAUSE I'M NOT GONNA GO BACK HOME ALL TAIL-BETWEEN-MY-LEGS.
LIKE A BITCH WHIPPED BACK TO HER KENNEL. NO WAY.
HE WON'T STOP AT A SERVICE STATION, SO I HAVE TO TAKE A PEE BEHIND SOME BUSHES.
I WATCH HIM SCRIBBLING NOTES IN SOME KIND OF KIDDIE EXERCISE BOOK KIND OF THING.
KEEP SMILING. KEEP ACTING DOCILE AND DUMB.
GOOD MONEY. YEAH.
YOU CAN BUY ME FOR A BAIL BOND AND A GREASY BREAKFAST.
BUT I'M NOBODY'S BITCH EXCEPT MY OWN.

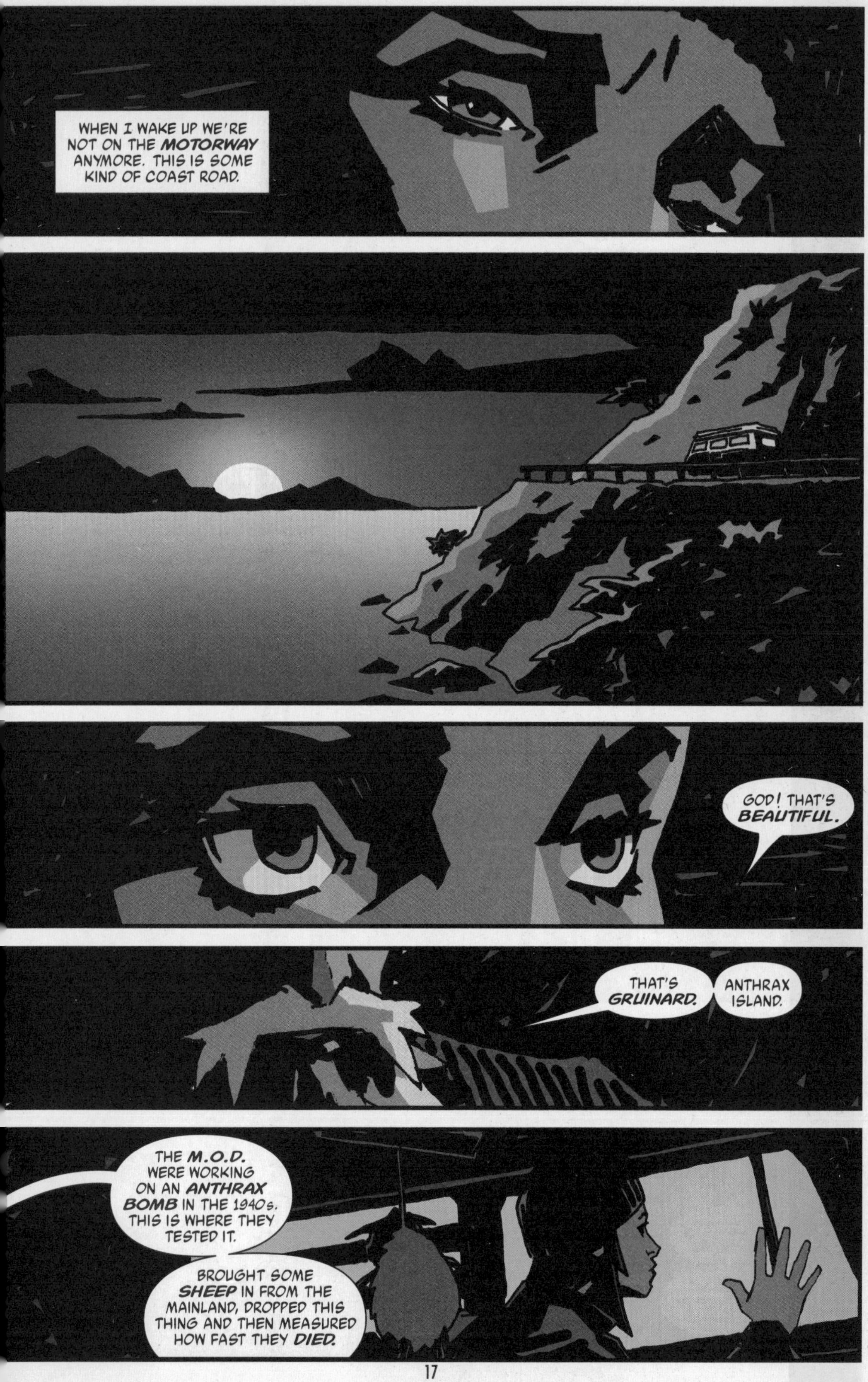
WHEN I WAKE UP WE'RE NOT ON THE MOTORWAY ANYMORE. THIS IS SOME KIND OF COAST ROAD.
GOD! THAT'S BEAUTIFUL.
THAT'S GRUINARD.
ANTHRAX ISLAND.
THE M.O.D. WERE WORKING ON AN ANTHRAX BOMB IN THE 1940s. THIS IS WHERE THEY TESTED IT.
BROUGHT SOME SHEEP IN FROM THE MAINLAND, DROPPED THIS THING AND THEN MEASURED HOW FAST THEY DIED.

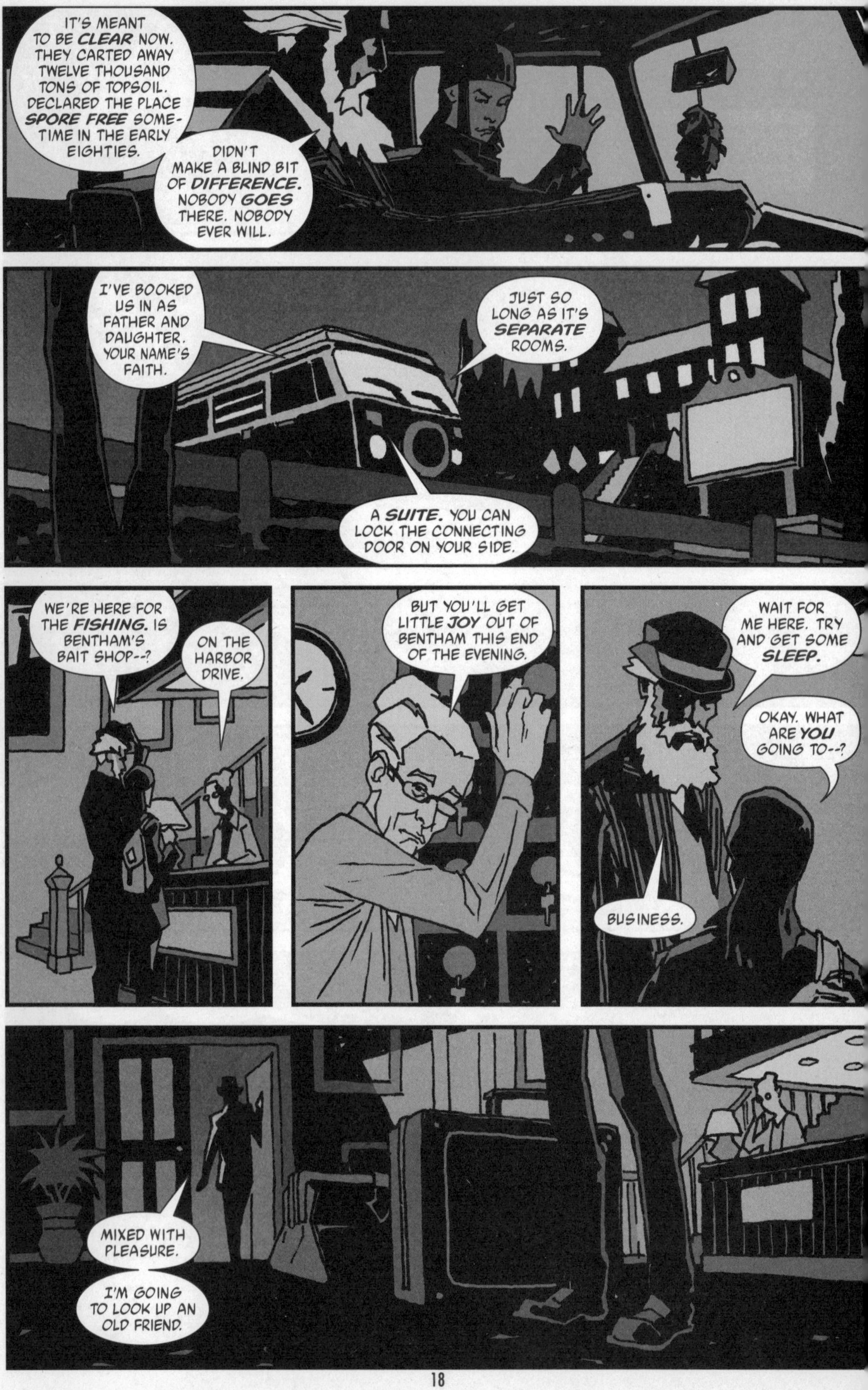
IT'S MEANT TO BE CLEAR NOW. THEY CARTED AWAY TWELVE THOUSAND TONS OF TOPSOIL. DECLARED THE PLACE SPORE FREE SOMETIME IN THE EARLY EIGHTIES.
DIDN'T MAKE A BLIND BIT OF DIFFERENCE. NOBODY GOES THERE. NOBODY EVER WILL.
I'VE BOOKED US IN AS FATHER AND DAUGHTER. YOUR NAME'S FAITH.
JUST SO LONG AS IT'S SEPARATE ROOMS.
A SUITE. YOU CAN LOCK THE CONNECTING DOOR ON YOUR SIDE.
WE'RE HERE FOR THE FISHING. IS BENTHAM'S BAIT SHOP--?
ON THE HARBOR DRIVE.
BUT YOU'LL GET LITTLE JOY OUT OF BENTHAM THIS END OF THE EVENING.
WAIT FOR ME HERE. TRY AND GET SOME SLEEP.
OKAY. WHAT ARE YOU GOING TO--?
BUSINESS.
MIXED WITH PLEASURE.
I'M GOING TO LOOK UP AN OLD FRIEND.

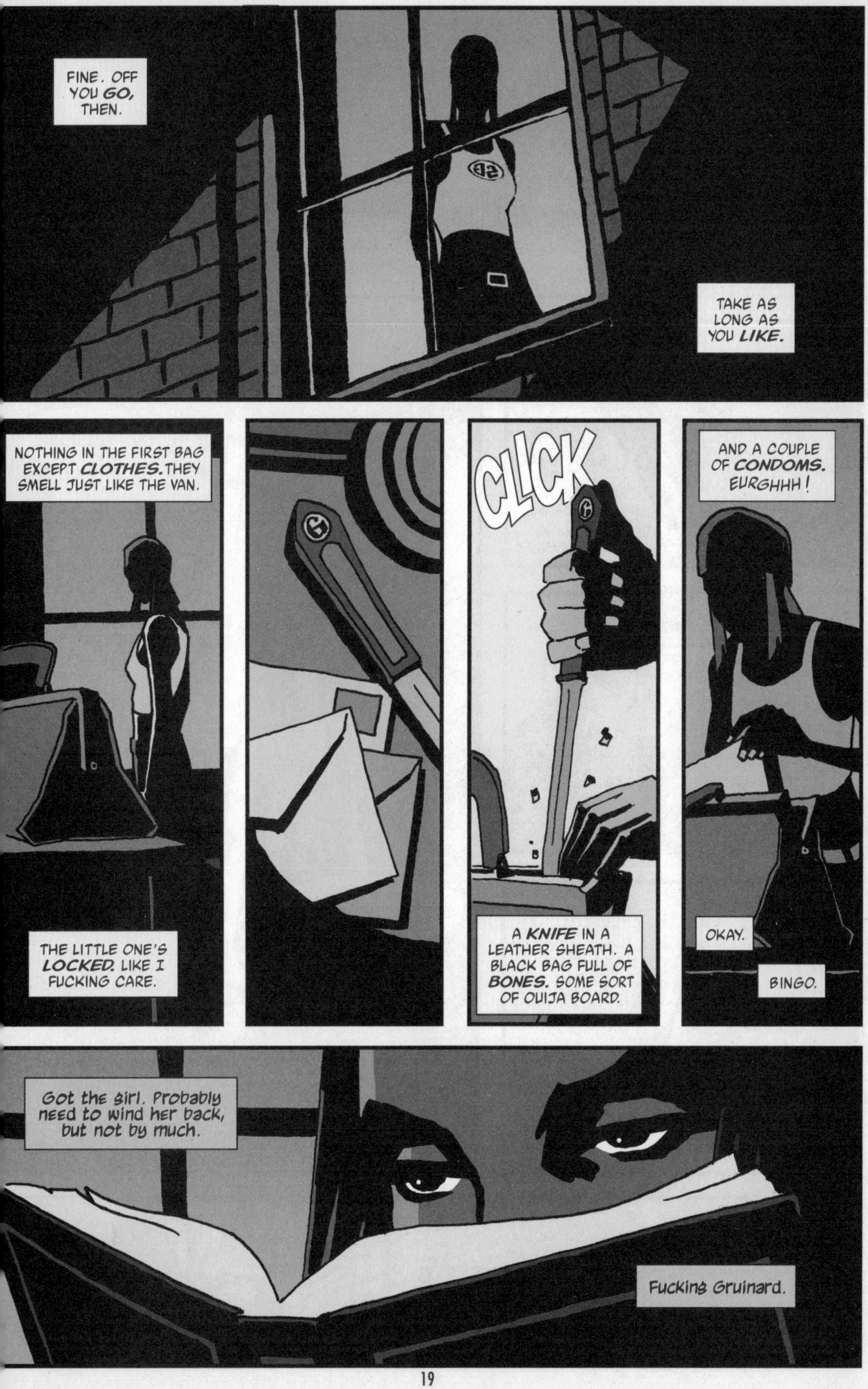

FINE. OFF YOU GO, THEN.
TAKE AS LONG AS YOU LIKE.
NOTHING IN THE FIRST BAG EXCEPT CLOTHES. THEY SMELL JUST LIKE THE VAN.
THE LITTLE ONE'S LOCKED. LIKE I FUCKING CARE.
CLICK
A KNIFE IN A LEATHER SHEATH. A BLACK BAG FULL OF BONES. SOME SORT OF OUIJA BOARD.
AND A COUPLE OF CONDOMS. EURGHHH!
OKAY.
BINGO.
Got the girl. Probably need to wind her back, but not by much.
Fucking Gruinard.

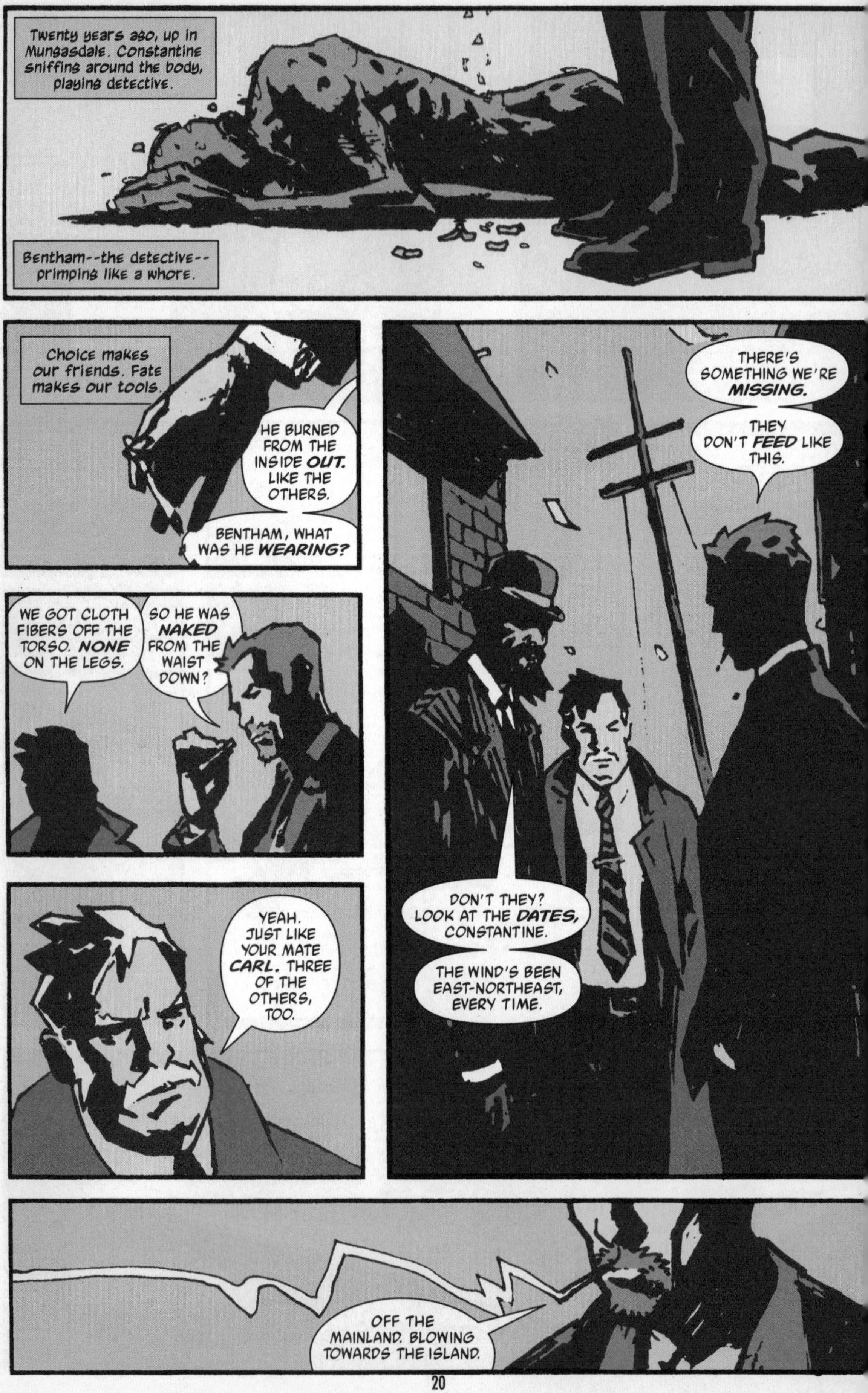

Twenty years ago, up in Mungasdale. Constantine sniffing around the body, playing detective.
Bentham--the detective--primping like a whore.
Choice makes our friends. Fate makes our tools.
HE BURNED FROM THE INSIDE OUT. LIKE THE OTHERS.
BENTHAM, WHAT WAS HE WEARING?
WE GOT CLOTH FIBERS OFF THE TORSO. NONE ON THE LEGS.
SO HE WAS NAKED FROM THE WAIST DOWN?
YEAH. JUST LIKE YOUR MATE CARL. THREE OF THE OTHERS, TOO.
THERE'S SOMETHING WE'RE MISSING.
THEY DON'T FEED LIKE THIS.
DON'T THEY? LOOK AT THE DATES, CONSTANTINE.
THE WIND'S BEEN EAST-NORTHEAST, EVERY TIME.
OFF THE MAINLAND. BLOWING TOWARDS THE ISLAND.

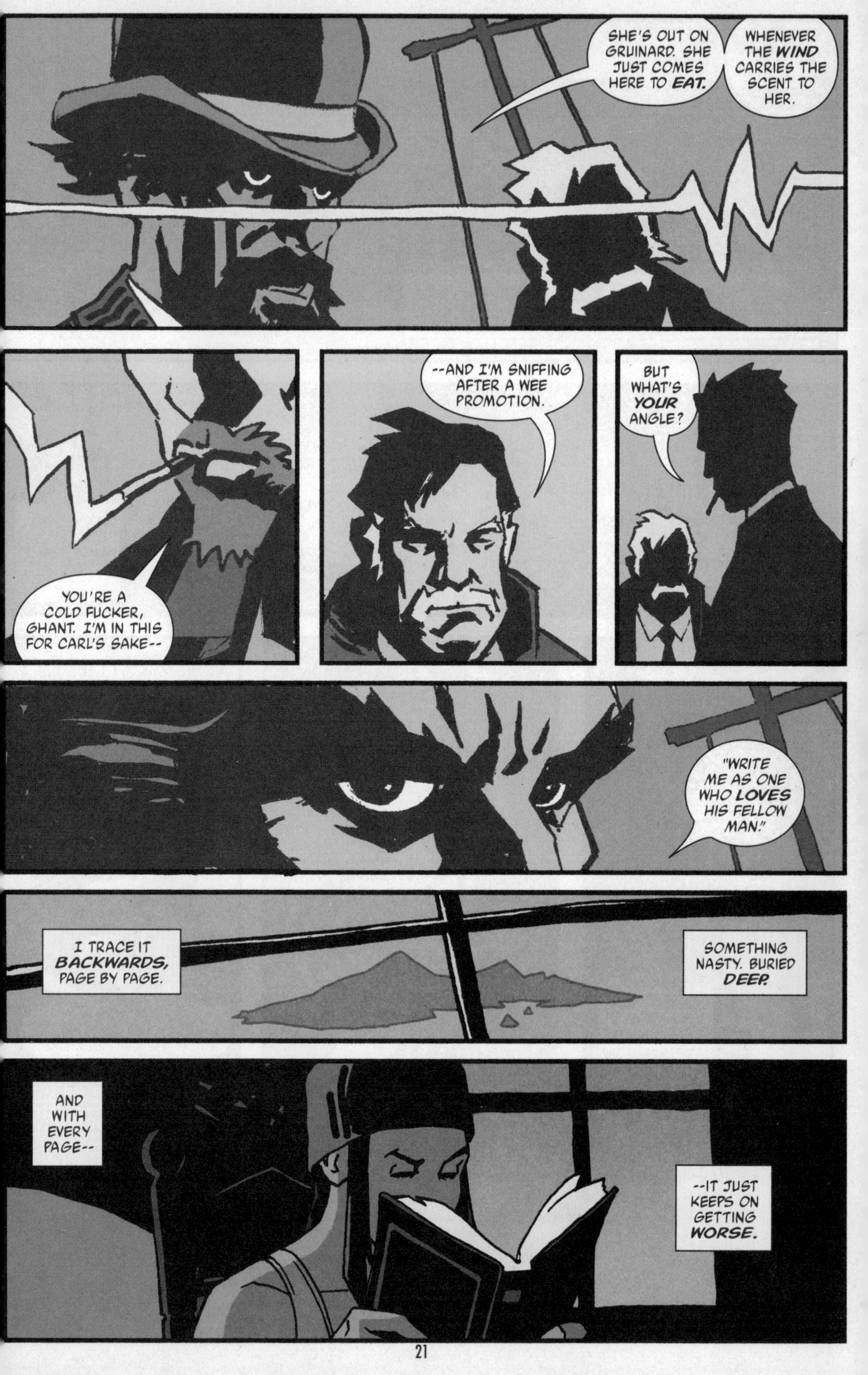
SHE'S OUT ON GRUINARD. SHE JUST COMES HERE TO EAT.
WHENEVER THE WIND CARRIES THE SCENT TO HER.
YOU'RE A COLD FUCKER, GHANT. I'M IN THIS FOR CARL'S SAKE--
--AND I'M SNIFFING AFTER A WEE PROMOTION.
BUT WHAT'S YOUR ANGLE?
"WRITE ME AS ONE WHO LOVES HIS FELLOW MAN."
I TRACE IT BACKWARDS, PAGE BY PAGE.
SOMETHING NASTY. BURIED DEEP.
AND WITH EVERY PAGE--
--IT JUST KEEPS ON GETTING WORSE.

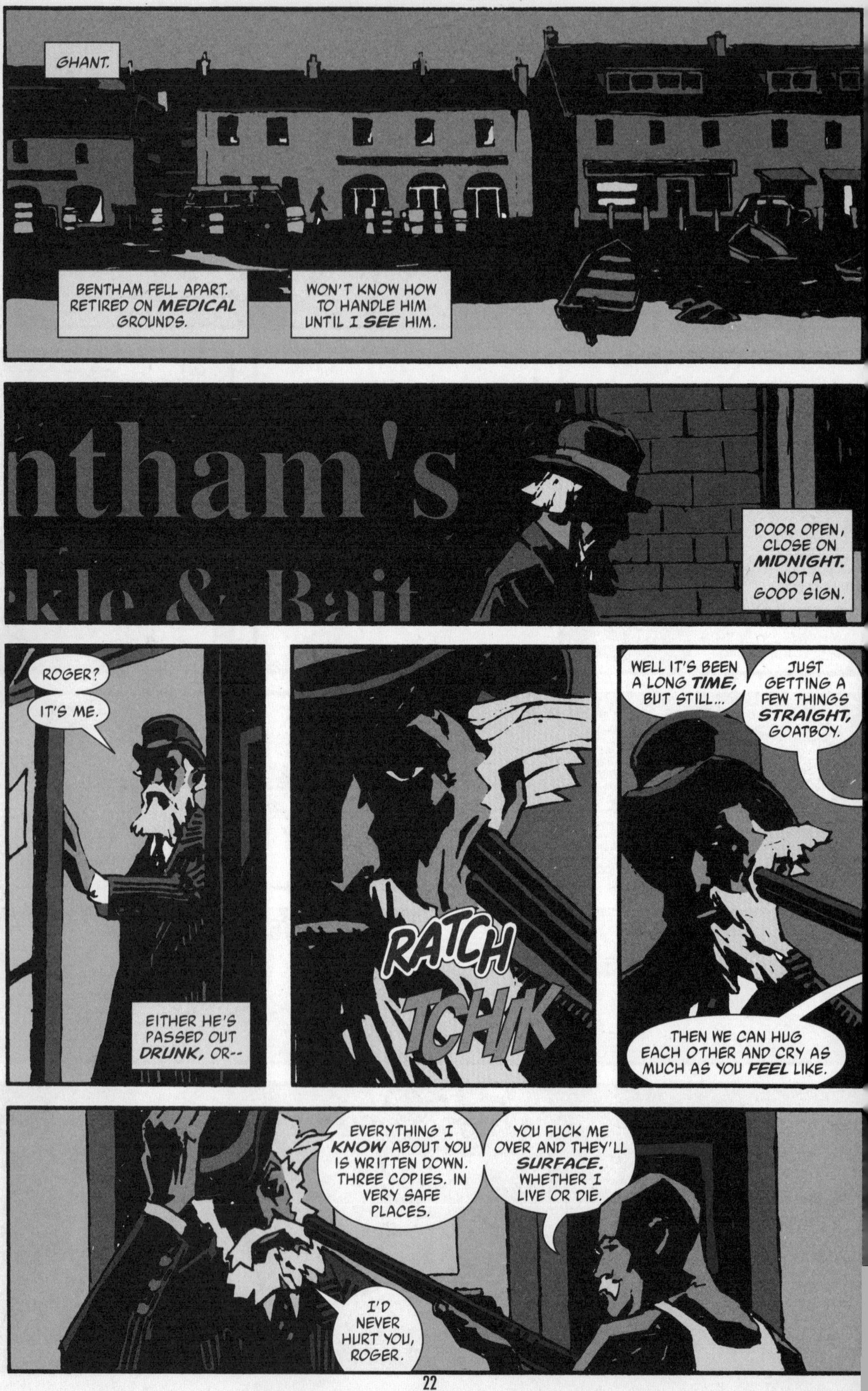
GHANT.
BENTHAM FELL APART. RETIRED ON MEDICAL GROUNDS.
WON'T KNOW HOW TO HANDLE HIM UNTIL I SEE HIM.
ntham's
kle & Bait
DOOR OPEN, CLOSE ON MIDNIGHT. NOT A GOOD SIGN.
ROGER?
IT'S ME.
EITHER HE'S PASSED OUT DRUNK, OR--
RATCH
TCHIK
WELL IT'S BEEN A LONG TIME, BUT STILL...
JUST GETTING A FEW THINGS STRAIGHT, GOATBOY.
THEN WE CAN HUG EACH OTHER AND CRY AS MUCH AS YOU FEEL LIKE.
EVERYTHING I KNOW ABOUT YOU IS WRITTEN DOWN. THREE COPIES. IN VERY SAFE PLACES.
YOU FUCK ME OVER AND THEY'LL SURFACE. WHETHER I LIVE OR DIE.
I'D NEVER HURT YOU, ROGER.

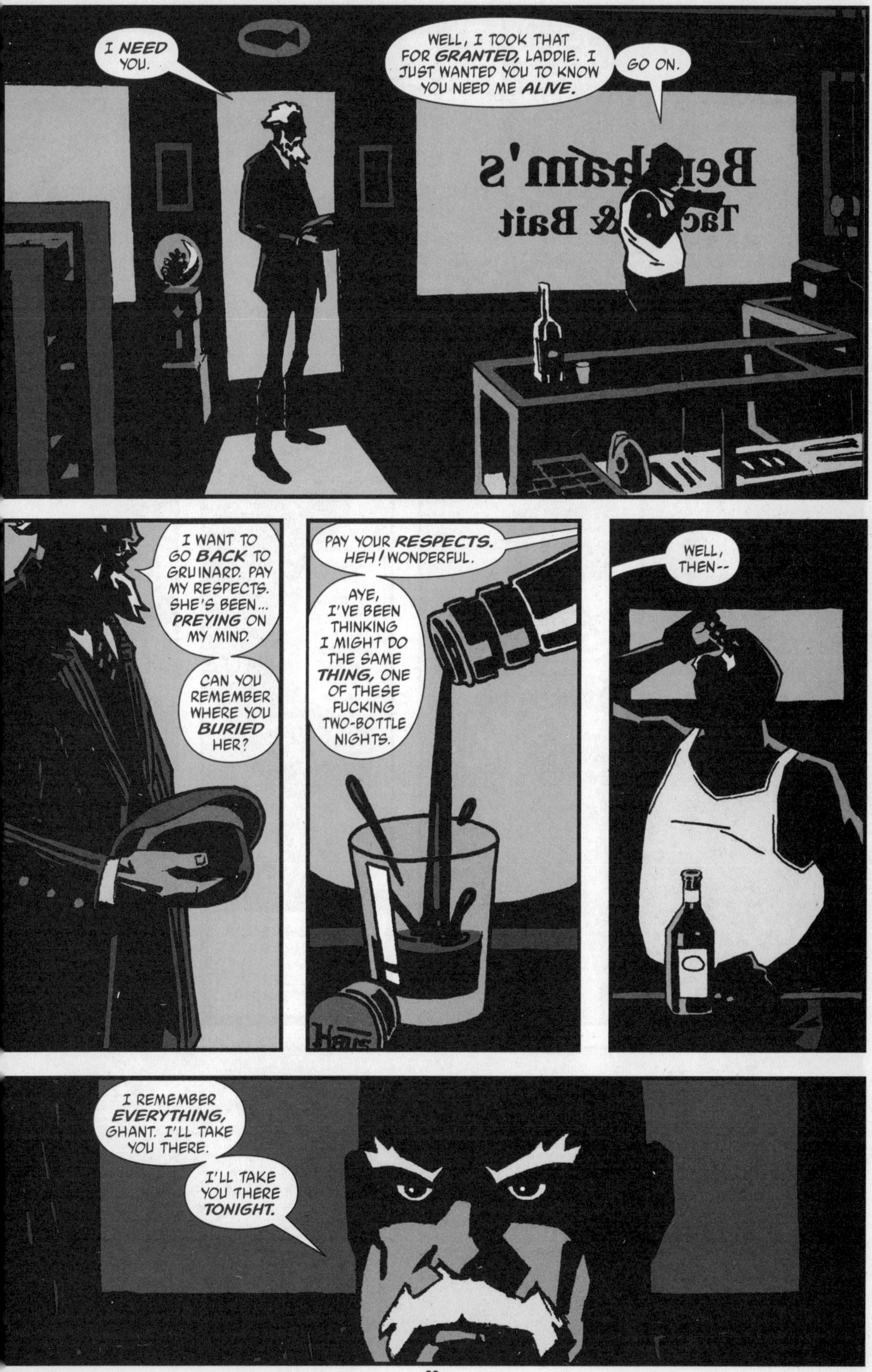

I NEED YOU.
WELL, I TOOK THAT FOR GRANTED, LADDIE. I JUST WANTED YOU TO KNOW YOU NEED ME ALIVE.
GO ON.
I WANT TO GO BACK TO GRUINARD. PAY MY RESPECTS. SHE'S BEEN... PREYING ON MY MIND.
CAN YOU REMEMBER WHERE YOU BURIED HER?
PAY YOUR RESPECTS. HEH! WONDERFUL.
AYE, I'VE BEEN THINKING I MIGHT DO THE SAME THING, ONE OF THESE FUCKING TWO-BOTTLE NIGHTS.
WELL, THEN--
I REMEMBER EVERYTHING, GHANT. I'LL TAKE YOU THERE.
I'LL TAKE YOU THERE TONIGHT.

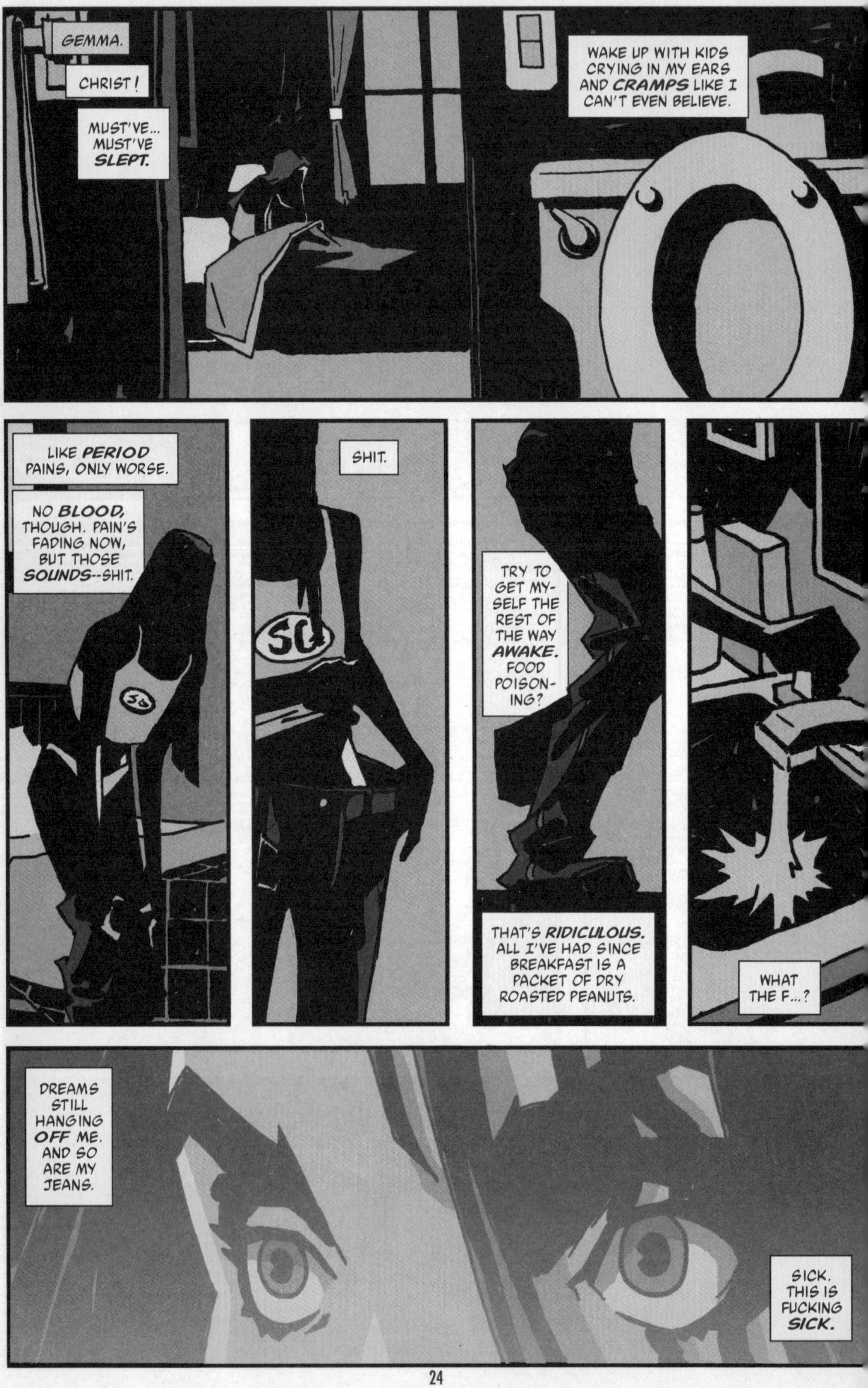

GEMMA.
CHRIST!
MUST'VE... MUST'VE SLEPT.
WAKE UP WITH KIDS CRYING IN MY EARS AND CRAMPS LIKE I CAN'T EVEN BELIEVE.
LIKE PERIOD PAINS, ONLY WORSE.
NO BLOOD, THOUGH. PAIN'S FADING NOW, BUT THOSE SOUNDS--SHIT.
SHIT.
TRY TO GET MY-SELF THE REST OF THE WAY AWAKE. FOOD POISON-ING?
THAT'S RIDICULOUS. ALL I'VE HAD SINCE BREAKFAST IS A PACKET OF DRY ROASTED PEANUTS.
WHAT THE F...?
DREAMS STILL HANGING OFF ME. AND SO ARE MY JEANS.
SICK. THIS IS FUCKING SICK.

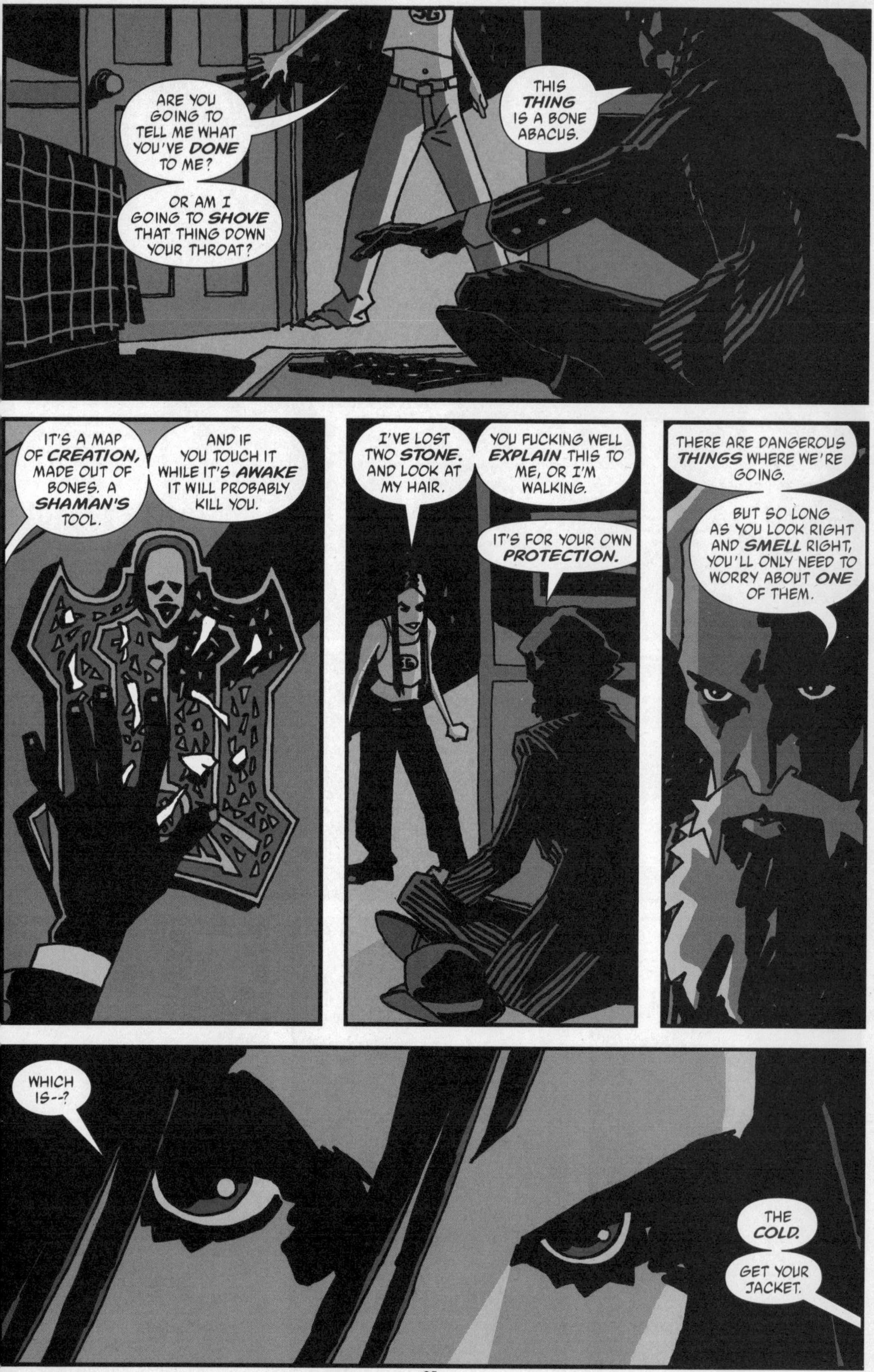
ARE YOU GOING TO TELL ME WHAT YOU'VE DONE TO ME?
OR AM I GOING TO SHOVE THAT THING DOWN YOUR THROAT?
THIS THING IS A BONE ABACUS.
IT'S A MAP OF CREATION, MADE OUT OF BONES. A SHAMAN'S TOOL.
AND IF YOU TOUCH IT WHILE IT'S AWAKE IT WILL PROBABLY KILL YOU.
I'VE LOST TWO STONE. AND LOOK AT MY HAIR.
YOU FUCKING WELL EXPLAIN THIS TO ME, OR I'M WALKING.
IT'S FOR YOUR OWN PROTECTION.
THERE ARE DANGEROUS THINGS WHERE WE'RE GOING.
BUT SO LONG AS YOU LOOK RIGHT AND SMELL RIGHT, YOU'LL ONLY NEED TO WORRY ABOUT ONE OF THEM.
WHICH IS--?
THE COLD.
GET YOUR JACKET.

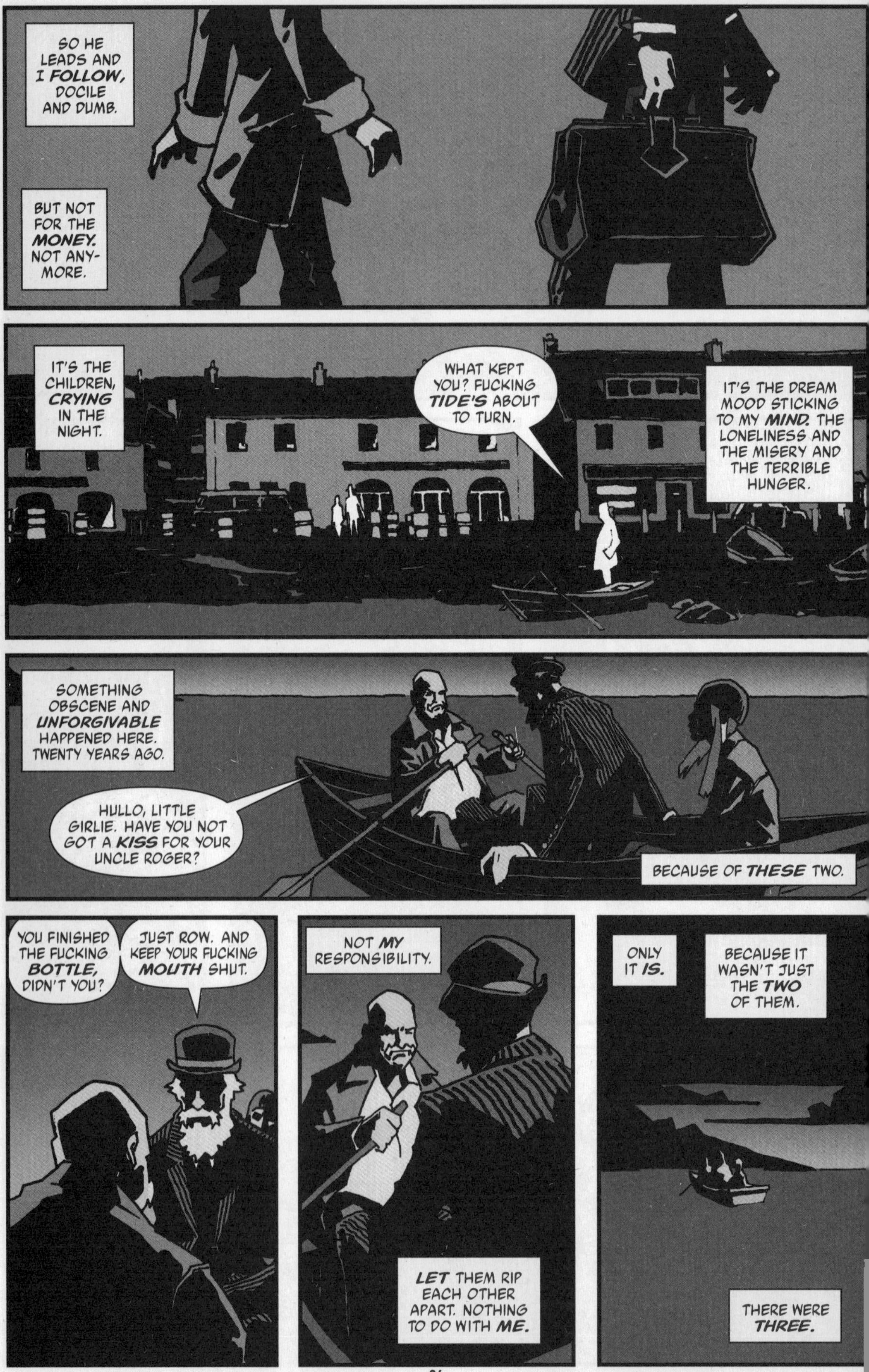
SO HE LEADS AND *I FOLLOW,* DOCILE AND DUMB.
BUT NOT FOR THE *MONEY.* NOT ANYMORE.
IT'S THE CHILDREN, *CRYING* IN THE NIGHT.
WHAT KEPT YOU? FUCKING *TIDE'S* ABOUT TO TURN.
IT'S THE DREAM MOOD STICKING TO MY *MIND.* THE LONELINESS AND THE MISERY AND THE TERRIBLE HUNGER.
SOMETHING OBSCENE AND *UNFORGIVABLE* HAPPENED HERE. TWENTY YEARS AGO.
HULLO, LITTLE GIRLIE. HAVE YOU NOT GOT A *KISS* FOR YOUR UNCLE ROGER?
BECAUSE OF *THESE* TWO.
YOU FINISHED THE FUCKING *BOTTLE,* DIDN'T YOU?
JUST ROW. AND KEEP YOUR FUCKING *MOUTH* SHUT.
NOT *MY* RESPONSIBILITY.
LET THEM RIP EACH OTHER APART. NOTHING TO DO WITH *ME.*
ONLY IT *IS.*
BECAUSE IT WASN'T JUST THE *TWO* OF THEM.
THERE WERE *THREE.*

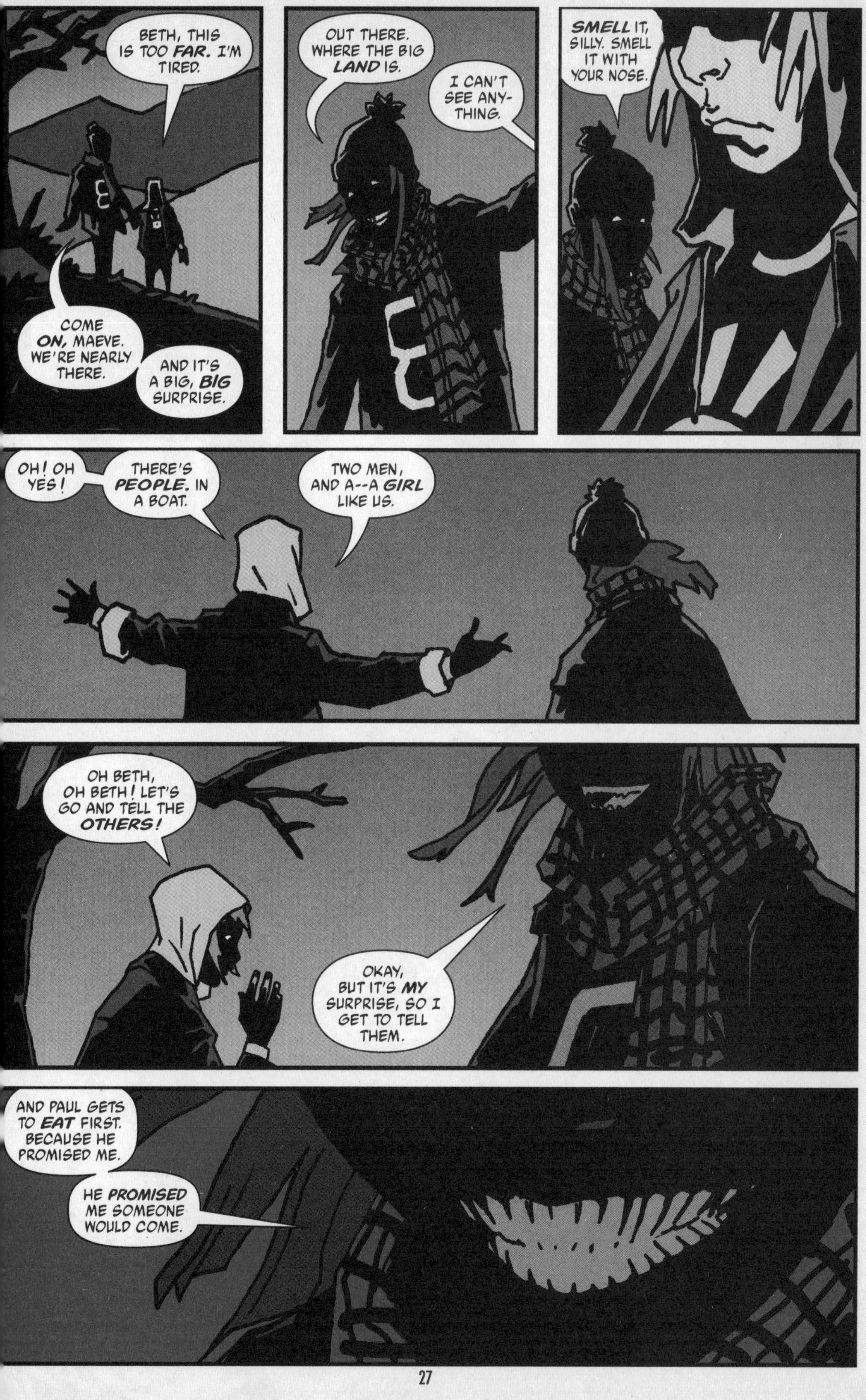
BETH, THIS IS TOO FAR. I'M TIRED.
COME ON, MAEVE. WE'RE NEARLY THERE.
AND IT'S A BIG, BIG SURPRISE.
OUT THERE. WHERE THE BIG LAND IS.
I CAN'T SEE ANY-THING.
SMELL IT, SILLY. SMELL IT WITH YOUR NOSE.
OH! OH YES!
THERE'S PEOPLE. IN A BOAT.
TWO MEN, AND A--A GIRL LIKE US.
OH BETH, OH BETH! LET'S GO AND TELL THE OTHERS!
OKAY, BUT IT'S MY SURPRISE, SO I GET TO TELL THEM.
AND PAUL GETS TO EAT FIRST. BECAUSE HE PROMISED ME.
HE PROMISED ME SOMEONE WOULD COME.

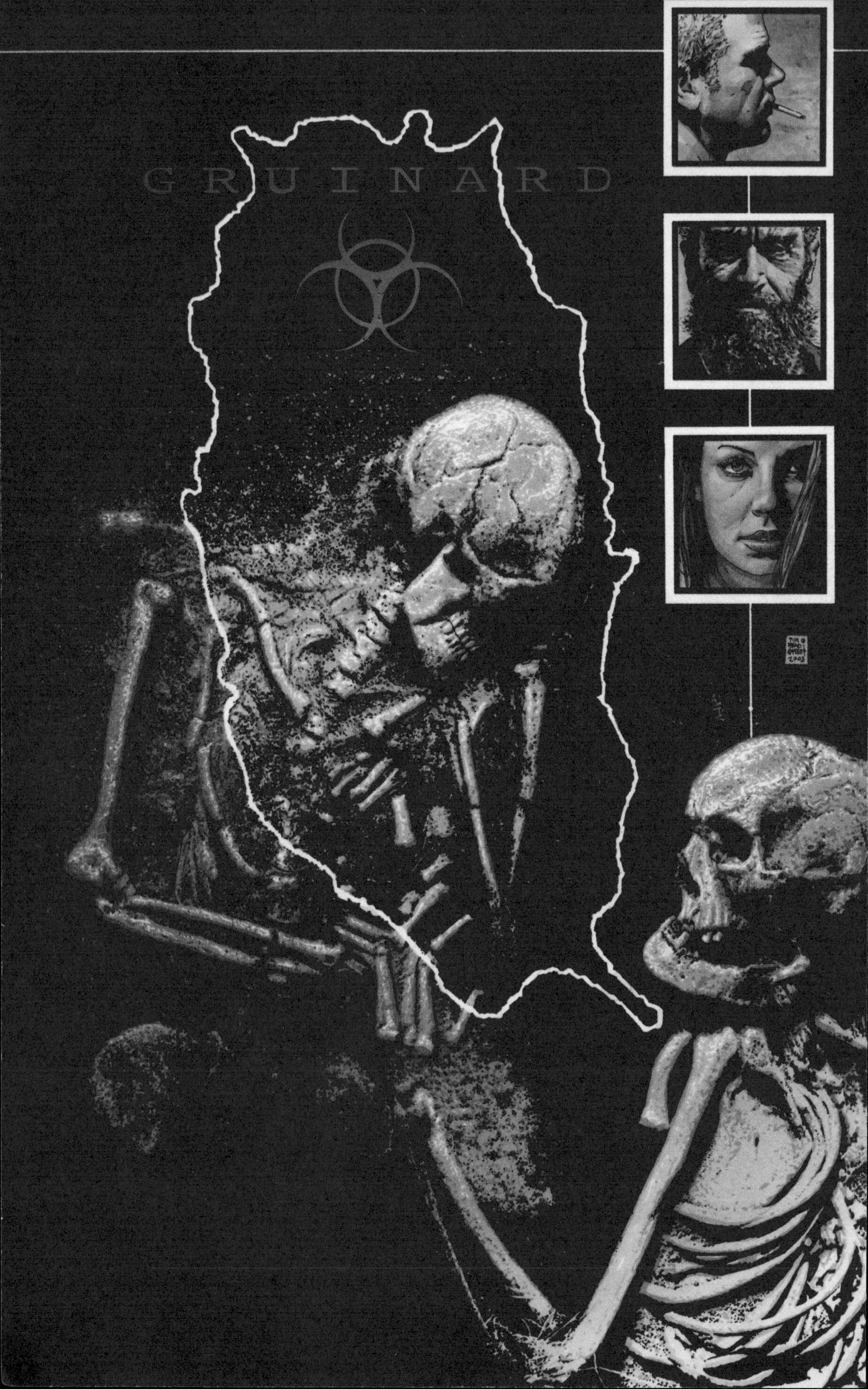
GRUINARD

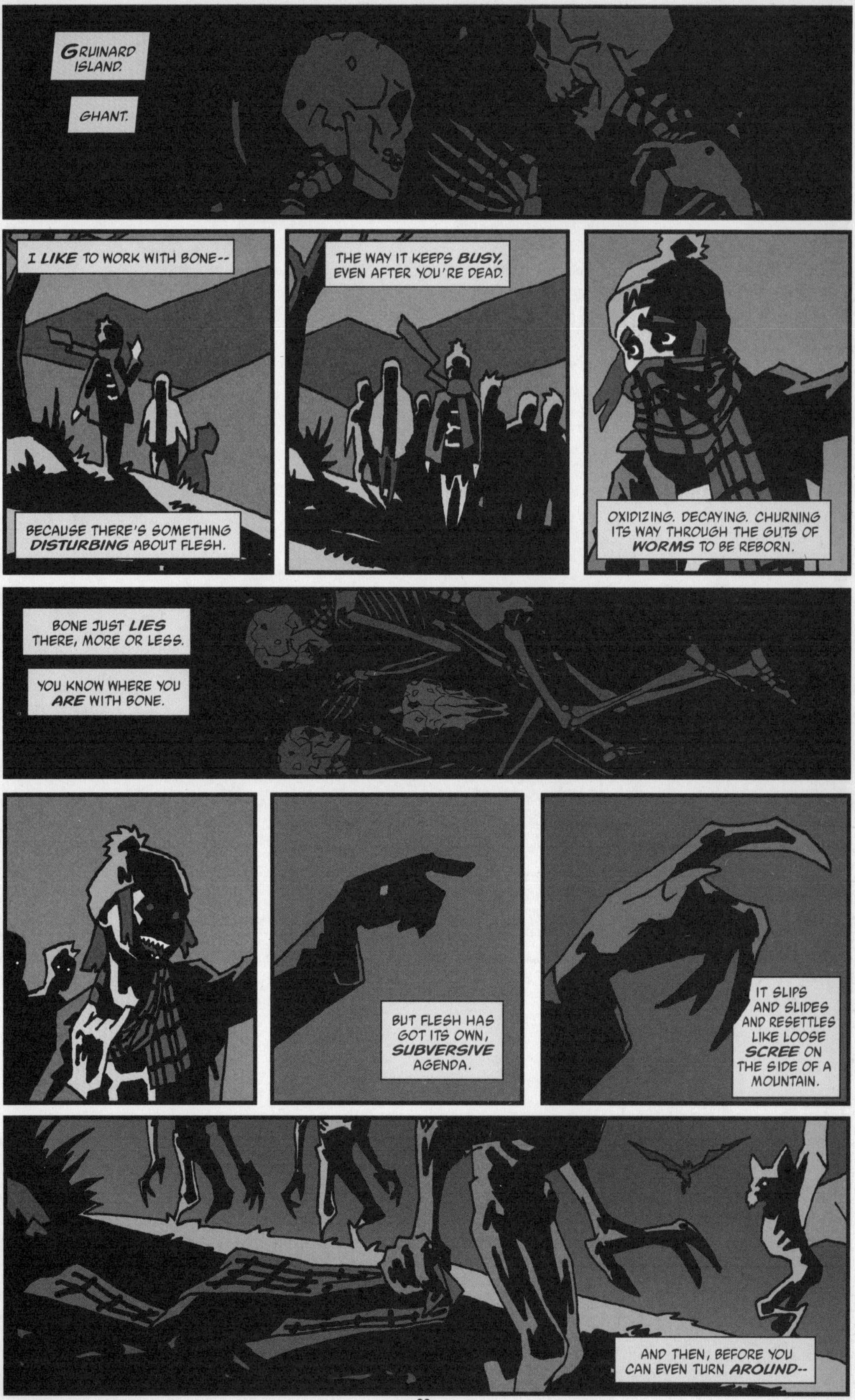
GRUINARD ISLAND.
GHANT.
I LIKE TO WORK WITH BONE--
BECAUSE THERE'S SOMETHING DISTURBING ABOUT FLESH.
THE WAY IT KEEPS BUSY, EVEN AFTER YOU'RE DEAD.
OXIDIZING. DECAYING. CHURNING ITS WAY THROUGH THE GUTS OF WORMS TO BE REBORN.
BONE JUST LIES THERE, MORE OR LESS.
YOU KNOW WHERE YOU ARE WITH BONE.
BUT FLESH HAS GOT ITS OWN, SUBVERSIVE AGENDA.
IT SLIPS AND SLIDES AND RESETTLES LIKE LOOSE SCREE ON THE SIDE OF A MOUNTAIN.
AND THEN, BEFORE YOU CAN EVEN TURN AROUND--

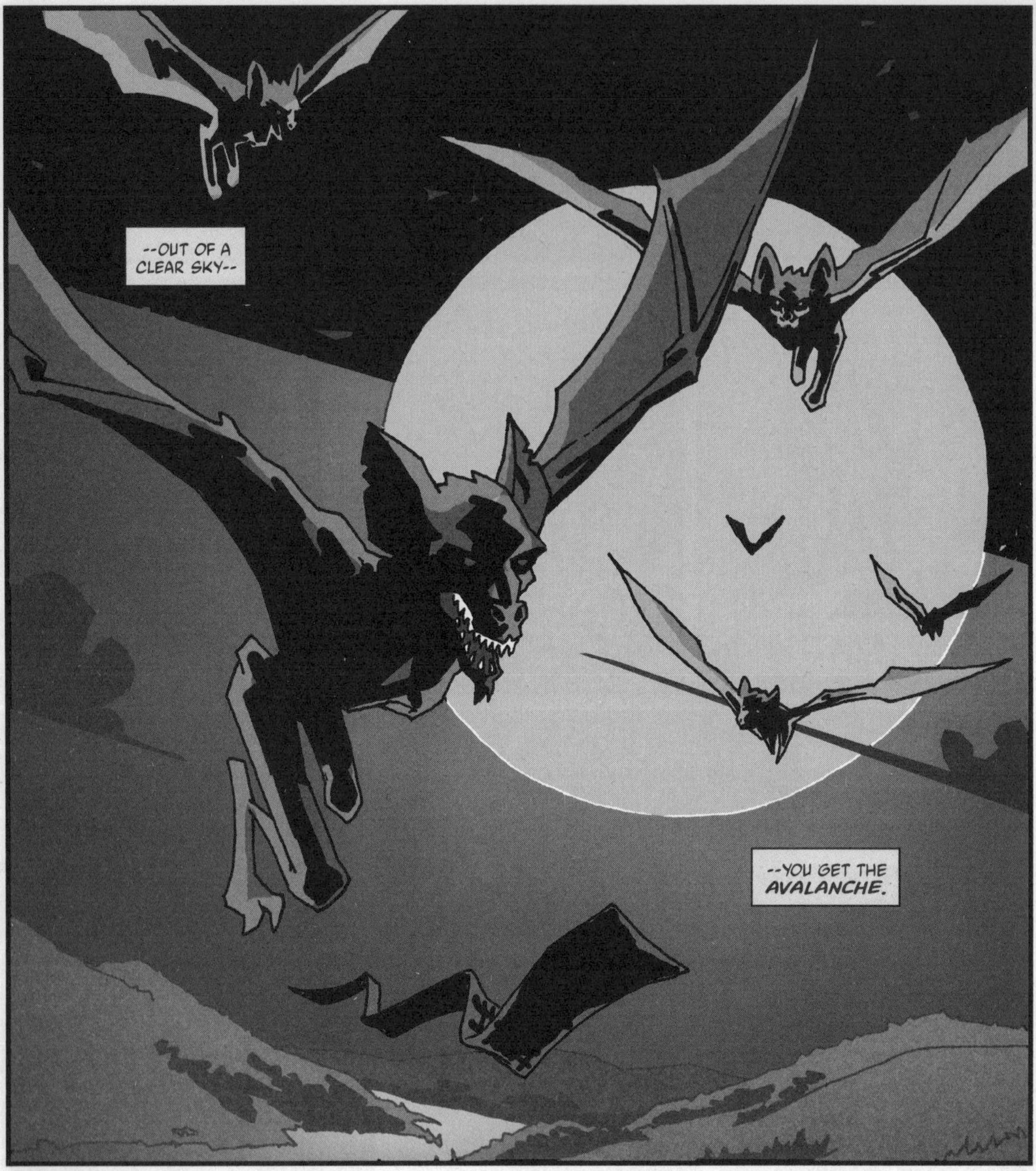
--OUT OF A CLEAR SKY--
--YOU GET THE AVALANCHE.

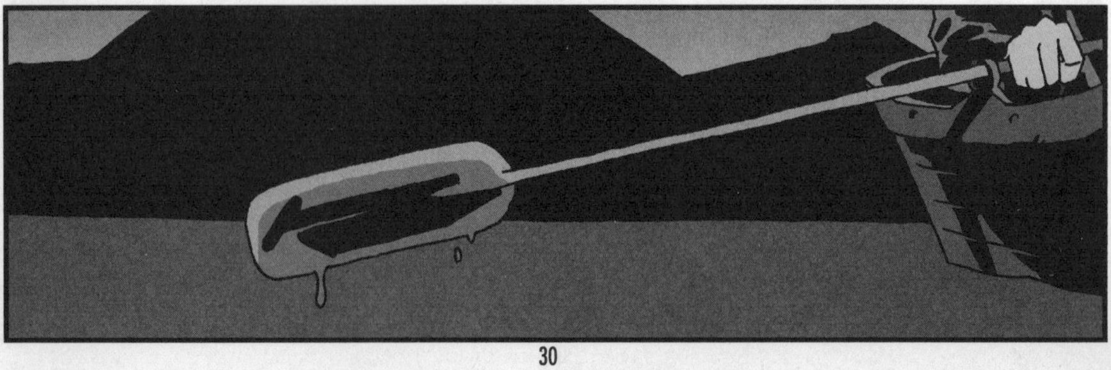

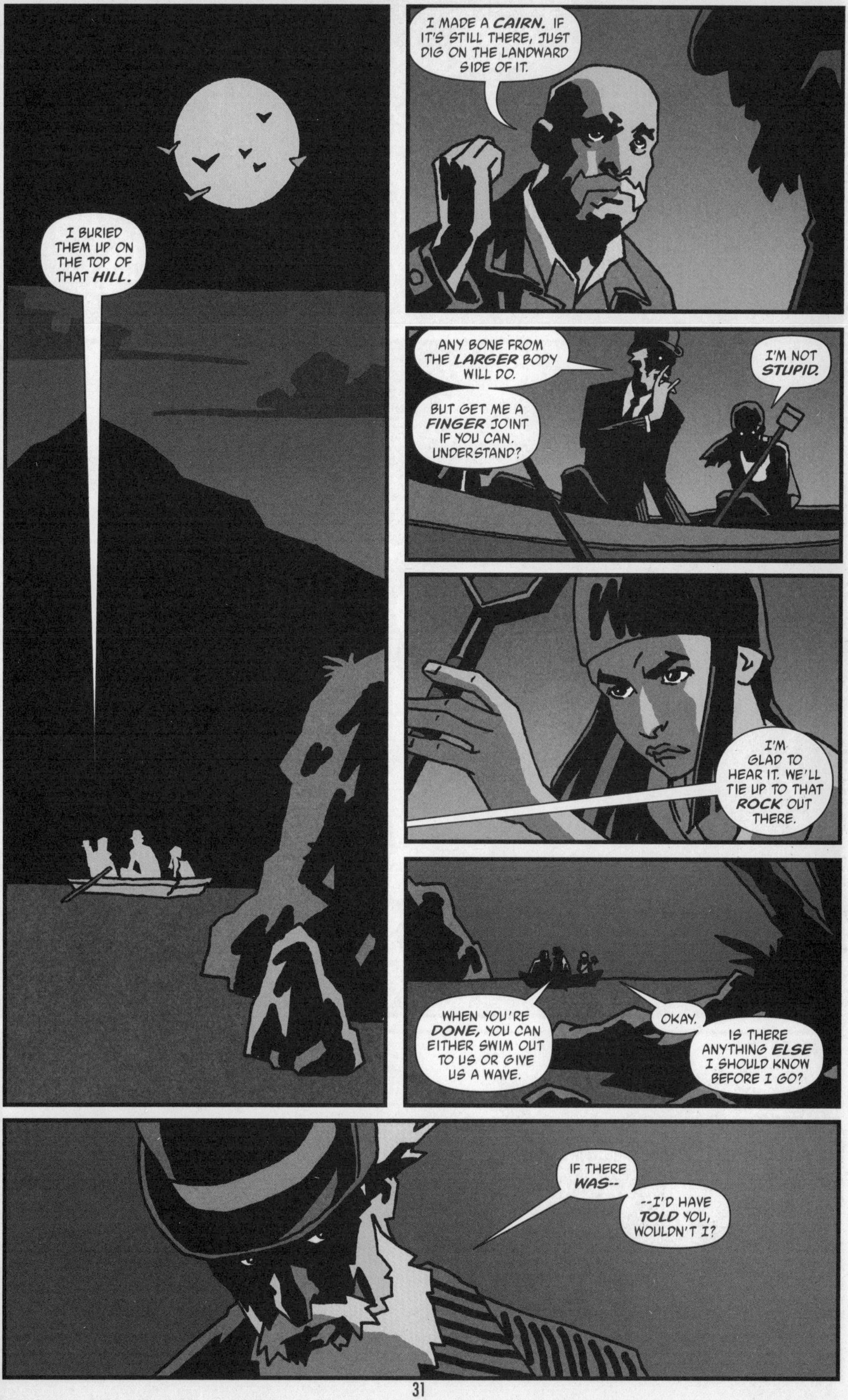
I BURIED THEM UP ON THE TOP OF THAT HILL.
I MADE A CAIRN. IF IT'S STILL THERE, JUST DIG ON THE LANDWARD SIDE OF IT.
ANY BONE FROM THE LARGER BODY WILL DO.
BUT GET ME A FINGER JOINT IF YOU CAN. UNDERSTAND?
I'M NOT STUPID.
I'M GLAD TO HEAR IT. WE'LL TIE UP TO THAT ROCK OUT THERE.
WHEN YOU'RE DONE, YOU CAN EITHER SWIM OUT TO US OR GIVE US A WAVE.
OKAY.
IS THERE ANYTHING ELSE I SHOULD KNOW BEFORE I GO?
IF THERE WAS--
--I'D HAVE TOLD YOU, WOULDN'T I?

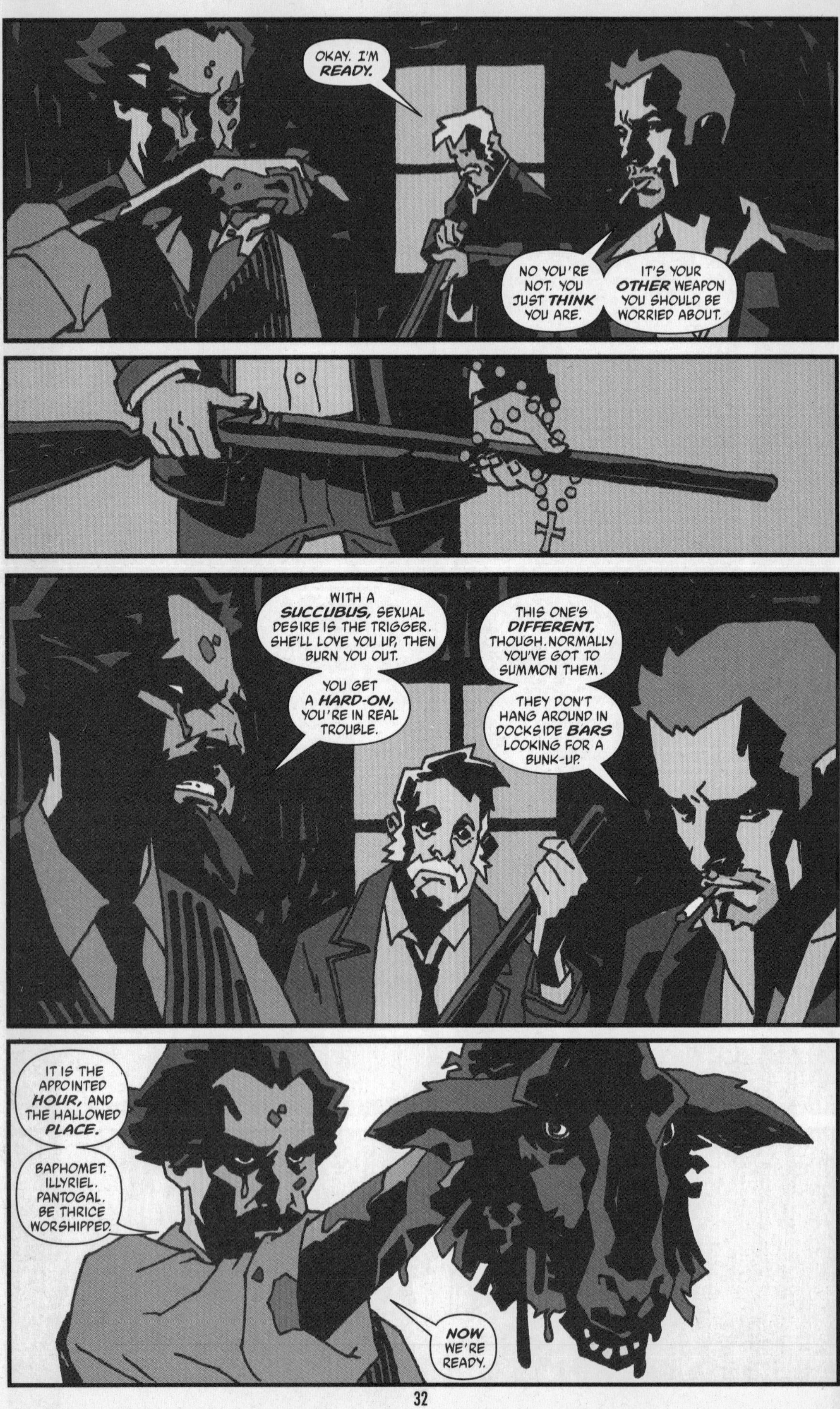
OKAY. I'M READY.
NO YOU'RE NOT. YOU JUST THINK YOU ARE.
IT'S YOUR OTHER WEAPON YOU SHOULD BE WORRIED ABOUT.
WITH A SUCCUBUS, SEXUAL DESIRE IS THE TRIGGER. SHE'LL LOVE YOU UP, THEN BURN YOU OUT.
YOU GET A HARD-ON, YOU'RE IN REAL TROUBLE.
THIS ONE'S DIFFERENT, THOUGH. NORMALLY YOU'VE GOT TO SUMMON THEM.
THEY DON'T HANG AROUND IN DOCKSIDE BARS LOOKING FOR A BUNK-UP.
IT IS THE APPOINTED HOUR, AND THE HALLOWED PLACE.
BAPHOMET. ILLYRIEL. PANTOGAL. BE THRICE WORSHIPPED.
NOW WE'RE READY.

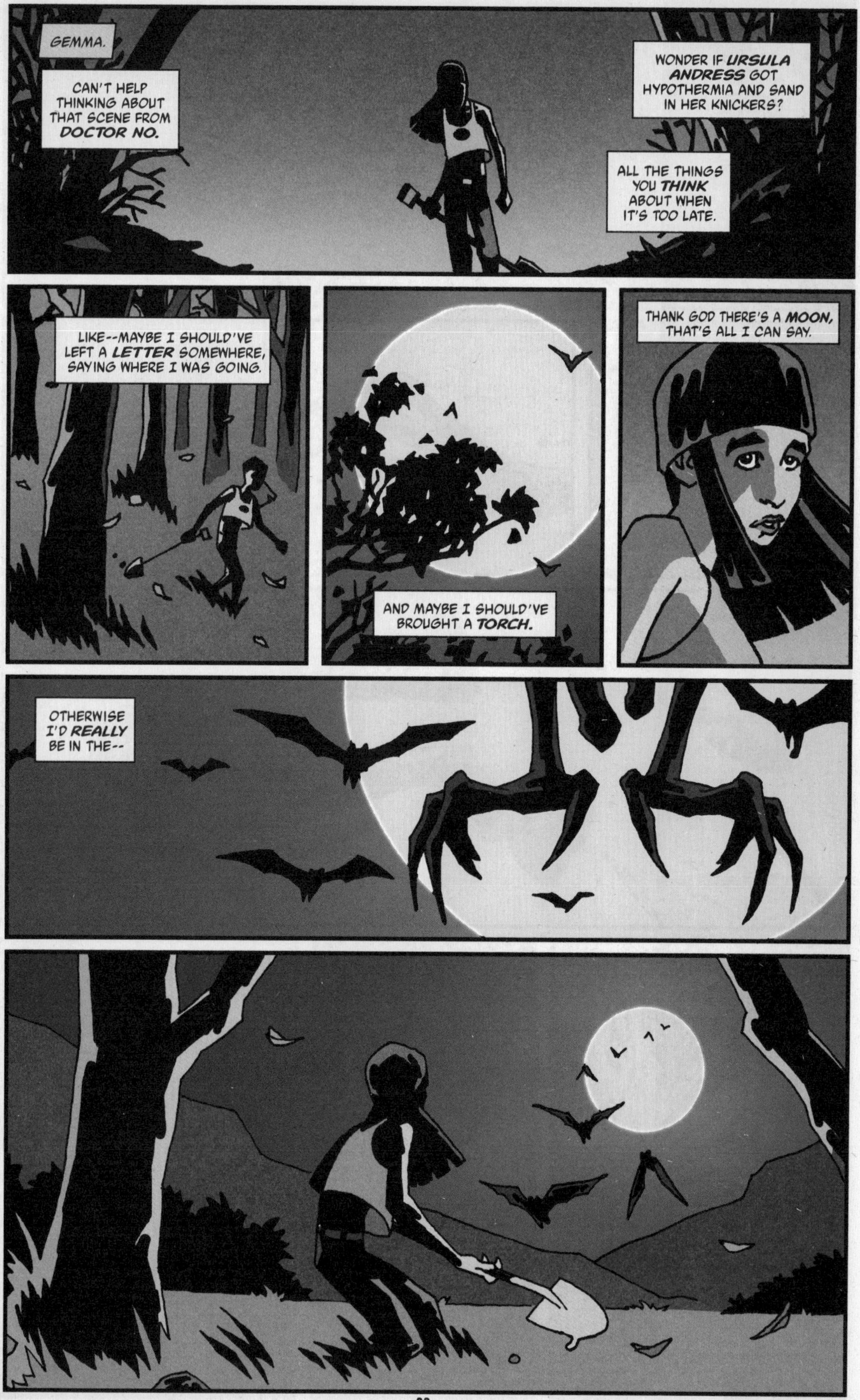
GEMMA.
CAN'T HELP THINKING ABOUT THAT SCENE FROM DOCTOR NO.
WONDER IF URSULA ANDRESS GOT HYPOTHERMIA AND SAND IN HER KNICKERS?
ALL THE THINGS YOU THINK ABOUT WHEN IT'S TOO LATE.
LIKE--MAYBE I SHOULD'VE LEFT A LETTER SOMEWHERE, SAYING WHERE I WAS GOING.
AND MAYBE I SHOULD'VE BROUGHT A TORCH.
THANK GOD THERE'S A MOON, THAT'S ALL I CAN SAY.
OTHERWISE I'D REALLY BE IN THE--

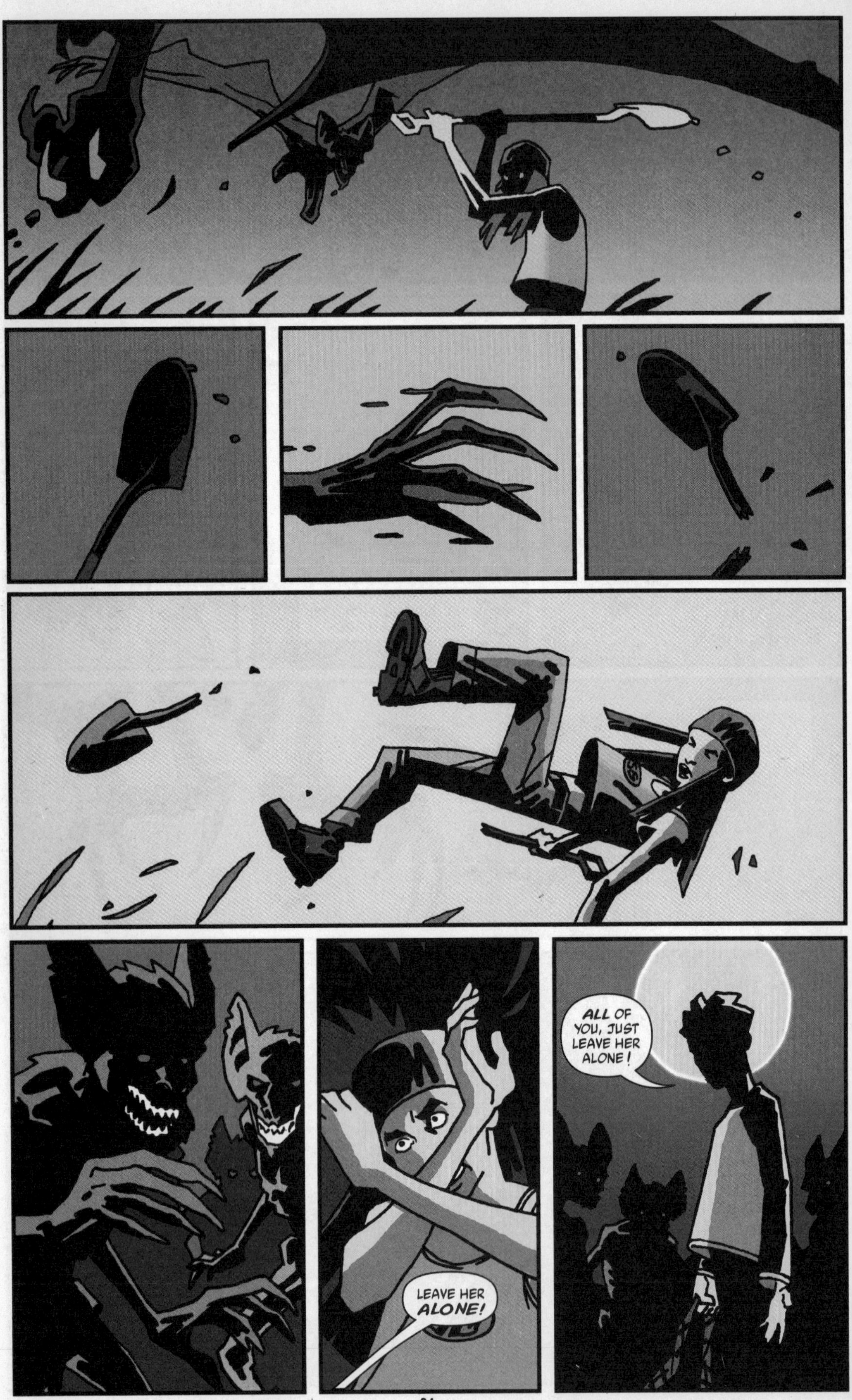
LEAVE HER
ALONE!
ALL OF
YOU, JUST
LEAVE HER
ALONE!

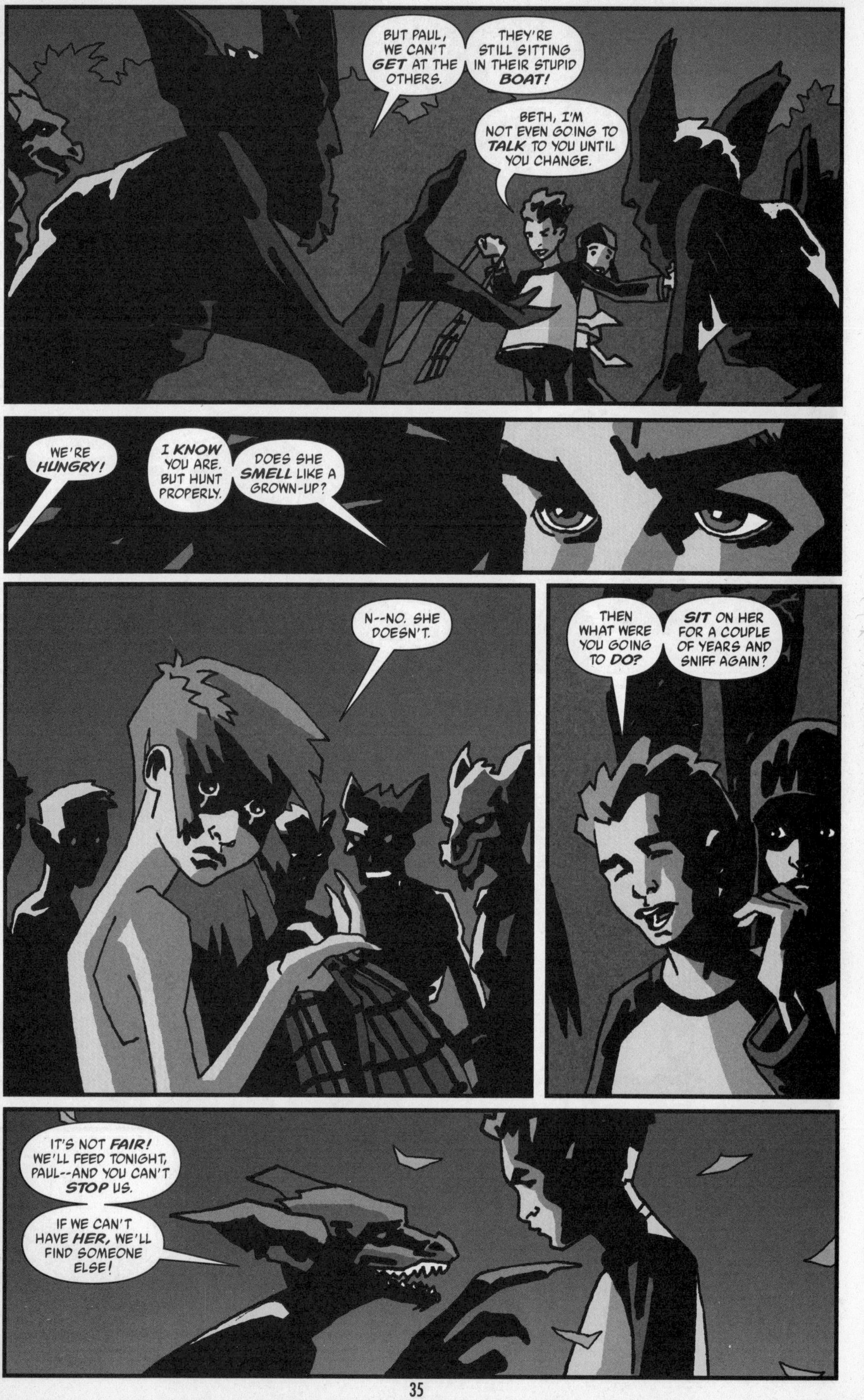

BUT PAUL, WE CAN'T GET AT THE OTHERS.
THEY'RE STILL SITTING IN THEIR STUPID BOAT!
BETH, I'M NOT EVEN GOING TO TALK TO YOU UNTIL YOU CHANGE.
WE'RE HUNGRY!
I KNOW YOU ARE. BUT HUNT PROPERLY.
DOES SHE SMELL LIKE A GROWN-UP?
N--NO. SHE DOESN'T.
THEN WHAT WERE YOU GOING TO DO?
SIT ON HER FOR A COUPLE OF YEARS AND SNIFF AGAIN?
IT'S NOT FAIR! WE'LL FEED TONIGHT, PAUL--AND YOU CAN'T STOP US.
IF WE CAN'T HAVE HER, WE'LL FIND SOMEONE ELSE!

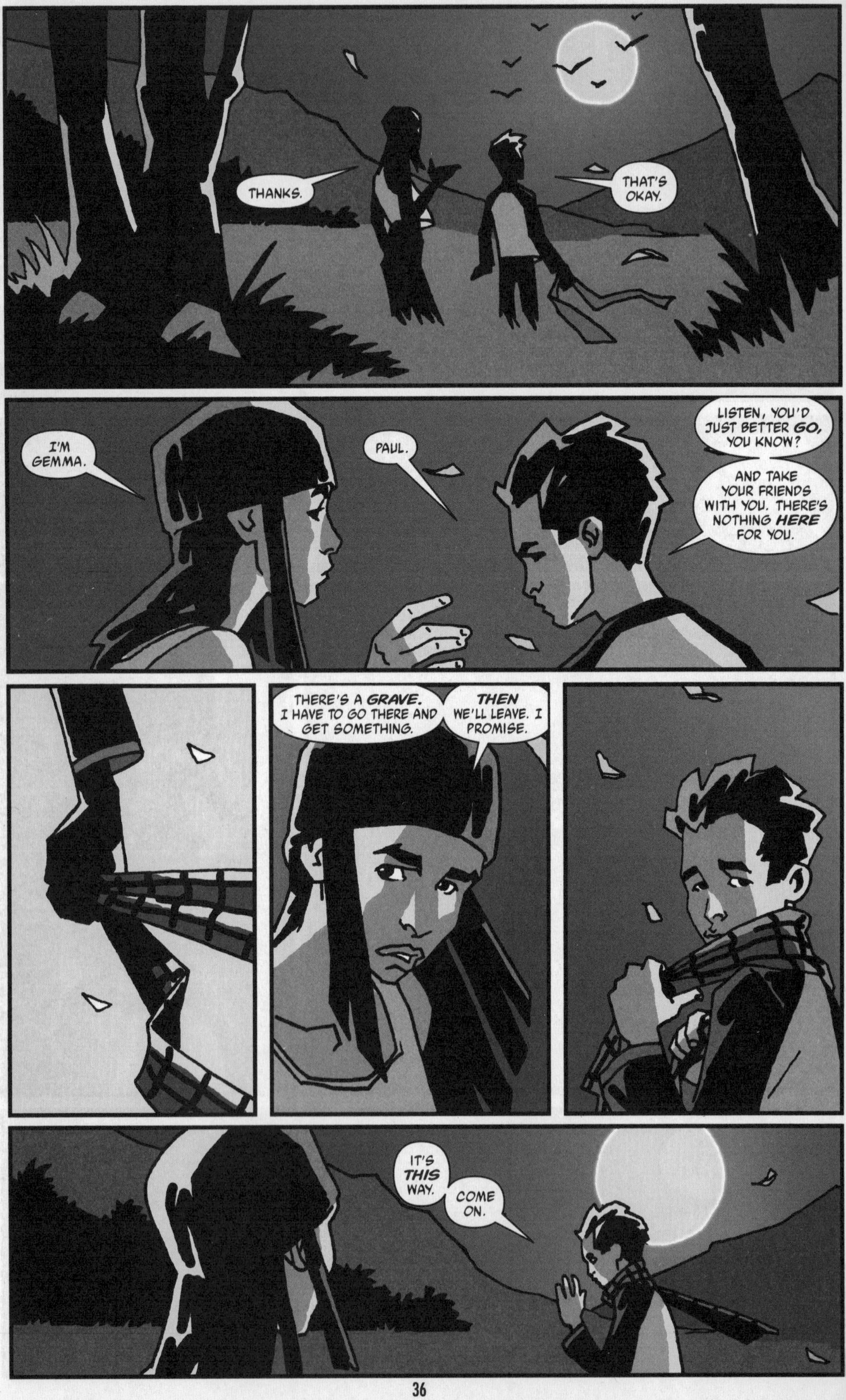
THANKS.
THAT'S OKAY.
I'M GEMMA.
PAUL.
LISTEN, YOU'D JUST BETTER GO, YOU KNOW?
AND TAKE YOUR FRIENDS WITH YOU. THERE'S NOTHING HERE FOR YOU.
THERE'S A GRAVE. I HAVE TO GO THERE AND GET SOMETHING.
THEN WE'LL LEAVE. I PROMISE.
IT'S THIS WAY.
COME ON.

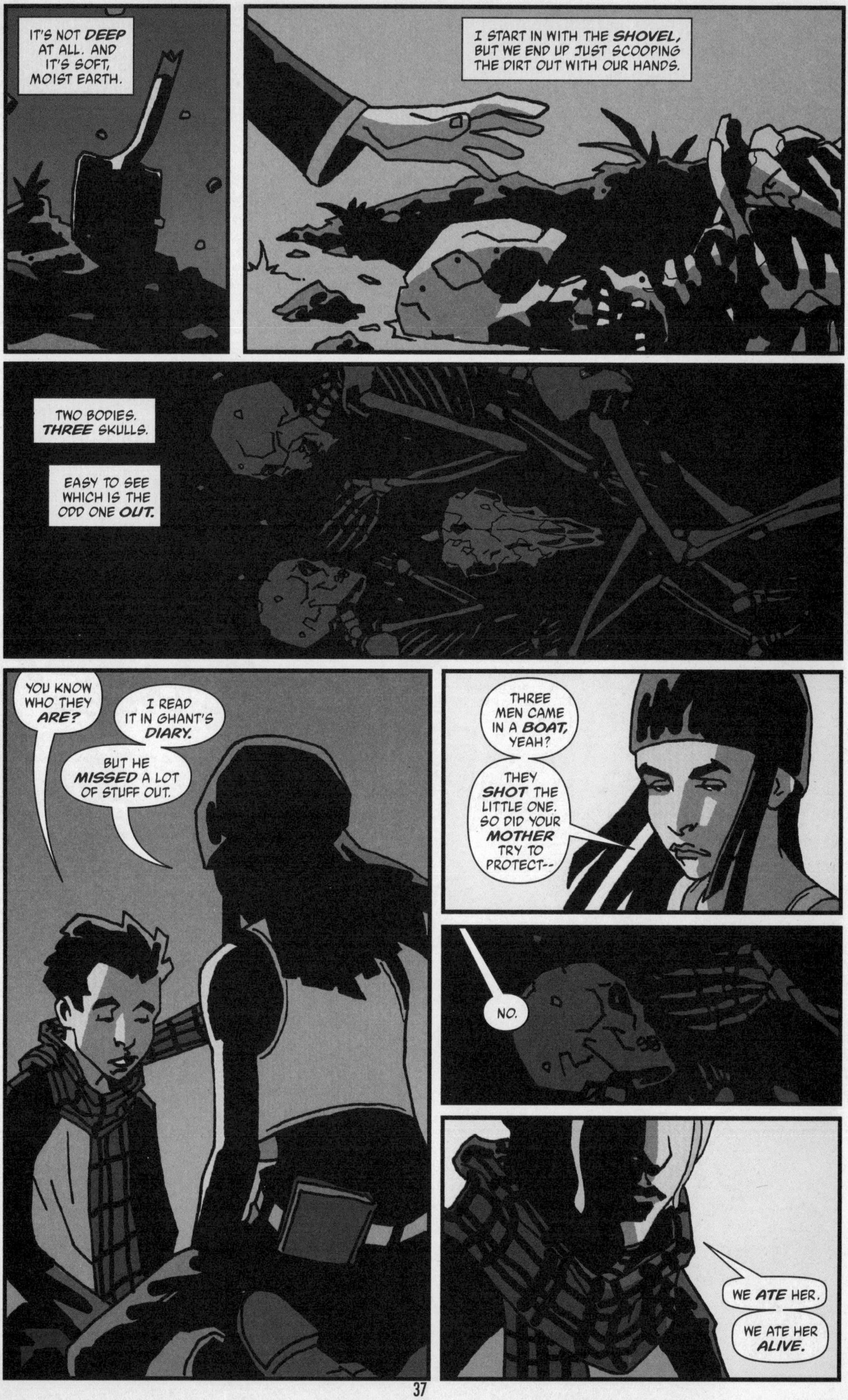
IT'S NOT DEEP AT ALL. AND IT'S SOFT, MOIST EARTH.
I START IN WITH THE SHOVEL, BUT WE END UP JUST SCOOPING THE DIRT OUT WITH OUR HANDS.
TWO BODIES. THREE SKULLS.
EASY TO SEE WHICH IS THE ODD ONE OUT.
YOU KNOW WHO THEY ARE?
I READ IT IN GHANT'S DIARY.
BUT HE MISSED A LOT OF STUFF OUT.
THREE MEN CAME IN A BOAT, YEAH?
THEY SHOT THE LITTLE ONE. SO DID YOUR MOTHER TRY TO PROTECT--
NO.
WE ATE HER.
WE ATE HER ALIVE.

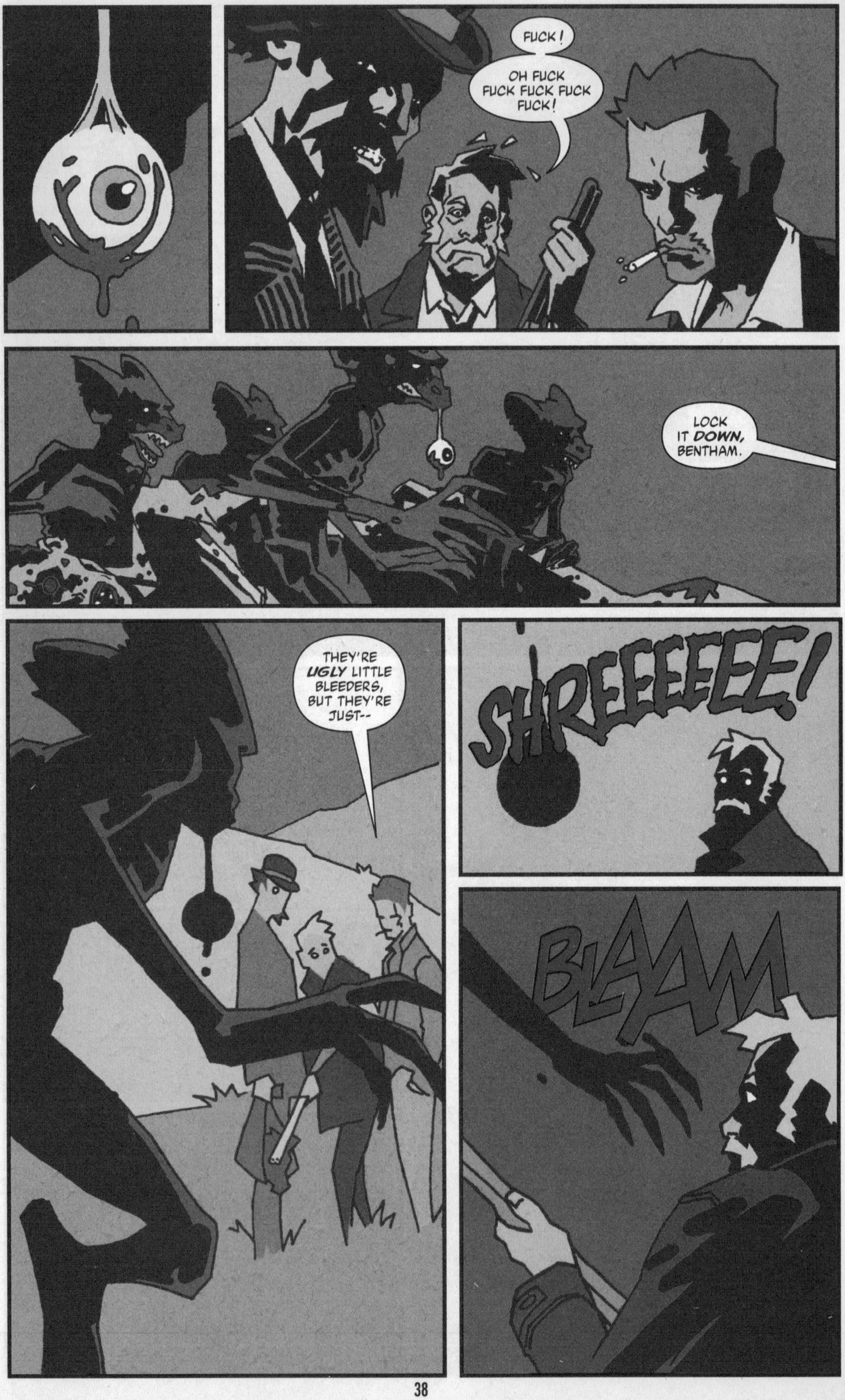
FUCK!
OH FUCK FUCK FUCK FUCK FUCK!
LOCK IT DOWN, BENTHAM.
THEY'RE UGLY LITTLE BLEEDERS, BUT THEY'RE JUST--
SHREEEEEEE!
BLAAM

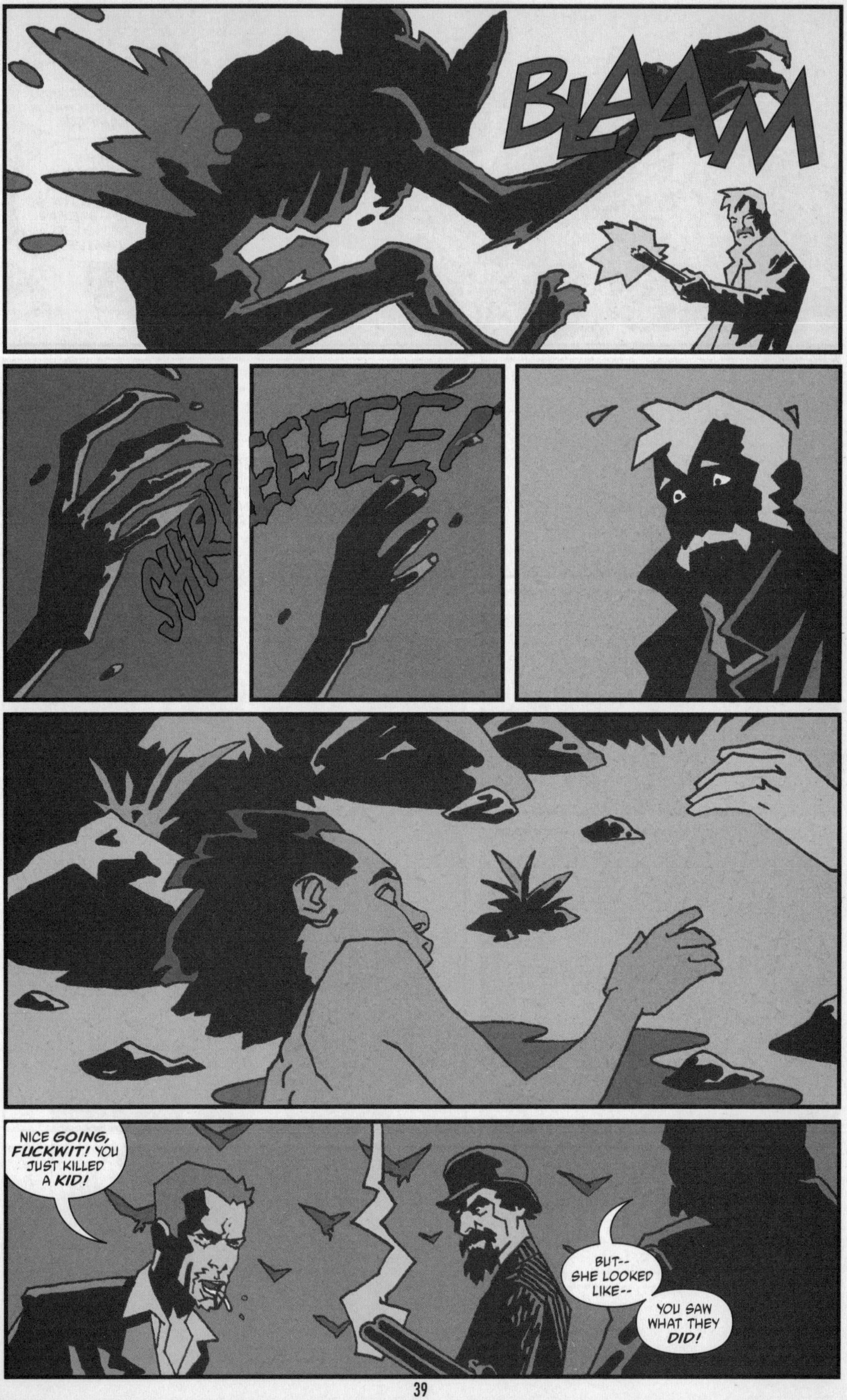
BLAAM
SHREEEEEEE!
NICE GOING, FUCKWIT! YOU JUST KILLED A KID!
BUT-- SHE LOOKED LIKE--
YOU SAW WHAT THEY DID!

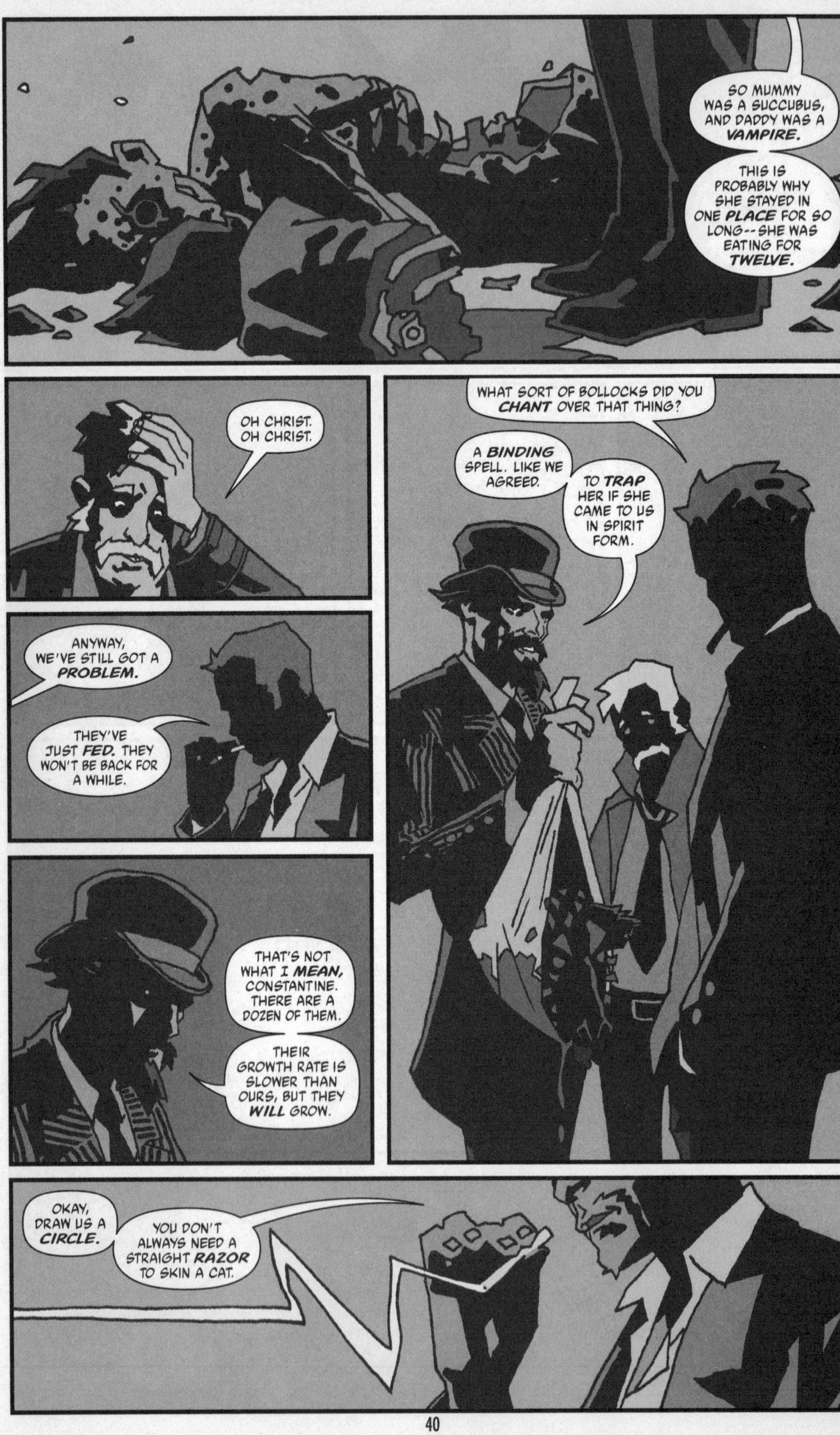

SO MUMMY WAS A SUCCUBUS, AND DADDY WAS A VAMPIRE.
THIS IS PROBABLY WHY SHE STAYED IN ONE PLACE FOR SO LONG--SHE WAS EATING FOR TWELVE.
OH CHRIST. OH CHRIST.
ANYWAY, WE'VE STILL GOT A PROBLEM.
THEY'VE JUST FED. THEY WON'T BE BACK FOR A WHILE.
THAT'S NOT WHAT I MEAN, CONSTANTINE. THERE ARE A DOZEN OF THEM.
THEIR GROWTH RATE IS SLOWER THAN OURS, BUT THEY WILL GROW.
WHAT SORT OF BOLLOCKS DID YOU CHANT OVER THAT THING?
A BINDING SPELL. LIKE WE AGREED.
TO TRAP HER IF SHE CAME TO US IN SPIRIT FORM.
OKAY, DRAW US A CIRCLE.
YOU DON'T ALWAYS NEED A STRAIGHT RAZOR TO SKIN A CAT.

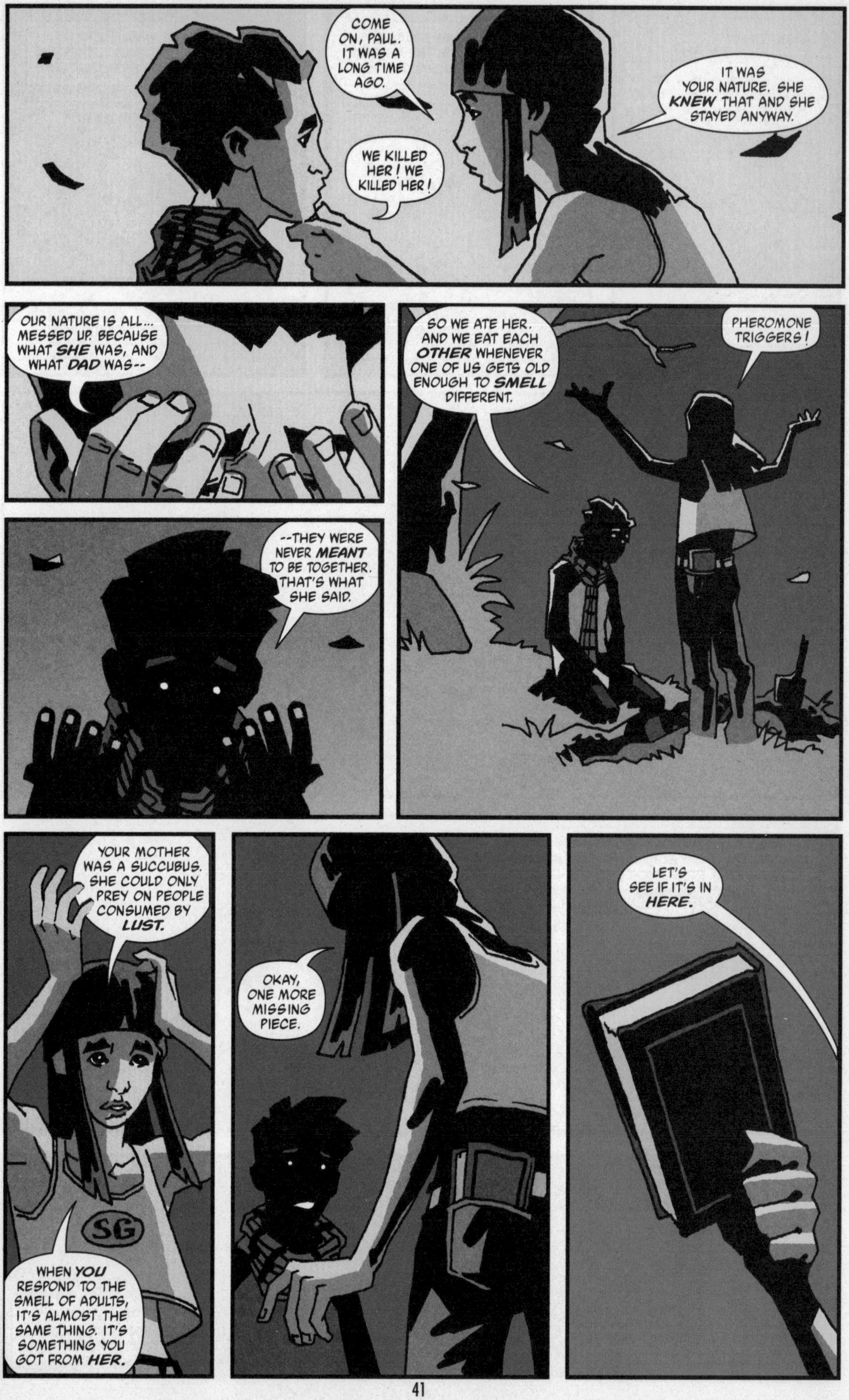
COME ON, PAUL. IT WAS A LONG TIME AGO.
WE KILLED HER! WE KILLED HER!
IT WAS YOUR NATURE. SHE KNEW THAT AND SHE STAYED ANYWAY.
OUR NATURE IS ALL... MESSED UP. BECAUSE WHAT SHE WAS, AND WHAT DAD WAS--
--THEY WERE NEVER MEANT TO BE TOGETHER. THAT'S WHAT SHE SAID.
SO WE ATE HER. AND WE EAT EACH OTHER WHENEVER ONE OF US GETS OLD ENOUGH TO SMELL DIFFERENT.
PHEROMONE TRIGGERS!
YOUR MOTHER WAS A SUCCUBUS. SHE COULD ONLY PREY ON PEOPLE CONSUMED BY LUST.
SG
WHEN YOU RESPOND TO THE SMELL OF ADULTS, IT'S ALMOST THE SAME THING. IT'S SOMETHING YOU GOT FROM HER.
OKAY, ONE MORE MISSING PIECE.
LET'S SEE IF IT'S IN HERE.

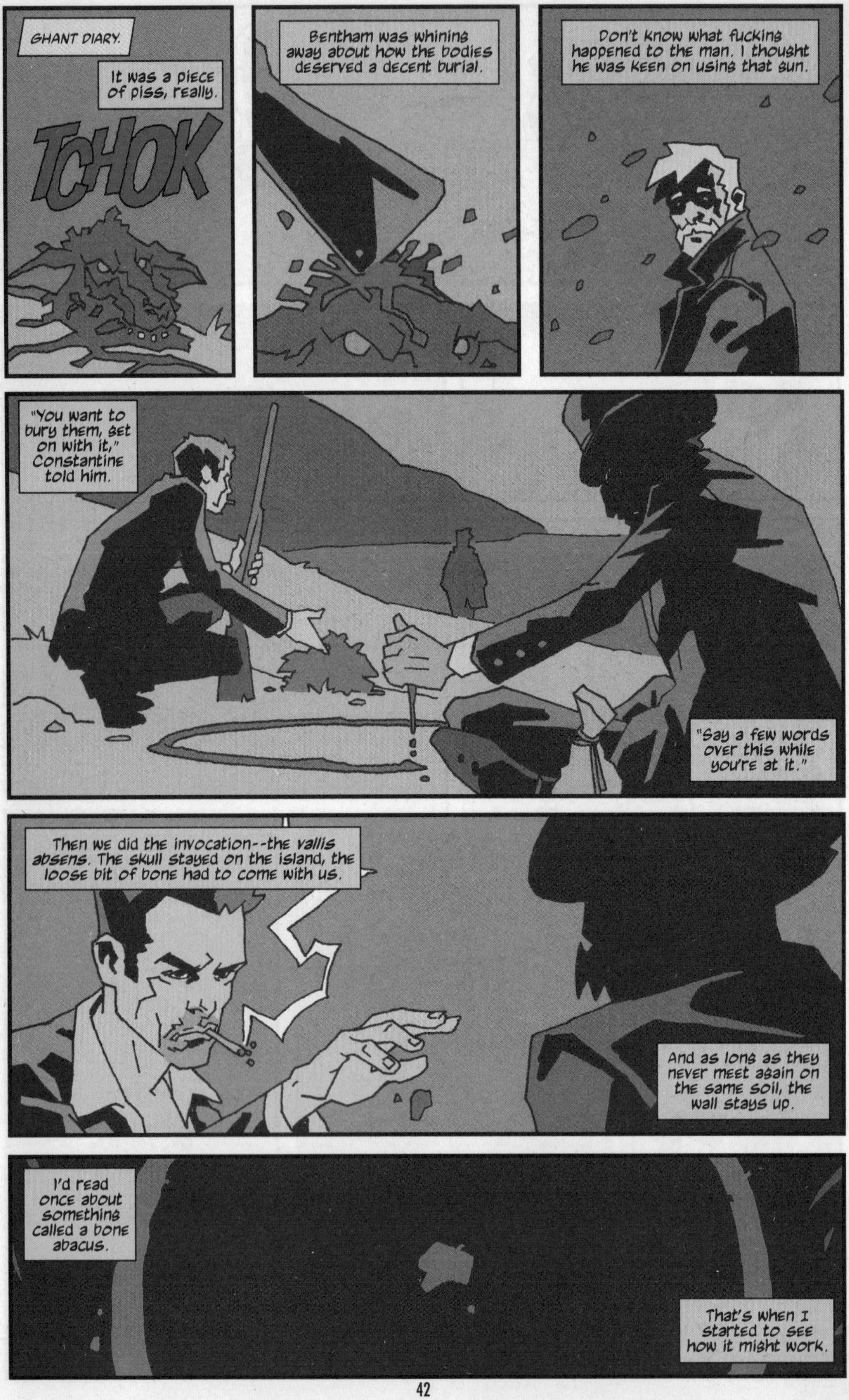
GHANT DIARY.
It was a piece of piss, really.
TCHOK
Bentham was whining away about how the bodies deserved a decent burial.
Don't know what fucking happened to the man. I thought he was keen on using that gun.
"You want to bury them, get on with it," Constantine told him.
"Say a few words over this while you're at it."
Then we did the invocation--the *vallis absens*. The skull stayed on the island, the loose bit of bone had to come with us.
And as long as they never meet again on the same soil, the wall stays up.
I'd read once about something called a bone abacus.
That's when I started to see how it might work.

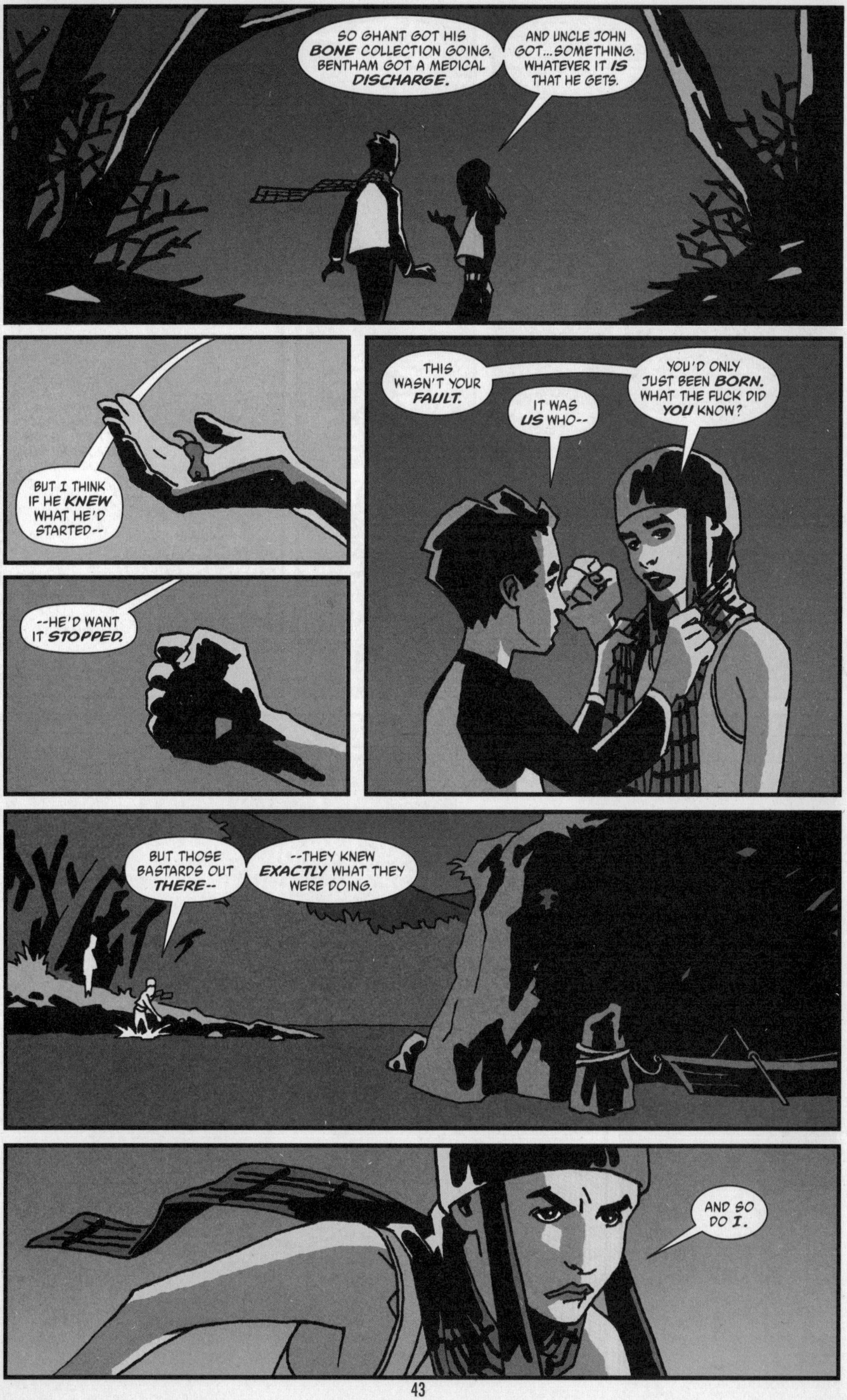
SO GHANT GOT HIS BONE COLLECTION GOING. BENTHAM GOT A MEDICAL DISCHARGE.
AND UNCLE JOHN GOT...SOMETHING. WHATEVER IT IS THAT HE GETS.
BUT I THINK IF HE KNEW WHAT HE'D STARTED--
--HE'D WANT IT STOPPED.
THIS WASN'T YOUR FAULT.
IT WAS US WHO--
YOU'D ONLY JUST BEEN BORN. WHAT THE FUCK DID YOU KNOW?
BUT THOSE BASTARDS OUT THERE--
--THEY KNEW EXACTLY WHAT THEY WERE DOING.
AND SO DO I.

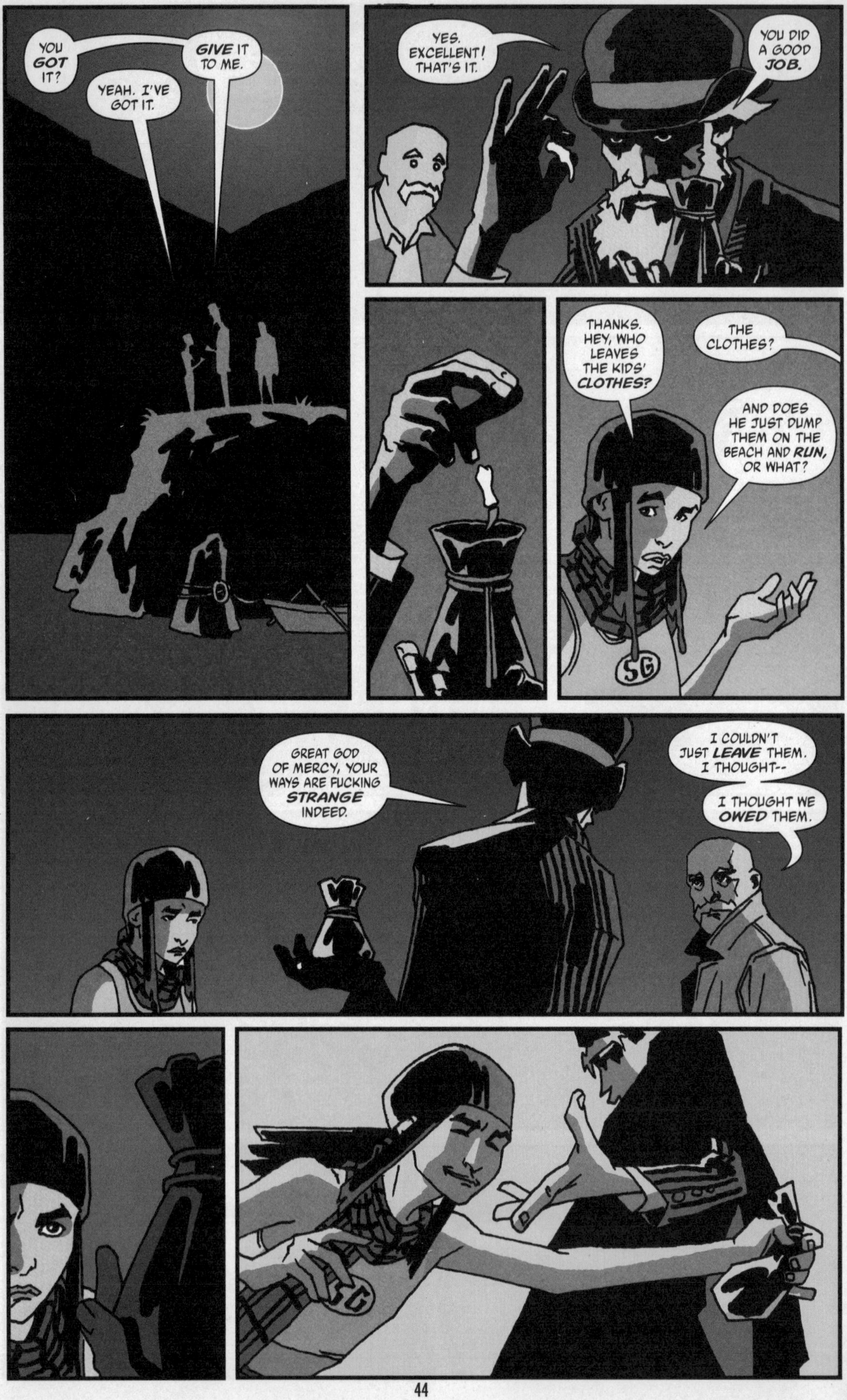
YOU **GOT** IT?
YEAH. I'VE GOT IT.
GIVE IT TO ME.
YES. EXCELLENT! THAT'S IT.
YOU DID A GOOD **JOB.**
THANKS. HEY, WHO LEAVES THE KIDS' **CLOTHES?**
THE CLOTHES?
AND DOES HE JUST DUMP THEM ON THE BEACH AND **RUN,** OR WHAT?
GREAT GOD OF MERCY, YOUR WAYS ARE FUCKING **STRANGE** INDEED.
I COULDN'T JUST **LEAVE** THEM. I THOUGHT--
I THOUGHT WE **OWED** THEM.

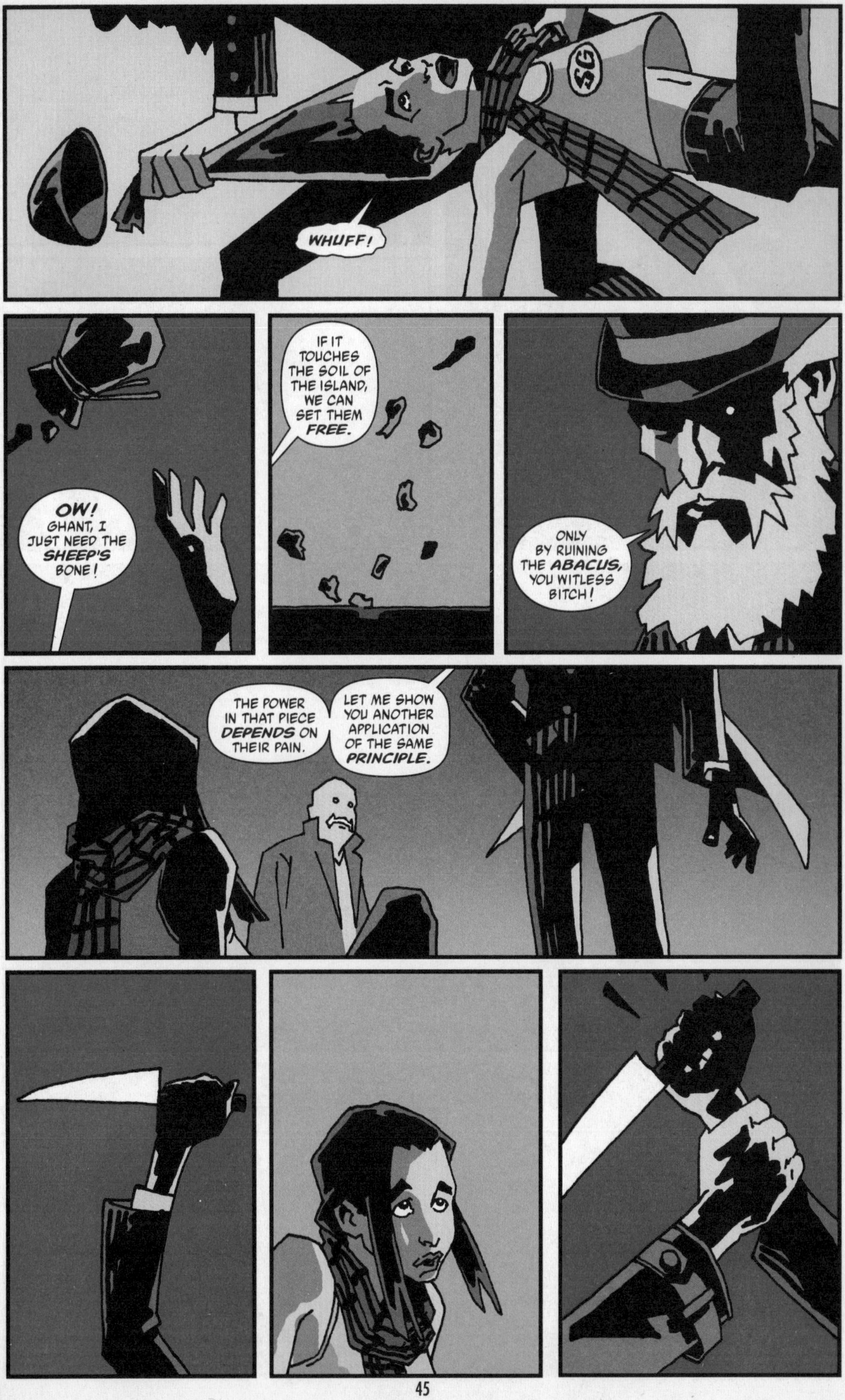
WHUFF!
OW! GHANT, I JUST NEED THE SHEEP'S BONE!
IF IT TOUCHES THE SOIL OF THE ISLAND, WE CAN SET THEM FREE.
ONLY BY RUINING THE ABACUS, YOU WITLESS BITCH!
THE POWER IN THAT PIECE DEPENDS ON THEIR PAIN.
LET ME SHOW YOU ANOTHER APPLICATION OF THE SAME PRINCIPLE.

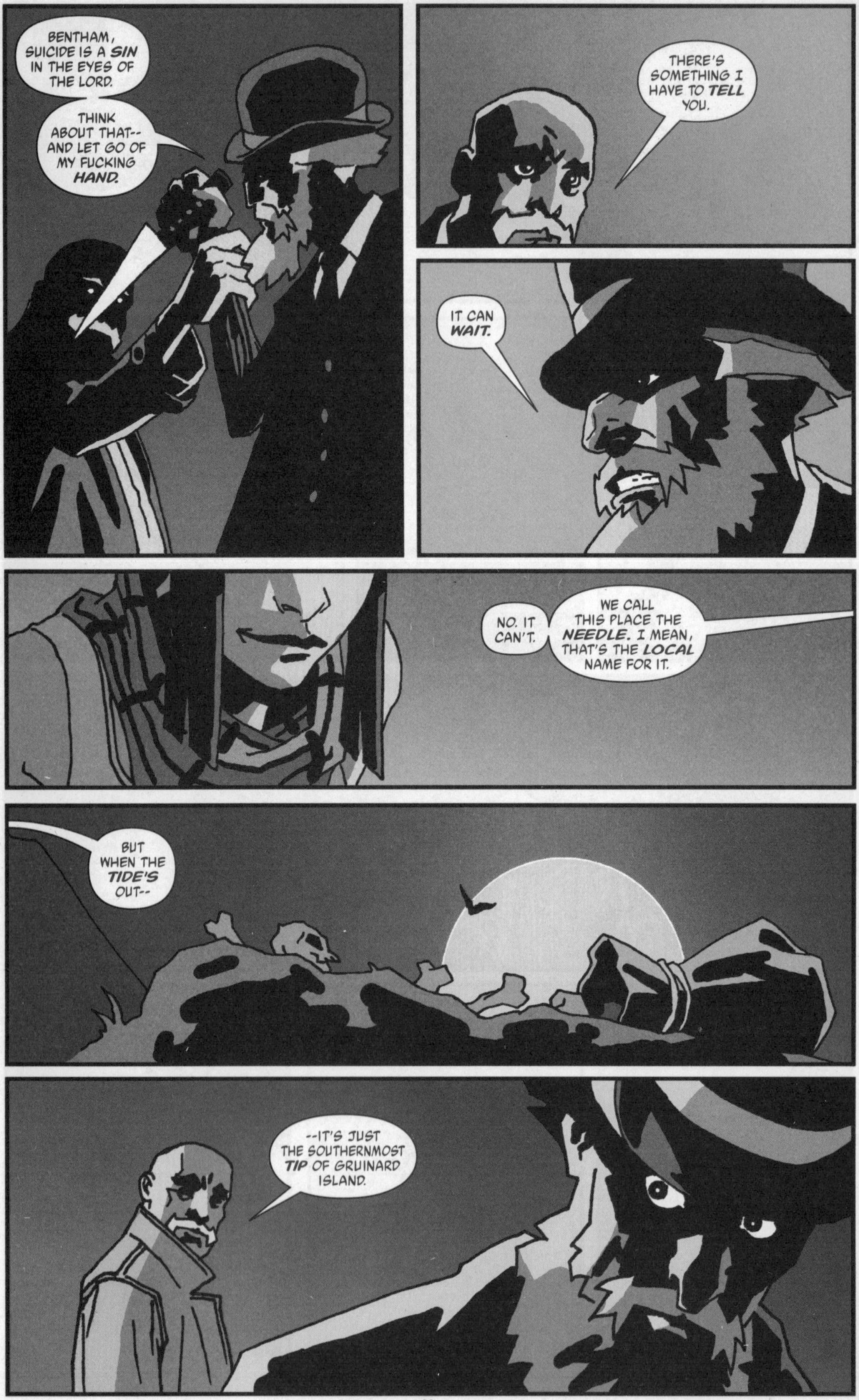
BENTHAM, SUICIDE IS A SIN IN THE EYES OF THE LORD.
THINK ABOUT THAT-- AND LET GO OF MY FUCKING HAND.
THERE'S SOMETHING I HAVE TO TELL YOU.
IT CAN WAIT.
NO. IT CAN'T.
WE CALL THIS PLACE THE NEEDLE. I MEAN, THAT'S THE LOCAL NAME FOR IT.
BUT WHEN THE TIDE'S OUT--
--IT'S JUST THE SOUTHERNMOST TIP OF GRUINARD ISLAND.

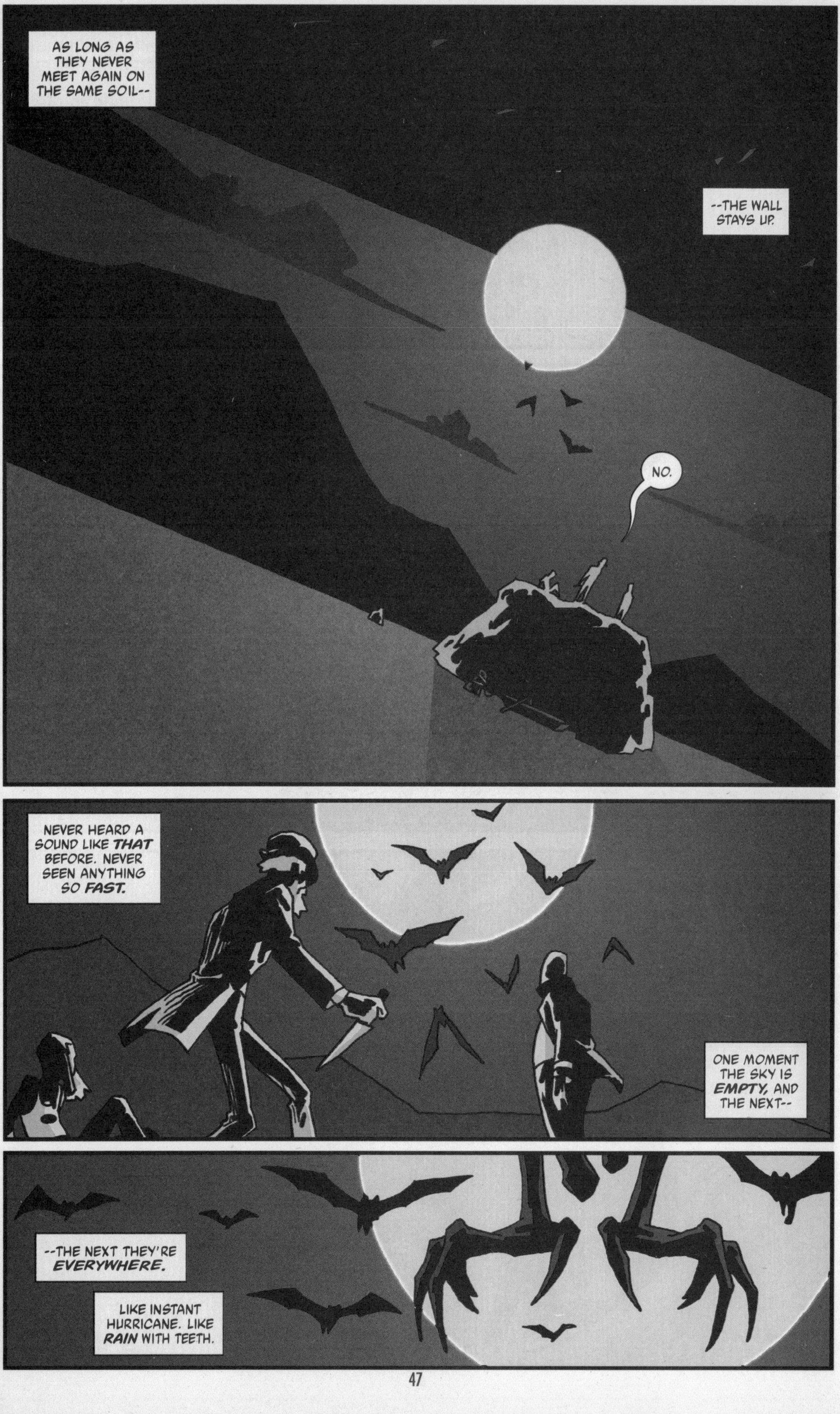
AS LONG AS THEY NEVER MEET AGAIN ON THE SAME SOIL--
--THE WALL STAYS UP.
NO.
NEVER HEARD A SOUND LIKE THAT BEFORE. NEVER SEEN ANYTHING SO FAST.
ONE MOMENT THE SKY IS EMPTY, AND THE NEXT--
--THE NEXT THEY'RE EVERYWHERE.
LIKE INSTANT HURRICANE. LIKE RAIN WITH TEETH.

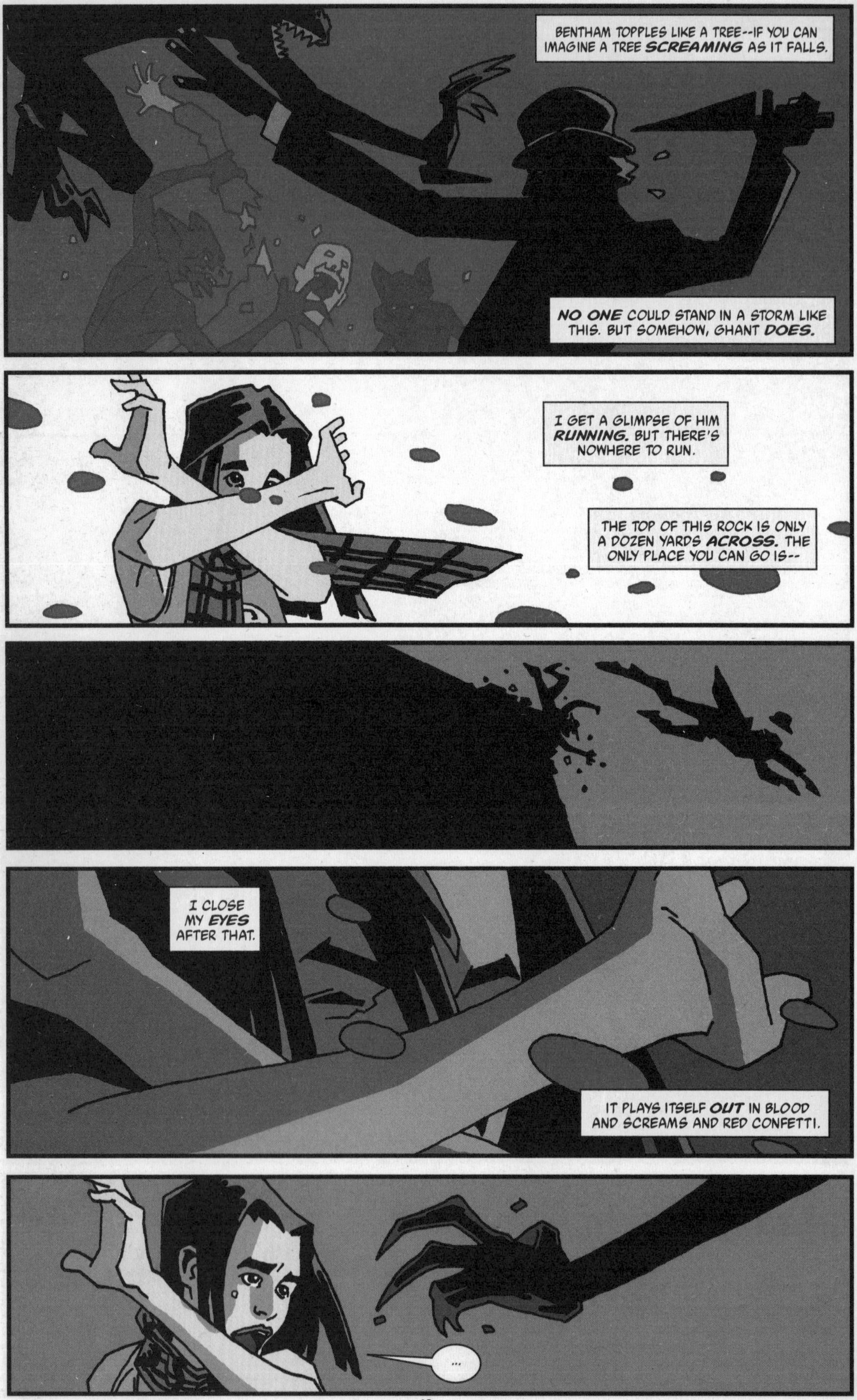
BENTHAM TOPPLES LIKE A TREE--IF YOU CAN IMAGINE A TREE SCREAMING AS IT FALLS.
NO ONE COULD STAND IN A STORM LIKE THIS. BUT SOMEHOW, GHANT DOES.
I GET A GLIMPSE OF HIM RUNNING. BUT THERE'S NOWHERE TO RUN.
THE TOP OF THIS ROCK IS ONLY A DOZEN YARDS ACROSS. THE ONLY PLACE YOU CAN GO IS--
I CLOSE MY EYES AFTER THAT.
IT PLAYS ITSELF OUT IN BLOOD AND SCREAMS AND RED CONFETTI.
...

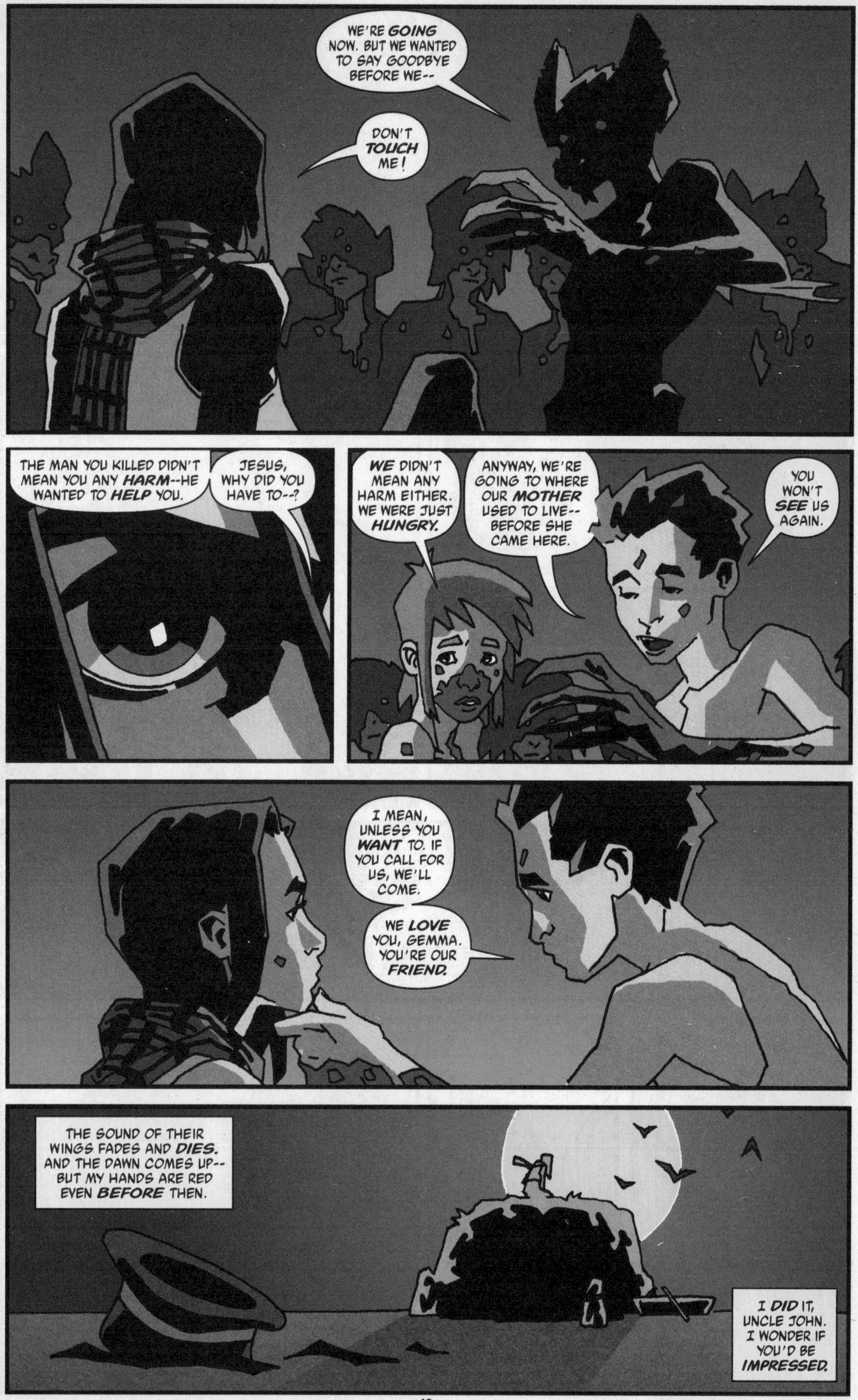
WE'RE **GOING** NOW. BUT WE WANTED TO SAY GOODBYE BEFORE WE--
DON'T **TOUCH** ME!
THE MAN YOU KILLED DIDN'T MEAN YOU ANY **HARM**--HE WANTED TO **HELP** YOU.
JESUS, WHY DID YOU HAVE TO--?
WE DIDN'T MEAN ANY HARM EITHER. WE WERE JUST **HUNGRY.**
ANYWAY, WE'RE GOING TO WHERE OUR **MOTHER** USED TO LIVE-- BEFORE SHE CAME HERE.
YOU WON'T **SEE** US AGAIN.
I MEAN, UNLESS YOU **WANT** TO. IF YOU CALL FOR US, WE'LL COME.
WE **LOVE** YOU, GEMMA. YOU'RE OUR **FRIEND.**
THE SOUND OF THEIR WINGS FADES AND **DIES.** AND THE DAWN COMES UP-- BUT MY HANDS ARE RED EVEN **BEFORE** THEN.
I **DID** IT, UNCLE JOHN. I WONDER IF YOU'D BE **IMPRESSED.**

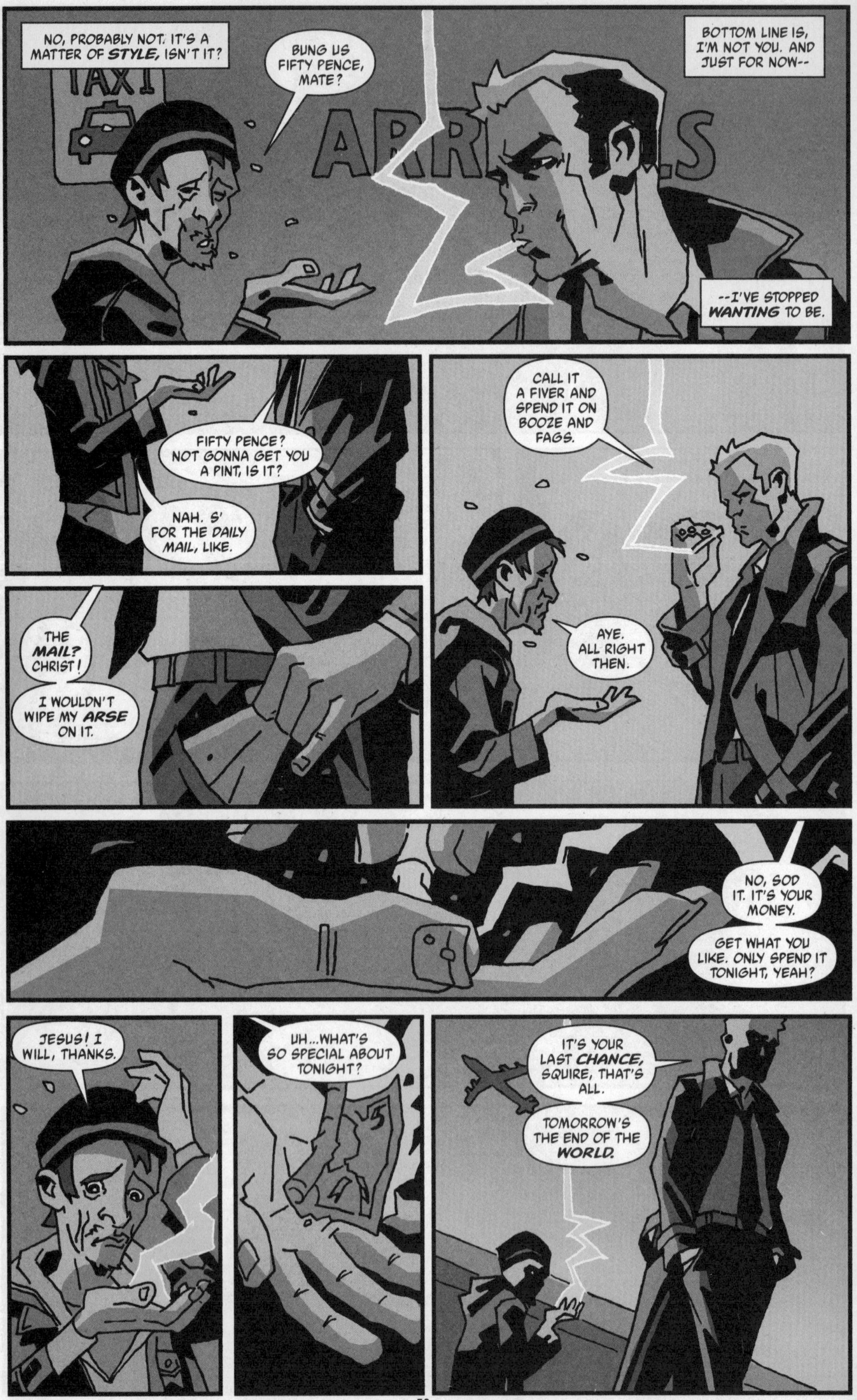
NO, PROBABLY NOT. IT'S A MATTER OF STYLE, ISN'T IT?
BUNG US FIFTY PENCE, MATE?
TAXI
ARRIVALS
BOTTOM LINE IS, I'M NOT YOU. AND JUST FOR NOW--
--I'VE STOPPED WANTING TO BE.
FIFTY PENCE? NOT GONNA GET YOU A PINT, IS IT?
NAH. S' FOR THE DAILY MAIL, LIKE.
CALL IT A FIVER AND SPEND IT ON BOOZE AND FAGS.
THE MAIL? CHRIST!
I WOULDN'T WIPE MY ARSE ON IT.
AYE. ALL RIGHT THEN.
NO, SOD IT. IT'S YOUR MONEY.
GET WHAT YOU LIKE. ONLY SPEND IT TONIGHT, YEAH?
JESUS! I WILL, THANKS.
UH...WHAT'S SO SPECIAL ABOUT TONIGHT?
IT'S YOUR LAST CHANCE, SQUIRE, THAT'S ALL.
TOMORROW'S THE END OF THE WORLD.

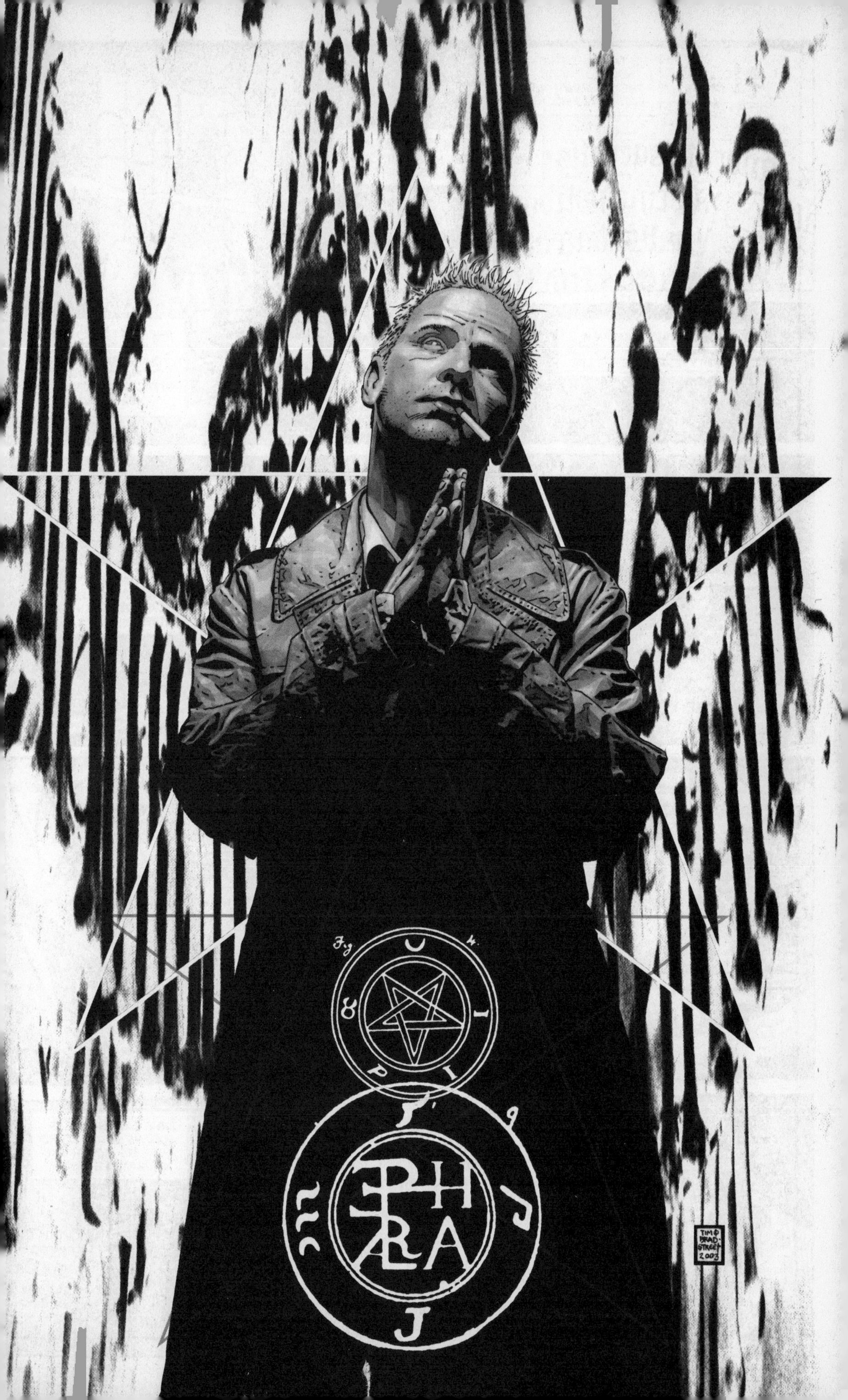
TIM BRAD-STREET 2003

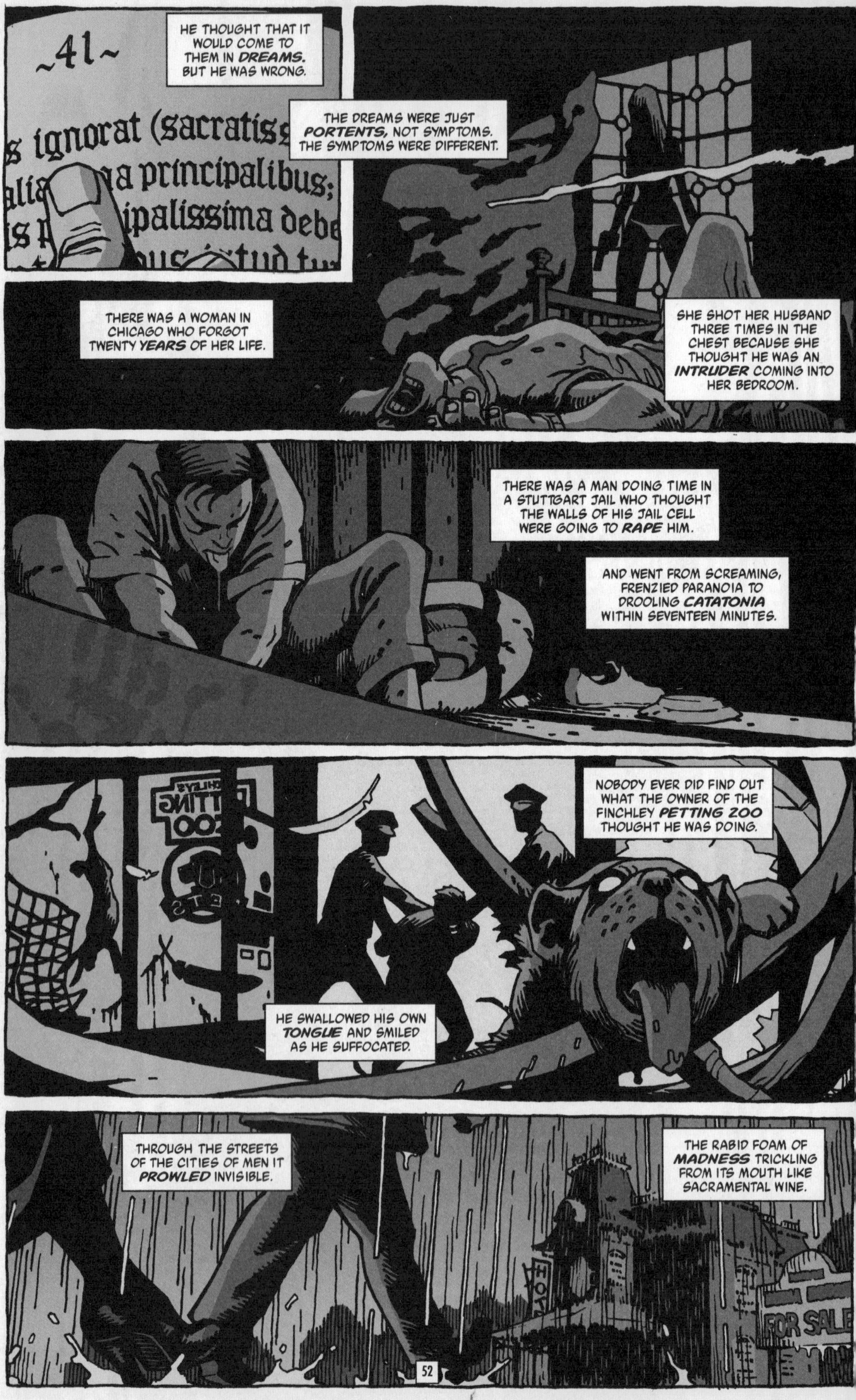
HE THOUGHT THAT IT WOULD COME TO THEM IN DREAMS. BUT HE WAS WRONG.
THE DREAMS WERE JUST PORTENTS, NOT SYMPTOMS. THE SYMPTOMS WERE DIFFERENT.
THERE WAS A WOMAN IN CHICAGO WHO FORGOT TWENTY YEARS OF HER LIFE.
SHE SHOT HER HUSBAND THREE TIMES IN THE CHEST BECAUSE SHE THOUGHT HE WAS AN INTRUDER COMING INTO HER BEDROOM.
THERE WAS A MAN DOING TIME IN A STUTTGART JAIL WHO THOUGHT THE WALLS OF HIS JAIL CELL WERE GOING TO RAPE HIM.
AND WENT FROM SCREAMING, FRENZIED PARANOIA TO DROOLING CATATONIA WITHIN SEVENTEEN MINUTES.
NOBODY EVER DID FIND OUT WHAT THE OWNER OF THE FINCHLEY PETTING ZOO THOUGHT HE WAS DOING.
HE SWALLOWED HIS OWN TONGUE AND SMILED AS HE SUFFOCATED.
THROUGH THE STREETS OF THE CITIES OF MEN IT PROWLED INVISIBLE.
THE RABID FOAM OF MADNESS TRICKLING FROM ITS MOUTH LIKE SACRAMENTAL WINE.

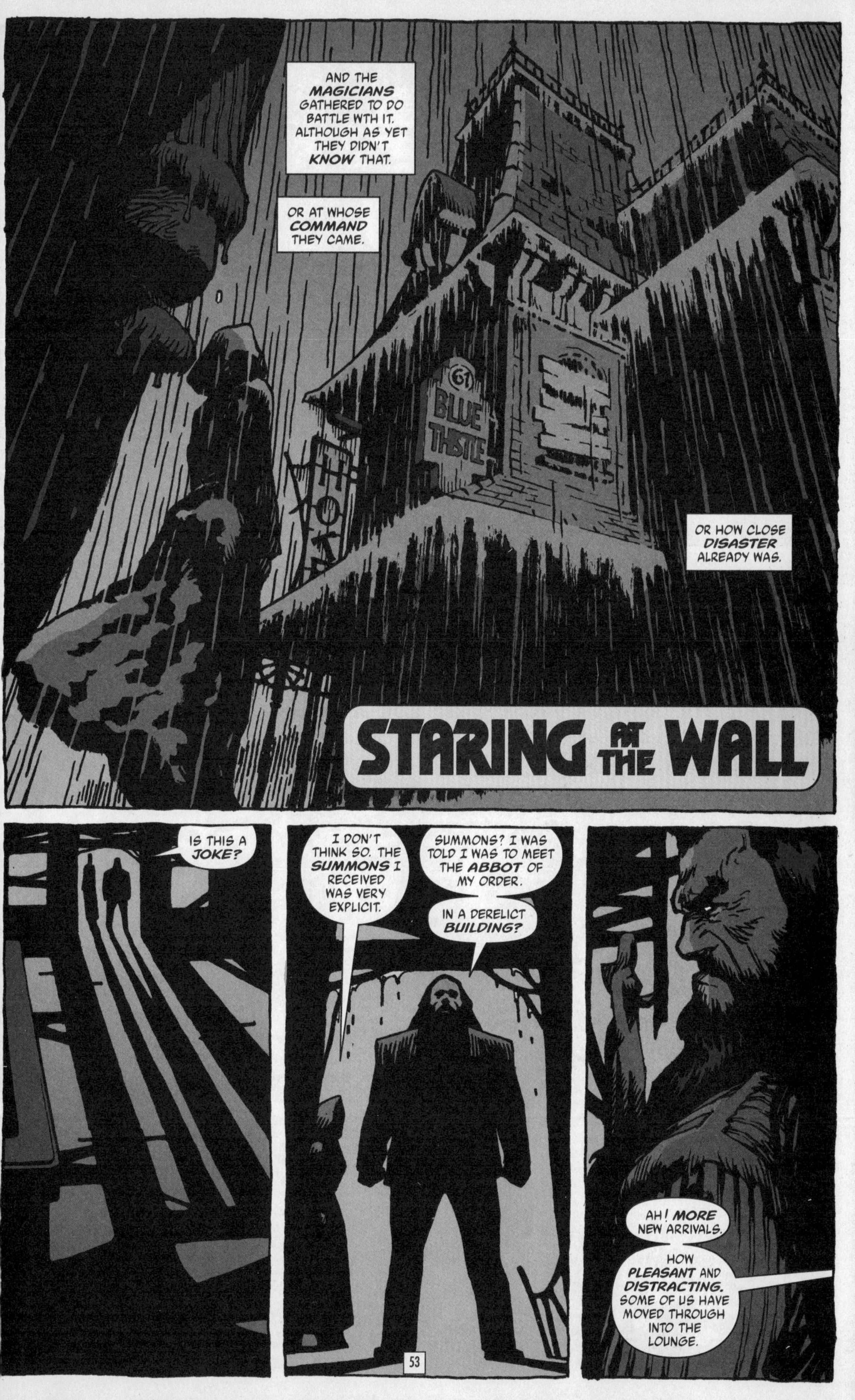
AND THE MAGICIANS GATHERED TO DO BATTLE WTH IT. ALTHOUGH AS YET THEY DIDN'T KNOW THAT.
OR AT WHOSE COMMAND THEY CAME.
BLUE THSTE
OR HOW CLOSE DISASTER ALREADY WAS.
STARING AT THE WALL
IS THIS A JOKE?
I DON'T THINK SO. THE SUMMONS I RECEIVED WAS VERY EXPLICIT.
SUMMONS? I WAS TOLD I WAS TO MEET THE ABBOT OF MY ORDER.
IN A DERELICT BUILDING?
AH! MORE NEW ARRIVALS.
HOW PLEASANT AND DISTRACTING. SOME OF US HAVE MOVED THROUGH INTO THE LOUNGE.

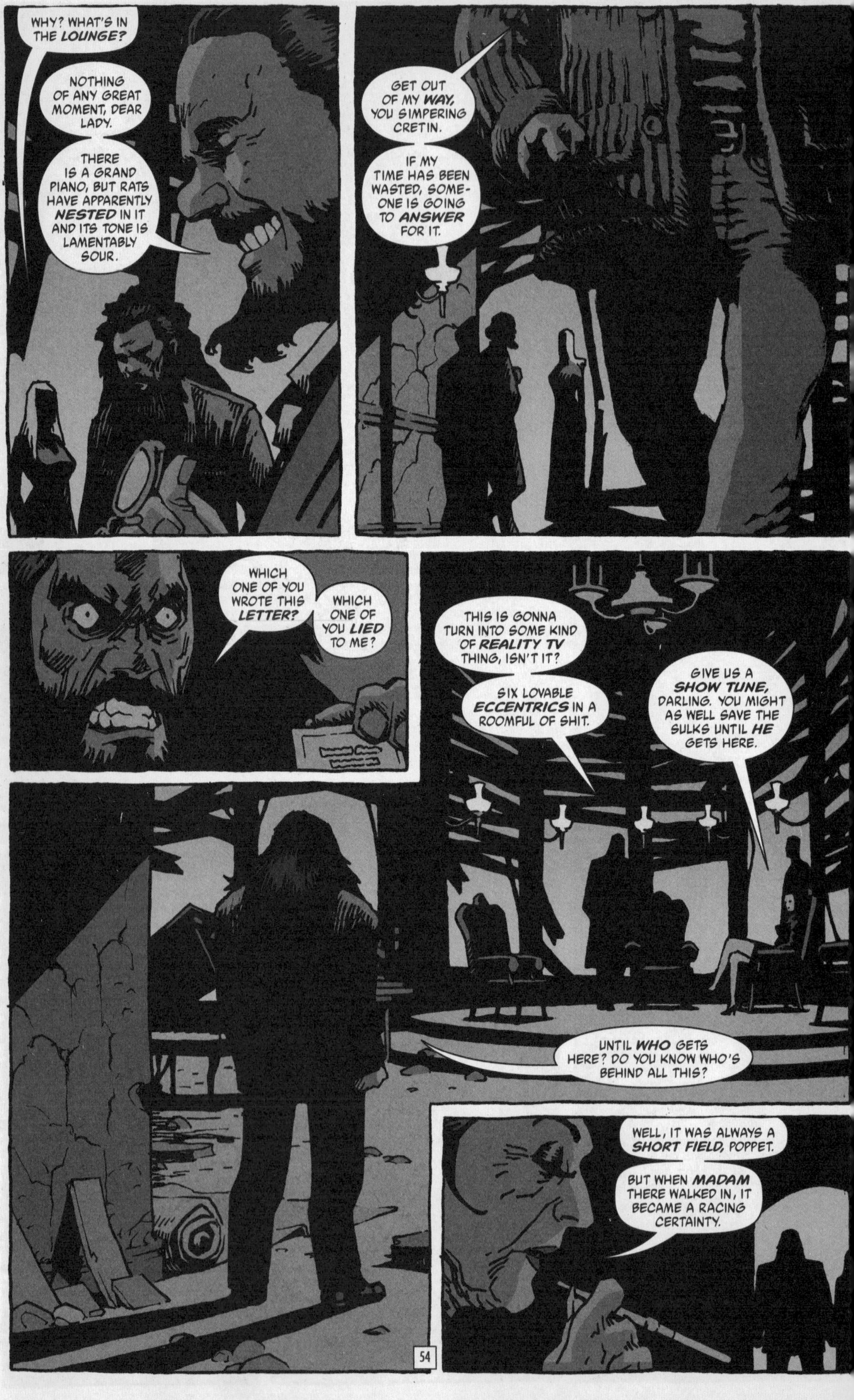
WHY? WHAT'S IN THE LOUNGE?
NOTHING OF ANY GREAT MOMENT, DEAR LADY.
THERE IS A GRAND PIANO, BUT RATS HAVE APPARENTLY NESTED IN IT AND ITS TONE IS LAMENTABLY SOUR.
GET OUT OF MY WAY, YOU SIMPERING CRETIN.
IF MY TIME HAS BEEN WASTED, SOME-ONE IS GOING TO ANSWER FOR IT.
WHICH ONE OF YOU WROTE THIS LETTER?
WHICH ONE OF YOU LIED TO ME?
THIS IS GONNA TURN INTO SOME KIND OF REALITY TV THING, ISN'T IT?
SIX LOVABLE ECCENTRICS IN A ROOMFUL OF SHIT.
GIVE US A SHOW TUNE, DARLING. YOU MIGHT AS WELL SAVE THE SULKS UNTIL HE GETS HERE.
UNTIL WHO GETS HERE? DO YOU KNOW WHO'S BEHIND ALL THIS?
WELL, IT WAS ALWAYS A SHORT FIELD, POPPET.
BUT WHEN MADAM THERE WALKED IN, IT BECAME A RACING CERTAINTY.

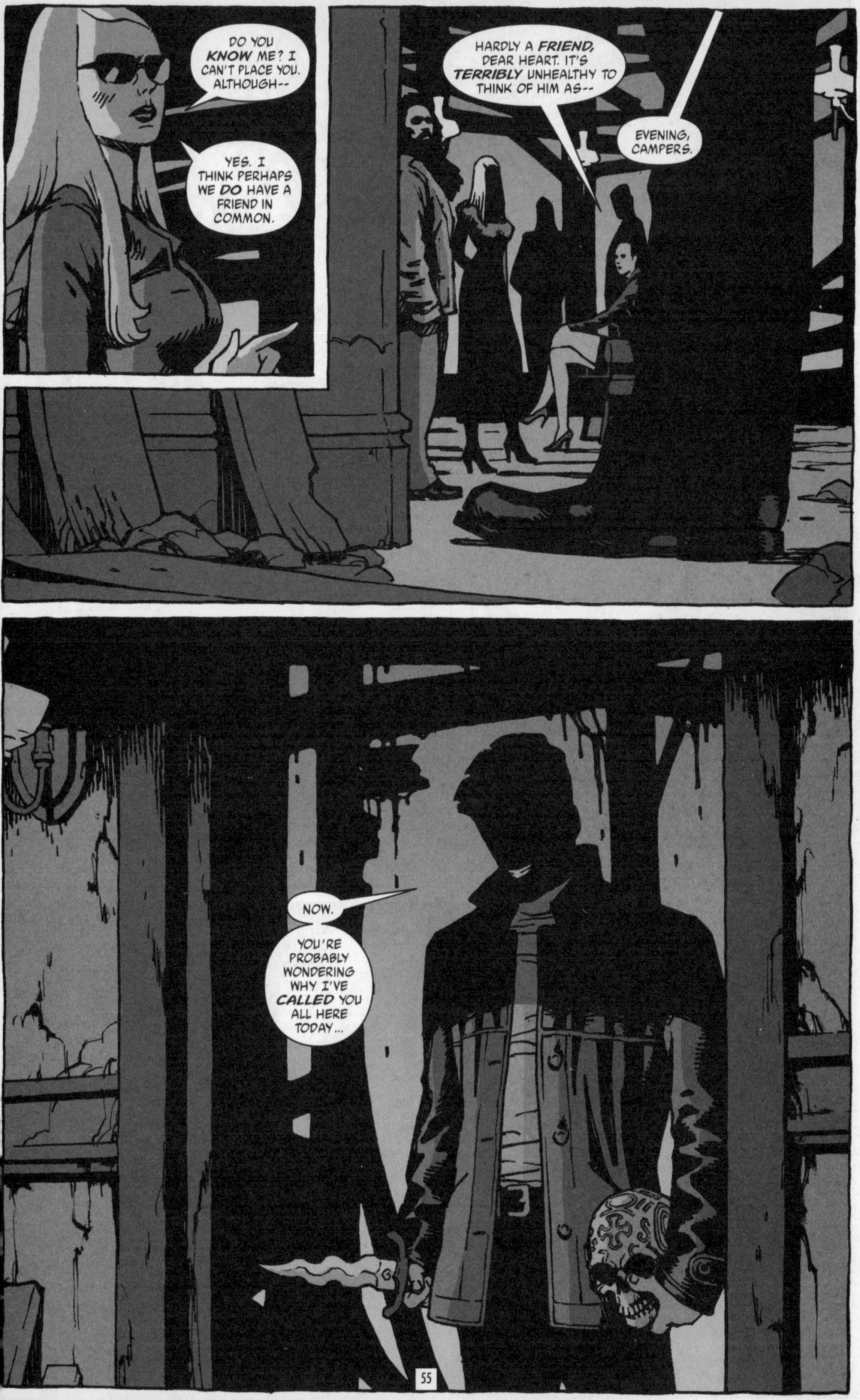
DO YOU KNOW ME? I CAN'T PLACE YOU. ALTHOUGH--
YES. I THINK PERHAPS WE DO HAVE A FRIEND IN COMMON.
HARDLY A FRIEND, DEAR HEART. IT'S TERRIBLY UNHEALTHY TO THINK OF HIM AS--
EVENING, CAMPERS.
NOW.
YOU'RE PROBABLY WONDERING WHY I'VE CALLED YOU ALL HERE TODAY...

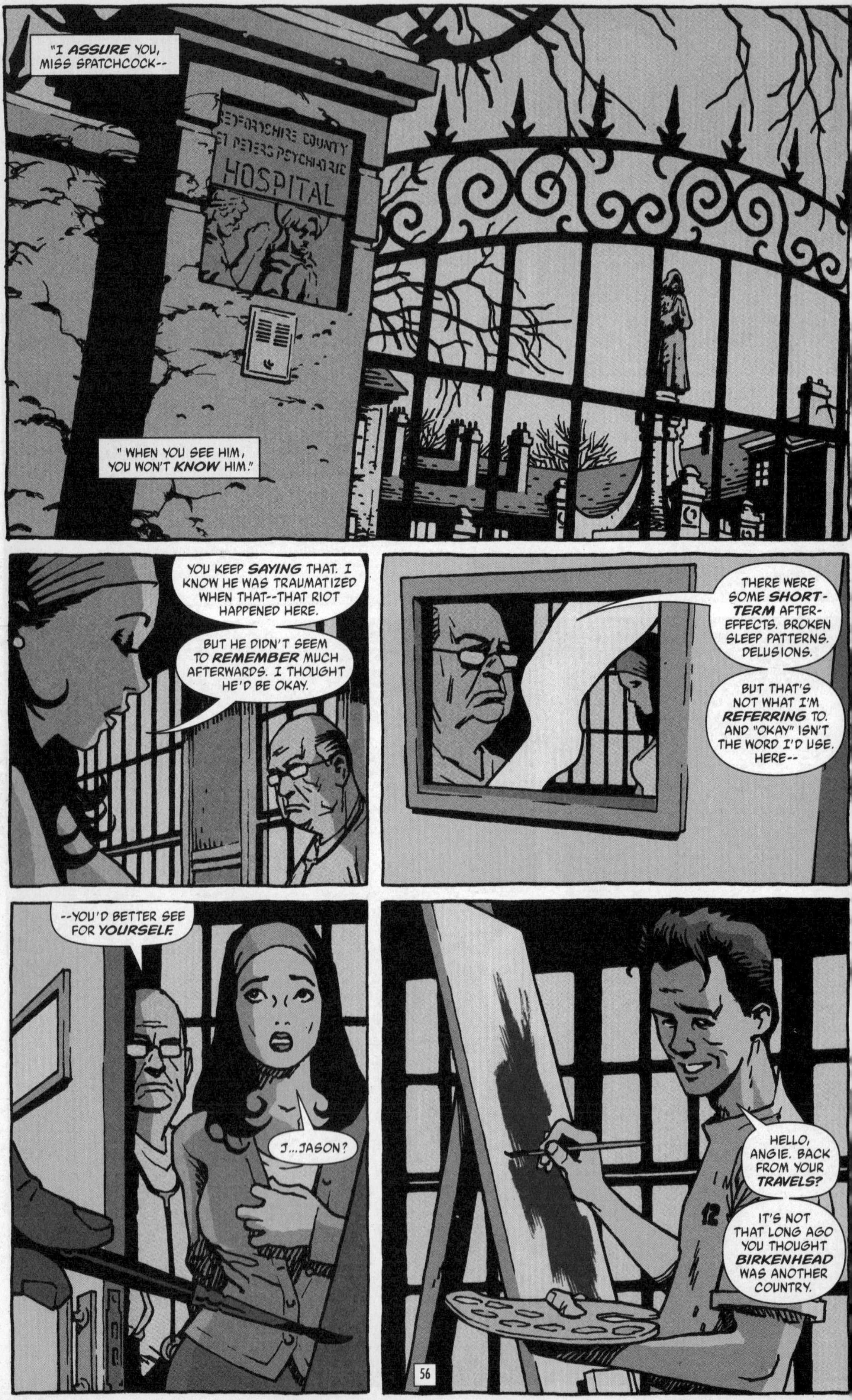
"I ASSURE YOU, MISS SPATCHCOCK--
BEDFORDSHIRE COUNTY ST PETERS PSYCHIATRIC HOSPITAL
"WHEN YOU SEE HIM, YOU WON'T KNOW HIM."
YOU KEEP SAYING THAT. I KNOW HE WAS TRAUMATIZED WHEN THAT--THAT RIOT HAPPENED HERE.
BUT HE DIDN'T SEEM TO REMEMBER MUCH AFTERWARDS. I THOUGHT HE'D BE OKAY.
THERE WERE SOME SHORT-TERM AFTER-EFFECTS. BROKEN SLEEP PATTERNS. DELUSIONS.
BUT THAT'S NOT WHAT I'M REFERRING TO. AND "OKAY" ISN'T THE WORD I'D USE. HERE--
--YOU'D BETTER SEE FOR YOURSELF.
J...JASON?
HELLO, ANGIE. BACK FROM YOUR TRAVELS?
IT'S NOT THAT LONG AGO YOU THOUGHT BIRKENHEAD WAS ANOTHER COUNTRY.

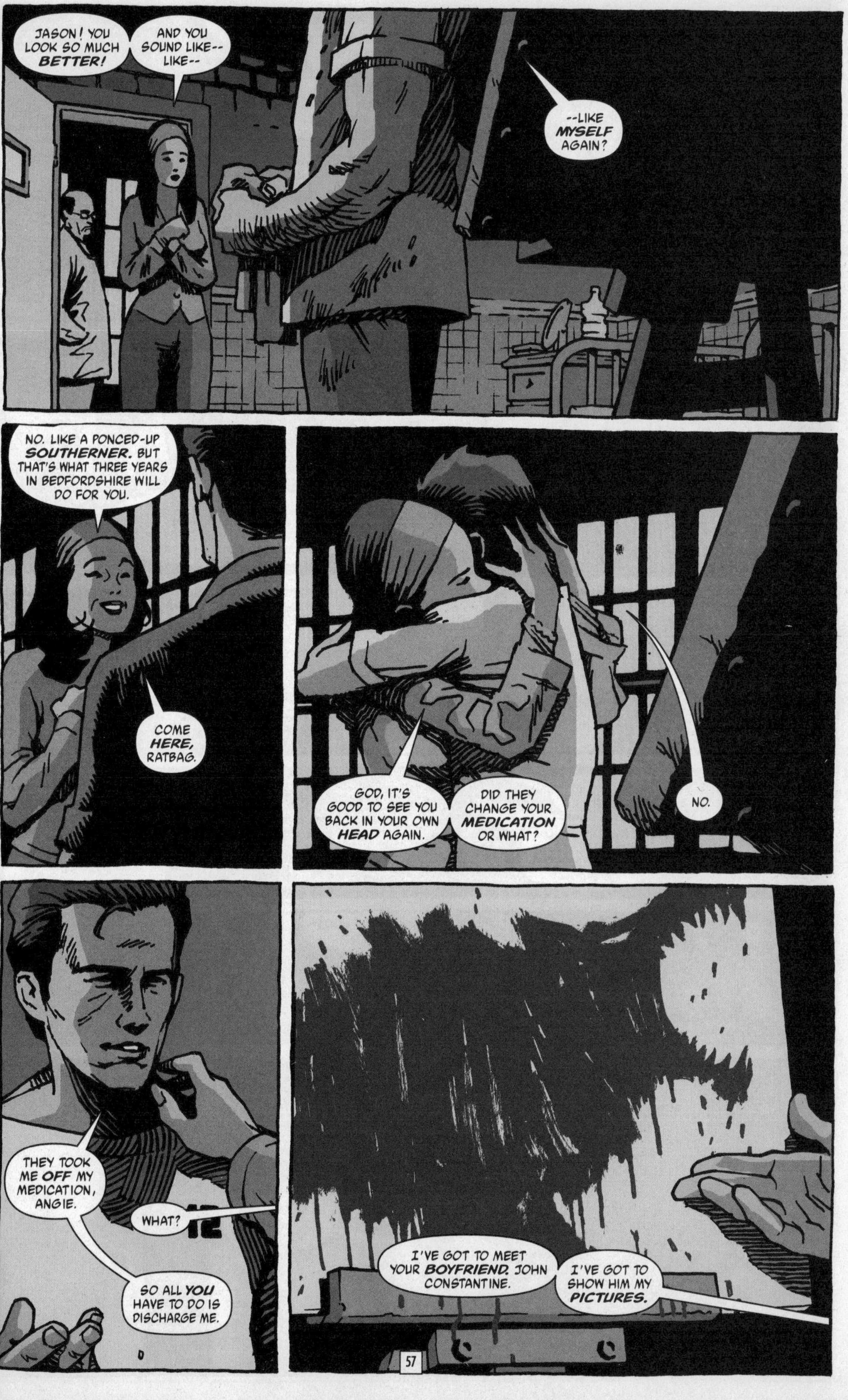
JASON! YOU LOOK SO MUCH BETTER!
AND YOU SOUND LIKE-- LIKE--
--LIKE MYSELF AGAIN?
NO. LIKE A PONCED-UP SOUTHERNER. BUT THAT'S WHAT THREE YEARS IN BEDFORDSHIRE WILL DO FOR YOU.
COME HERE, RATBAG.
GOD, IT'S GOOD TO SEE YOU BACK IN YOUR OWN HEAD AGAIN.
DID THEY CHANGE YOUR MEDICATION OR WHAT?
NO.
THEY TOOK ME OFF MY MEDICATION, ANGIE.
WHAT?
SO ALL YOU HAVE TO DO IS DISCHARGE ME.
I'VE GOT TO MEET YOUR BOYFRIEND. JOHN CONSTANTINE.
I'VE GOT TO SHOW HIM MY PICTURES.

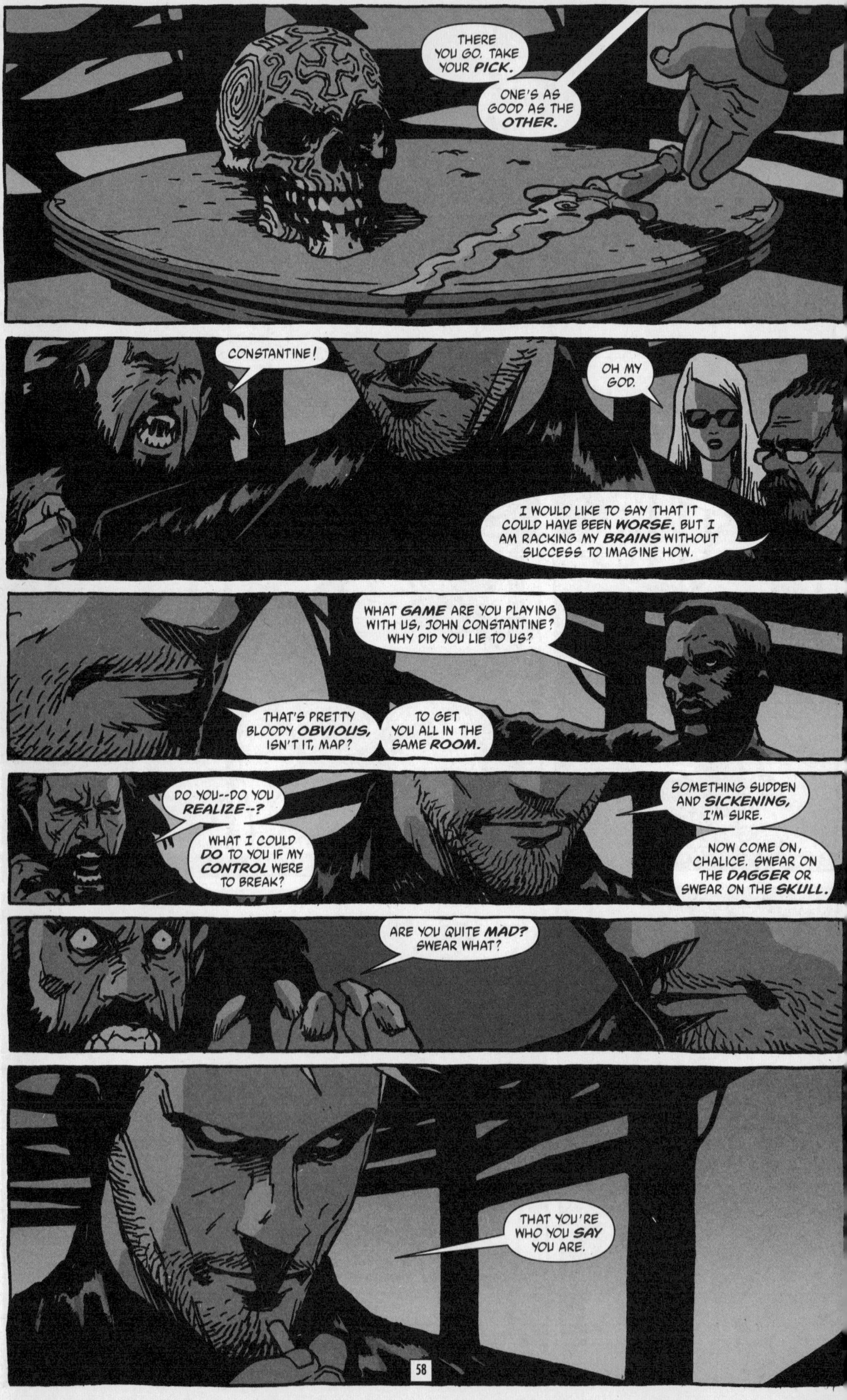
THERE YOU GO. TAKE YOUR PICK.
ONE'S AS GOOD AS THE OTHER.
CONSTANTINE!
OH MY GOD.
I WOULD LIKE TO SAY THAT IT COULD HAVE BEEN WORSE. BUT I AM RACKING MY BRAINS WITHOUT SUCCESS TO IMAGINE HOW.
WHAT GAME ARE YOU PLAYING WITH US, JOHN CONSTANTINE? WHY DID YOU LIE TO US?
THAT'S PRETTY BLOODY OBVIOUS, ISN'T IT, MAP?
TO GET YOU ALL IN THE SAME ROOM.
DO YOU--DO YOU REALIZE--?
WHAT I COULD DO TO YOU IF MY CONTROL WERE TO BREAK?
SOMETHING SUDDEN AND SICKENING, I'M SURE.
NOW COME ON, CHALICE. SWEAR ON THE DAGGER OR SWEAR ON THE SKULL.
ARE YOU QUITE MAD? SWEAR WHAT?
THAT YOU'RE WHO YOU SAY YOU ARE.

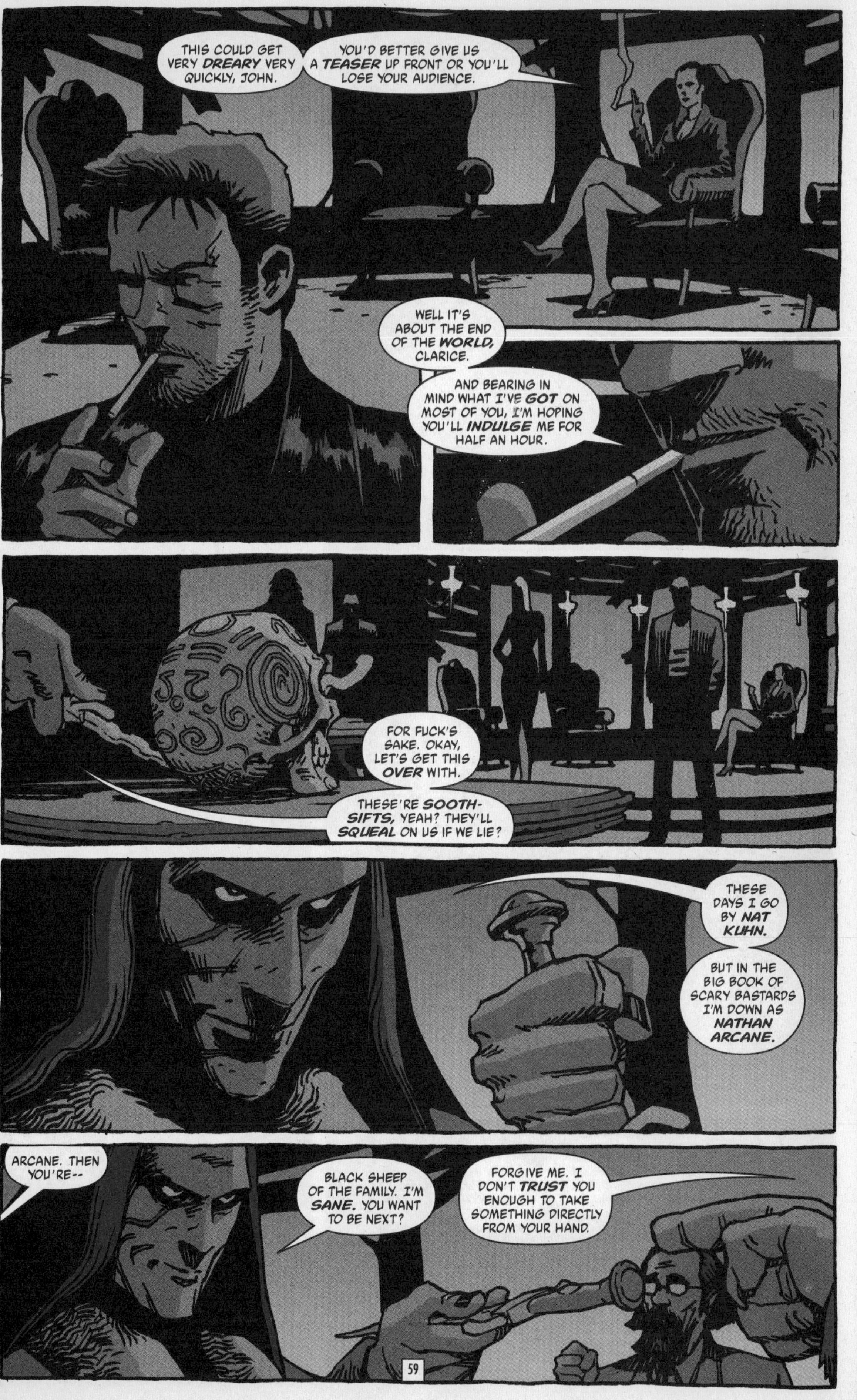
THIS COULD GET VERY DREARY VERY QUICKLY, JOHN.
YOU'D BETTER GIVE US A TEASER UP FRONT OR YOU'LL LOSE YOUR AUDIENCE.
WELL IT'S ABOUT THE END OF THE WORLD, CLARICE.
AND BEARING IN MIND WHAT I'VE GOT ON MOST OF YOU, I'M HOPING YOU'LL INDULGE ME FOR HALF AN HOUR.
FOR FUCK'S SAKE. OKAY, LET'S GET THIS OVER WITH.
THESE'RE SOOTH-SIFTS, YEAH? THEY'LL SQUEAL ON US IF WE LIE?
THESE DAYS I GO BY NAT KUHN.
BUT IN THE BIG BOOK OF SCARY BASTARDS I'M DOWN AS NATHAN ARCANE.
ARCANE. THEN YOU'RE--
BLACK SHEEP OF THE FAMILY. I'M SANE. YOU WANT TO BE NEXT?
FORGIVE ME. I DON'T TRUST YOU ENOUGH TO TAKE SOMETHING DIRECTLY FROM YOUR HAND.

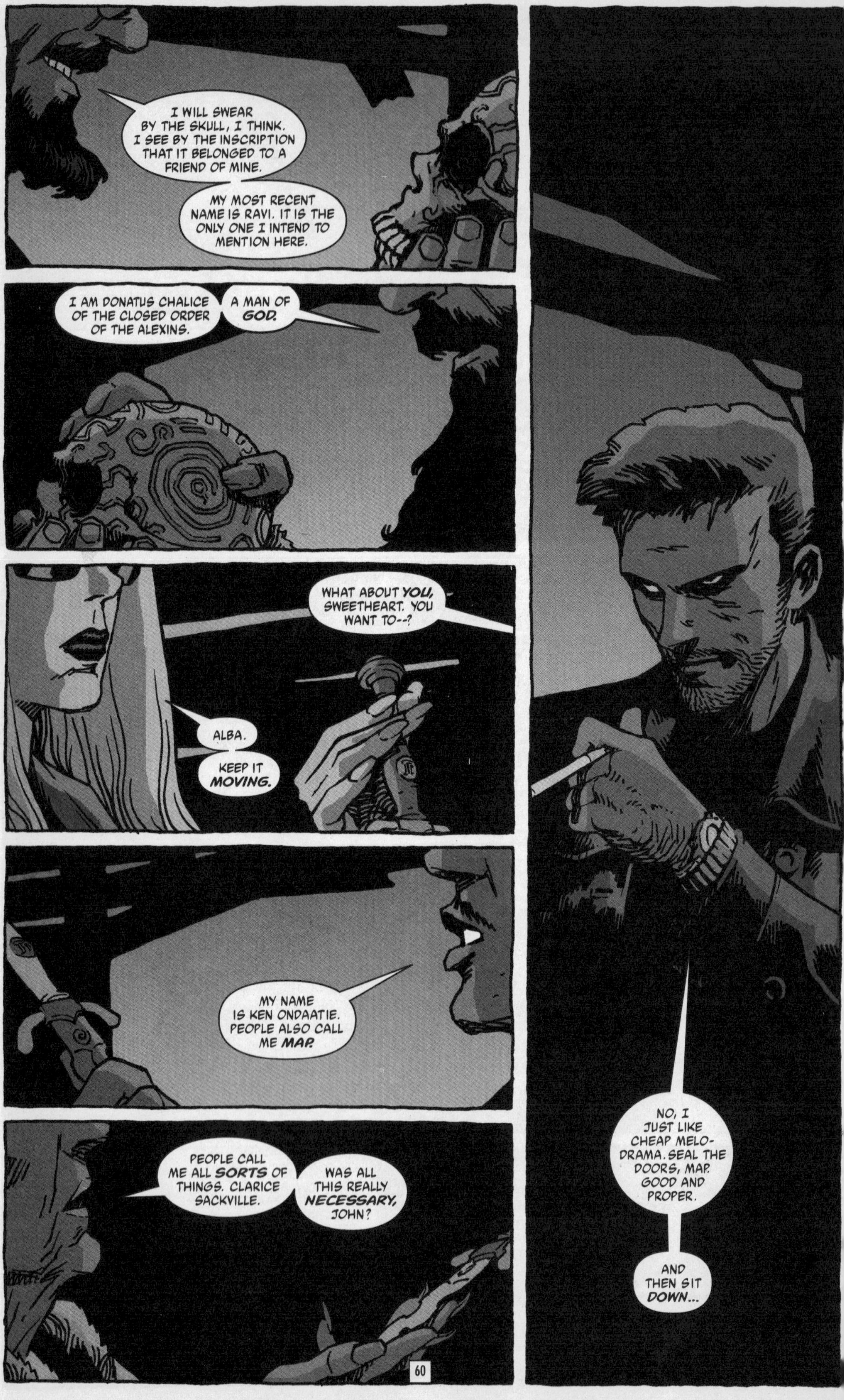
I WILL SWEAR BY THE SKULL, I THINK. I SEE BY THE INSCRIPTION THAT IT BELONGED TO A FRIEND OF MINE.
MY MOST RECENT NAME IS RAVI. IT IS THE ONLY ONE I INTEND TO MENTION HERE.
I AM DONATUS CHALICE OF THE CLOSED ORDER OF THE ALEXINS.
A MAN OF GOD.
WHAT ABOUT YOU, SWEETHEART. YOU WANT TO--?
ALBA.
KEEP IT MOVING.
MY NAME IS KEN ONDAATIE. PEOPLE ALSO CALL ME MAP.
PEOPLE CALL ME ALL SORTS OF THINGS. CLARICE SACKVILLE.
WAS ALL THIS REALLY NECESSARY, JOHN?
NO, I JUST LIKE CHEAP MELO-DRAMA. SEAL THE DOORS, MAP. GOOD AND PROPER.
AND THEN SIT DOWN...

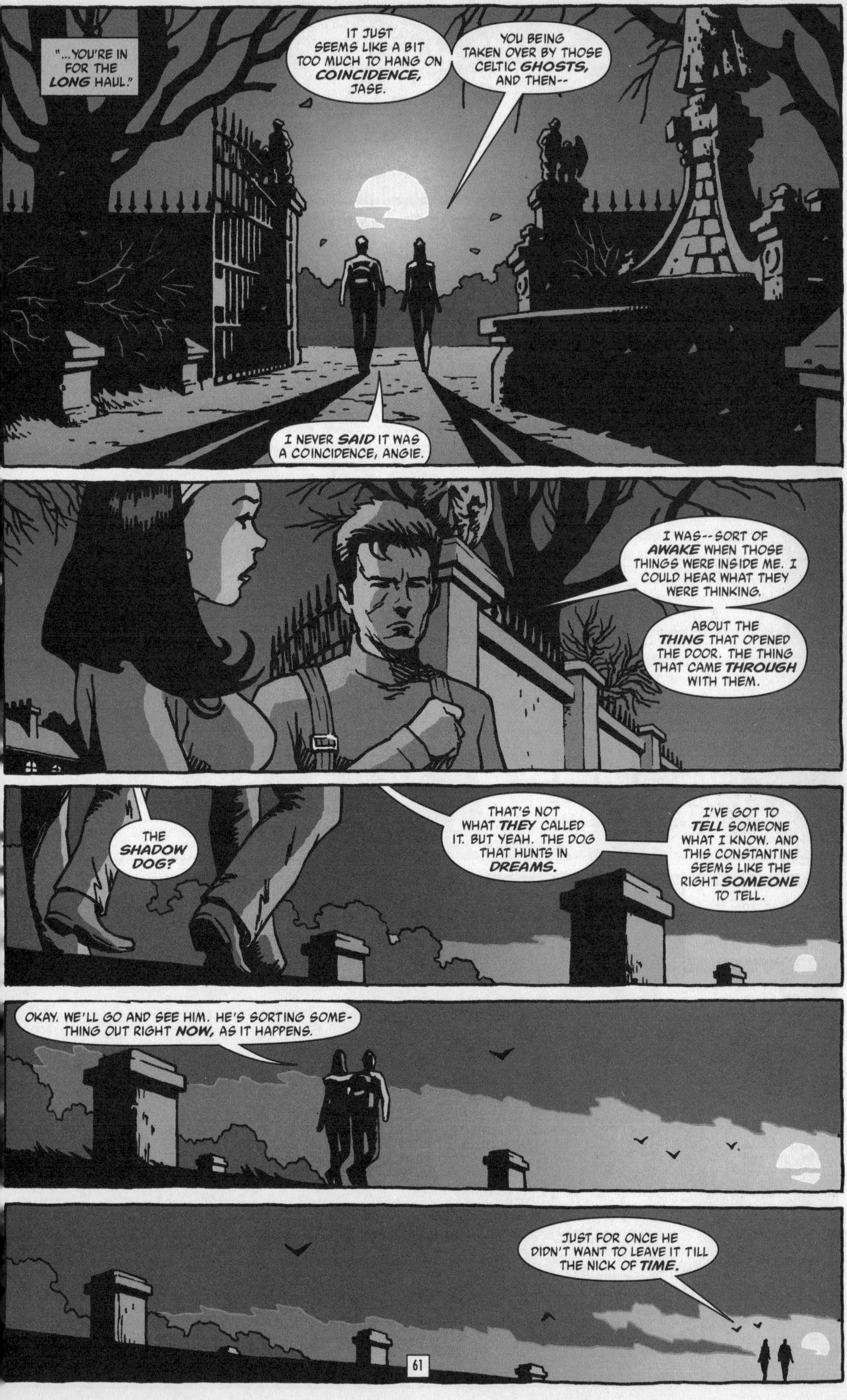
"...YOU'RE IN FOR THE LONG HAUL."
IT JUST SEEMS LIKE A BIT TOO MUCH TO HANG ON COINCIDENCE, JASE.
YOU BEING TAKEN OVER BY THOSE CELTIC GHOSTS, AND THEN--
I NEVER SAID IT WAS A COINCIDENCE, ANGIE.
I WAS--SORT OF AWAKE WHEN THOSE THINGS WERE INSIDE ME. I COULD HEAR WHAT THEY WERE THINKING.
ABOUT THE THING THAT OPENED THE DOOR. THE THING THAT CAME THROUGH WITH THEM.
THE SHADOW DOG?
THAT'S NOT WHAT THEY CALLED IT. BUT YEAH. THE DOG THAT HUNTS IN DREAMS.
I'VE GOT TO TELL SOMEONE WHAT I KNOW. AND THIS CONSTANTINE SEEMS LIKE THE RIGHT SOMEONE TO TELL.
OKAY. WE'LL GO AND SEE HIM. HE'S SORTING SOMETHING OUT RIGHT NOW, AS IT HAPPENS.
JUST FOR ONCE HE DIDN'T WANT TO LEAVE IT TILL THE NICK OF TIME.

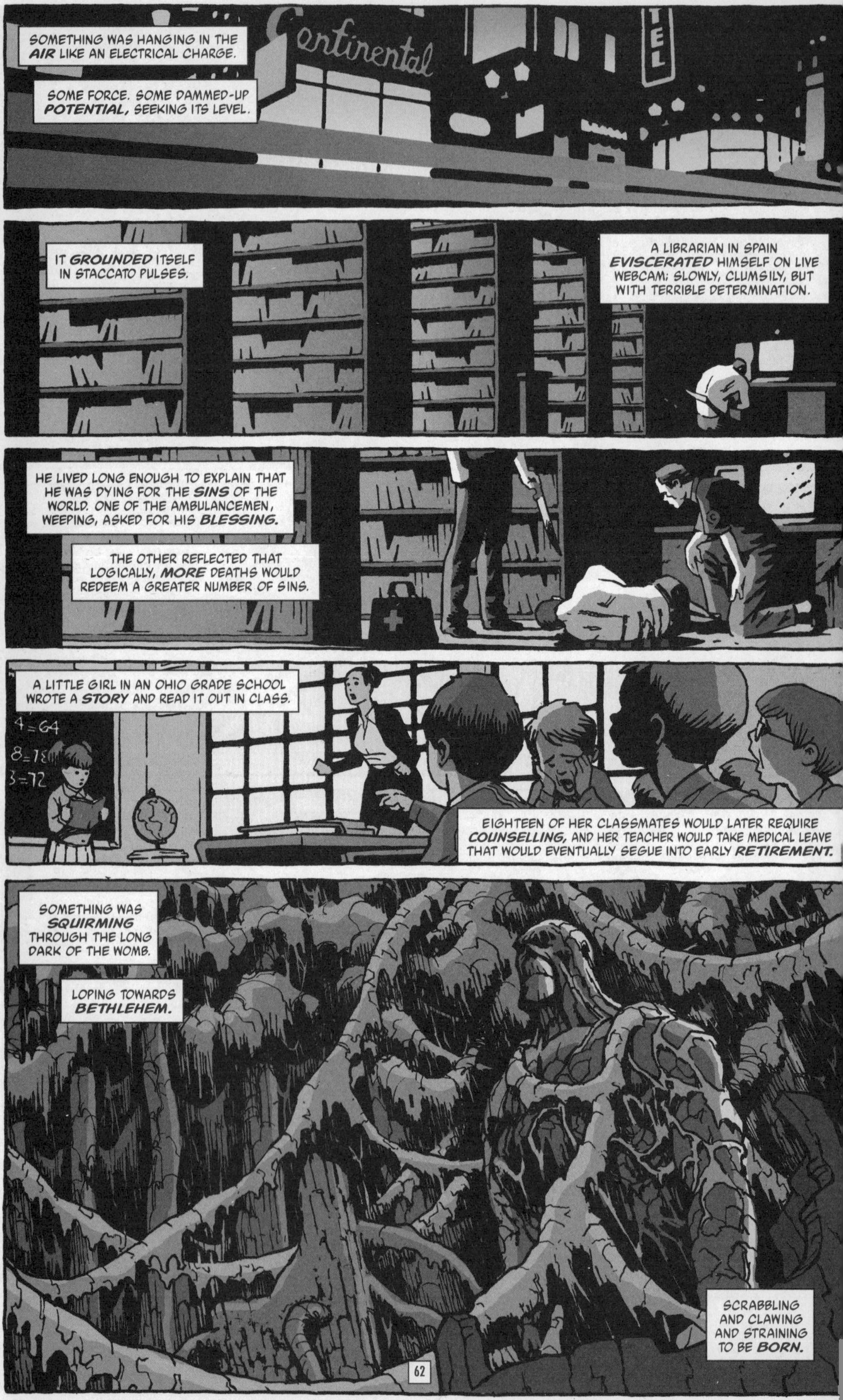
SOMETHING WAS HANGING IN THE AIR LIKE AN ELECTRICAL CHARGE.
SOME FORCE. SOME DAMMED-UP POTENTIAL, SEEKING ITS LEVEL.
IT GROUNDED ITSELF IN STACCATO PULSES.
A LIBRARIAN IN SPAIN EVISCERATED HIMSELF ON LIVE WEBCAM; SLOWLY, CLUMSILY, BUT WITH TERRIBLE DETERMINATION.
HE LIVED LONG ENOUGH TO EXPLAIN THAT HE WAS DYING FOR THE SINS OF THE WORLD. ONE OF THE AMBULANCEMEN, WEEPING, ASKED FOR HIS BLESSING.
THE OTHER REFLECTED THAT LOGICALLY, MORE DEATHS WOULD REDEEM A GREATER NUMBER OF SINS.
A LITTLE GIRL IN AN OHIO GRADE SCHOOL WROTE A STORY AND READ IT OUT IN CLASS.
EIGHTEEN OF HER CLASSMATES WOULD LATER REQUIRE COUNSELLING, AND HER TEACHER WOULD TAKE MEDICAL LEAVE THAT WOULD EVENTUALLY SEGUE INTO EARLY RETIREMENT.
SOMETHING WAS SQUIRMING THROUGH THE LONG DARK OF THE WOMB.
LOPING TOWARDS BETHLEHEM.
SCRABBLING AND CLAWING AND STRAINING TO BE BORN.

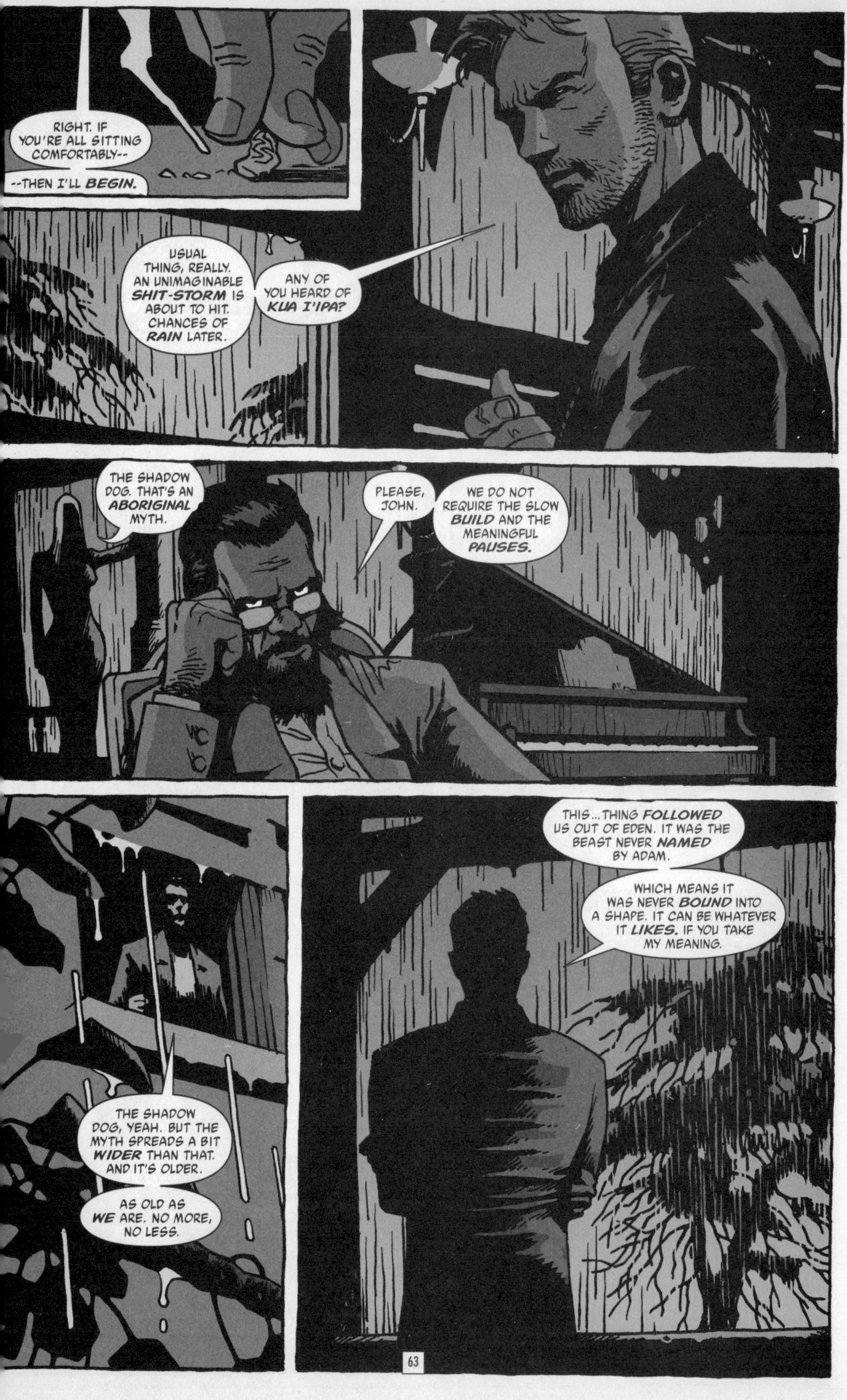
RIGHT. IF YOU'RE ALL SITTING COMFORTABLY--
--THEN I'LL BEGIN.
USUAL THING, REALLY. AN UNIMAGINABLE SHIT-STORM IS ABOUT TO HIT. CHANCES OF RAIN LATER.
ANY OF YOU HEARD OF KUA I'IPA?
THE SHADOW DOG. THAT'S AN ABORIGINAL MYTH.
PLEASE, JOHN.
WE DO NOT REQUIRE THE SLOW BUILD AND THE MEANINGFUL PAUSES.
THE SHADOW DOG, YEAH. BUT THE MYTH SPREADS A BIT WIDER THAN THAT. AND IT'S OLDER.
AS OLD AS WE ARE. NO MORE, NO LESS.
THIS...THING FOLLOWED US OUT OF EDEN. IT WAS THE BEAST NEVER NAMED BY ADAM.
WHICH MEANS IT WAS NEVER BOUND INTO A SHAPE. IT CAN BE WHATEVER IT LIKES. IF YOU TAKE MY MEANING.

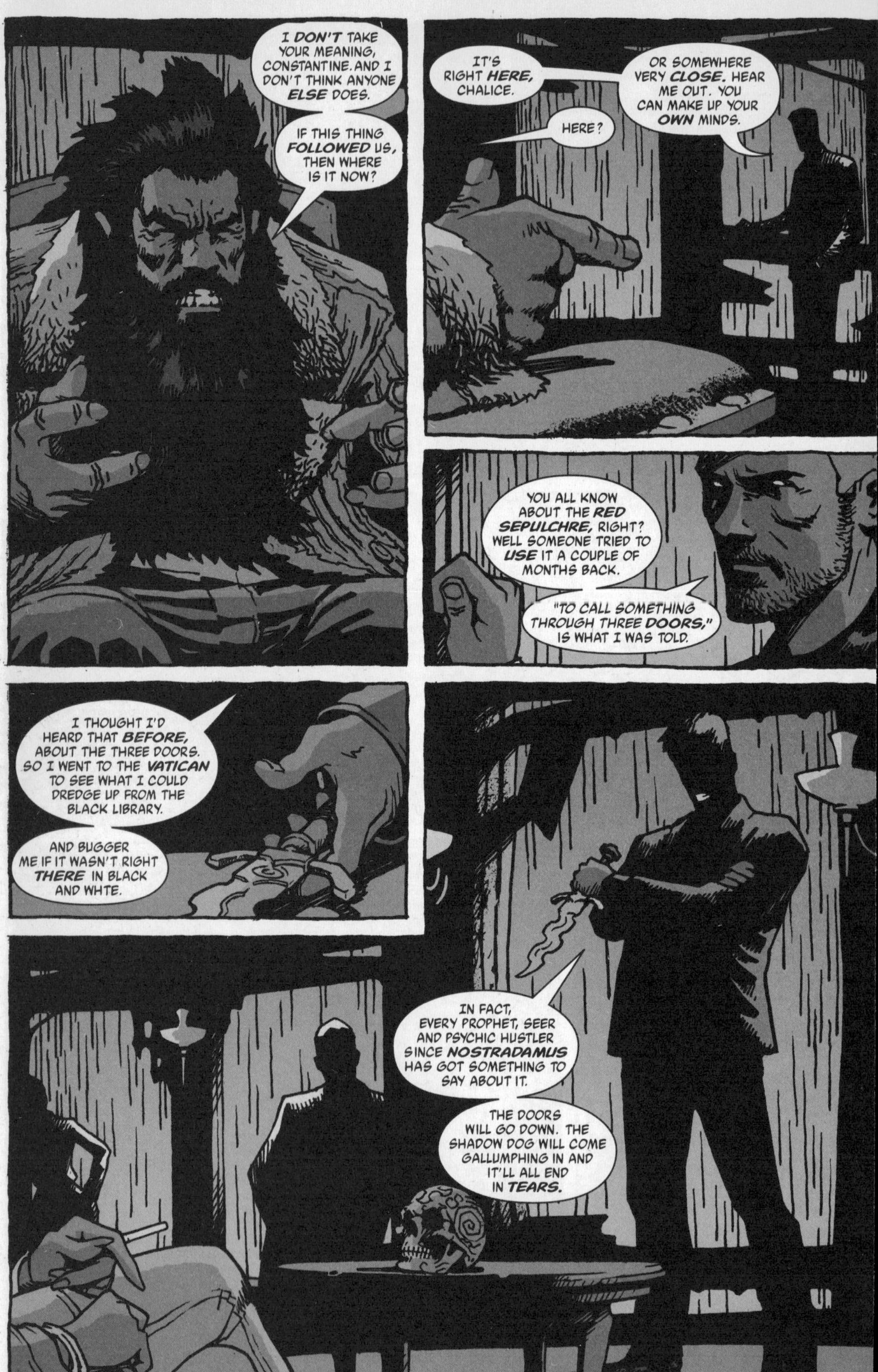
I DON'T TAKE YOUR MEANING, CONSTANTINE. AND I DON'T THINK ANYONE ELSE DOES.
IF THIS THING FOLLOWED US, THEN WHERE IS IT NOW?
IT'S RIGHT HERE, CHALICE.
HERE?
OR SOMEWHERE VERY CLOSE. HEAR ME OUT. YOU CAN MAKE UP YOUR OWN MINDS.
YOU ALL KNOW ABOUT THE RED SEPULCHRE, RIGHT? WELL SOMEONE TRIED TO USE IT A COUPLE OF MONTHS BACK.
"TO CALL SOMETHING THROUGH THREE DOORS," IS WHAT I WAS TOLD.
I THOUGHT I'D HEARD THAT BEFORE, ABOUT THE THREE DOORS. SO I WENT TO THE VATICAN TO SEE WHAT I COULD DREDGE UP FROM THE BLACK LIBRARY.
AND BUGGER ME IF IT WASN'T RIGHT THERE IN BLACK AND WHTE.
IN FACT, EVERY PROPHET, SEER AND PSYCHIC HUSTLER SINCE NOSTRADAMUS HAS GOT SOMETHING TO SAY ABOUT IT.
THE DOORS WILL GO DOWN. THE SHADOW DOG WILL COME GALLUMPHING IN AND IT'LL ALL END IN TEARS.

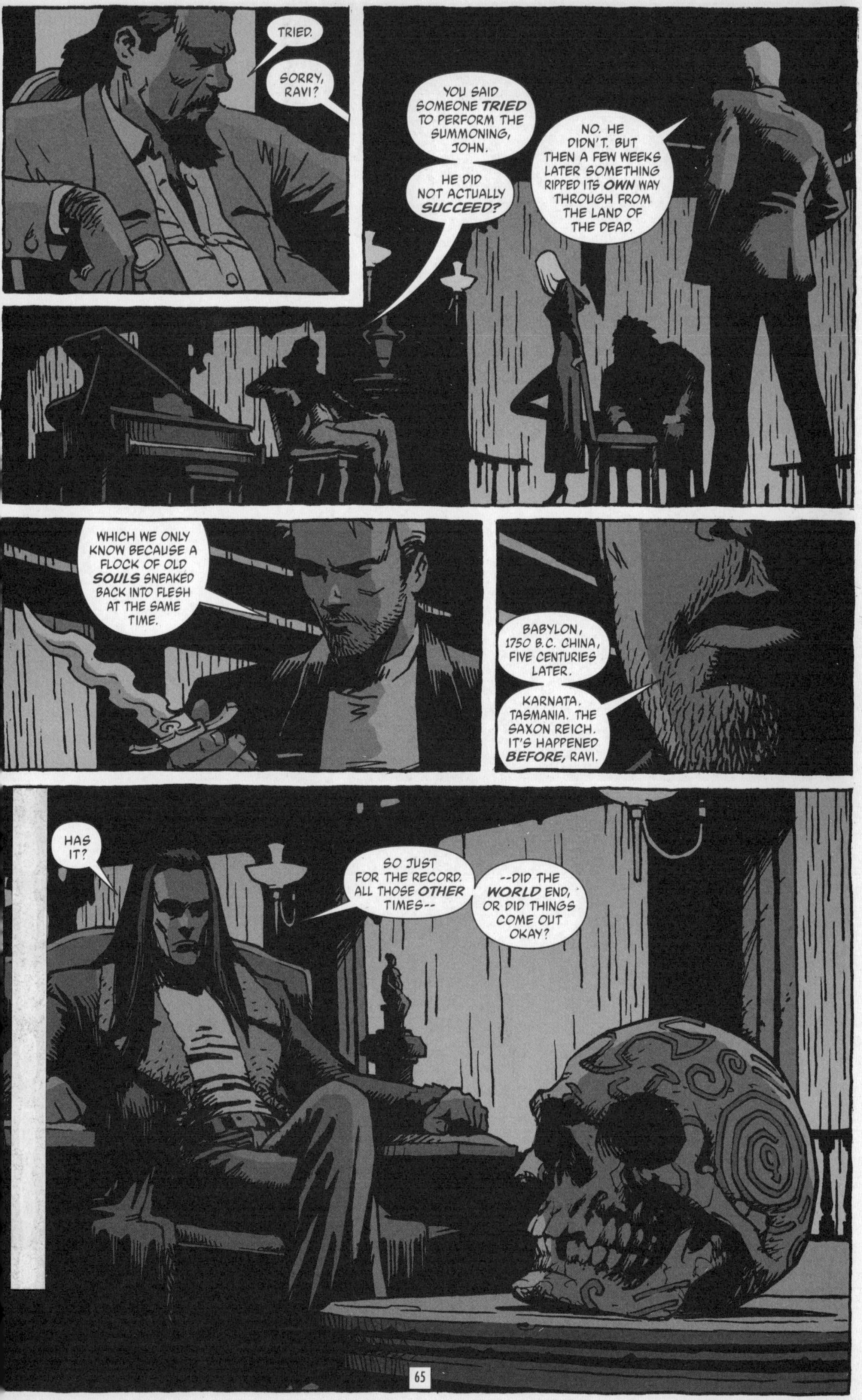
TRIED.
SORRY, RAVI?
YOU SAID SOMEONE TRIED TO PERFORM THE SUMMONING, JOHN.
HE DID NOT ACTUALLY SUCCEED?
NO. HE DIDN'T. BUT THEN A FEW WEEKS LATER SOMETHING RIPPED ITS OWN WAY THROUGH FROM THE LAND OF THE DEAD.
WHICH WE ONLY KNOW BECAUSE A FLOCK OF OLD SOULS SNEAKED BACK INTO FLESH AT THE SAME TIME.
BABYLON, 1750 B.C. CHINA, FIVE CENTURIES LATER.
KARNATA. TASMANIA. THE SAXON REICH. IT'S HAPPENED BEFORE, RAVI.
HAS IT?
SO JUST FOR THE RECORD. ALL THOSE OTHER TIMES--
--DID THE WORLD END, OR DID THINGS COME OUT OKAY?

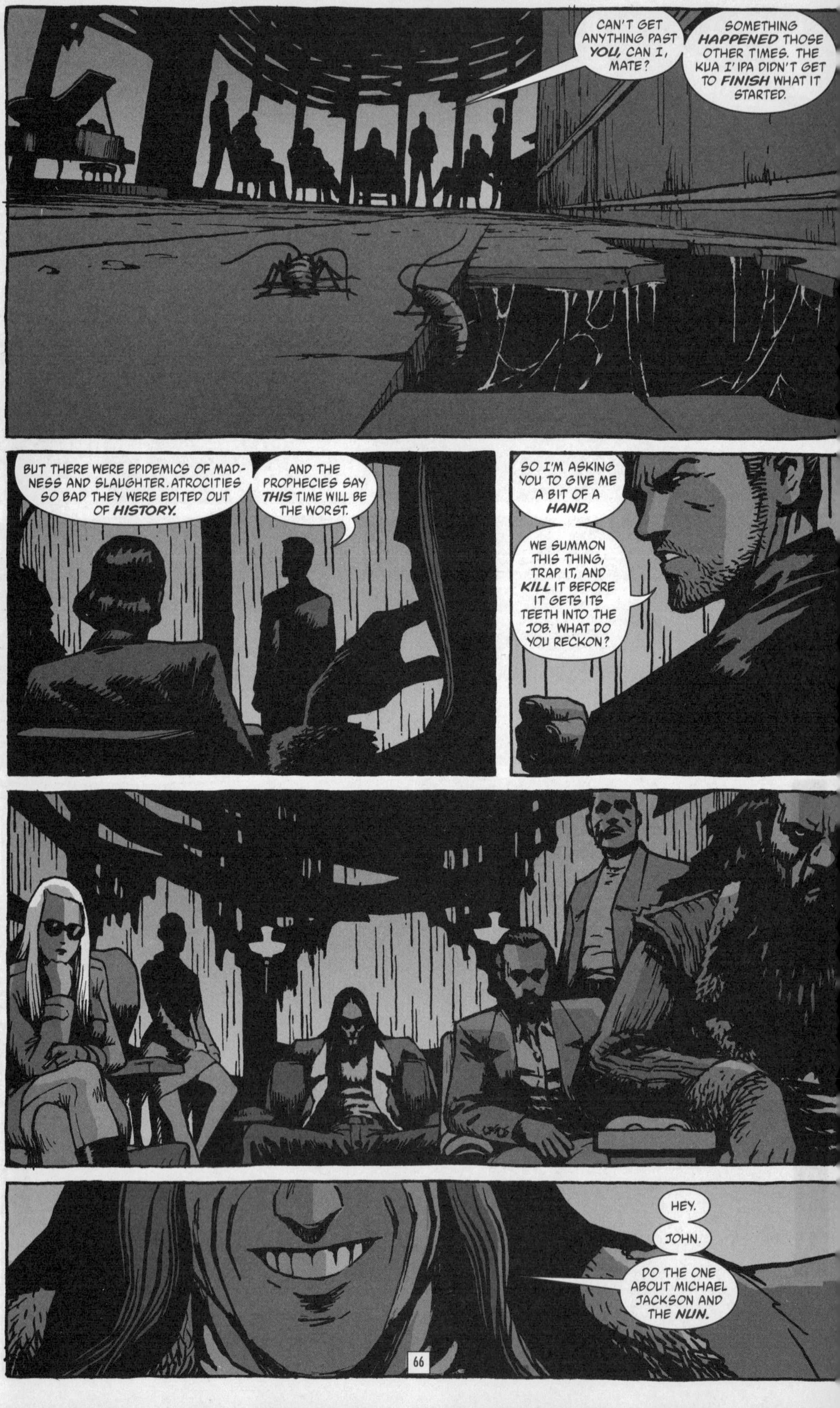

CAN'T GET ANYTHING PAST YOU, CAN I, MATE?
SOMETHING HAPPENED THOSE OTHER TIMES. THE KUA I'IPA DIDN'T GET TO FINISH WHAT IT STARTED.
BUT THERE WERE EPIDEMICS OF MADNESS AND SLAUGHTER. ATROCITIES SO BAD THEY WERE EDITED OUT OF HISTORY.
AND THE PROPHECIES SAY THIS TIME WILL BE THE WORST.
SO I'M ASKING YOU TO GIVE ME A BIT OF A HAND.
WE SUMMON THIS THING, TRAP IT, AND KILL IT BEFORE IT GETS ITS TEETH INTO THE JOB. WHAT DO YOU RECKON?
HEY.
JOHN.
DO THE ONE ABOUT MICHAEL JACKSON AND THE NUN.

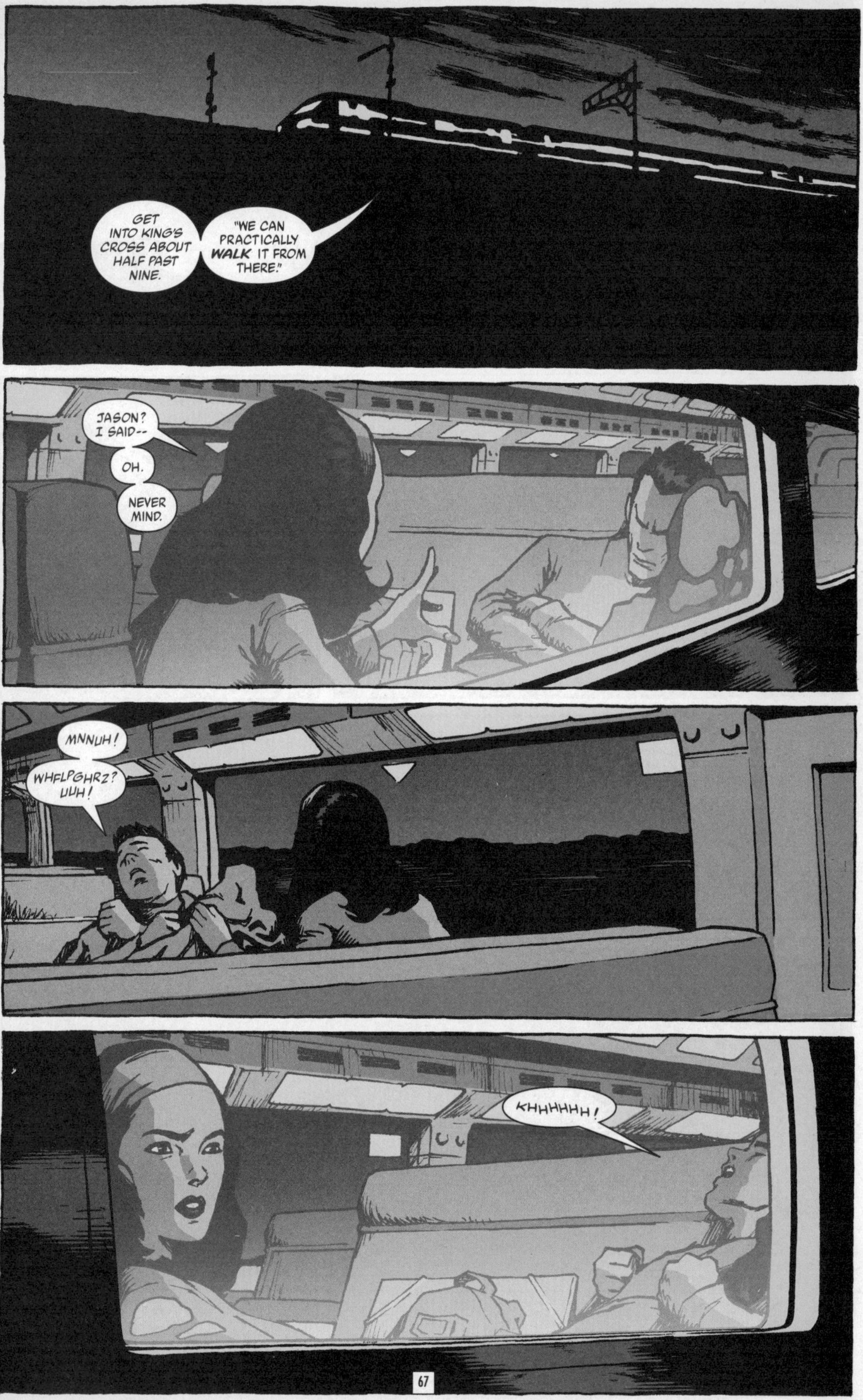
GET INTO KING'S CROSS ABOUT HALF PAST NINE.
"WE CAN PRACTICALLY **WALK** IT FROM THERE."
JASON? I SAID--
OH.
NEVER MIND.
MNNUH!
WHFLPGHRZ? UUH!
KHHHHHH!

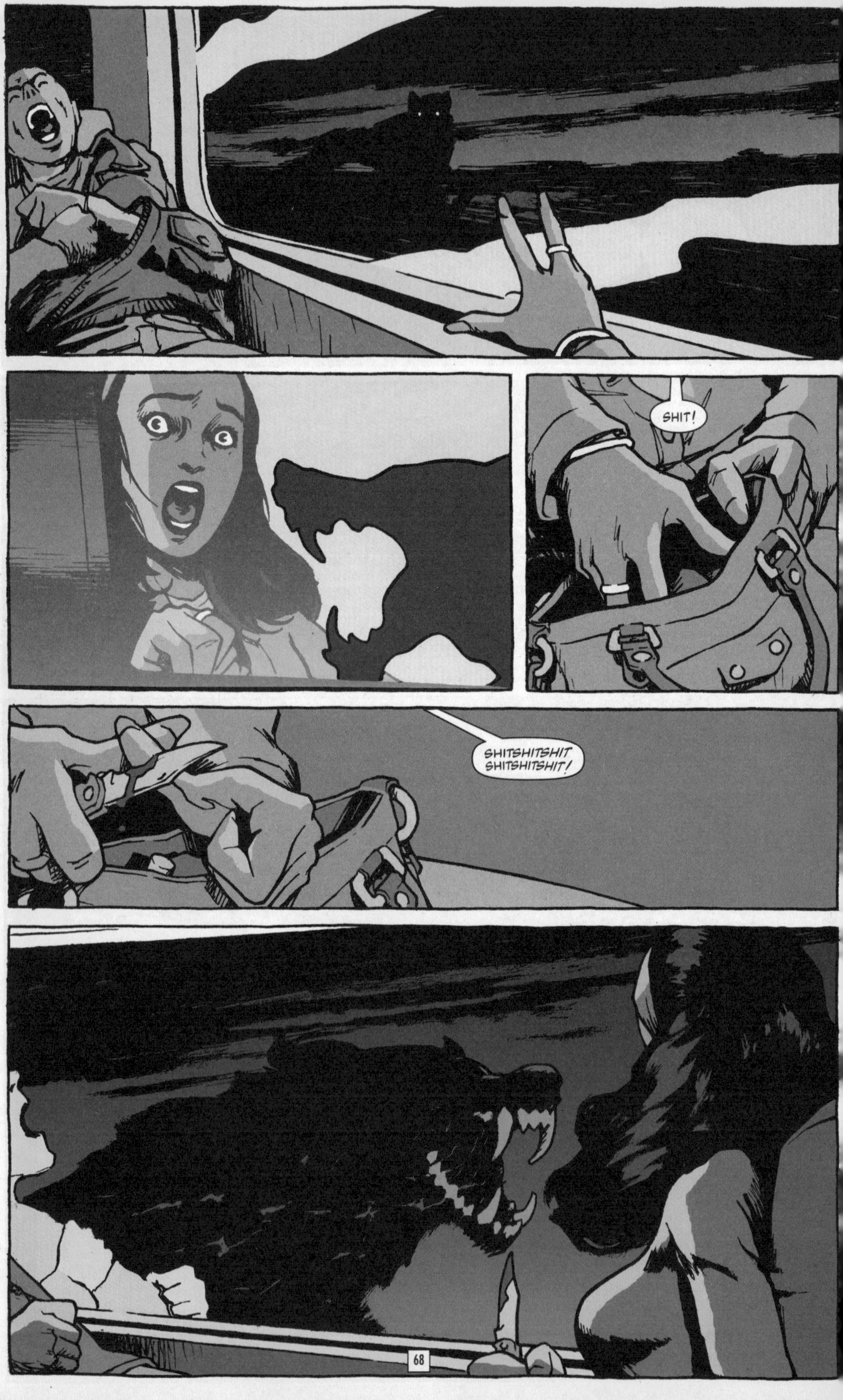
SHIT!
SHITSHITSHIT
SHITSHITSHIT!

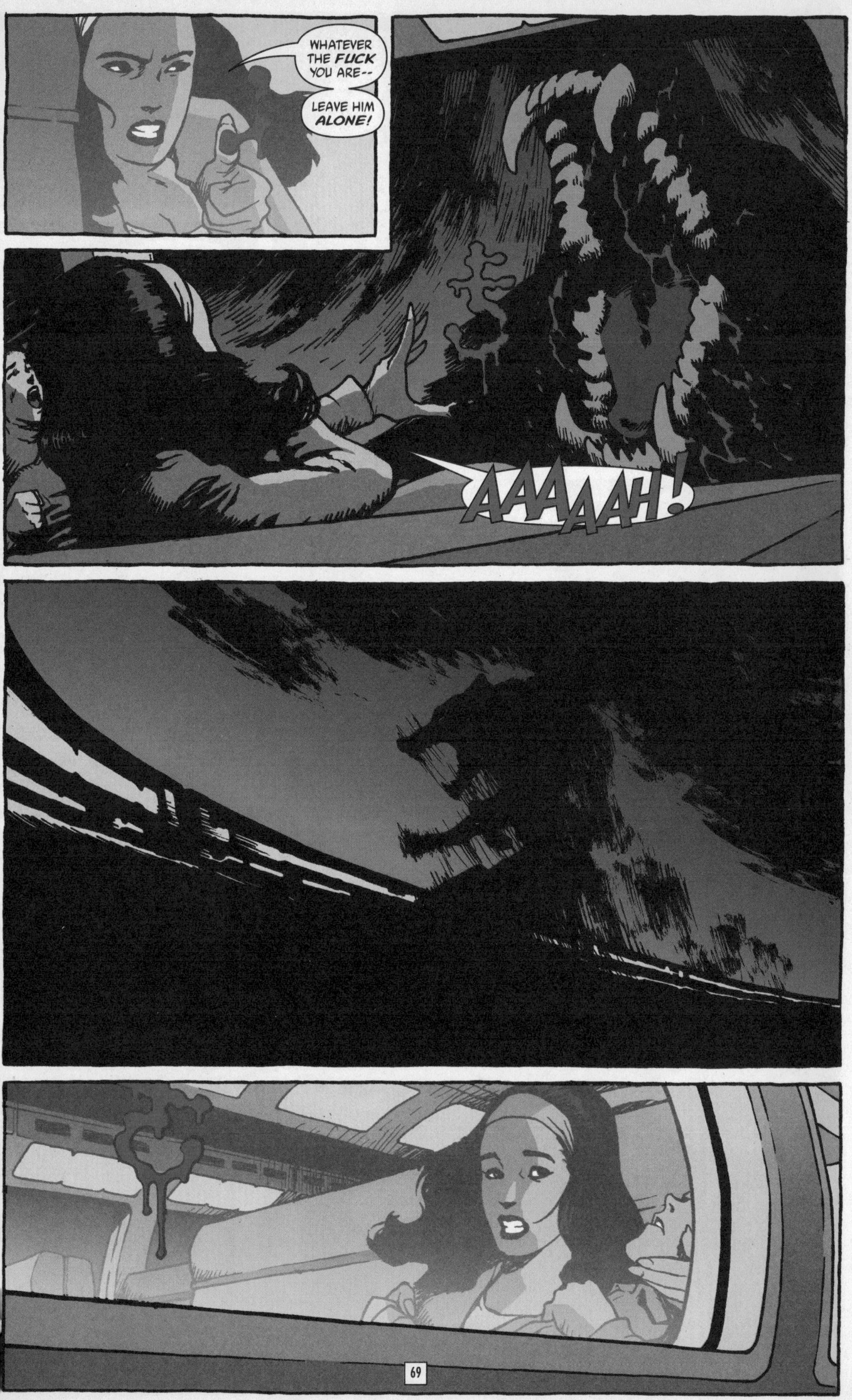
WHATEVER THE FUCK YOU ARE--
LEAVE HIM ALONE!
AAAAAH!

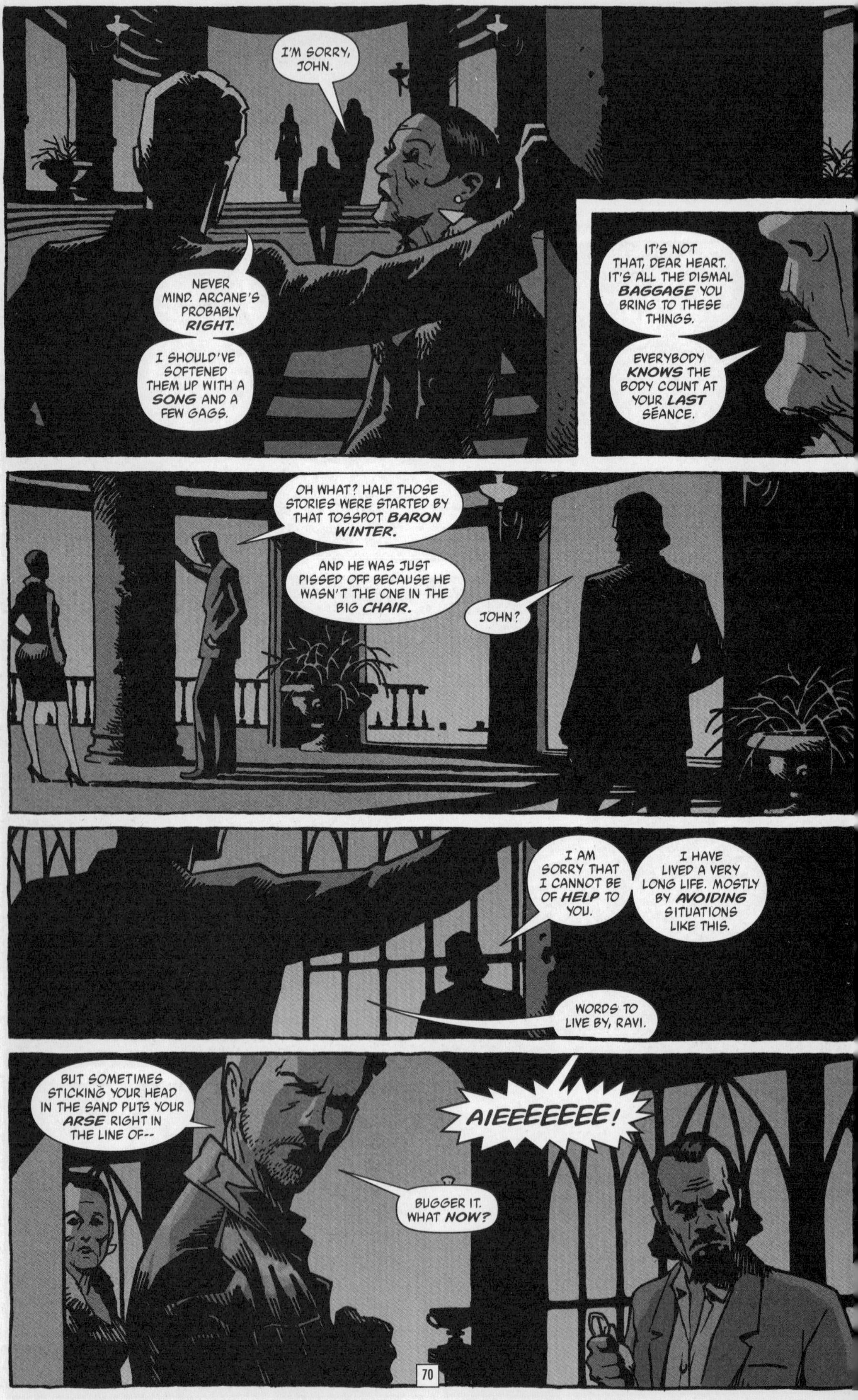
I'M SORRY, JOHN.
NEVER MIND. ARCANE'S PROBABLY RIGHT.
I SHOULD'VE SOFTENED THEM UP WITH A SONG AND A FEW GAGS.
IT'S NOT THAT, DEAR HEART. IT'S ALL THE DISMAL BAGGAGE YOU BRING TO THESE THINGS.
EVERYBODY KNOWS THE BODY COUNT AT YOUR LAST SÉANCE.
OH WHAT? HALF THOSE STORIES WERE STARTED BY THAT TOSSPOT BARON WINTER.
AND HE WAS JUST PISSED OFF BECAUSE HE WASN'T THE ONE IN THE BIG CHAIR.
JOHN?
I AM SORRY THAT I CANNOT BE OF HELP TO YOU.
I HAVE LIVED A VERY LONG LIFE. MOSTLY BY AVOIDING SITUATIONS LIKE THIS.
WORDS TO LIVE BY, RAVI.
BUT SOMETIMES STICKING YOUR HEAD IN THE SAND PUTS YOUR ARSE RIGHT IN THE LINE OF--
AIEEEEEEE!
BUGGER IT. WHAT NOW?

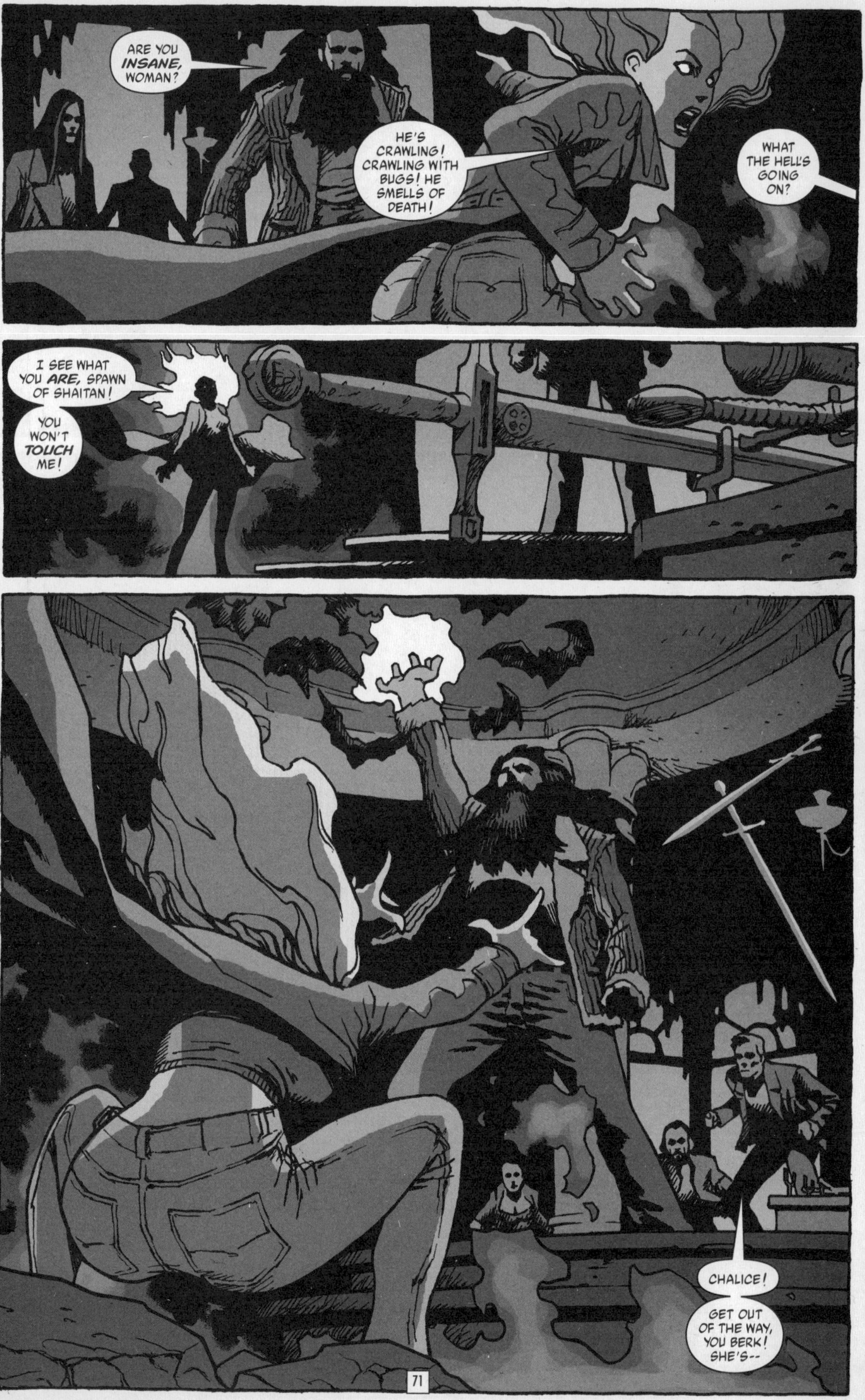

ARE YOU **INSANE,** WOMAN?
HE'S CRAWLING! CRAWLING WITH BUGS! HE SMELLS OF DEATH!
WHAT THE HELL'S GOING ON?
I SEE WHAT YOU **ARE,** SPAWN OF SHAITAN!
YOU WON'T **TOUCH** ME!
CHALICE!
GET OUT OF THE WAY, YOU BERK! SHE'S--

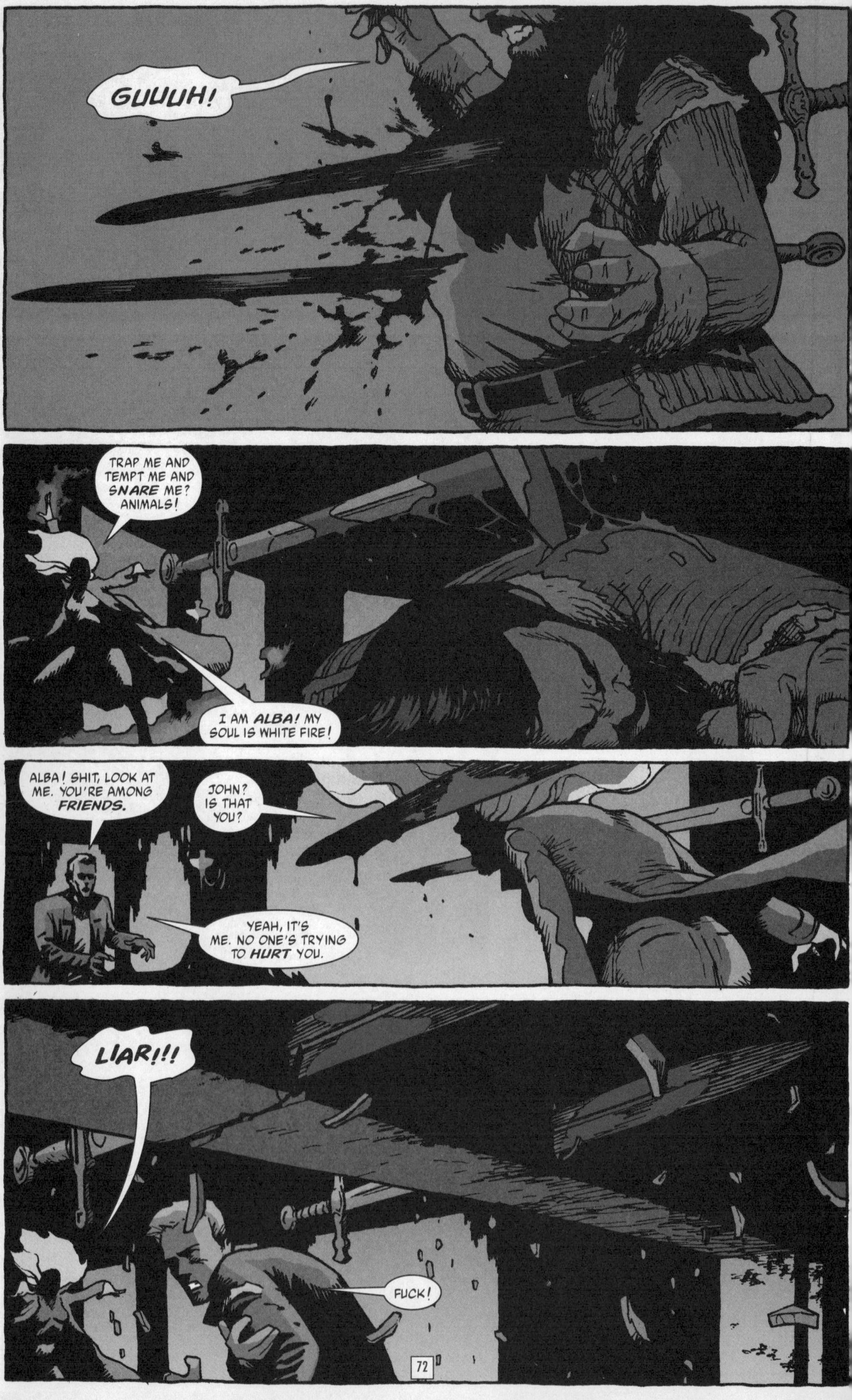
GUUUH!
TRAP ME AND TEMPT ME AND SNARE ME? ANIMALS!
I AM ALBA! MY SOUL IS WHITE FIRE!
ALBA! SHIT, LOOK AT ME. YOU'RE AMONG FRIENDS.
JOHN? IS THAT YOU?
YEAH, IT'S ME. NO ONE'S TRYING TO HURT YOU.
LIAR!!!
FUCK!

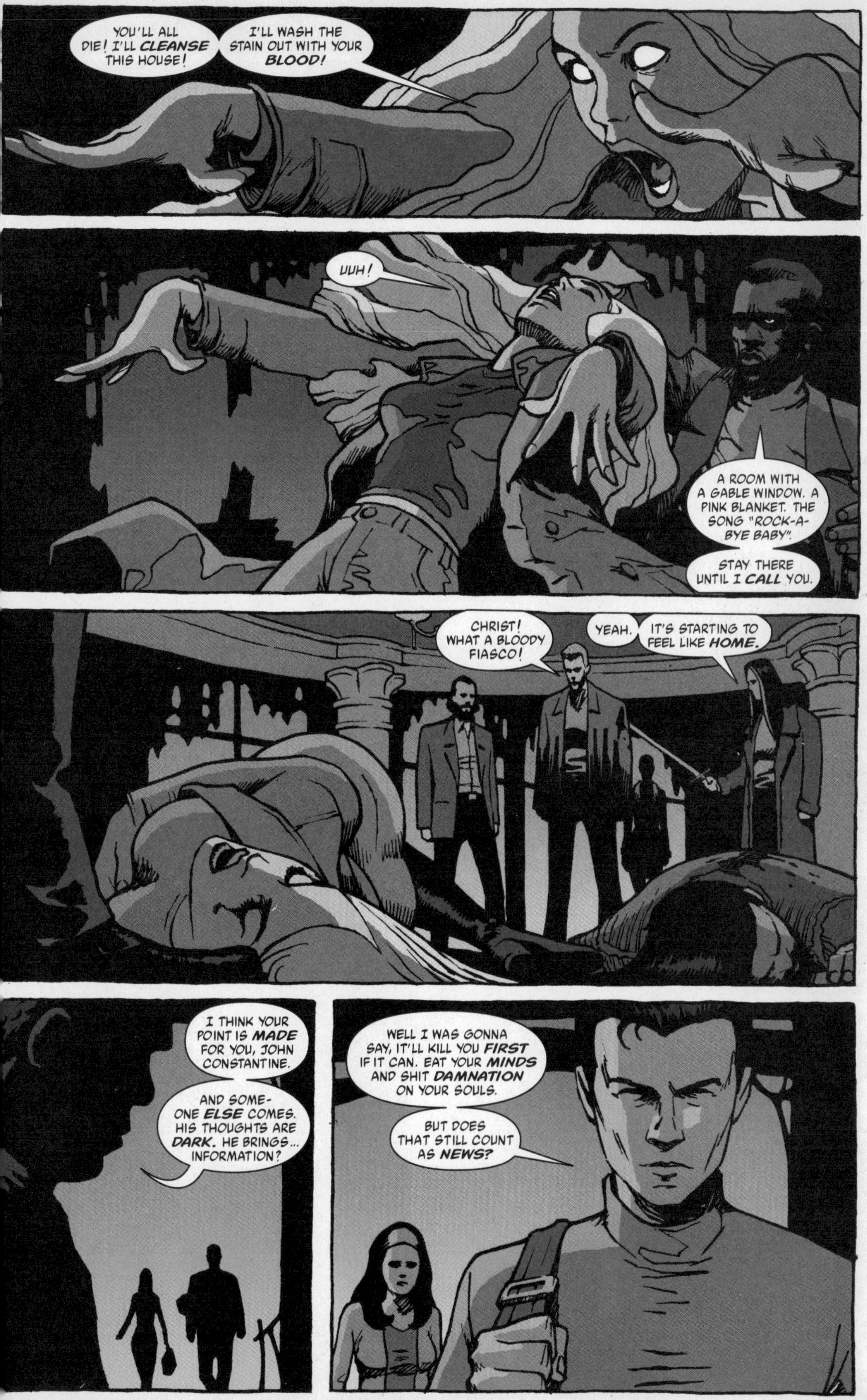
YOU'LL ALL DIE! I'LL CLEANSE THIS HOUSE!
I'LL WASH THE STAIN OUT WITH YOUR BLOOD!
UUH!
A ROOM WITH A GABLE WINDOW. A PINK BLANKET. THE SONG "ROCK-A-BYE BABY".
STAY THERE UNTIL I CALL YOU.
CHRIST! WHAT A BLOODY FIASCO!
YEAH.
IT'S STARTING TO FEEL LIKE HOME.
I THINK YOUR POINT IS MADE FOR YOU, JOHN CONSTANTINE.
AND SOME-ONE ELSE COMES. HIS THOUGHTS ARE DARK. HE BRINGS... INFORMATION?
WELL I WAS GONNA SAY, IT'LL KILL YOU FIRST IF IT CAN. EAT YOUR MINDS AND SHIT DAMNATION ON YOUR SOULS.
BUT DOES THAT STILL COUNT AS NEWS?

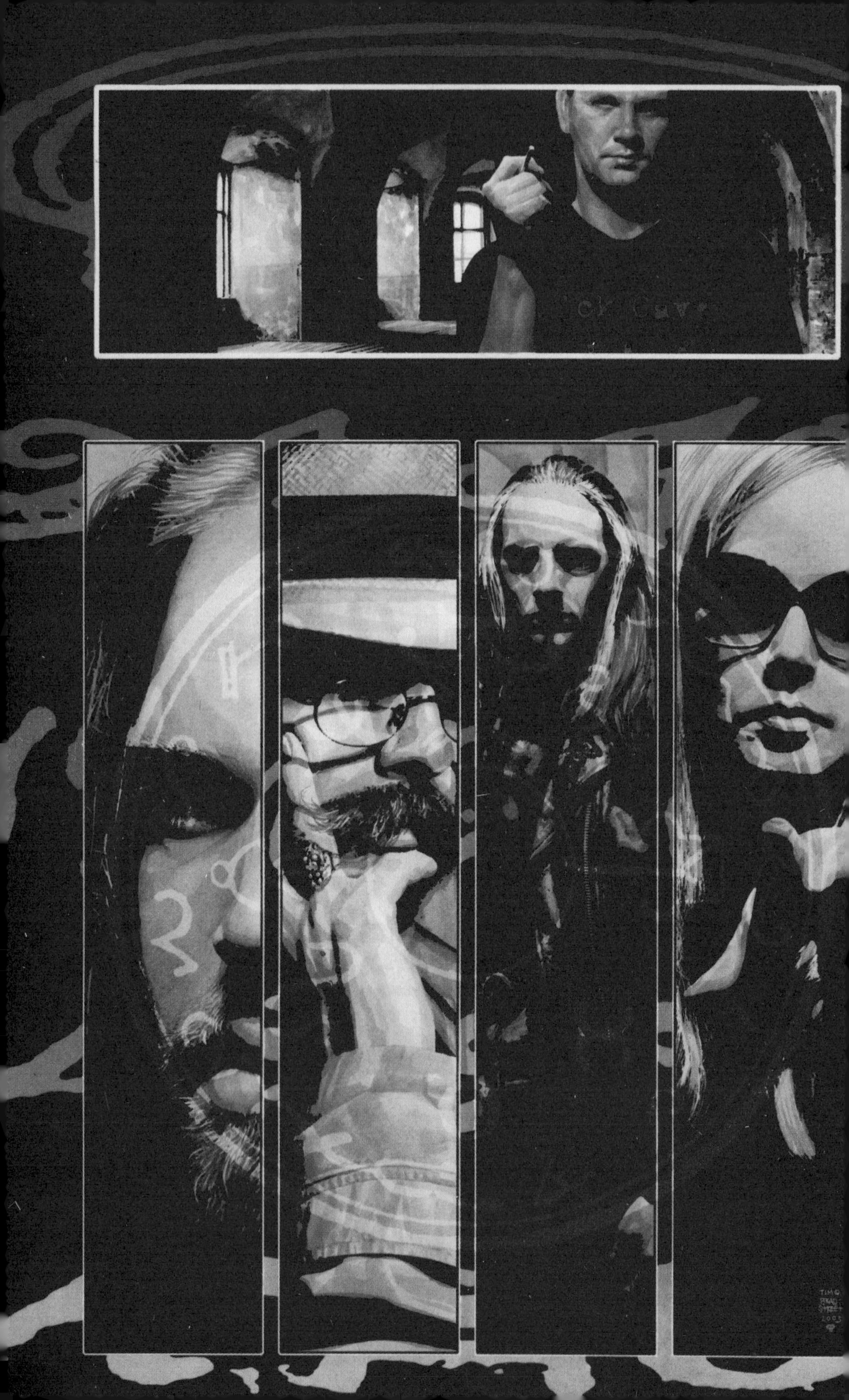

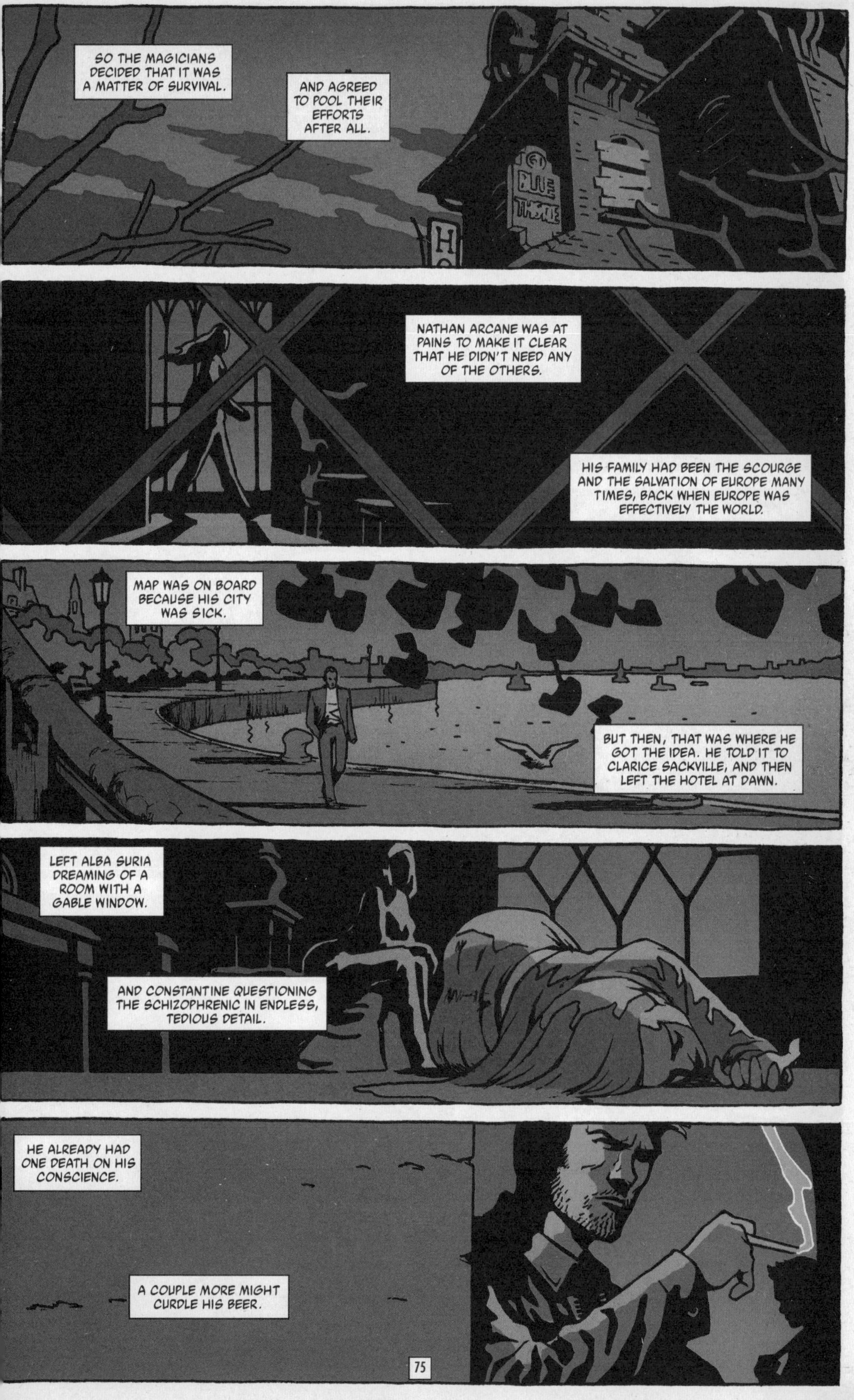
SO THE MAGICIANS DECIDED THAT IT WAS A MATTER OF SURVIVAL.
AND AGREED TO POOL THEIR EFFORTS AFTER ALL.
NATHAN ARCANE WAS AT PAINS TO MAKE IT CLEAR THAT HE DIDN'T NEED ANY OF THE OTHERS.
HIS FAMILY HAD BEEN THE SCOURGE AND THE SALVATION OF EUROPE MANY TIMES, BACK WHEN EUROPE WAS EFFECTIVELY THE WORLD.
MAP WAS ON BOARD BECAUSE HIS CITY WAS SICK.
BUT THEN, THAT WAS WHERE HE GOT THE IDEA. HE TOLD IT TO CLARICE SACKVILLE, AND THEN LEFT THE HOTEL AT DAWN.
LEFT ALBA SURIA DREAMING OF A ROOM WITH A GABLE WINDOW.
AND CONSTANTINE QUESTIONING THE SCHIZOPHRENIC IN ENDLESS, TEDIOUS DETAIL.
HE ALREADY HAD ONE DEATH ON HIS CONSCIENCE.
A COUPLE MORE MIGHT CURDLE HIS BEER.

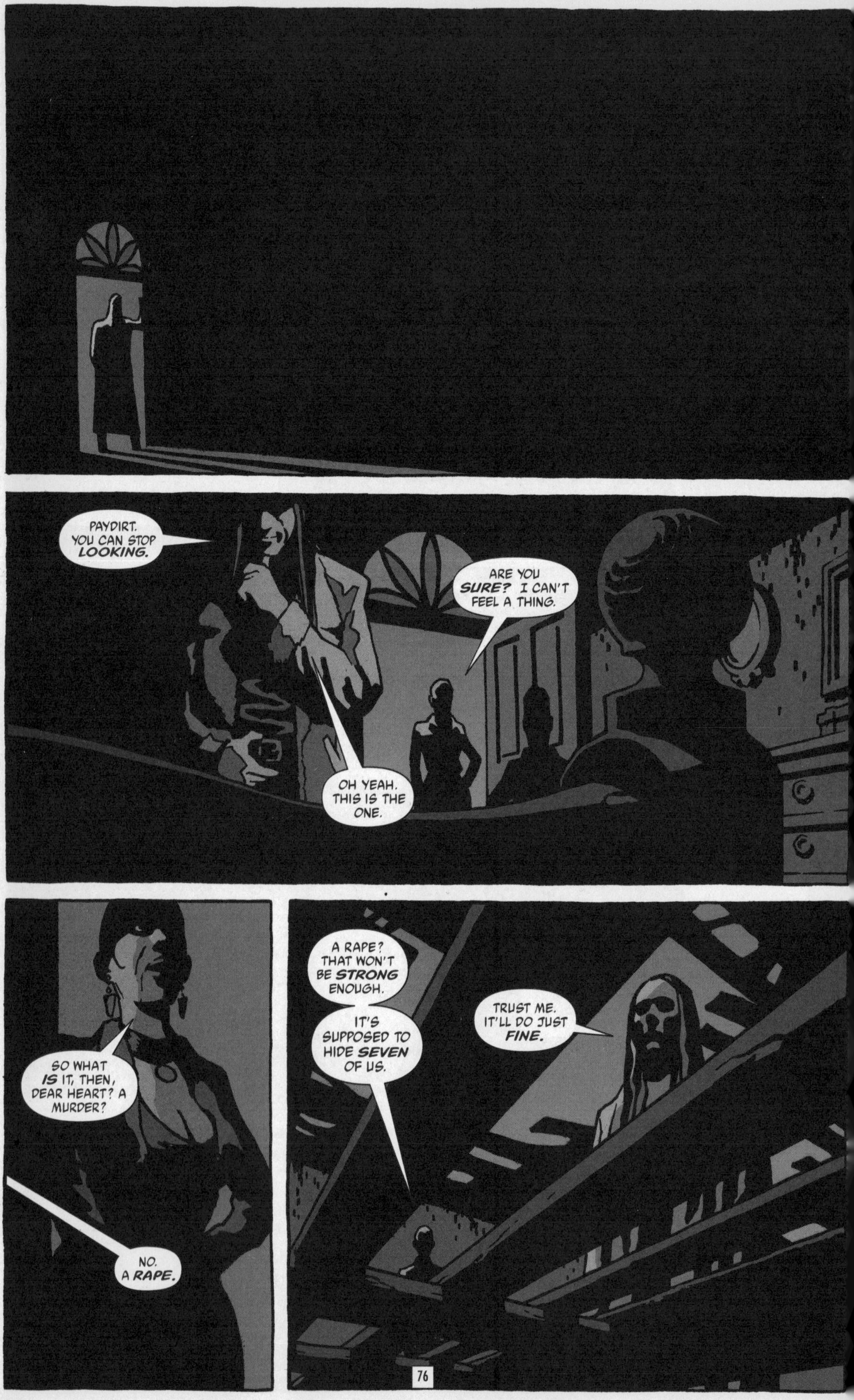
PAYDIRT. YOU CAN STOP LOOKING.
ARE YOU SURE? I CAN'T FEEL A THING.
OH YEAH. THIS IS THE ONE.
SO WHAT IS IT, THEN, DEAR HEART? A MURDER?
NO. A RAPE.
A RAPE? THAT WON'T BE STRONG ENOUGH.
IT'S SUPPOSED TO HIDE SEVEN OF US.
TRUST ME. IT'LL DO JUST FINE.

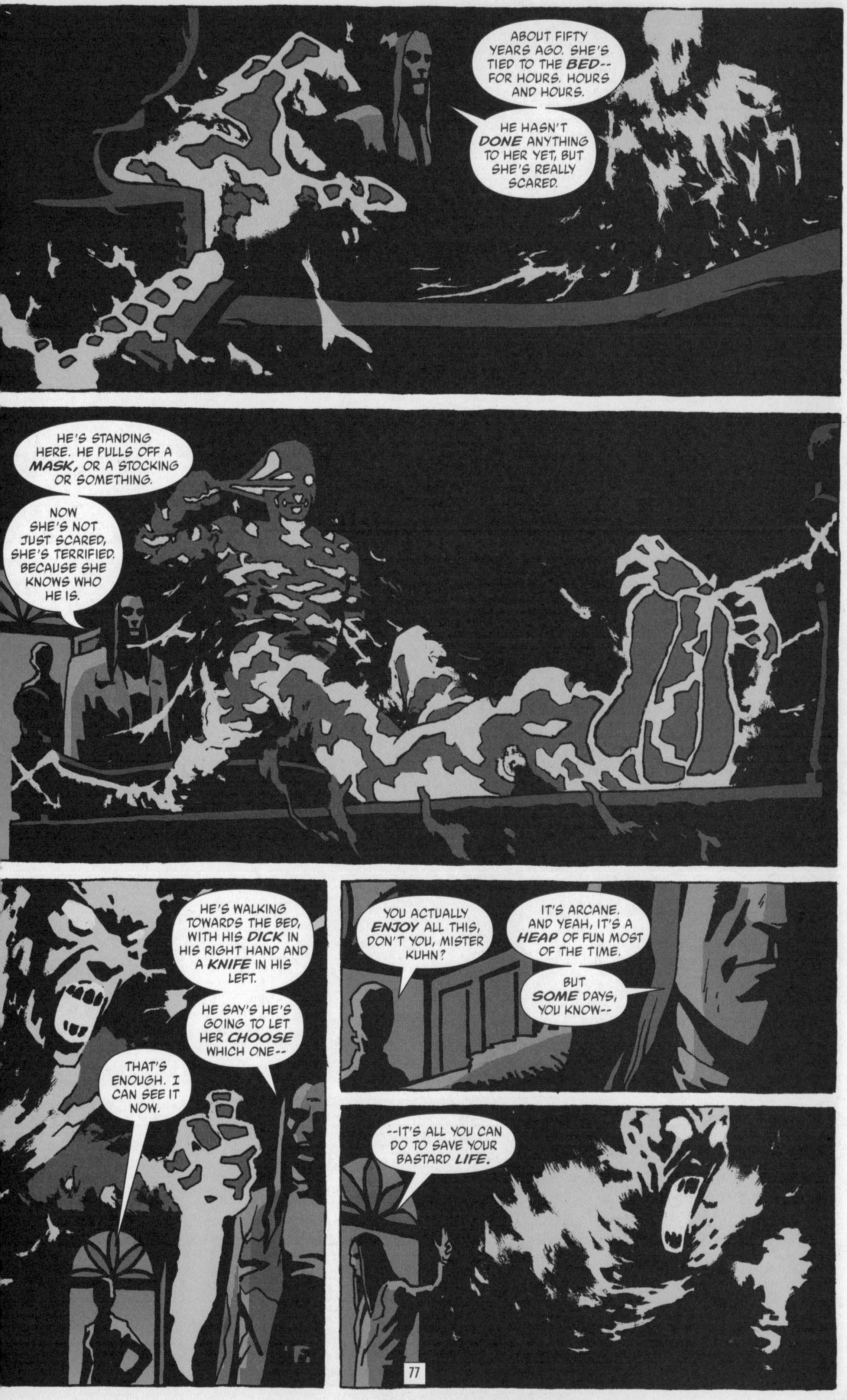
ABOUT FIFTY YEARS AGO. SHE'S TIED TO THE BED--FOR HOURS. HOURS AND HOURS.
HE HASN'T DONE ANYTHING TO HER YET, BUT SHE'S REALLY SCARED.
HE'S STANDING HERE. HE PULLS OFF A MASK, OR A STOCKING OR SOMETHING.
NOW SHE'S NOT JUST SCARED, SHE'S TERRIFIED. BECAUSE SHE KNOWS WHO HE IS.
HE'S WALKING TOWARDS THE BED, WITH HIS DICK IN HIS RIGHT HAND AND A KNIFE IN HIS LEFT.
HE SAY'S HE'S GOING TO LET HER CHOOSE WHICH ONE--
THAT'S ENOUGH. I CAN SEE IT NOW.
YOU ACTUALLY ENJOY ALL THIS, DON'T YOU, MISTER KUHN?
IT'S ARCANE. AND YEAH, IT'S A HEAP OF FUN MOST OF THE TIME.
BUT SOME DAYS, YOU KNOW--
--IT'S ALL YOU CAN DO TO SAVE YOUR BASTARD LIFE.

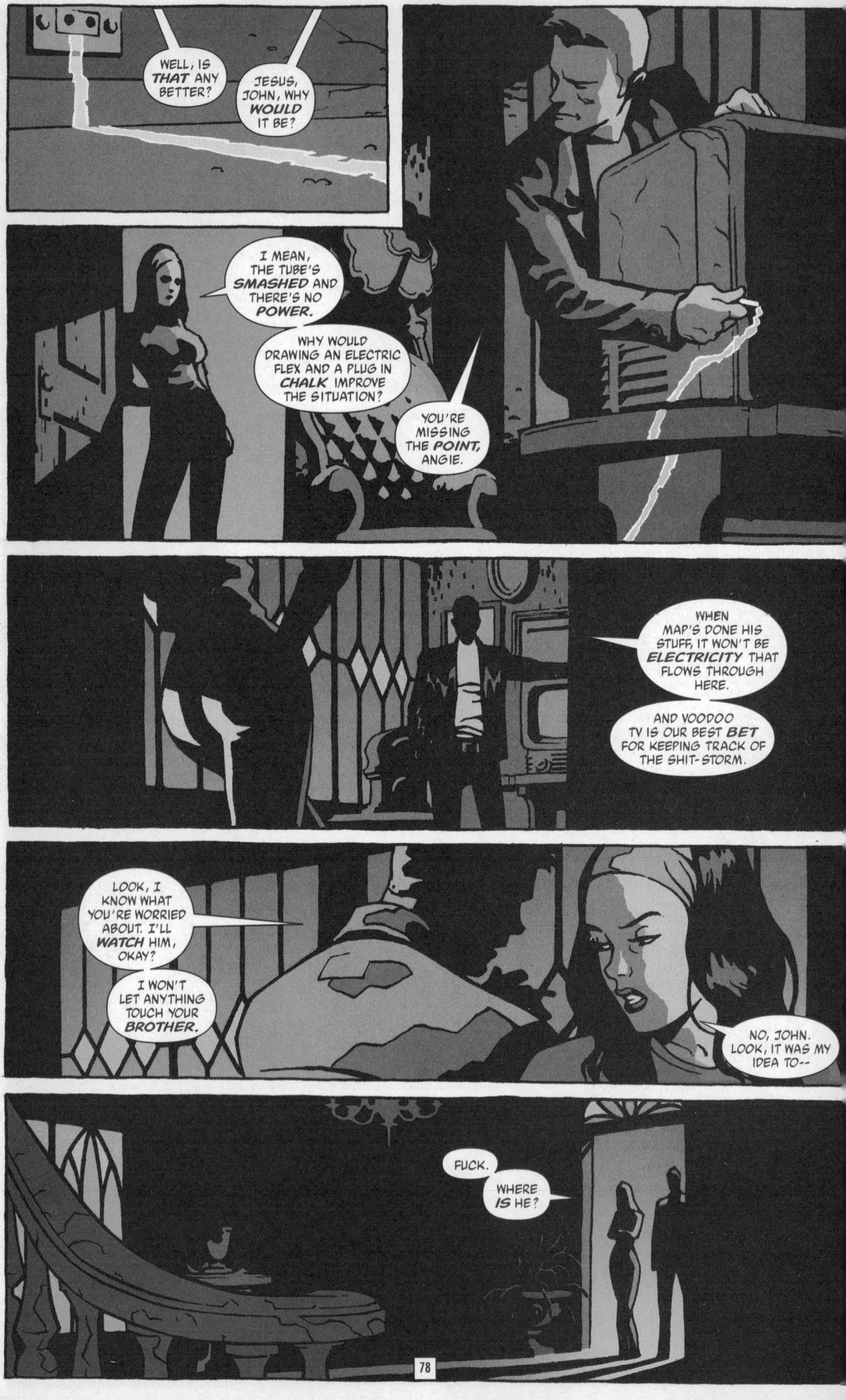
WELL, IS THAT ANY BETTER?
JESUS, JOHN, WHY WOULD IT BE?
I MEAN, THE TUBE'S SMASHED AND THERE'S NO POWER.
WHY WOULD DRAWING AN ELECTRIC FLEX AND A PLUG IN CHALK IMPROVE THE SITUATION?
YOU'RE MISSING THE POINT, ANGIE.
WHEN MAP'S DONE HIS STUFF, IT WON'T BE ELECTRICITY THAT FLOWS THROUGH HERE.
AND VOODOO TV IS OUR BEST BET FOR KEEPING TRACK OF THE SHIT-STORM.
LOOK, I KNOW WHAT YOU'RE WORRIED ABOUT. I'LL WATCH HIM, OKAY?
I WON'T LET ANYTHING TOUCH YOUR BROTHER.
NO, JOHN. LOOK, IT WAS MY IDEA TO--
FUCK.
WHERE IS HE?

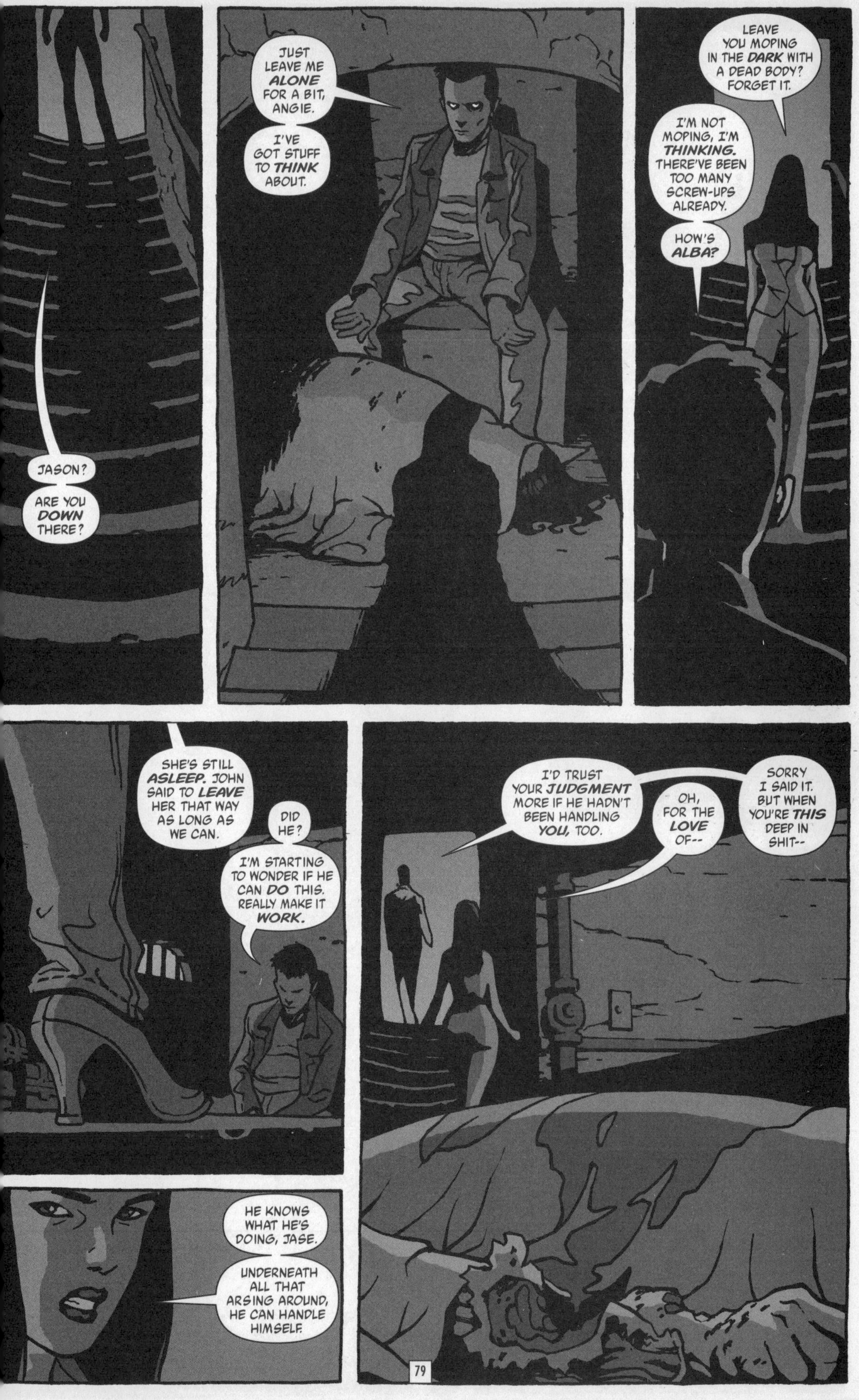

JASON?
ARE YOU DOWN THERE?
JUST LEAVE ME ALONE FOR A BIT, ANGIE.
I'VE GOT STUFF TO THINK ABOUT.
LEAVE YOU MOPING IN THE DARK WITH A DEAD BODY? FORGET IT.
I'M NOT MOPING, I'M THINKING. THERE'VE BEEN TOO MANY SCREW-UPS ALREADY.
HOW'S ALBA?
SHE'S STILL ASLEEP. JOHN SAID TO LEAVE HER THAT WAY AS LONG AS WE CAN.
DID HE?
I'M STARTING TO WONDER IF HE CAN DO THIS. REALLY MAKE IT WORK.
HE KNOWS WHAT HE'S DOING, JASE.
UNDERNEATH ALL THAT ARSING AROUND, HE CAN HANDLE HIMSELF.
I'D TRUST YOUR JUDGMENT MORE IF HE HADN'T BEEN HANDLING YOU, TOO.
OH, FOR THE LOVE OF--
SORRY I SAID IT. BUT WHEN YOU'RE THIS DEEP IN SHIT--

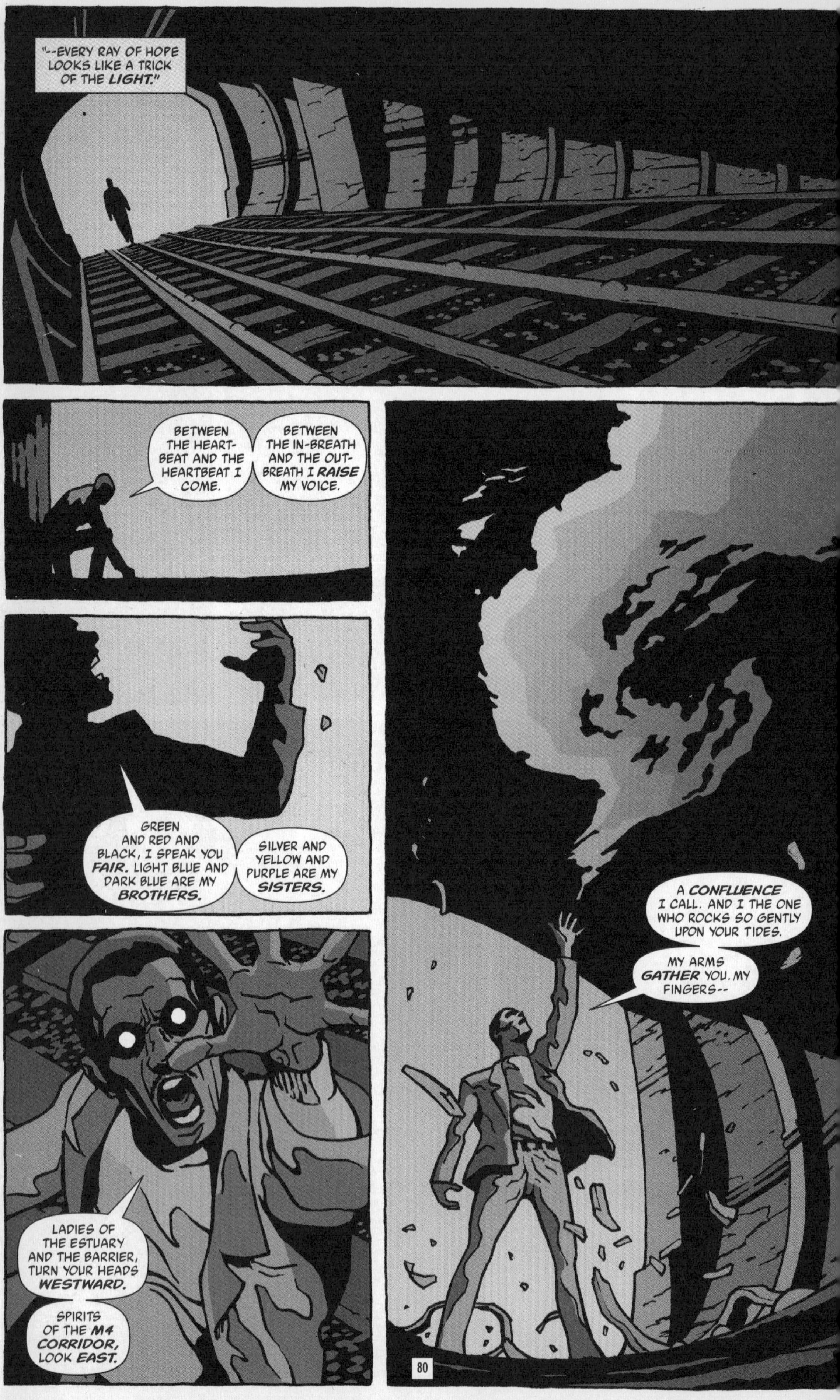
"--EVERY RAY OF HOPE LOOKS LIKE A TRICK OF THE LIGHT."
BETWEEN THE HEART-BEAT AND THE HEARTBEAT I COME.
BETWEEN THE IN-BREATH AND THE OUT-BREATH I RAISE MY VOICE.
GREEN AND BLACK AND RED AND BLACK, I SPEAK YOU FAIR. LIGHT BLUE AND DARK BLUE ARE MY BROTHERS.
SILVER AND YELLOW AND PURPLE ARE MY SISTERS.
LADIES OF THE ESTUARY AND THE BARRIER, TURN YOUR HEADS WESTWARD.
SPIRITS OF THE M4 CORRIDOR, LOOK EAST.
A CONFLUENCE I CALL. AND I THE ONE WHO ROCKS SO GENTLY UPON YOUR TIDES.
MY ARMS GATHER YOU. MY FINGERS--

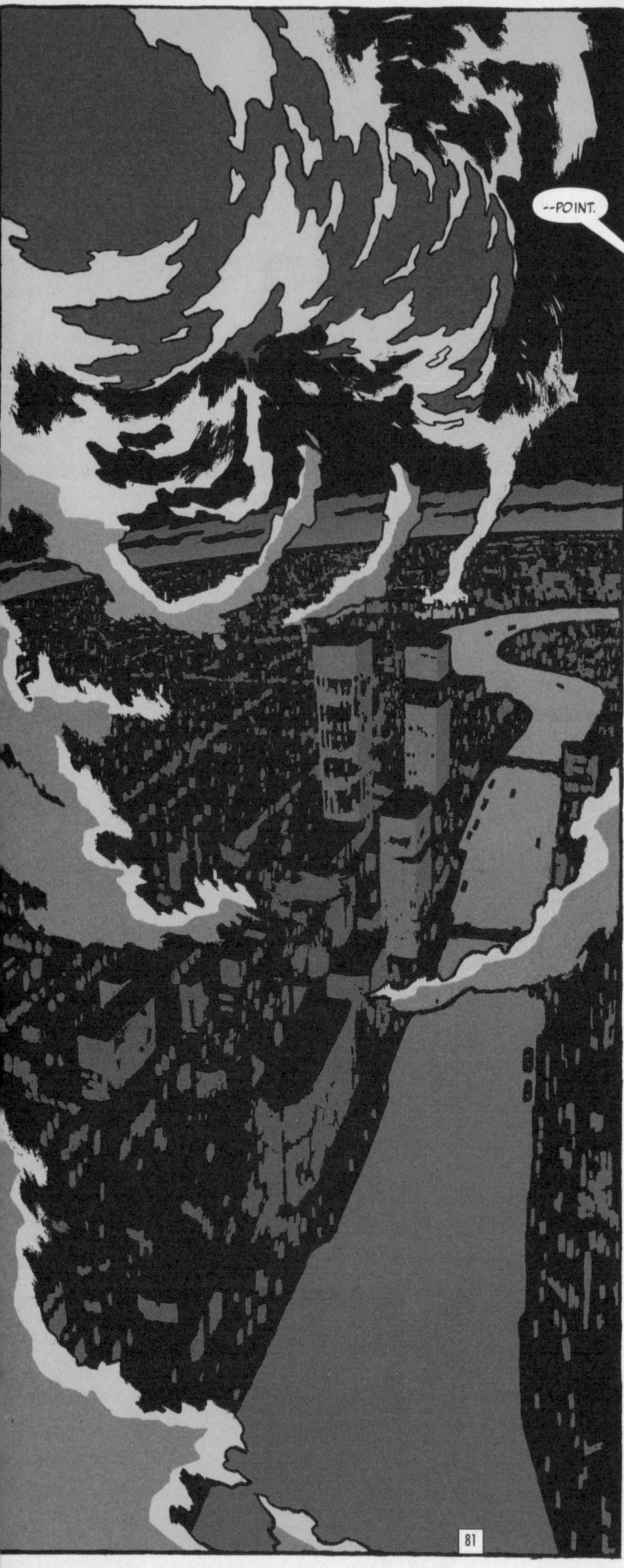

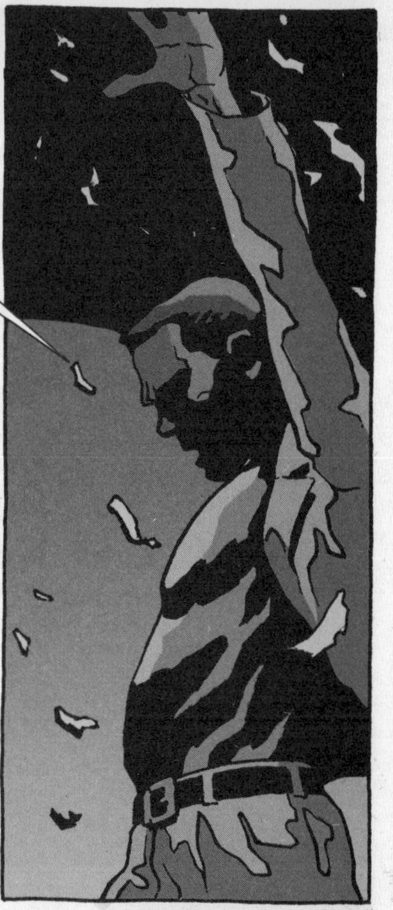
--POINT.

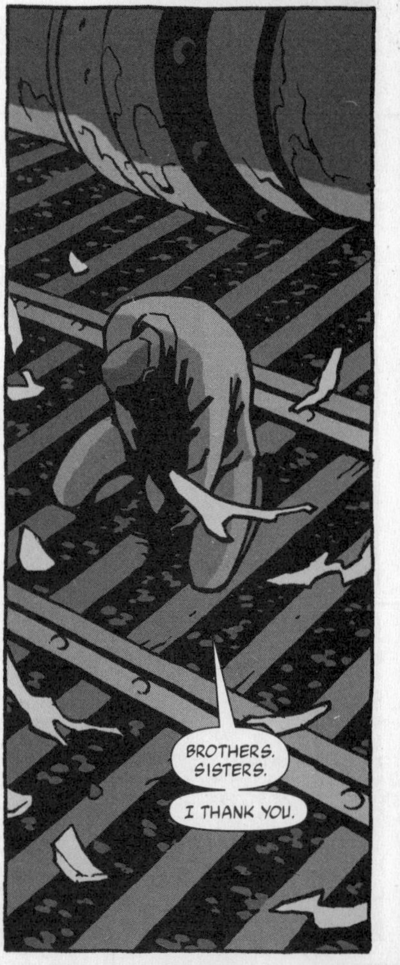
BROTHERS. SISTERS.
I THANK YOU.

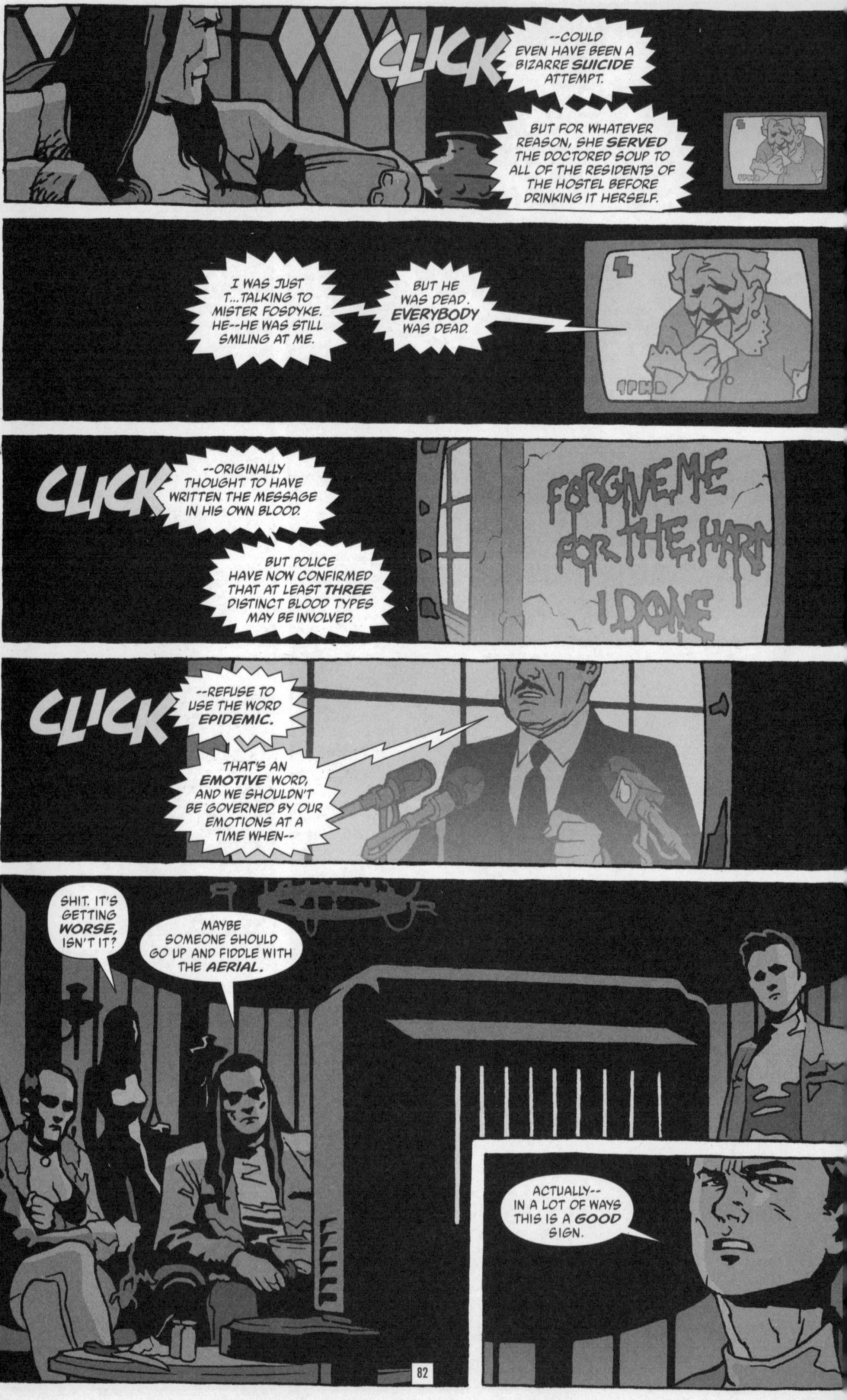
CLICK
--COULD EVEN HAVE BEEN A BIZARRE SUICIDE ATTEMPT.
BUT FOR WHATEVER REASON, SHE SERVED THE DOCTORED SOUP TO ALL OF THE RESIDENTS OF THE HOSTEL BEFORE DRINKING IT HERSELF.
I WAS JUST T...TALKING TO MISTER FOSDYKE. HE--HE WAS STILL SMILING AT ME.
BUT HE WAS DEAD. EVERYBODY WAS DEAD.
CLICK
--ORIGINALLY THOUGHT TO HAVE WRITTEN THE MESSAGE IN HIS OWN BLOOD.
BUT POLICE HAVE NOW CONFIRMED THAT AT LEAST THREE DISTINCT BLOOD TYPES MAY BE INVOLVED.
FORGIVE ME
FOR THE HARM
I DONE
CLICK
--REFUSE TO USE THE WORD EPIDEMIC.
THAT'S AN EMOTIVE WORD, AND WE SHOULDN'T BE GOVERNED BY OUR EMOTIONS AT A TIME WHEN--
SHIT. IT'S GETTING WORSE, ISN'T IT?
MAYBE SOMEONE SHOULD GO UP AND FIDDLE WITH THE AERIAL.
ACTUALLY-- IN A LOT OF WAYS THIS IS A GOOD SIGN.

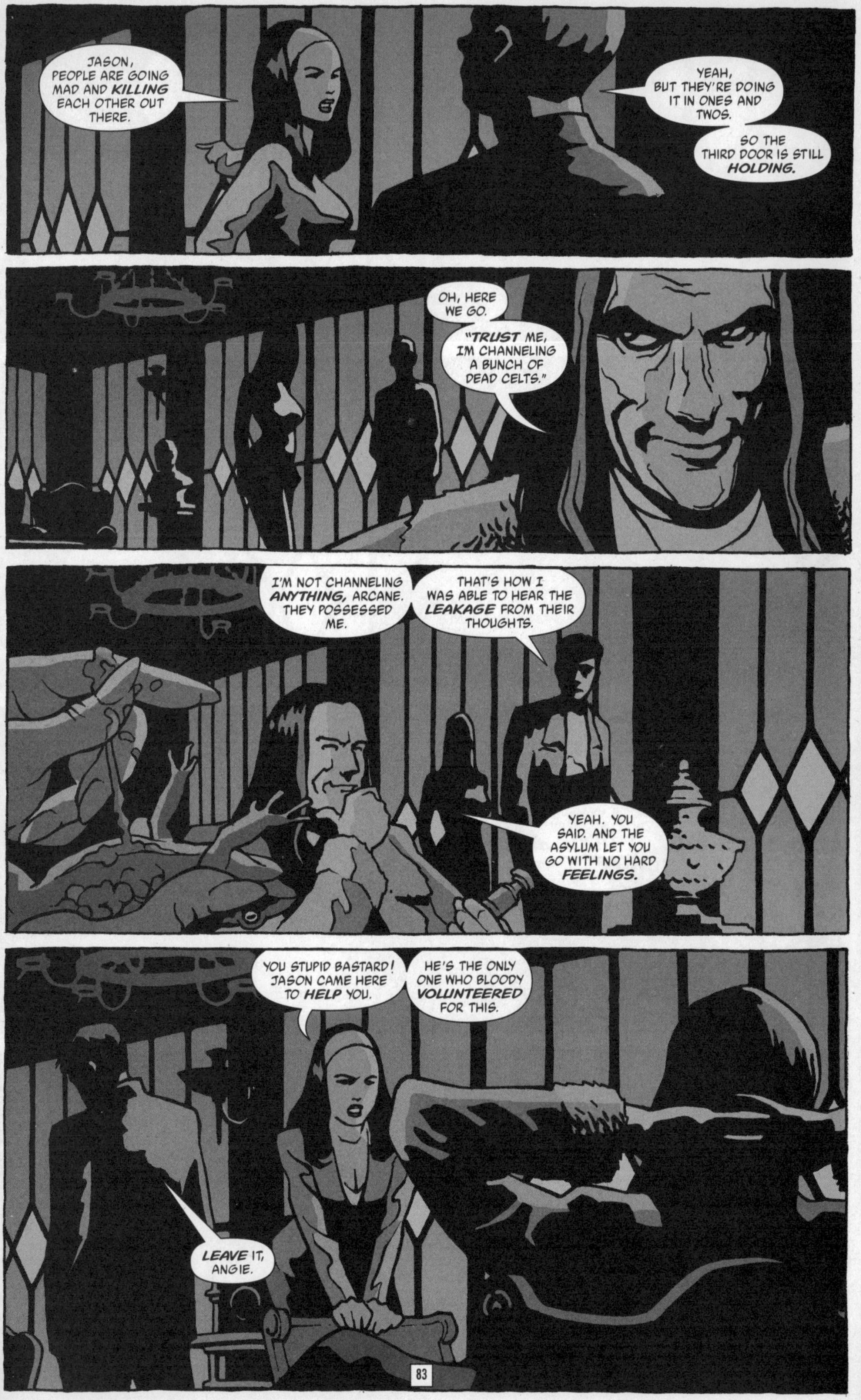
JASON, PEOPLE ARE GOING MAD AND KILLING EACH OTHER OUT THERE.
YEAH, BUT THEY'RE DOING IT IN ONES AND TWOS.
SO THE THIRD DOOR IS STILL HOLDING.
OH, HERE WE GO.
"TRUST ME, I'M CHANNELING A BUNCH OF DEAD CELTS."
I'M NOT CHANNELING ANYTHING, ARCANE. THEY POSSESSED ME.
THAT'S HOW I WAS ABLE TO HEAR THE LEAKAGE FROM THEIR THOUGHTS.
YEAH. YOU SAID. AND THE ASYLUM LET YOU GO WITH NO HARD FEELINGS.
YOU STUPID BASTARD! JASON CAME HERE TO HELP YOU.
HE'S THE ONLY ONE WHO BLOODY VOLUNTEERED FOR THIS.
LEAVE IT, ANGIE.

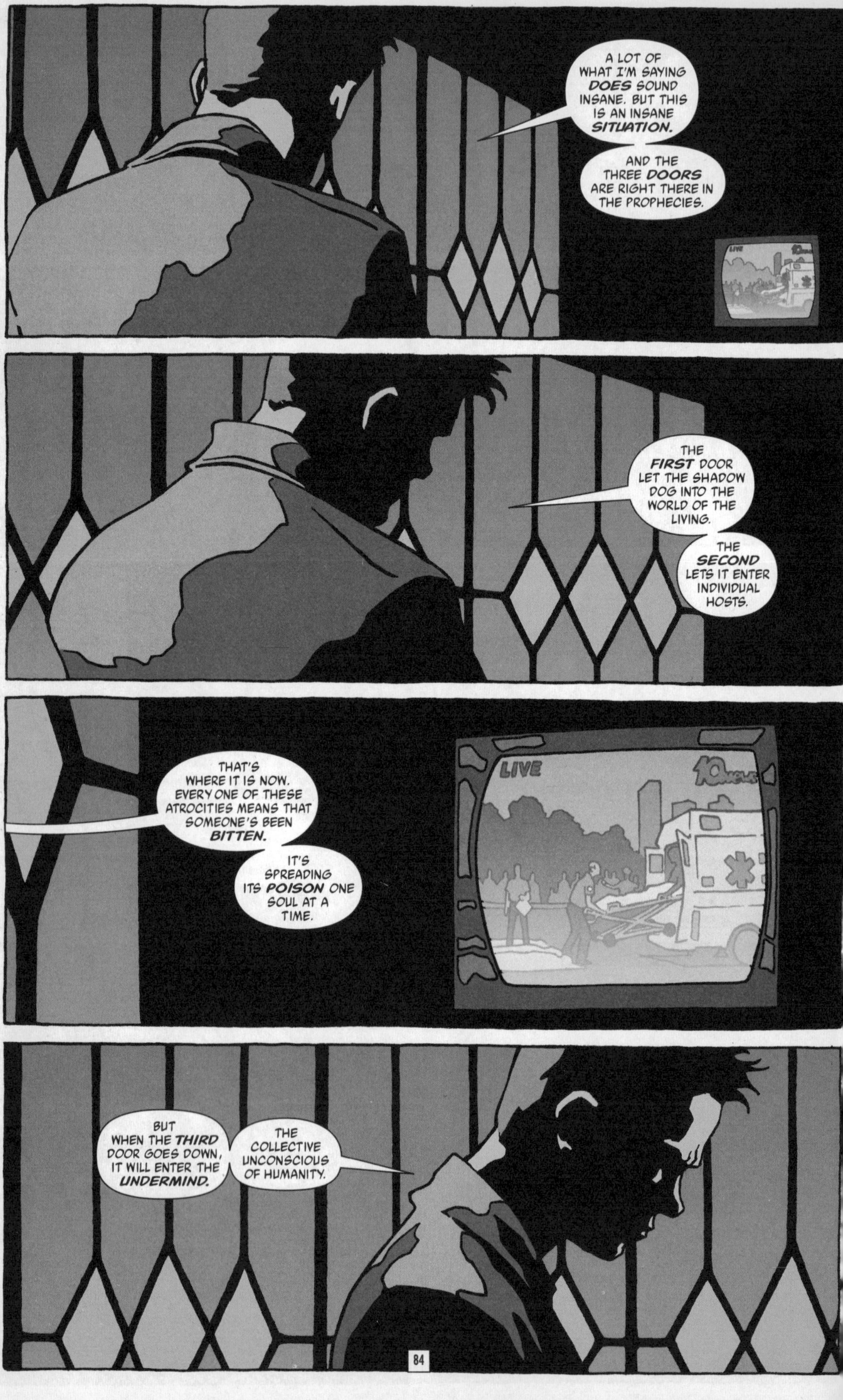

A LOT OF WHAT I'M SAYING DOES SOUND INSANE. BUT THIS IS AN INSANE SITUATION.
AND THE THREE DOORS ARE RIGHT THERE IN THE PROPHECIES.
LIVE
THE FIRST DOOR LET THE SHADOW DOG INTO THE WORLD OF THE LIVING.
THE SECOND LETS IT ENTER INDIVIDUAL HOSTS.
THAT'S WHERE IT IS NOW. EVERY ONE OF THESE ATROCITIES MEANS THAT SOMEONE'S BEEN BITTEN.
IT'S SPREADING ITS POISON ONE SOUL AT A TIME.
LIVE
BUT WHEN THE THIRD DOOR GOES DOWN, IT WILL ENTER THE UNDERMIND.
THE COLLECTIVE UNCONSCIOUS OF HUMANITY.

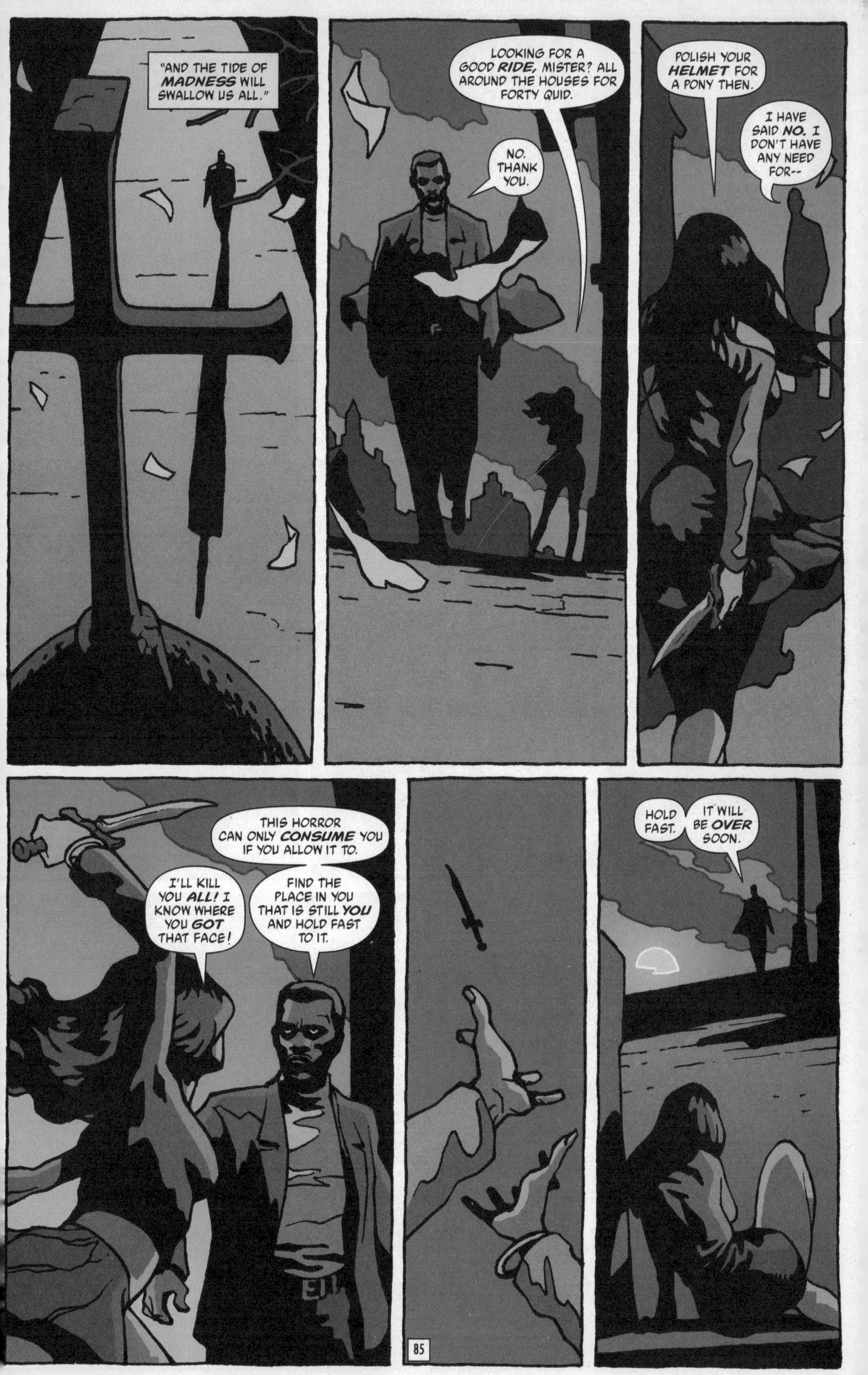
"AND THE TIDE OF MADNESS WILL SWALLOW US ALL."
LOOKING FOR A GOOD RIDE, MISTER? ALL AROUND THE HOUSES FOR FORTY QUID.
NO. THANK YOU.
POLISH YOUR HELMET FOR A PONY THEN.
I HAVE SAID NO. I DON'T HAVE ANY NEED FOR--
THIS HORROR CAN ONLY CONSUME YOU IF YOU ALLOW IT TO.
I'LL KILL YOU ALL! I KNOW WHERE YOU GOT THAT FACE!
FIND THE PLACE IN YOU THAT IS STILL YOU AND HOLD FAST TO IT.
HOLD FAST.
IT WILL BE OVER SOON.

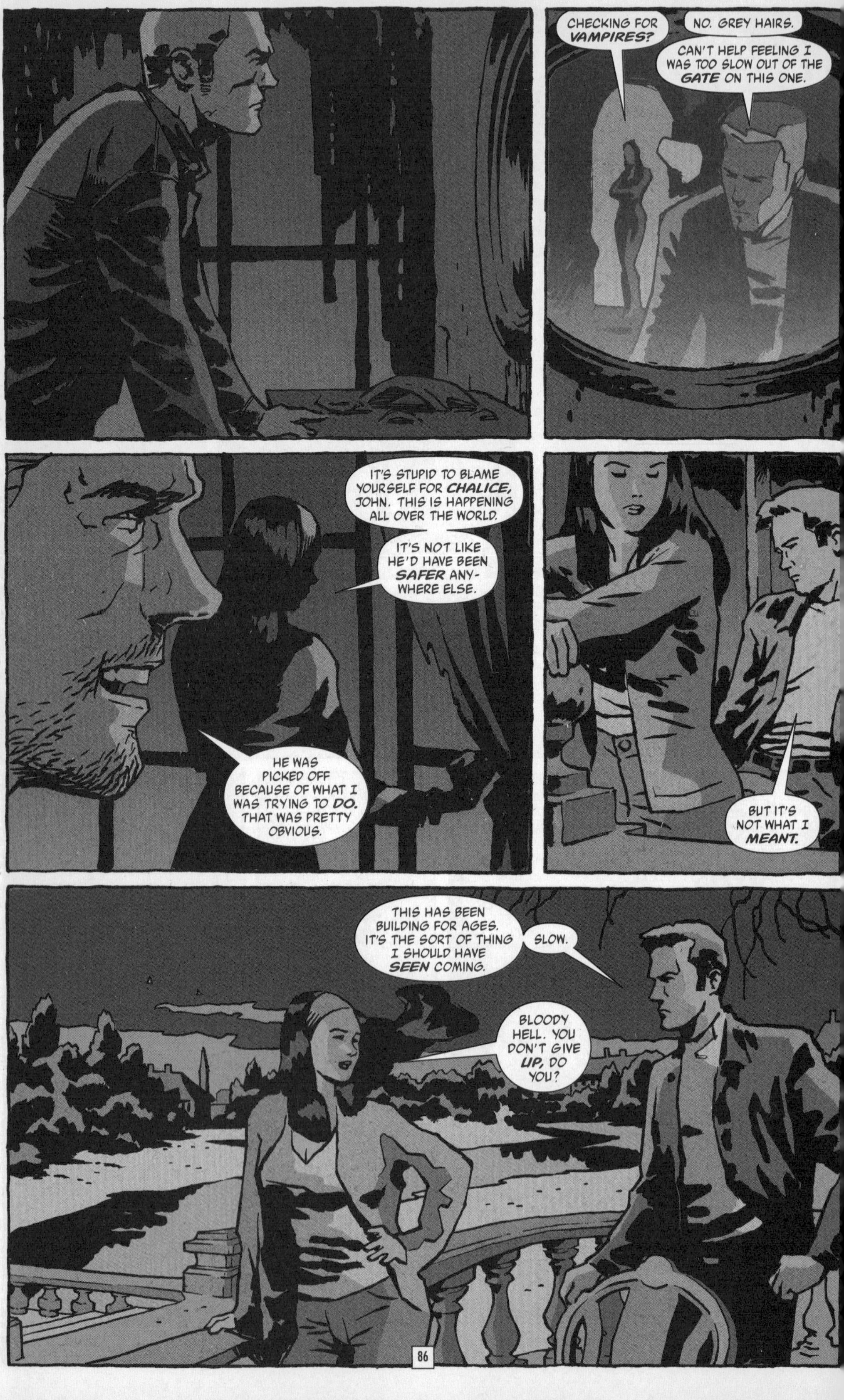

CHECKING FOR VAMPIRES?
NO. GREY HAIRS.
CAN'T HELP FEELING I WAS TOO SLOW OUT OF THE GATE ON THIS ONE.
IT'S STUPID TO BLAME YOURSELF FOR CHALICE, JOHN. THIS IS HAPPENING ALL OVER THE WORLD.
IT'S NOT LIKE HE'D HAVE BEEN SAFER ANYWHERE ELSE.
HE WAS PICKED OFF BECAUSE OF WHAT I WAS TRYING TO DO. THAT WAS PRETTY OBVIOUS.
BUT IT'S NOT WHAT I MEANT.
THIS HAS BEEN BUILDING FOR AGES. IT'S THE SORT OF THING I SHOULD HAVE SEEN COMING.
SLOW.
BLOODY HELL. YOU DON'T GIVE UP, DO YOU?

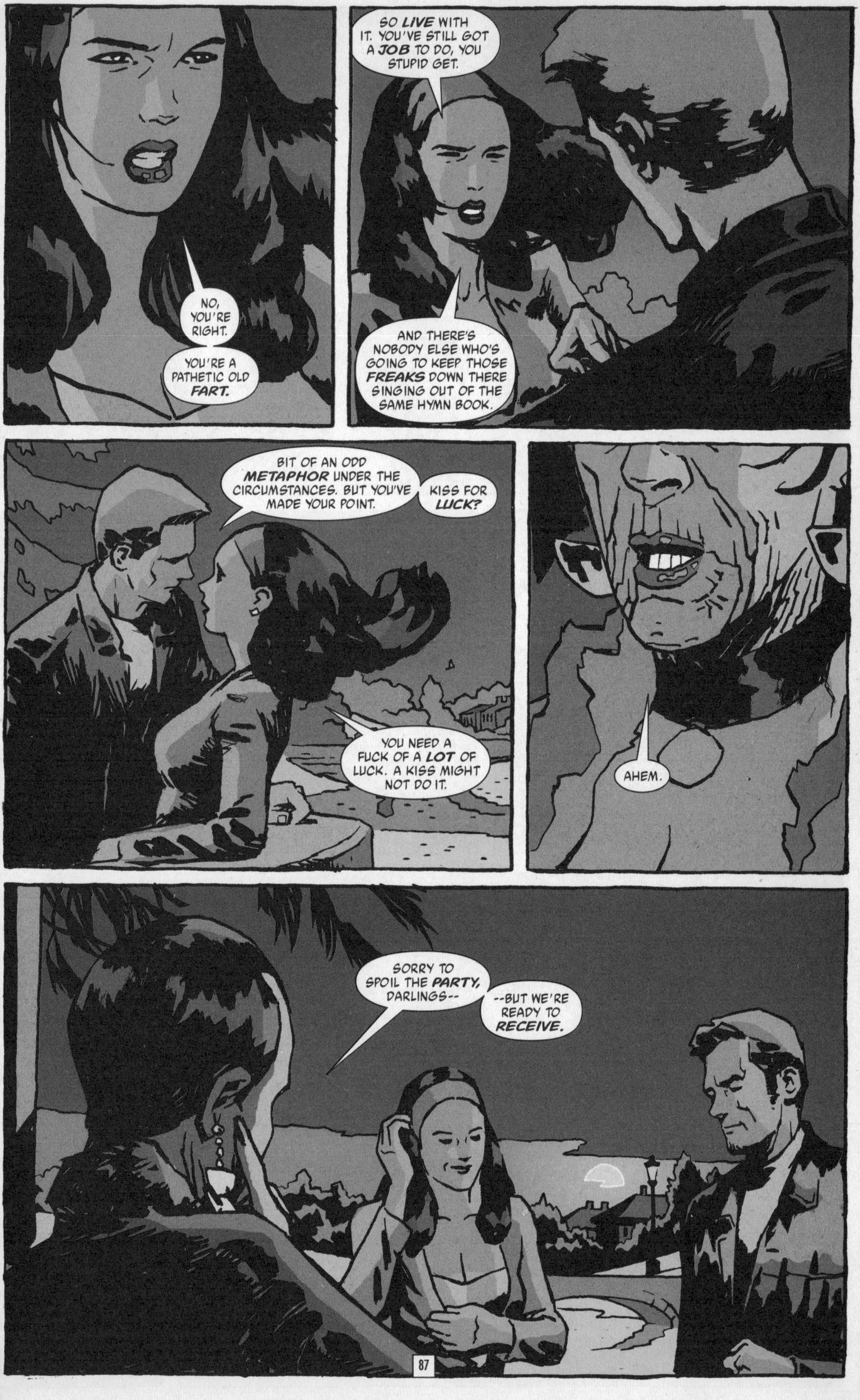
NO, YOU'RE RIGHT.
YOU'RE A PATHETIC OLD FART.
SO LIVE WITH IT. YOU'VE STILL GOT A JOB TO DO, YOU STUPID GET.
AND THERE'S NOBODY ELSE WHO'S GOING TO KEEP THOSE FREAKS DOWN THERE SINGING OUT OF THE SAME HYMN BOOK.
BIT OF AN ODD METAPHOR UNDER THE CIRCUMSTANCES. BUT YOU'VE MADE YOUR POINT.
KISS FOR LUCK?
YOU NEED A FUCK OF A LOT OF LUCK. A KISS MIGHT NOT DO IT.
AHEM.
SORRY TO SPOIL THE PARTY, DARLINGS--
--BUT WE'RE READY TO RECEIVE.

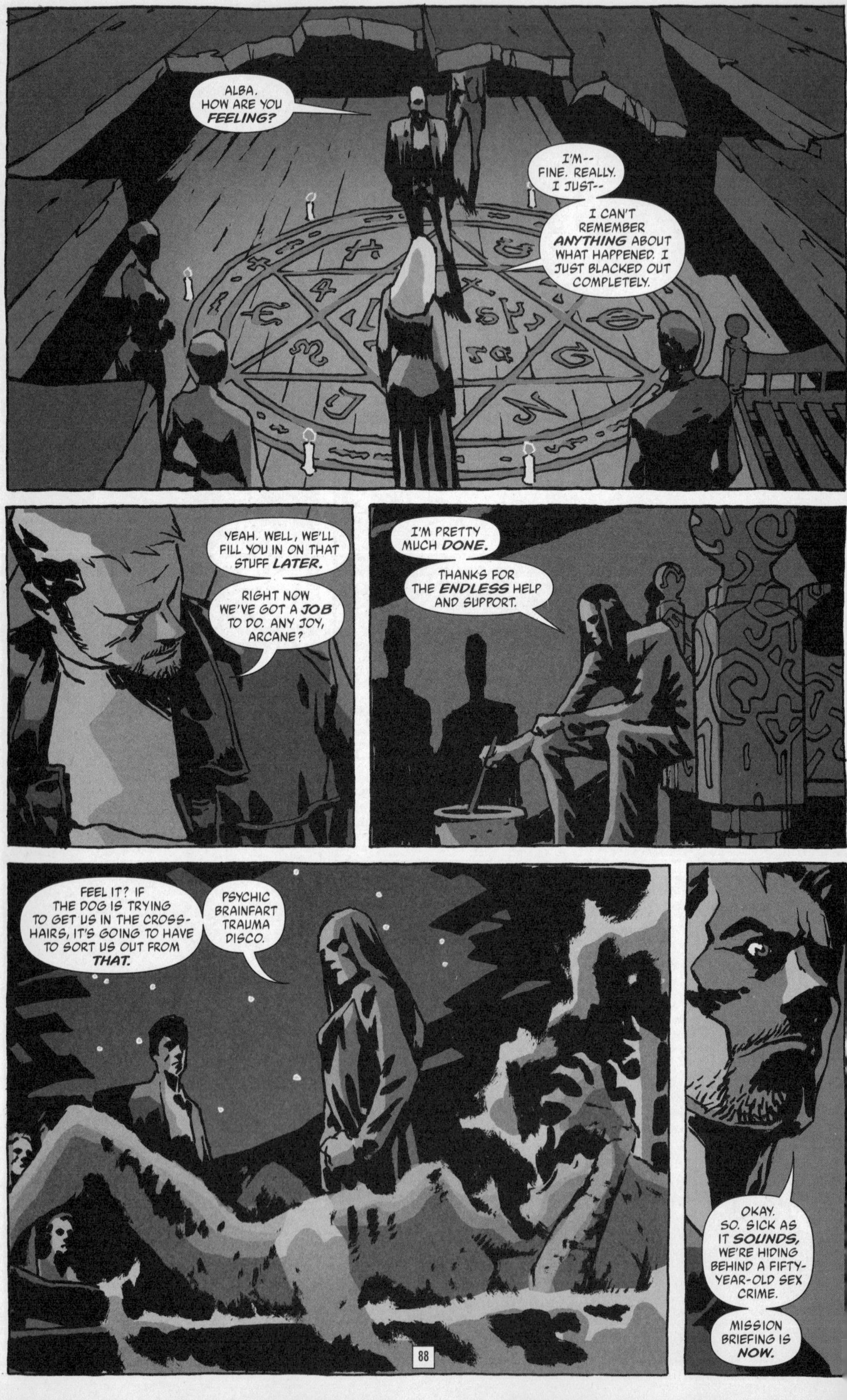
ALBA. HOW ARE YOU FEELING?
I'M-- FINE. REALLY. I JUST--
I CAN'T REMEMBER ANYTHING ABOUT WHAT HAPPENED. I JUST BLACKED OUT COMPLETELY.
YEAH. WELL, WE'LL FILL YOU IN ON THAT STUFF LATER.
RIGHT NOW WE'VE GOT A JOB TO DO. ANY JOY, ARCANE?
I'M PRETTY MUCH DONE.
THANKS FOR THE ENDLESS HELP AND SUPPORT.
FEEL IT? IF THE DOG IS TRYING TO GET US IN THE CROSS-HAIRS, IT'S GOING TO HAVE TO SORT US OUT FROM THAT.
PSYCHIC BRAINFART TRAUMA DISCO.
OKAY. SO. SICK AS IT SOUNDS, WE'RE HIDING BEHIND A FIFTY-YEAR-OLD SEX CRIME.
MISSION BRIEFING IS NOW.

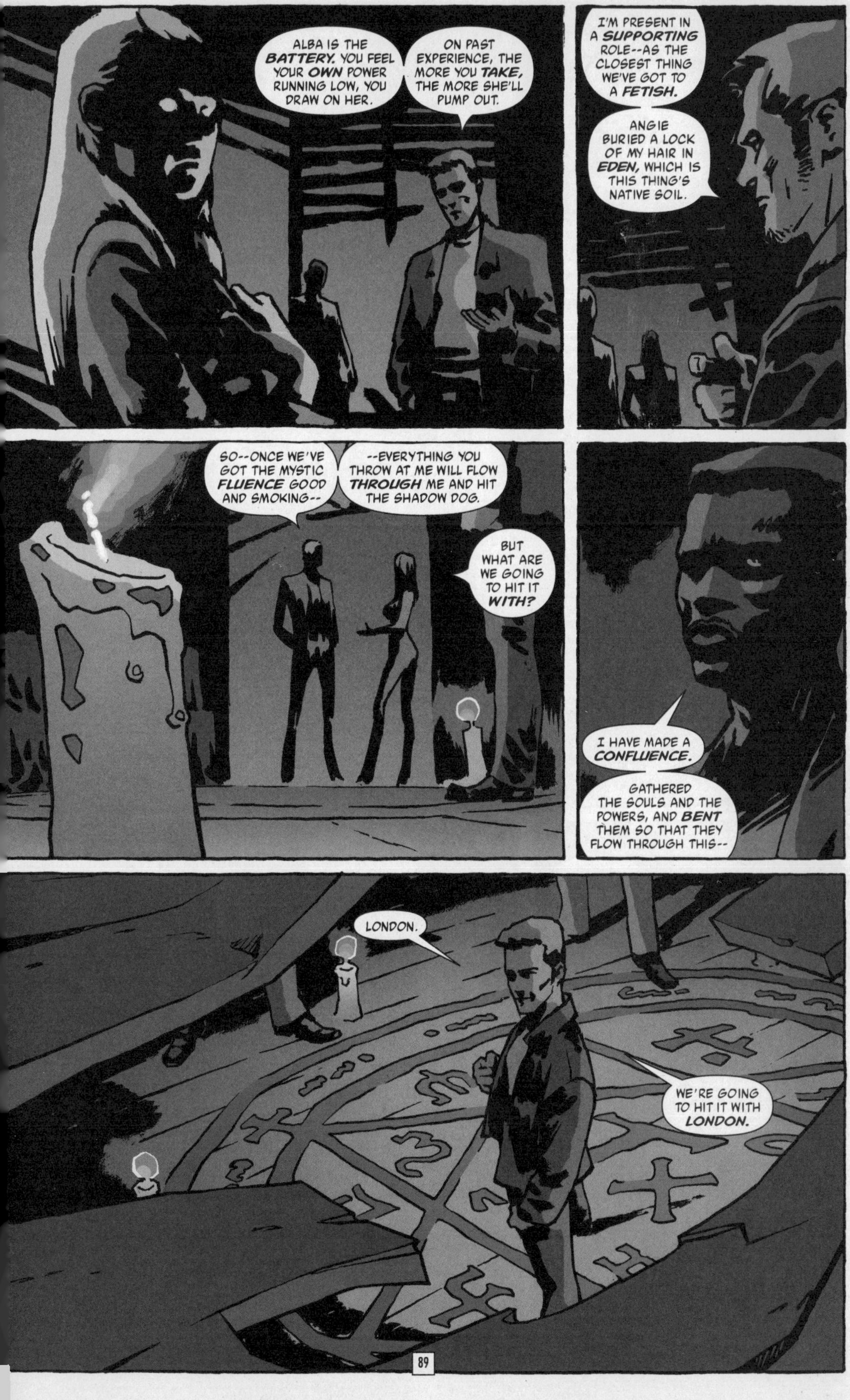

ALBA IS THE BATTERY. YOU FEEL YOUR OWN POWER RUNNING LOW, YOU DRAW ON HER.
ON PAST EXPERIENCE, THE MORE YOU TAKE, THE MORE SHE'LL PUMP OUT.
I'M PRESENT IN A SUPPORTING ROLE--AS THE CLOSEST THING WE'VE GOT TO A FETISH.
ANGIE BURIED A LOCK OF MY HAIR IN EDEN, WHICH IS THIS THING'S NATIVE SOIL.
SO--ONCE WE'VE GOT THE MYSTIC FLUENCE GOOD AND SMOKING--
--EVERYTHING YOU THROW AT ME WILL FLOW THROUGH ME AND HIT THE SHADOW DOG.
BUT WHAT ARE WE GOING TO HIT IT WITH?
I HAVE MADE A CONFLUENCE.
GATHERED THE SOULS AND THE POWERS, AND BENT THEM SO THAT THEY FLOW THROUGH THIS--
LONDON.
WE'RE GOING TO HIT IT WITH LONDON.

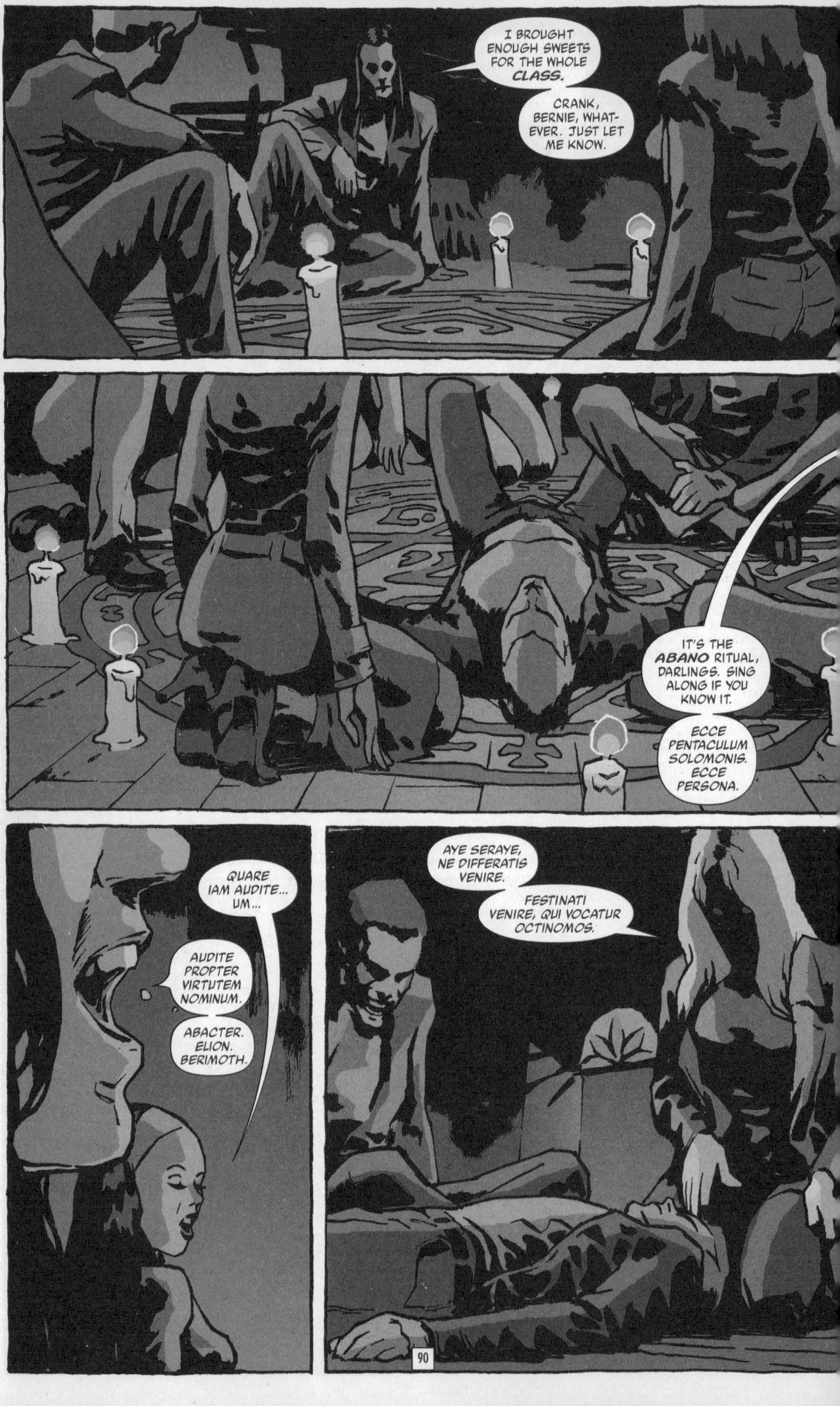
I BROUGHT ENOUGH SWEETS FOR THE WHOLE CLASS.
CRANK, BERNIE, WHAT-EVER. JUST LET ME KNOW.
IT'S THE ABANO RITUAL, DARLINGS. SING ALONG IF YOU KNOW IT.
ECCE PENTACULUM SOLOMONIS. ECCE PERSONA.
QUARE IAM AUDITE... UM...
AUDITE PROPTER VIRTUTEM NOMINUM.
ABACTER. ELION. BERIMOTH.
AYE SERAYE, NE DIFFERATIS VENIRE.
FESTINATI VENIRE, QUI VOCATUR OCTINOMOS.

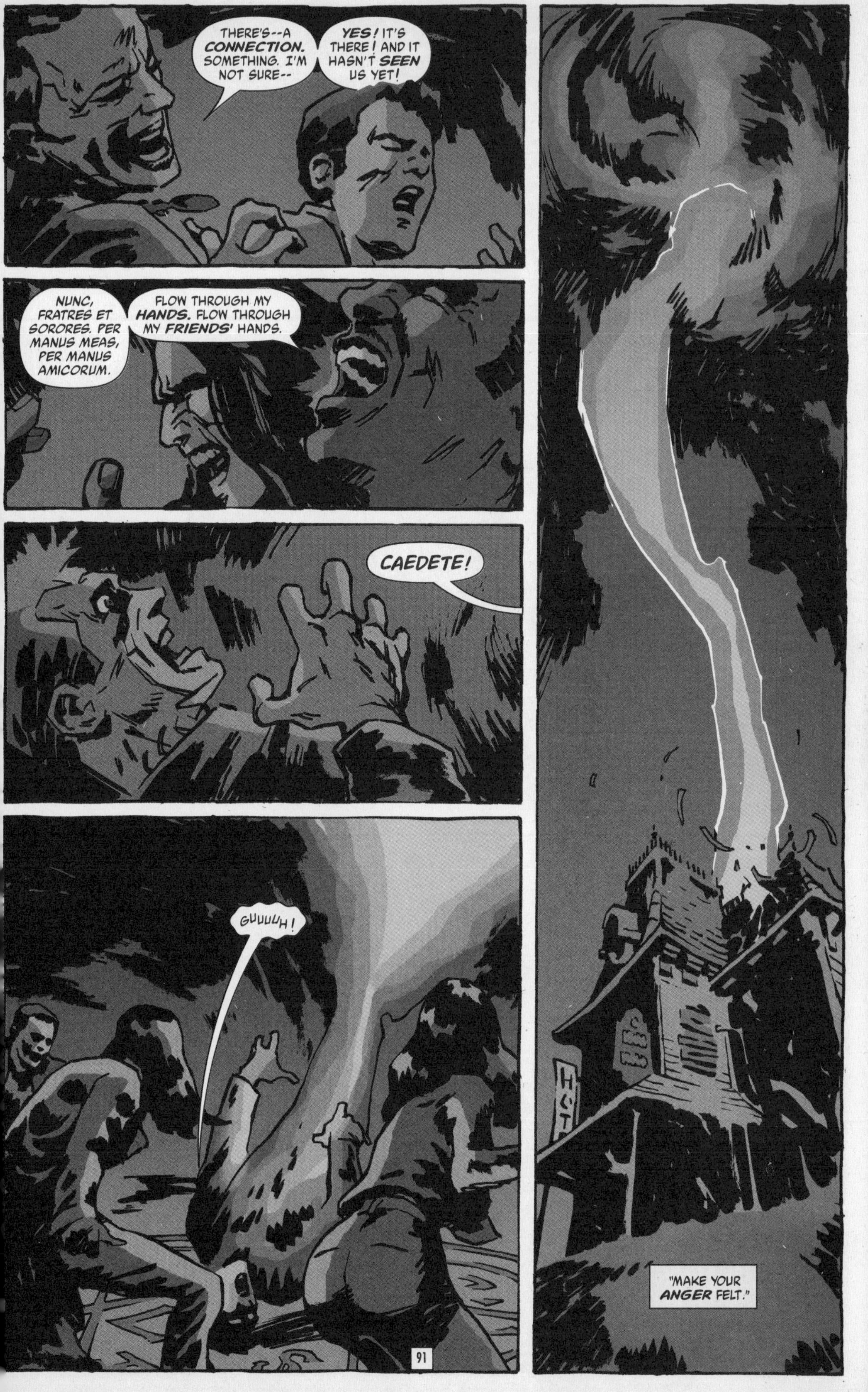
THERE'S--A CONNECTION. SOMETHING. I'M NOT SURE--
YES! IT'S THERE! AND IT HASN'T SEEN US YET!
NUNC, FRATRES ET SORORES. PER MANUS MEAS, PER MANUS AMICORUM.
FLOW THROUGH MY HANDS. FLOW THROUGH MY FRIENDS' HANDS.
CAEDETE!
GUUUUH!
"MAKE YOUR ANGER FELT."

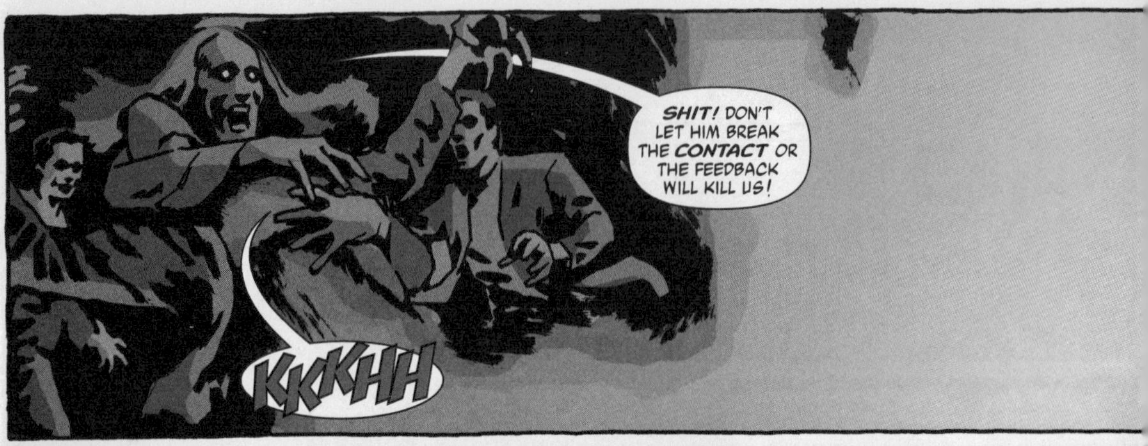
SHIT! DON'T LET HIM BREAK THE CONTACT OR THE FEEDBACK WILL KILL US!
KKKHH

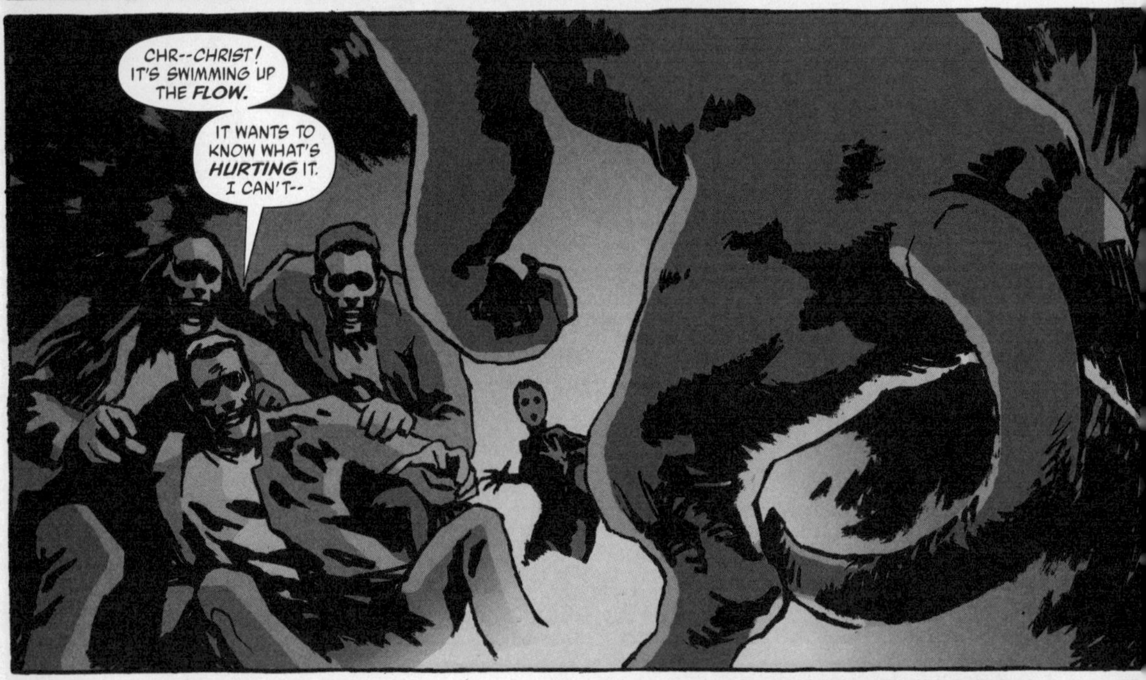
CHR--CHRIST! IT'S SWIMMING UP THE FLOW.
IT WANTS TO KNOW WHAT'S HURTING IT. I CAN'T--

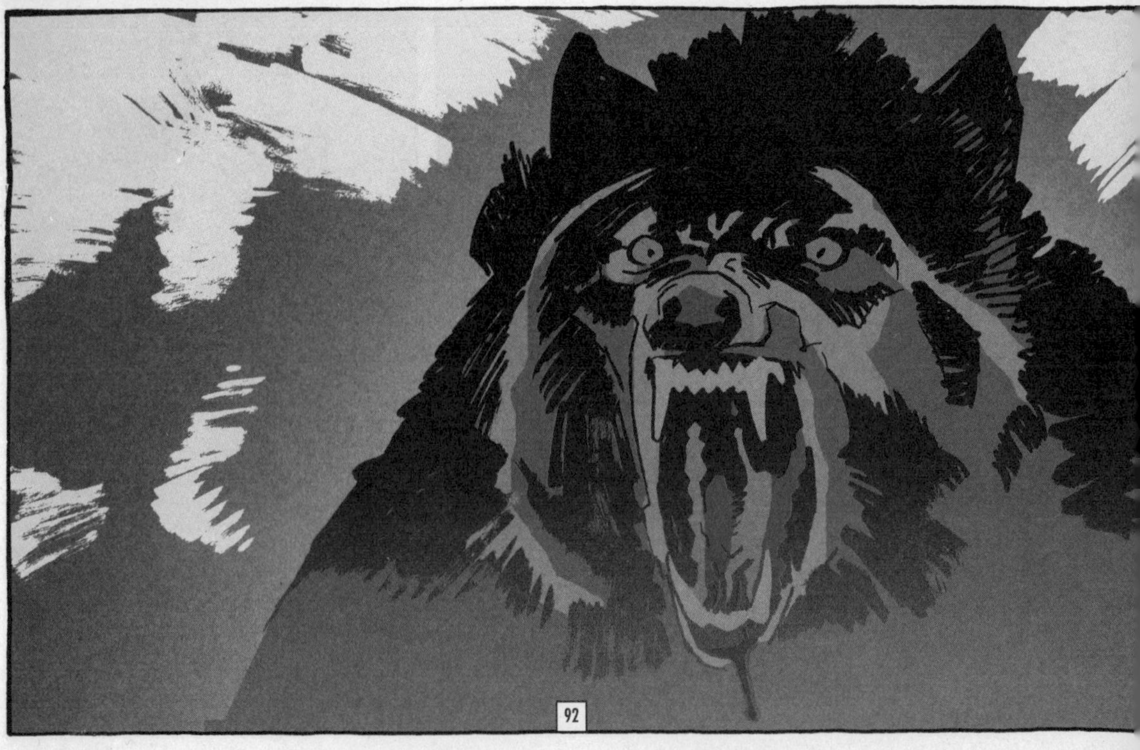

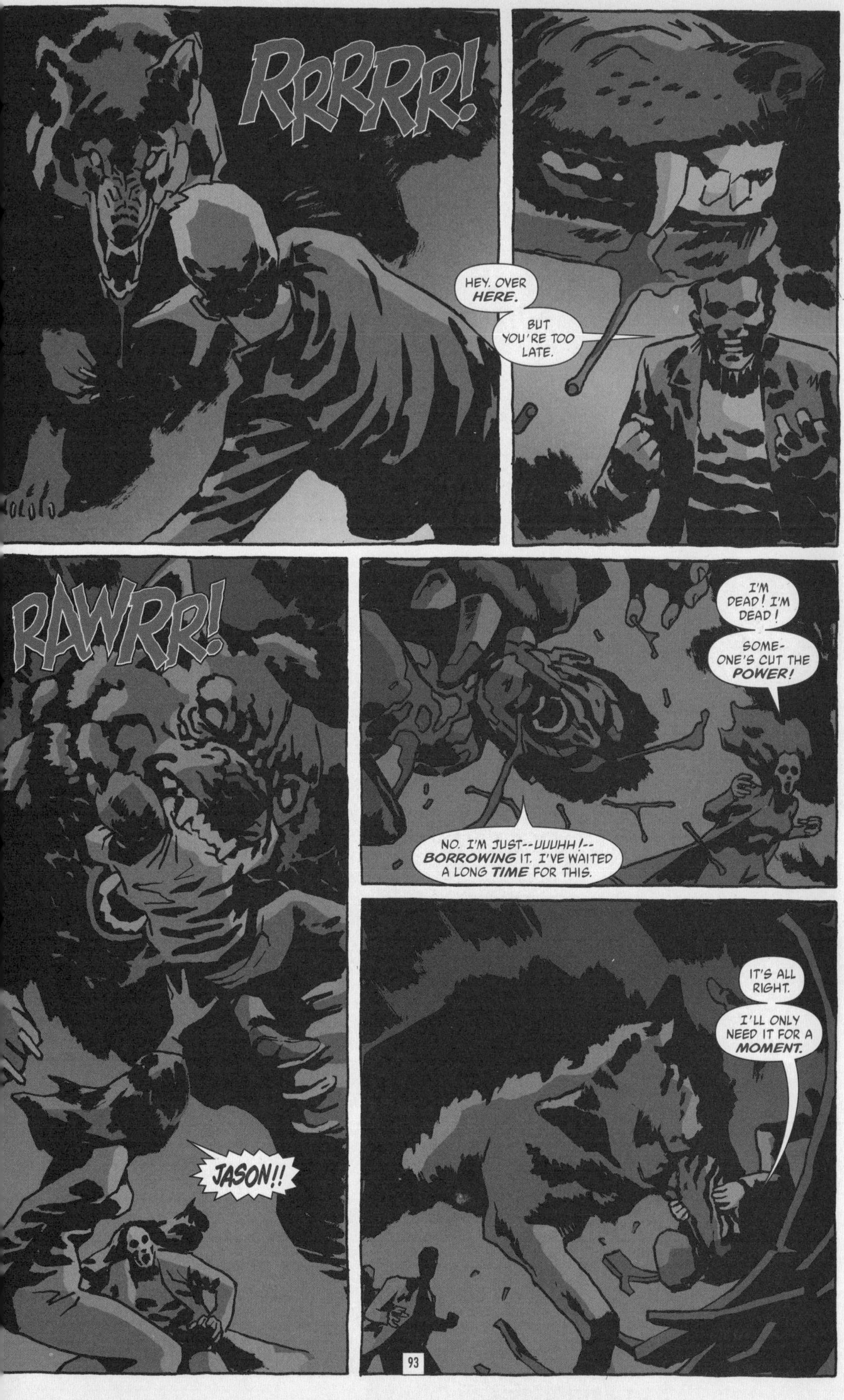
RRRRR!
HEY. OVER HERE.
BUT YOU'RE TOO LATE.
RAWRR!
JASON!!
I'M DEAD! I'M DEAD!
SOME-ONE'S CUT THE POWER!
NO. I'M JUST--UUUHH!--BORROWING IT. I'VE WAITED A LONG TIME FOR THIS.
IT'S ALL RIGHT.
I'LL ONLY NEED IT FOR A MOMENT.

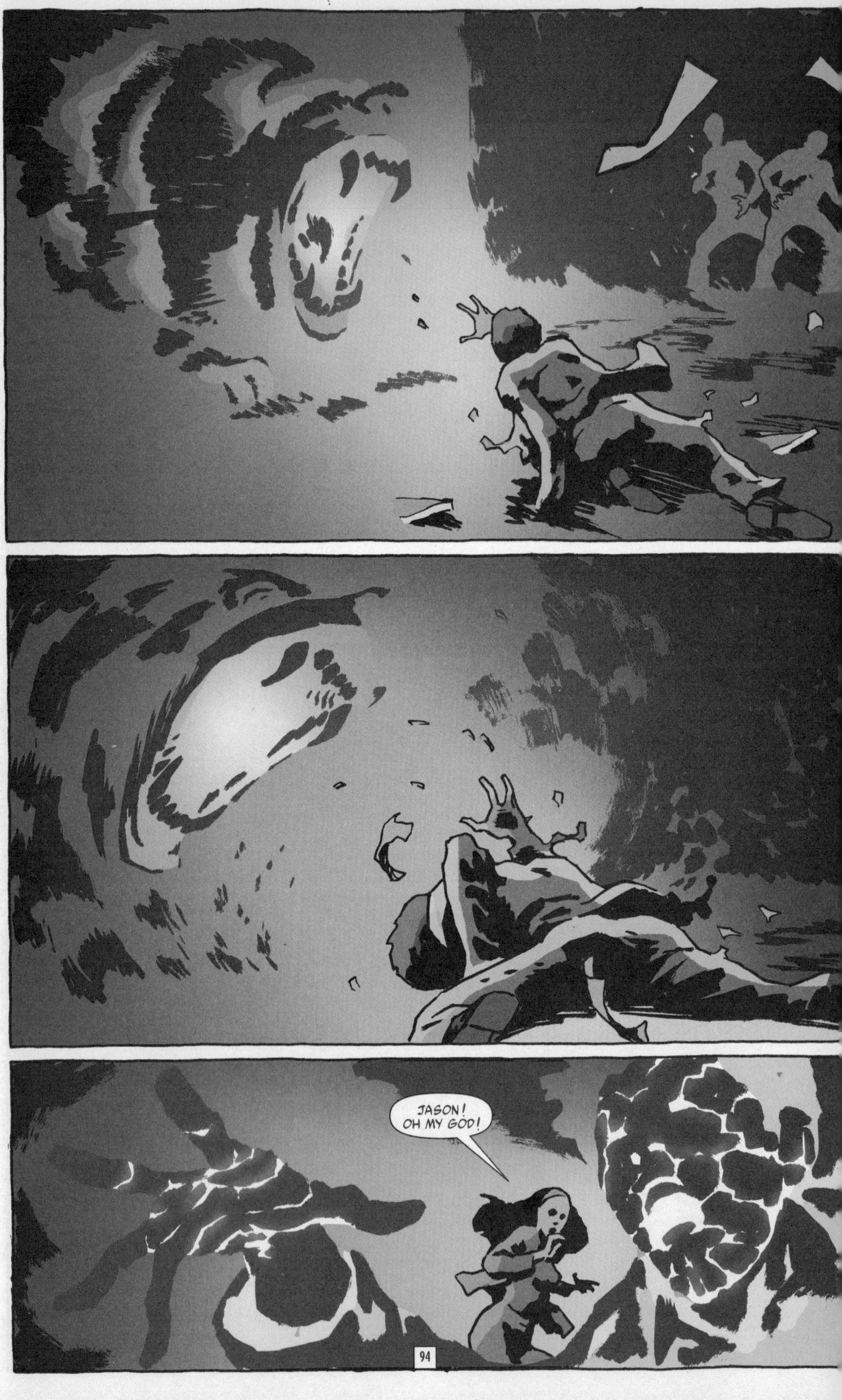
JASON! OH MY GOD!

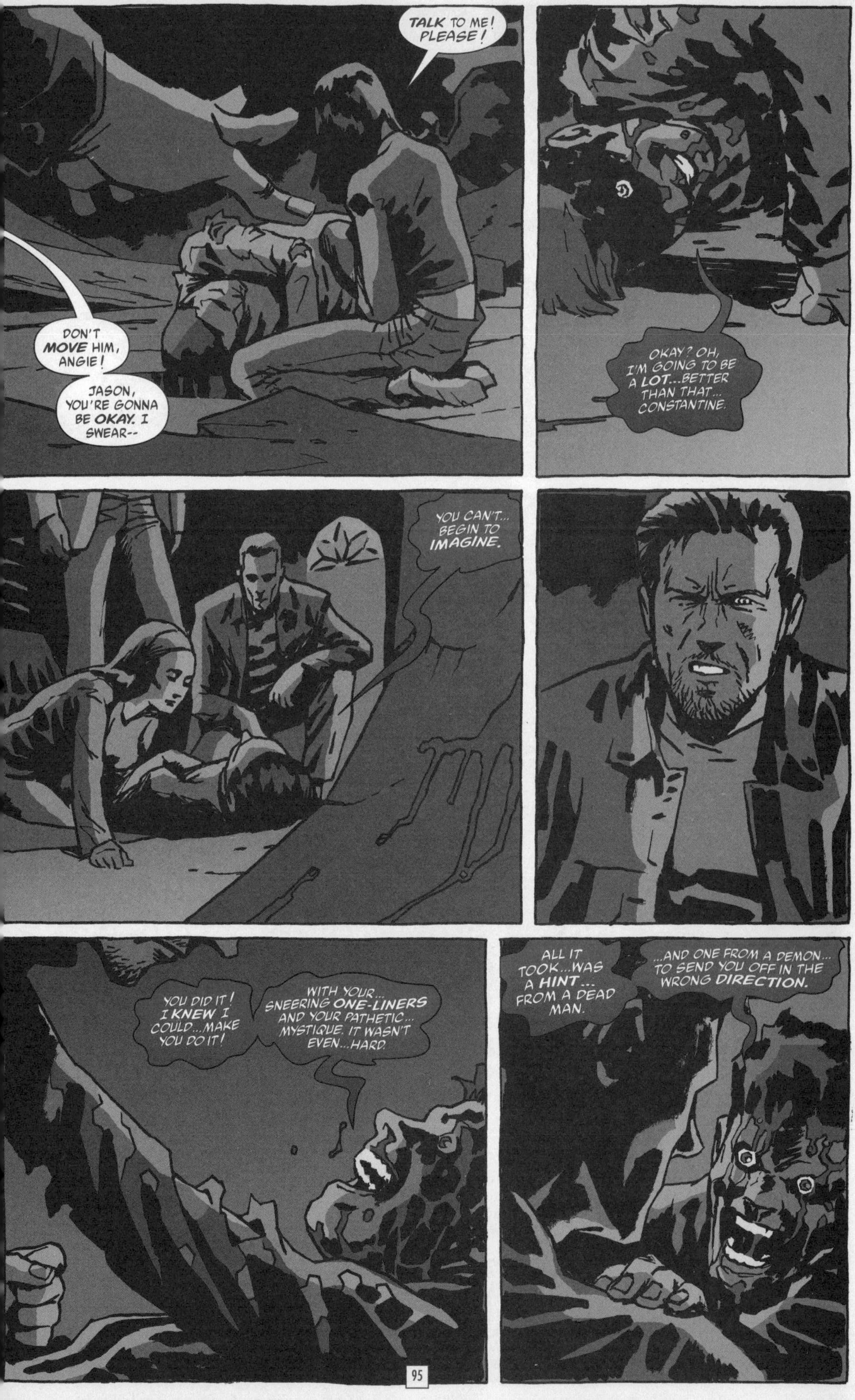
TALK TO ME! PLEASE!
DON'T MOVE HIM, ANGIE!
JASON, YOU'RE GONNA BE OKAY. I SWEAR--
OKAY? OH, I'M GOING TO BE A LOT...BETTER THAN THAT... CONSTANTINE.
YOU CAN'T... BEGIN TO IMAGINE.
YOU DID IT! I KNEW I COULD...MAKE YOU DO IT!
WITH YOUR... SNEERING ONE-LINERS AND YOUR PATHETIC... MYSTIQUE. IT WASN'T EVEN...HARD.
ALL IT TOOK...WAS A HINT... FROM A DEAD MAN.
...AND ONE FROM A DEMON... TO SEND YOU OFF IN THE WRONG DIRECTION.

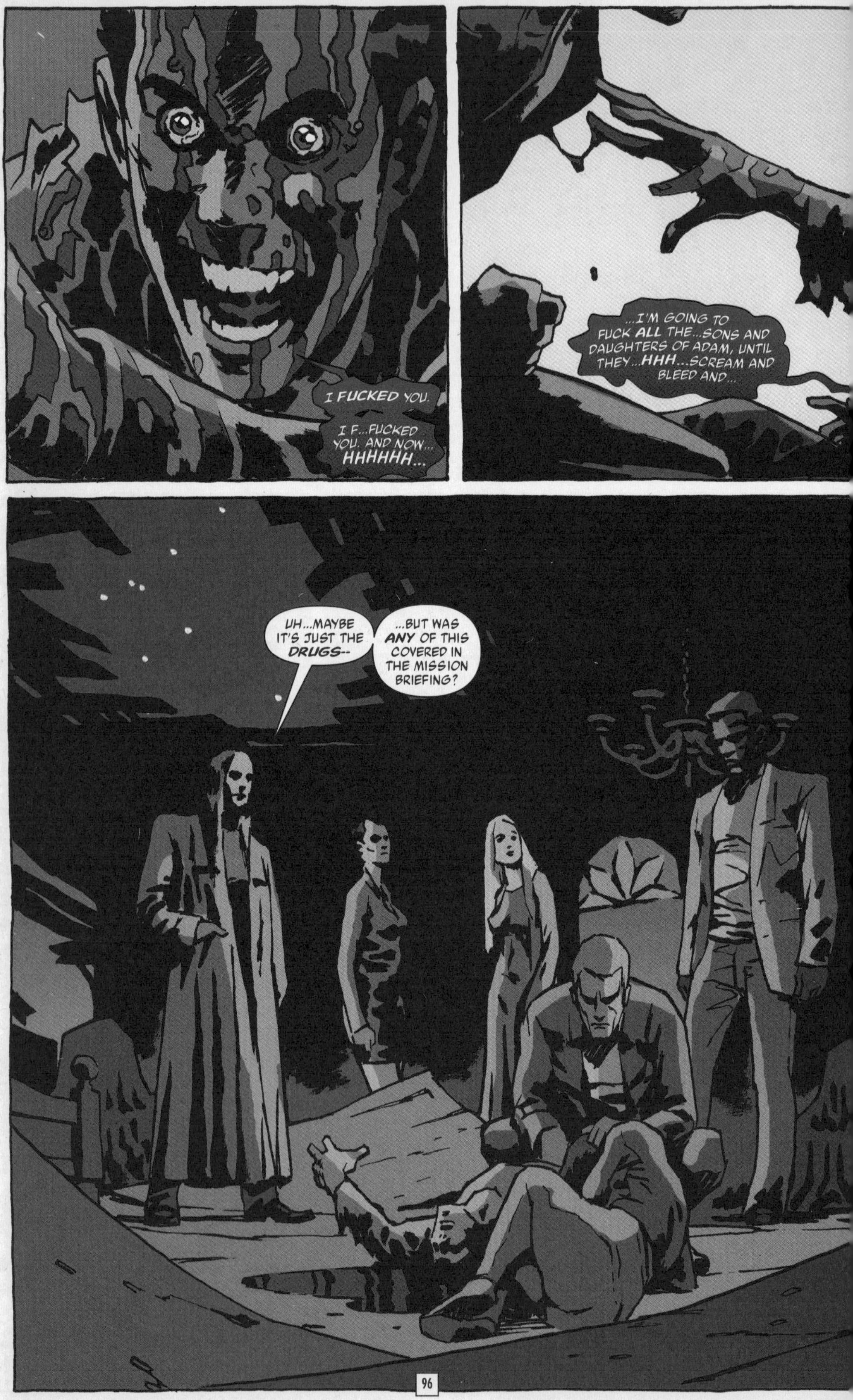

I FUCKED YOU.
I F...FUCKED YOU. AND NOW... HHHHHH...
...I'M GOING TO FUCK ALL THE...SONS AND DAUGHTERS OF ADAM, UNTIL THEY...HHH...SCREAM AND BLEED AND...
UH...MAYBE IT'S JUST THE DRUGS--
...BUT WAS ANY OF THIS COVERED IN THE MISSION BRIEFING?

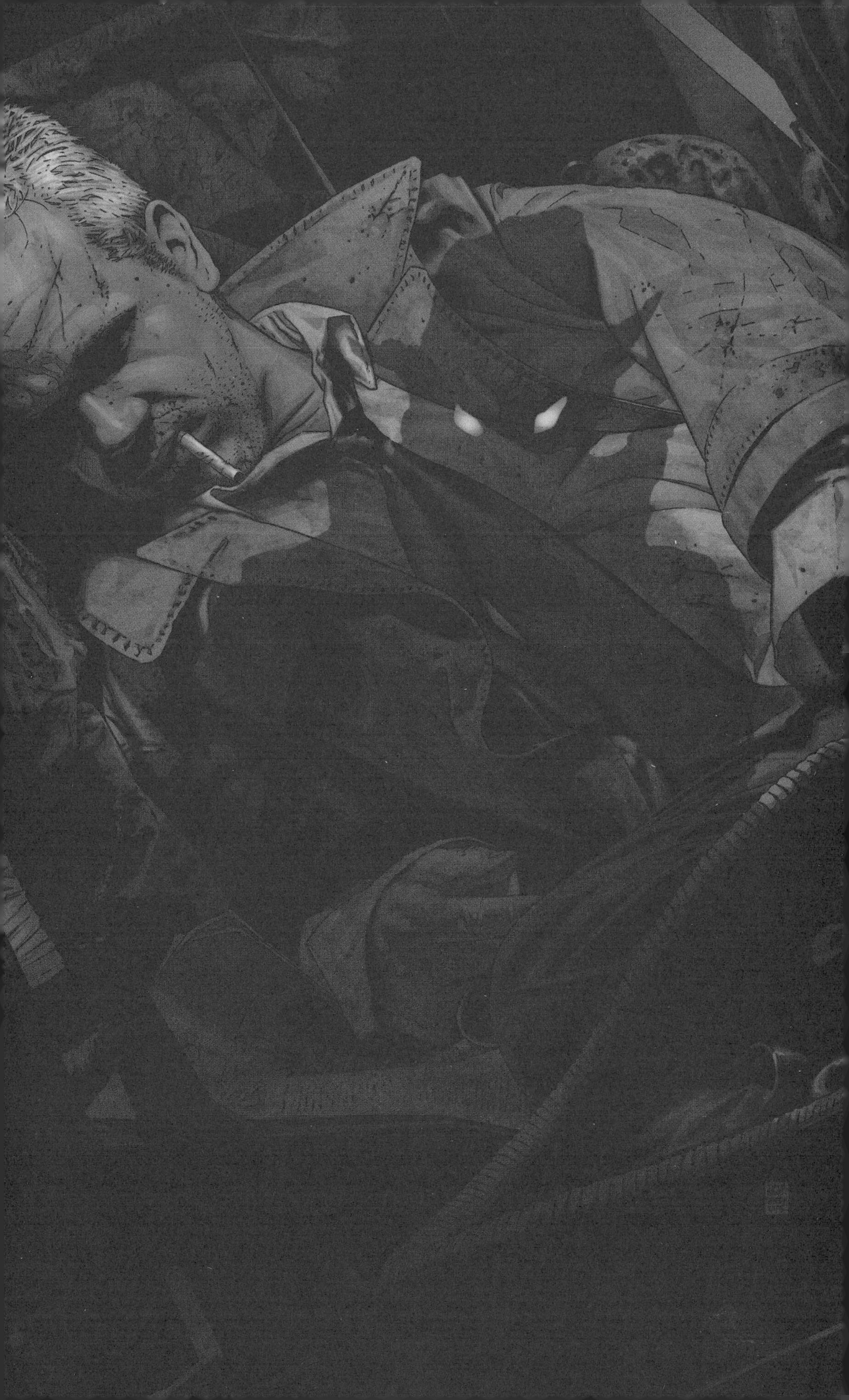

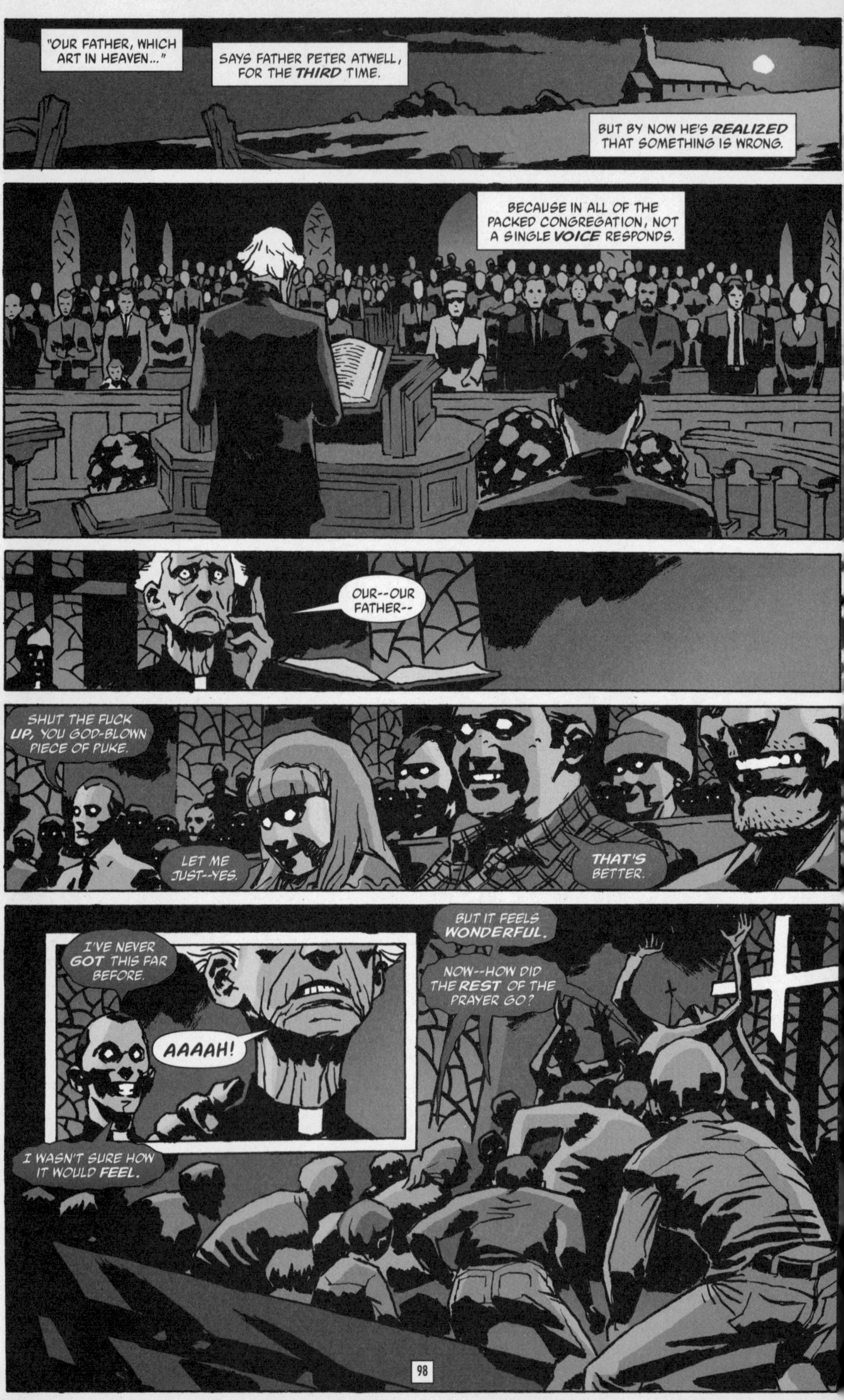
"OUR FATHER, WHICH ART IN HEAVEN..."
SAYS FATHER PETER ATWELL, FOR THE THIRD TIME.
BUT BY NOW HE'S REALIZED THAT SOMETHING IS WRONG.
BECAUSE IN ALL OF THE PACKED CONGREGATION, NOT A SINGLE VOICE RESPONDS.
OUR--OUR FATHER--
SHUT THE FUCK UP, YOU GOD-BLOWN PIECE OF PUKE.
LET ME JUST--YES.
THAT'S BETTER.
I'VE NEVER GOT THIS FAR BEFORE.
AAAAH!
I WASN'T SURE HOW IT WOULD FEEL.
BUT IT FEELS WONDERFUL.
NOW--HOW DID THE REST OF THE PRAYER GO?

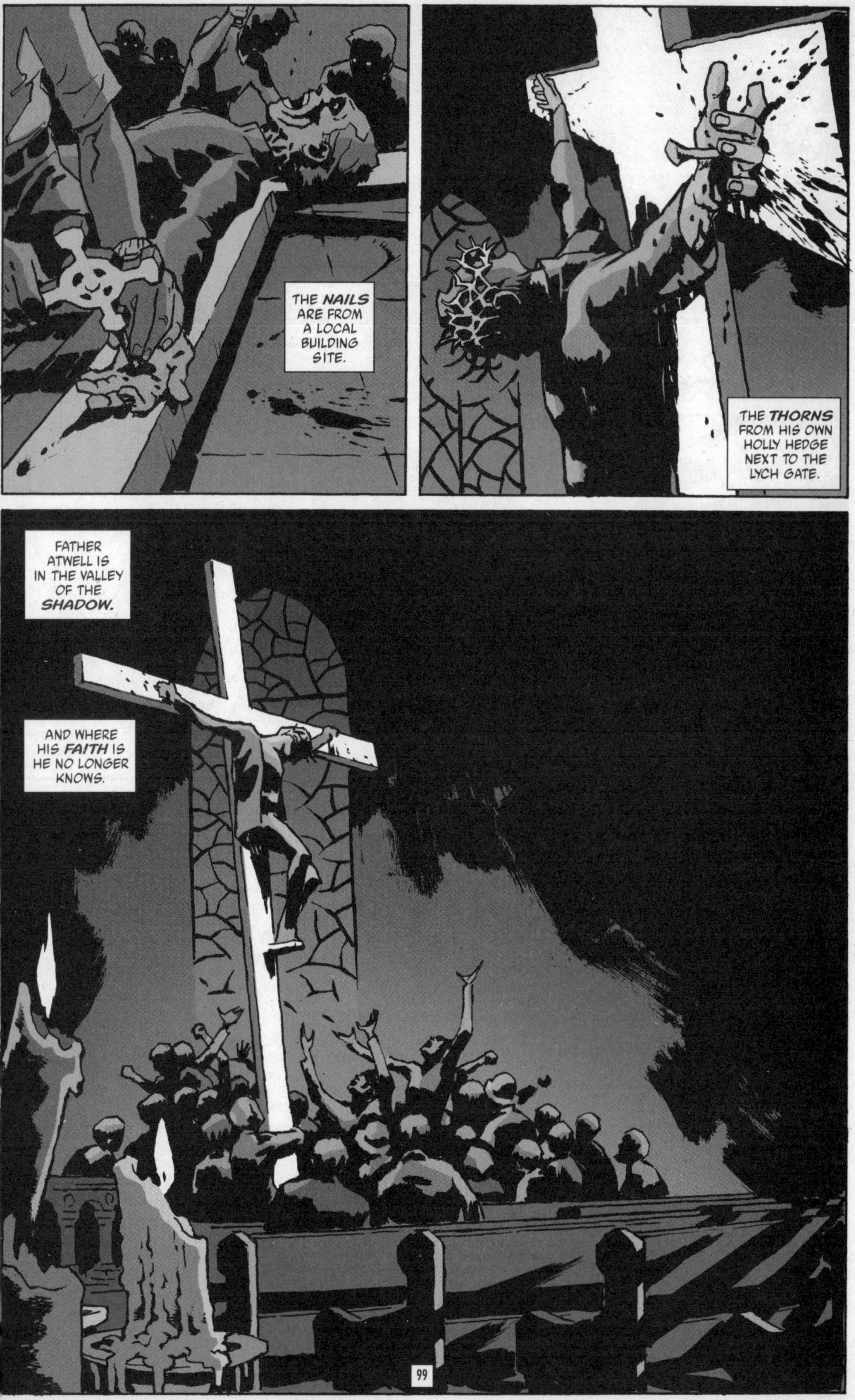
THE NAILS ARE FROM A LOCAL BUILDING SITE.
THE THORNS FROM HIS OWN HOLLY HEDGE NEXT TO THE LYCH GATE.
FATHER ATWELL IS IN THE VALLEY OF THE SHADOW.
AND WHERE HIS FAITH IS HE NO LONGER KNOWS.

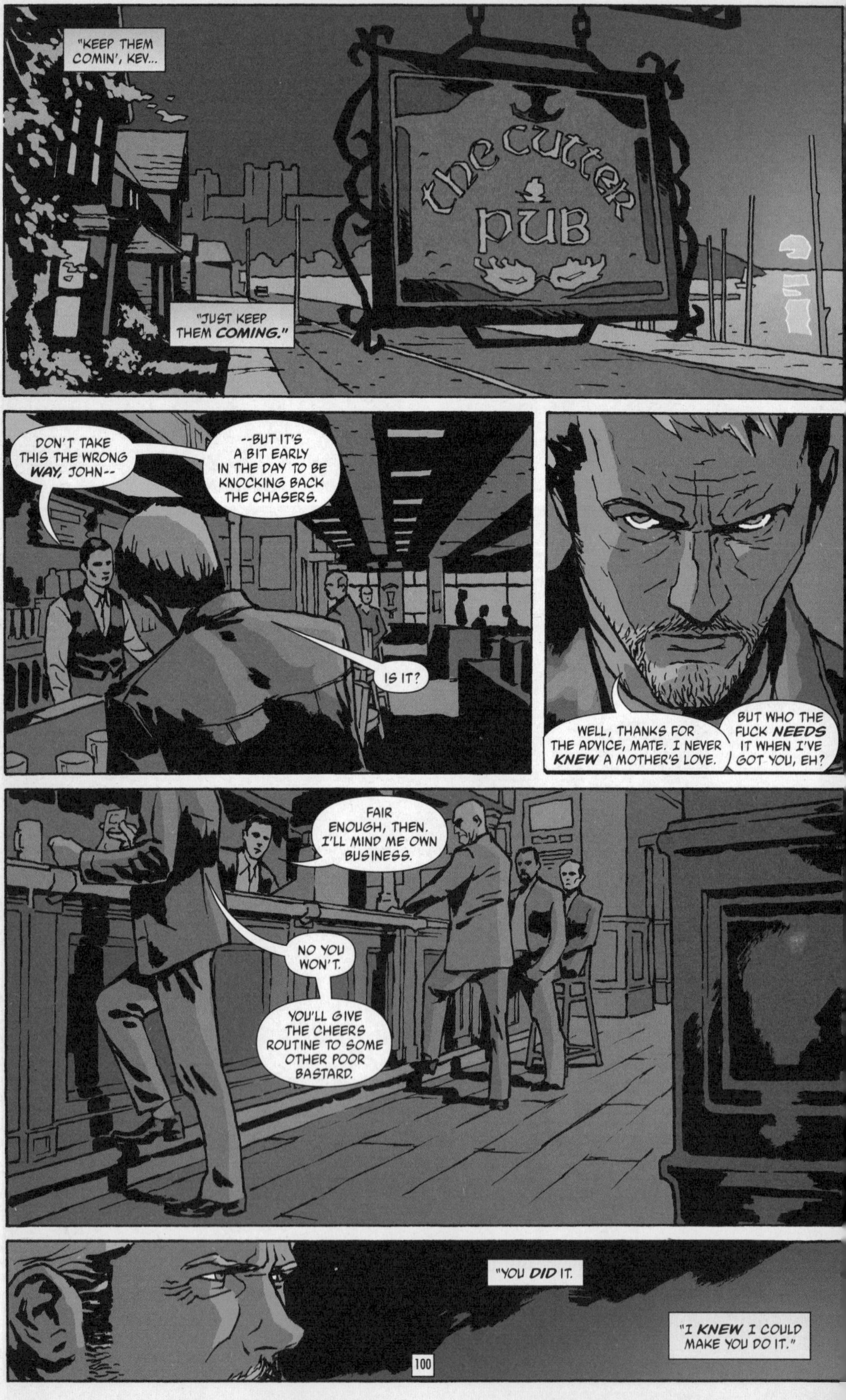

"KEEP THEM COMIN', KEV...
THE CUTTER PUB
"JUST KEEP THEM COMING."
DON'T TAKE THIS THE WRONG WAY, JOHN--
--BUT IT'S A BIT EARLY IN THE DAY TO BE KNOCKING BACK THE CHASERS.
IS IT?
WELL, THANKS FOR THE ADVICE, MATE. I NEVER KNEW A MOTHER'S LOVE.
BUT WHO THE FUCK NEEDS IT WHEN I'VE GOT YOU, EH?
FAIR ENOUGH, THEN. I'LL MIND ME OWN BUSINESS.
NO YOU WON'T.
YOU'LL GIVE THE CHEERS ROUTINE TO SOME OTHER POOR BASTARD.
"YOU DID IT.
"I KNEW I COULD MAKE YOU DO IT."

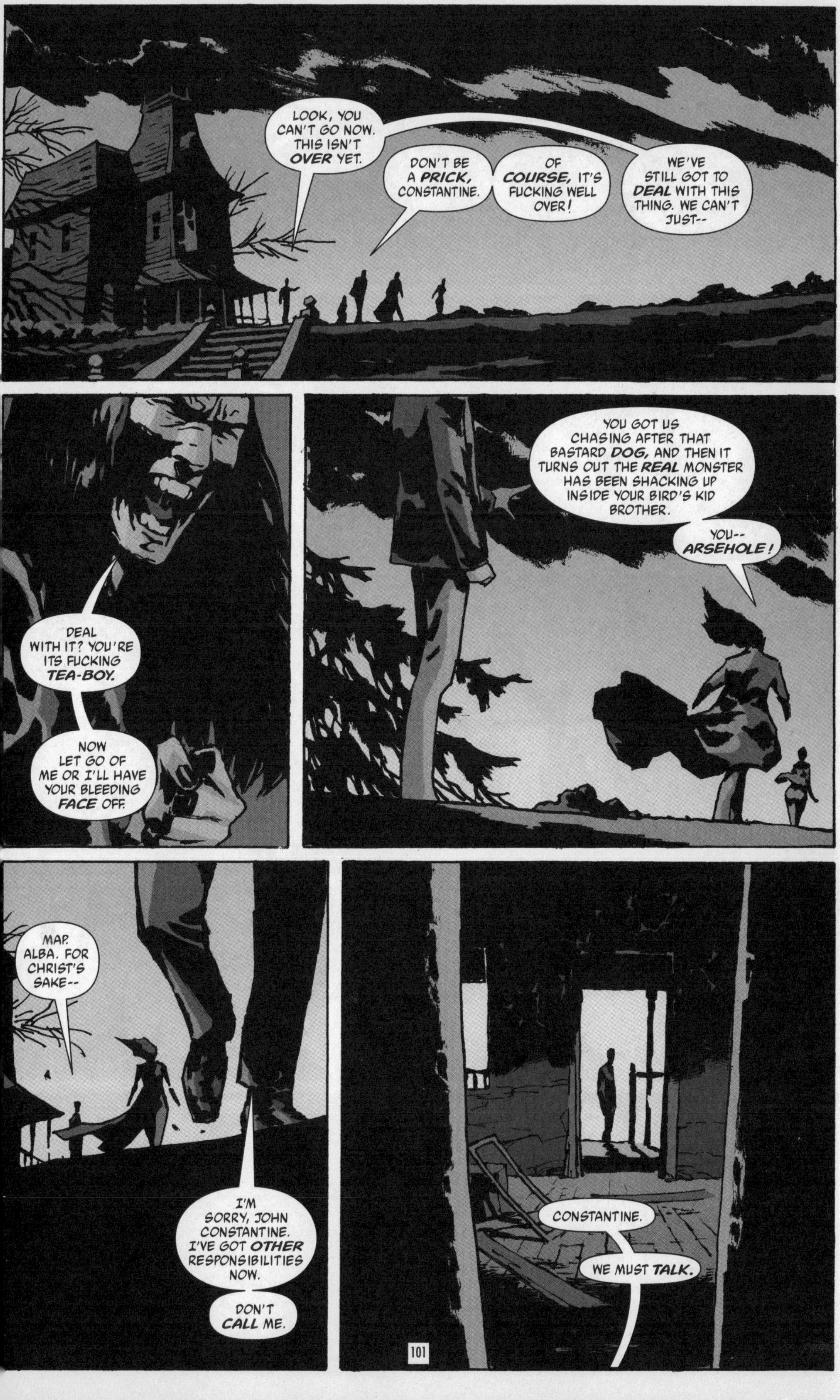
LOOK, YOU CAN'T GO NOW. THIS ISN'T OVER YET.
DON'T BE A PRICK, CONSTANTINE.
OF COURSE, IT'S FUCKING WELL OVER!
WE'VE STILL GOT TO DEAL WITH THIS THING. WE CAN'T JUST--
DEAL WITH IT? YOU'RE ITS FUCKING TEA-BOY.
NOW LET GO OF ME OR I'LL HAVE YOUR BLEEDING FACE OFF.
YOU GOT US CHASING AFTER THAT BASTARD DOG, AND THEN IT TURNS OUT THE REAL MONSTER HAS BEEN SHACKING UP INSIDE YOUR BIRD'S KID BROTHER.
YOU-- ARSEHOLE!
MAP. ALBA. FOR CHRIST'S SAKE--
I'M SORRY, JOHN CONSTANTINE. I'VE GOT OTHER RESPONSIBILITIES NOW.
DON'T CALL ME.
CONSTANTINE.
WE MUST TALK.

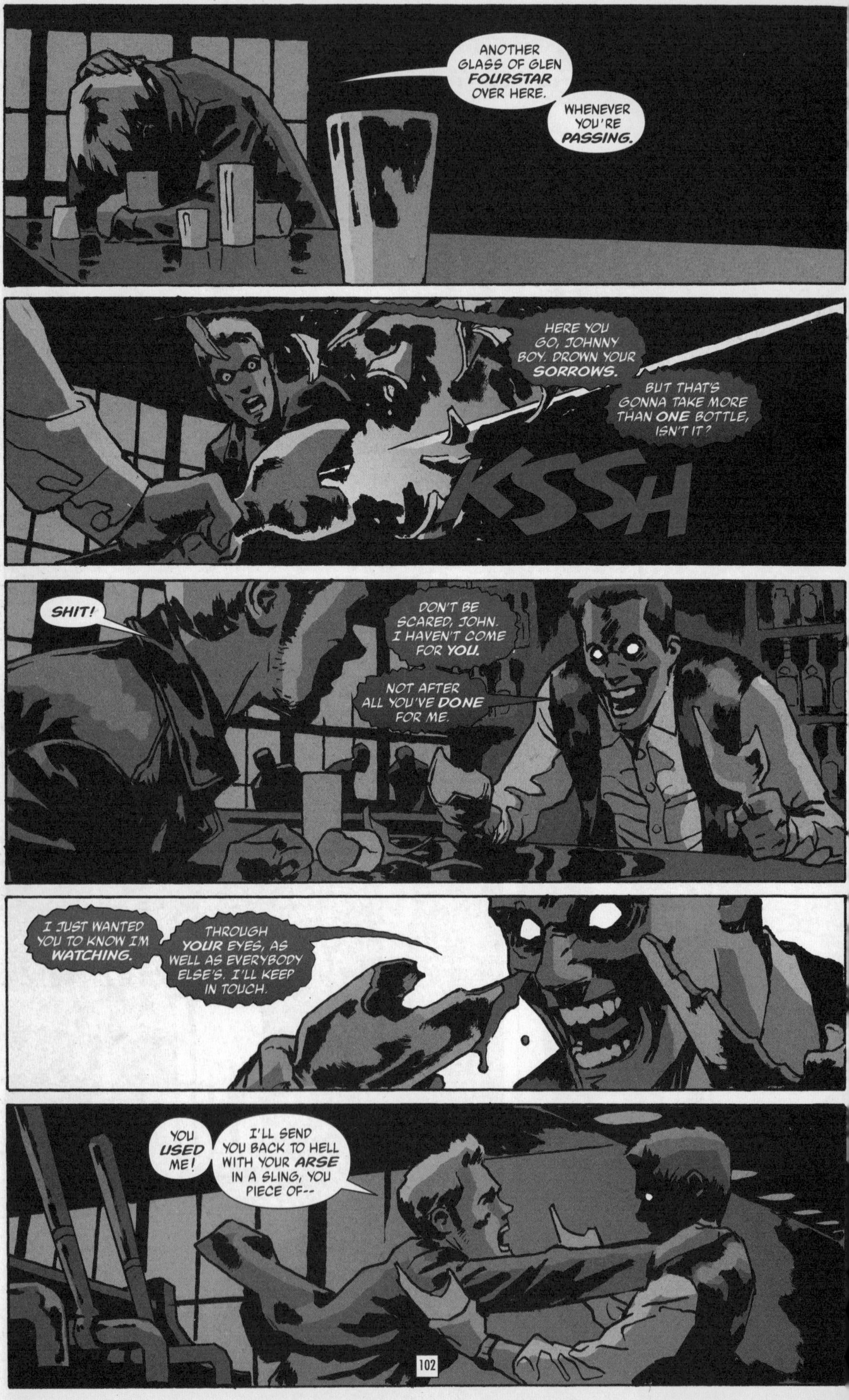
ANOTHER GLASS OF GLEN FOURSTAR OVER HERE.
WHENEVER YOU'RE PASSING.
HERE YOU GO, JOHNNY BOY. DROWN YOUR SORROWS.
BUT THAT'S GONNA TAKE MORE THAN ONE BOTTLE, ISN'T IT?
KSSH
SHIT!
DON'T BE SCARED, JOHN. I HAVEN'T COME FOR YOU.
NOT AFTER ALL YOU'VE DONE FOR ME.
I JUST WANTED YOU TO KNOW I'M WATCHING.
THROUGH YOUR EYES, AS WELL AS EVERYBODY ELSE'S. I'LL KEEP IN TOUCH.
YOU USED ME!
I'LL SEND YOU BACK TO HELL WITH YOUR ARSE IN A SLING, YOU PIECE OF--

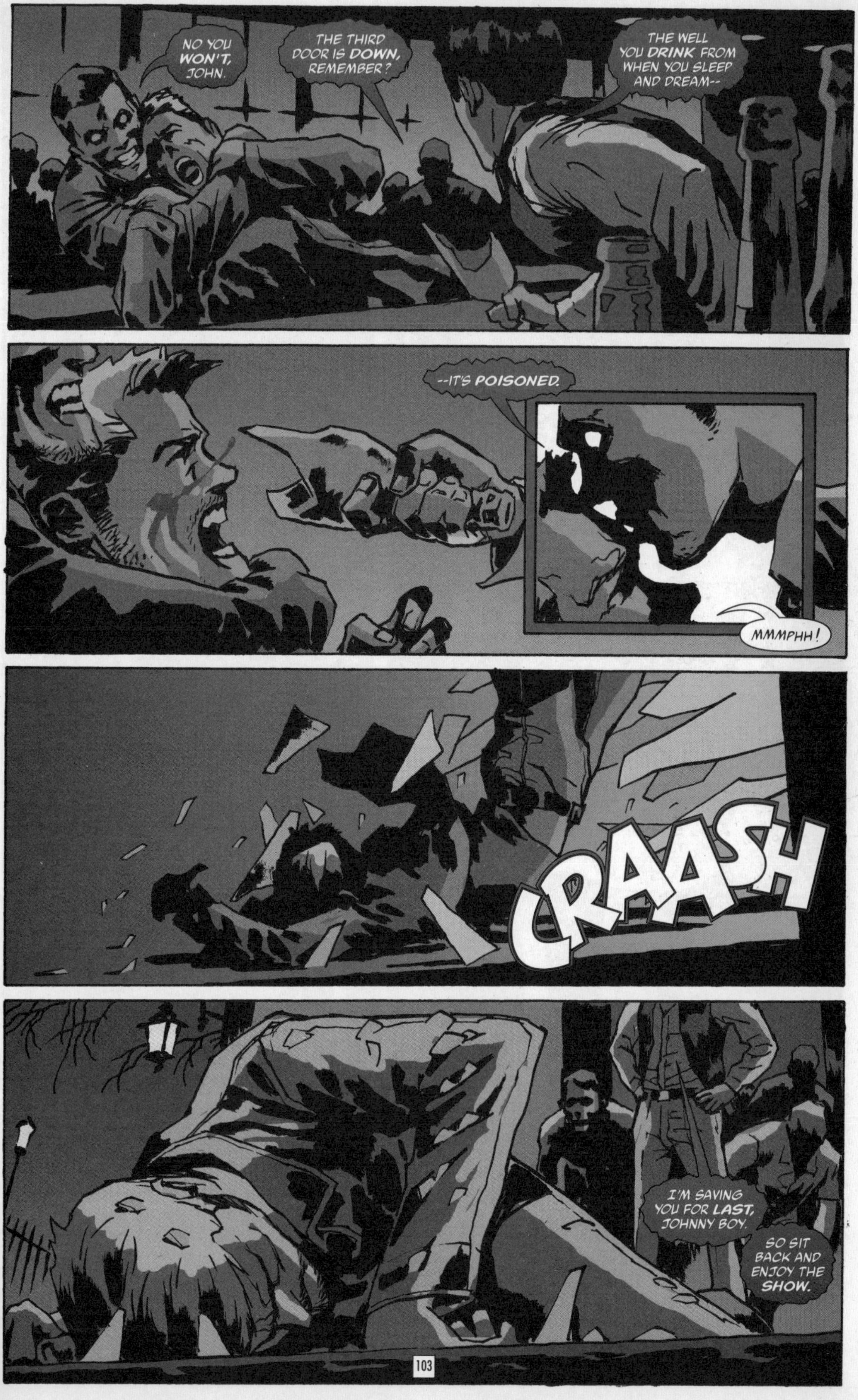

NO YOU **WON'T,** JOHN.
THE THIRD DOOR IS **DOWN,** REMEMBER?
THE WELL YOU **DRINK** FROM WHEN YOU SLEEP AND DREAM--
--IT'S **POISONED.**
MMMPHH!
CRAASH
I'M SAVING YOU FOR **LAST,** JOHNNY BOY.
SO SIT BACK AND ENJOY THE **SHOW.**

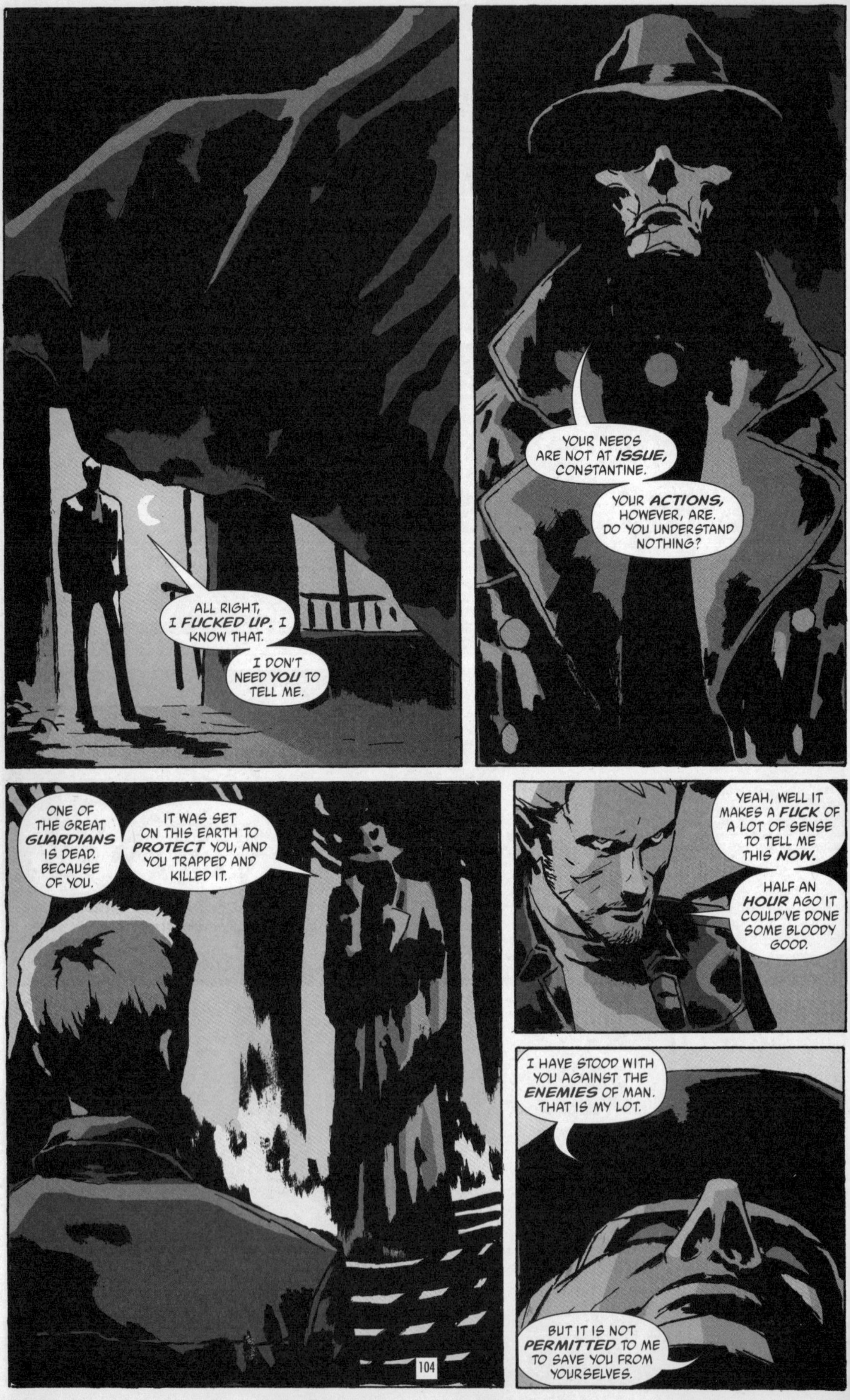
ALL RIGHT, I FUCKED UP. I KNOW THAT.
I DON'T NEED YOU TO TELL ME.
YOUR NEEDS ARE NOT AT ISSUE, CONSTANTINE.
YOUR ACTIONS, HOWEVER, ARE. DO YOU UNDERSTAND NOTHING?
ONE OF THE GREAT GUARDIANS IS DEAD. BECAUSE OF YOU.
IT WAS SET ON THIS EARTH TO PROTECT YOU, AND YOU TRAPPED AND KILLED IT.
YEAH, WELL IT MAKES A FUCK OF A LOT OF SENSE TO TELL ME THIS NOW.
HALF AN HOUR AGO IT COULD'VE DONE SOME BLOODY GOOD.
I HAVE STOOD WITH YOU AGAINST THE ENEMIES OF MAN. THAT IS MY LOT.
BUT IT IS NOT PERMITTED TO ME TO SAVE YOU FROM YOURSELVES.

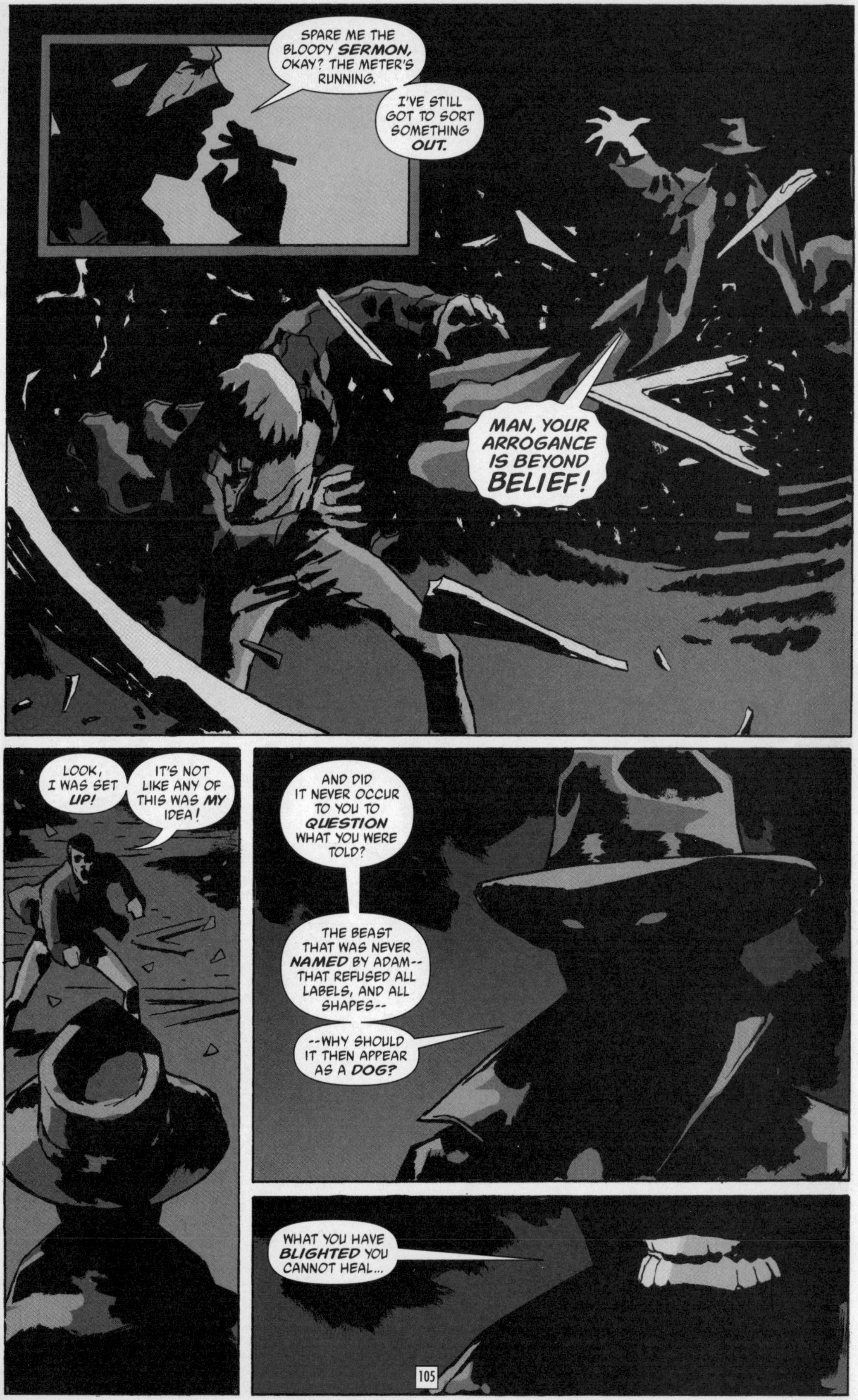
SPARE ME THE BLOODY SERMON, OKAY? THE METER'S RUNNING.
I'VE STILL GOT TO SORT SOMETHING OUT.
MAN, YOUR ARROGANCE IS BEYOND BELIEF!
LOOK, I WAS SET UP!
IT'S NOT LIKE ANY OF THIS WAS MY IDEA!
AND DID IT NEVER OCCUR TO YOU TO QUESTION WHAT YOU WERE TOLD?
THE BEAST THAT WAS NEVER NAMED BY ADAM-- THAT REFUSED ALL LABELS, AND ALL SHAPES--
--WHY SHOULD IT THEN APPEAR AS A DOG?
WHAT YOU HAVE BLIGHTED YOU CANNOT HEAL...

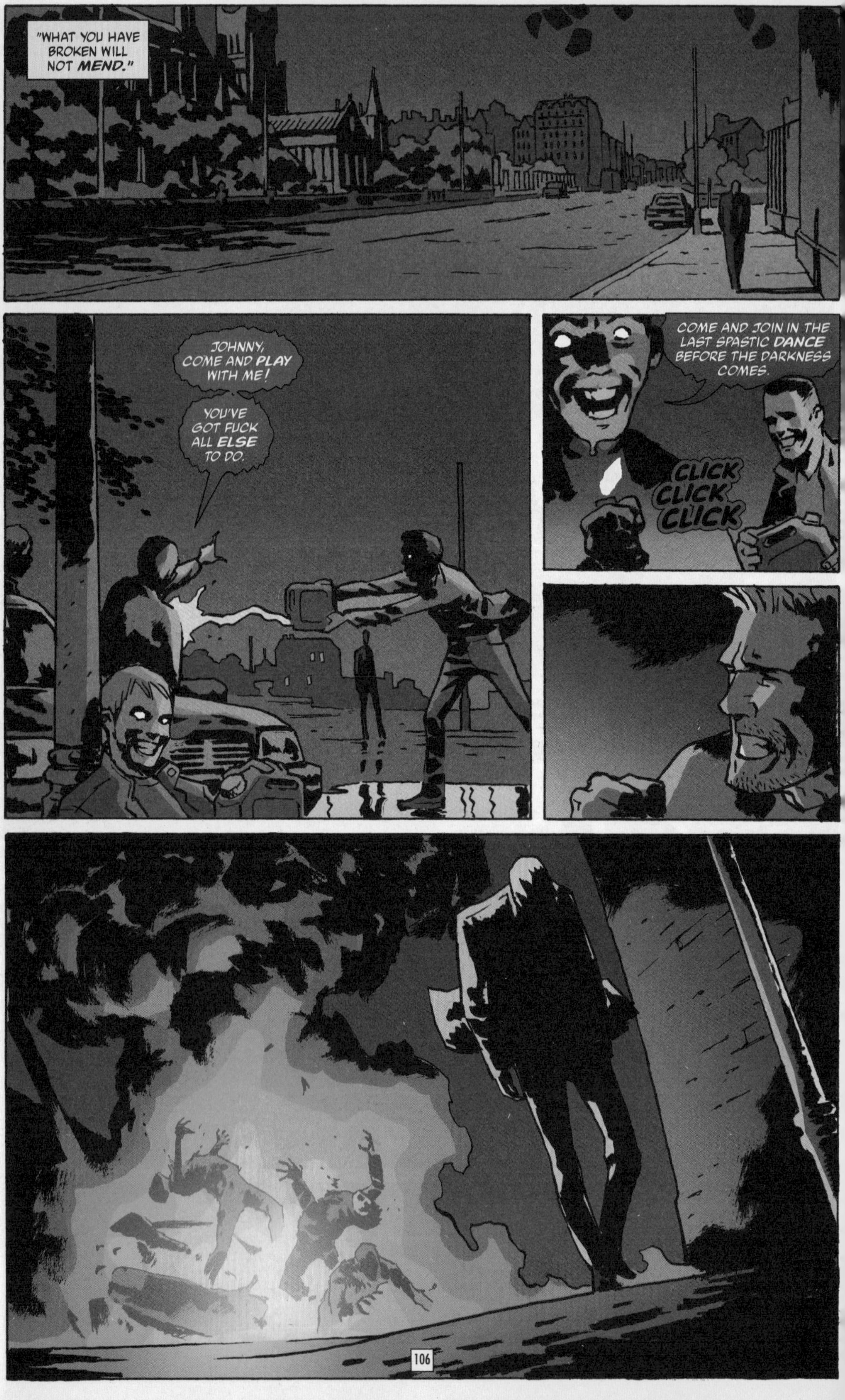
"WHAT YOU HAVE BROKEN WILL NOT MEND."
JOHNNY, COME AND PLAY WITH ME!
YOU'VE GOT FUCK ALL ELSE TO DO.
COME AND JOIN IN THE LAST SPASTIC DANCE BEFORE THE DARKNESS COMES.
CLICK CLICK CLICK

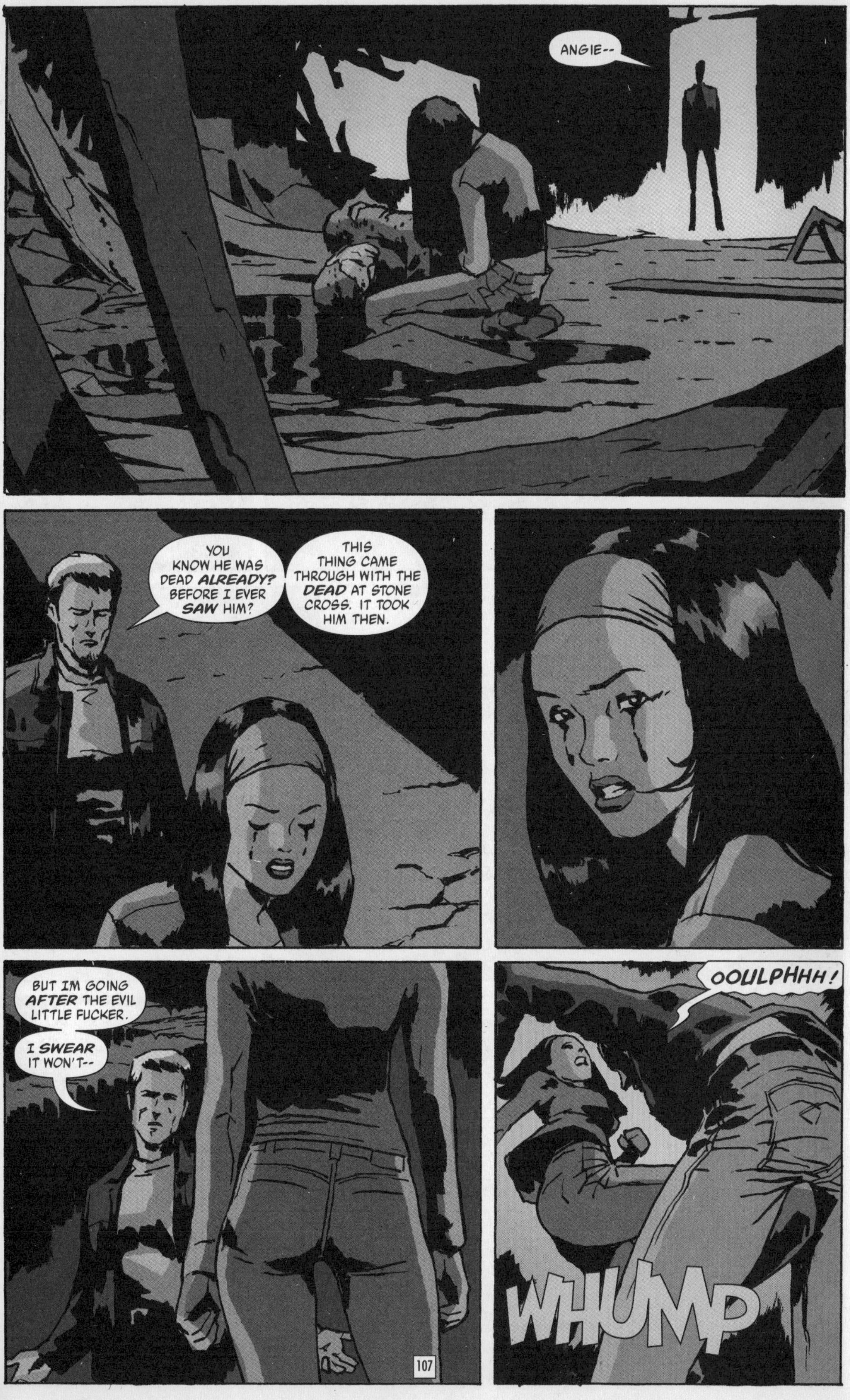
ANGIE--
YOU KNOW HE WAS DEAD ALREADY? BEFORE I EVER SAW HIM?
THIS THING CAME THROUGH WITH THE DEAD AT STONE CROSS. IT TOOK HIM THEN.
BUT IM GOING AFTER THE EVIL LITTLE FUCKER.
I SWEAR IT WON'T--
OOULPHHH!
WHUMP

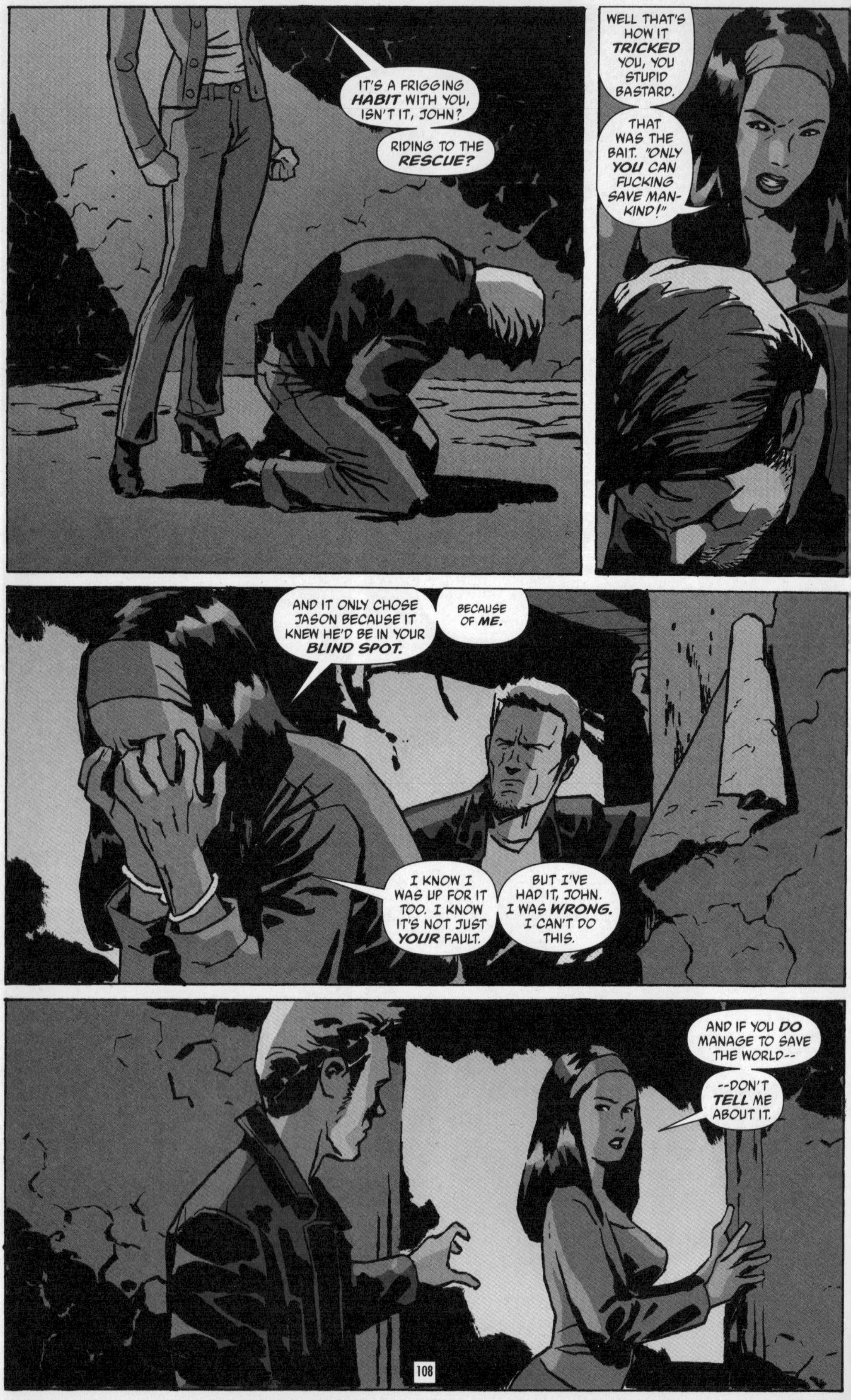
IT'S A FRIGGING HABIT WITH YOU, ISN'T IT, JOHN?
RIDING TO THE RESCUE?
WELL THAT'S HOW IT TRICKED YOU, YOU STUPID BASTARD.
THAT WAS THE BAIT. "ONLY YOU CAN FUCKING SAVE MAN-KIND!"
AND IT ONLY CHOSE JASON BECAUSE IT KNEW HE'D BE IN YOUR BLIND SPOT.
BECAUSE OF ME.
I KNOW I WAS UP FOR IT TOO. I KNOW IT'S NOT JUST YOUR FAULT.
BUT I'VE HAD IT, JOHN. I WAS WRONG. I CAN'T DO THIS.
AND IF YOU DO MANAGE TO SAVE THE WORLD--
--DON'T TELL ME ABOUT IT.

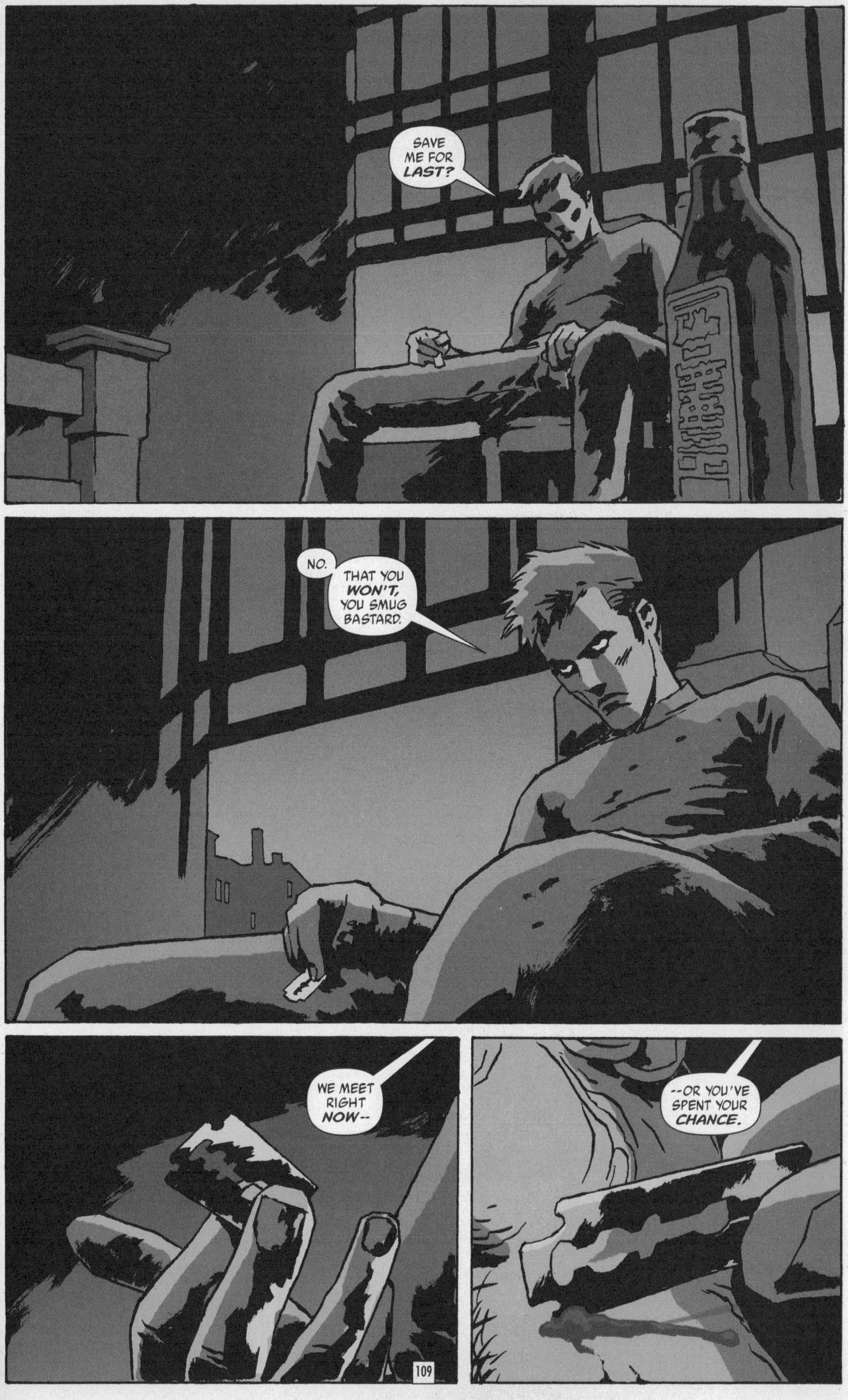
SAVE ME FOR LAST?
NO.
THAT YOU WON'T, YOU SMUG BASTARD.
WE MEET RIGHT NOW--
--OR YOU'VE SPENT YOUR CHANCE.

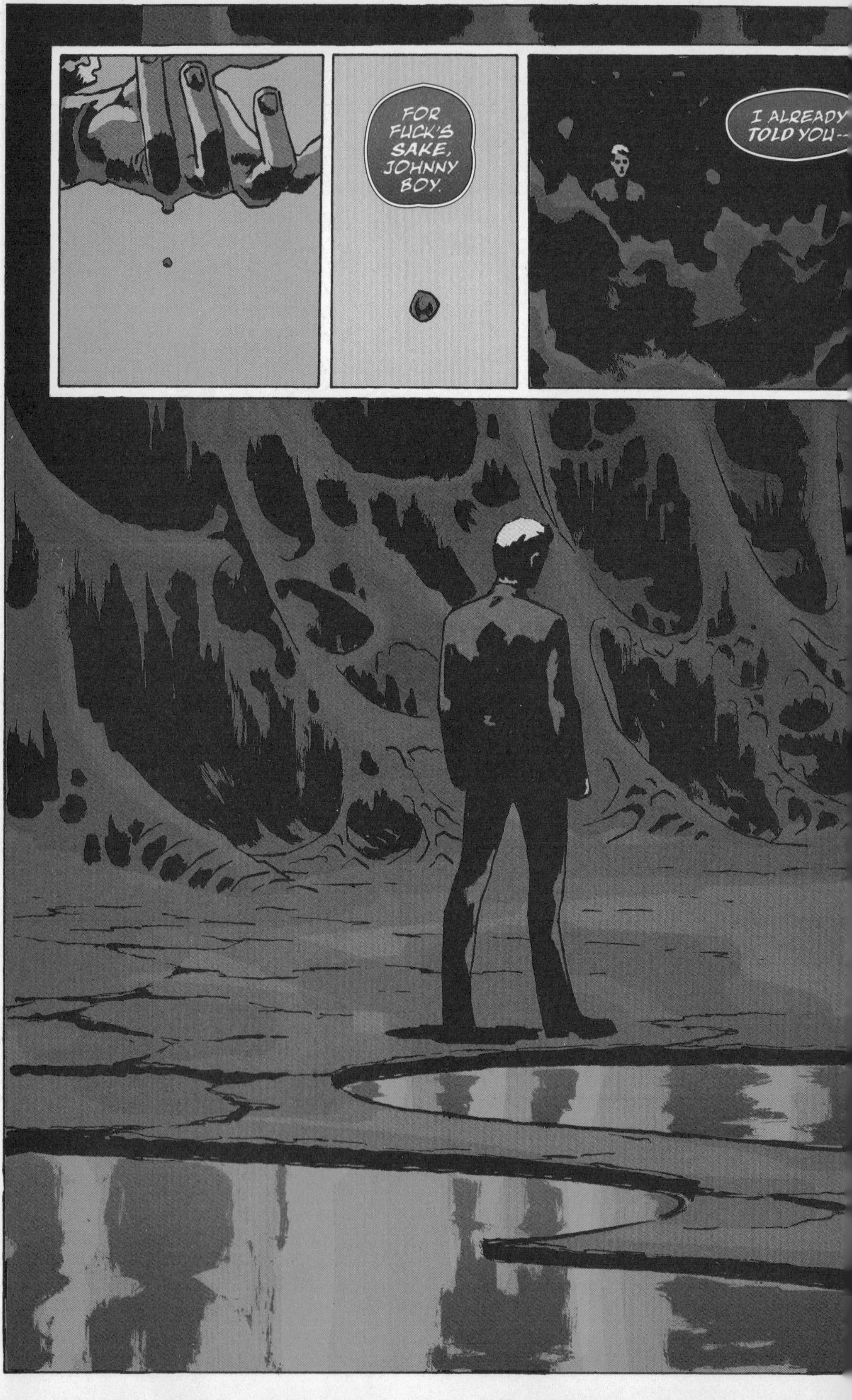
FOR FUCK'S SAKE, JOHNNY BOY.
I ALREADY TOLD YOU--

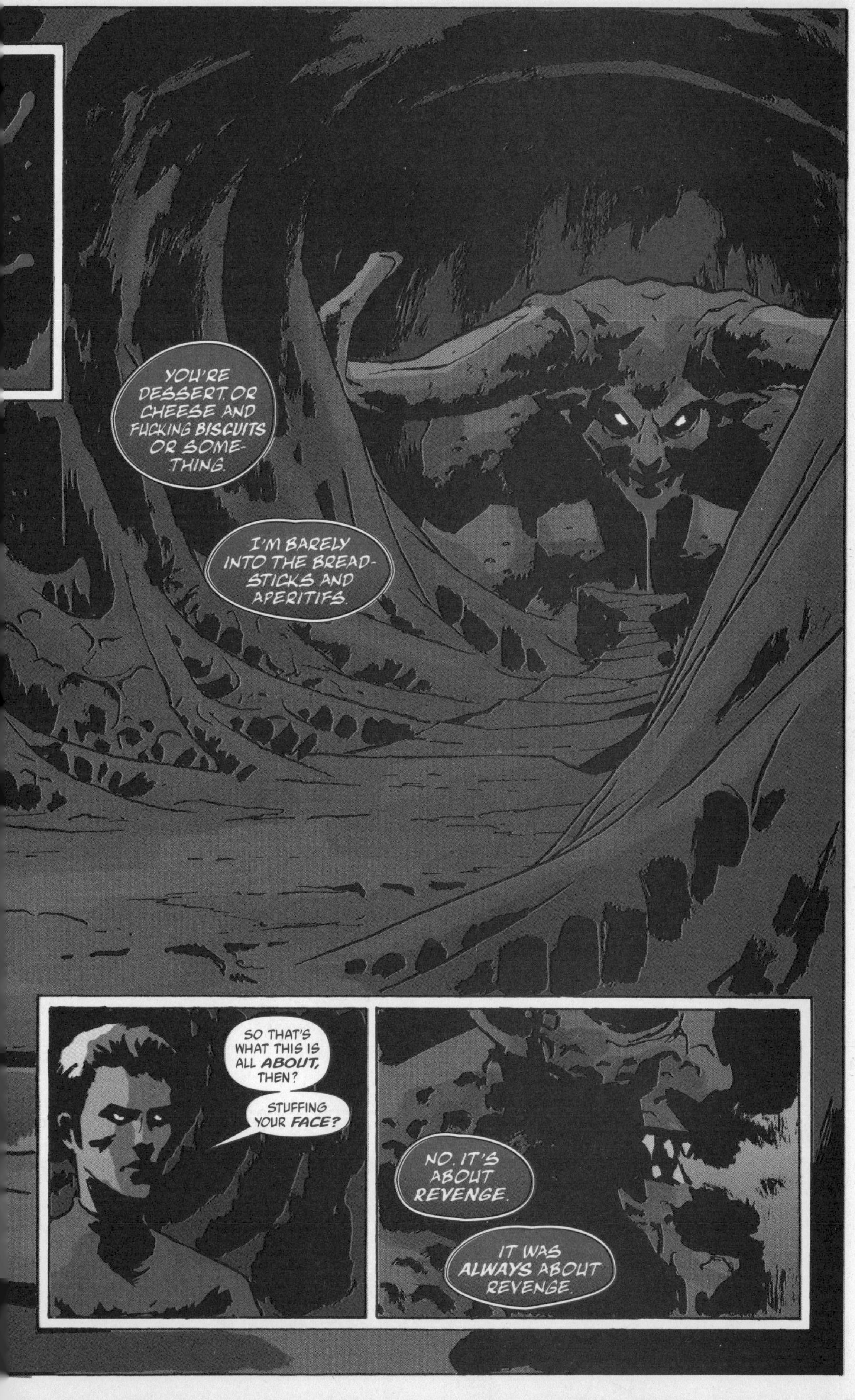
YOU'RE DESSERT. OR CHEESE AND FUCKING **BISCUITS** OR SOME-THING.
I'M BARELY INTO THE BREAD-STICKS AND APERITIFS.
SO THAT'S WHAT THIS IS ALL **ABOUT,** THEN?
STUFFING YOUR **FACE?**
NO. IT'S ABOUT **REVENGE.**
IT WAS **ALWAYS** ABOUT REVENGE.

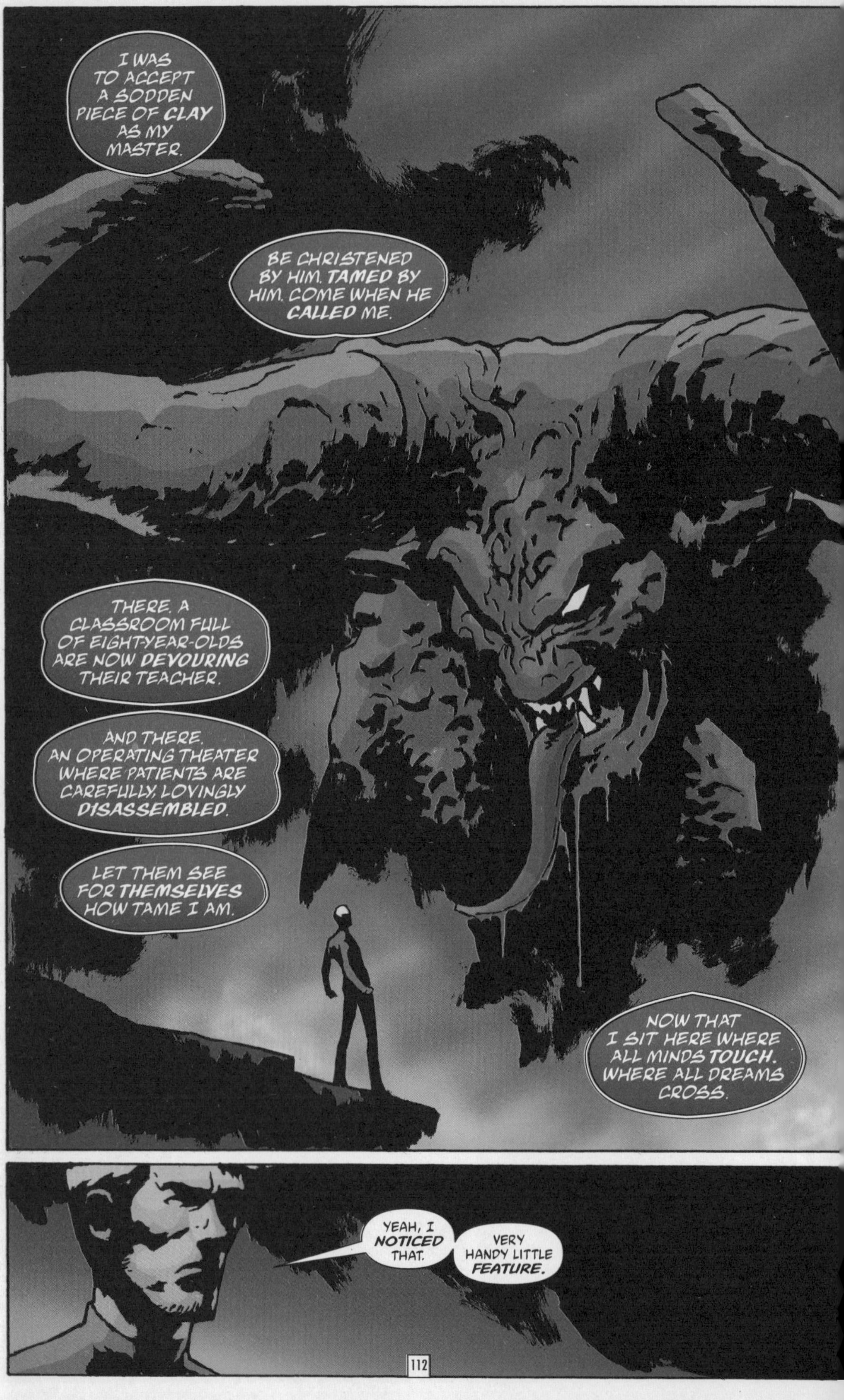
I WAS TO ACCEPT A SODDEN PIECE OF CLAY AS MY MASTER.
BE CHRISTENED BY HIM. TAMED BY HIM. COME WHEN HE CALLED ME.
THERE. A CLASSROOM FULL OF EIGHT-YEAR-OLDS ARE NOW DEVOURING THEIR TEACHER.
AND THERE. AN OPERATING THEATER WHERE PATIENTS ARE CAREFULLY, LOVINGLY DISASSEMBLED.
LET THEM SEE FOR THEMSELVES HOW TAME I AM.
NOW THAT I SIT HERE WHERE ALL MINDS TOUCH. WHERE ALL DREAMS CROSS.
YEAH, I NOTICED THAT.
VERY HANDY LITTLE FEATURE.

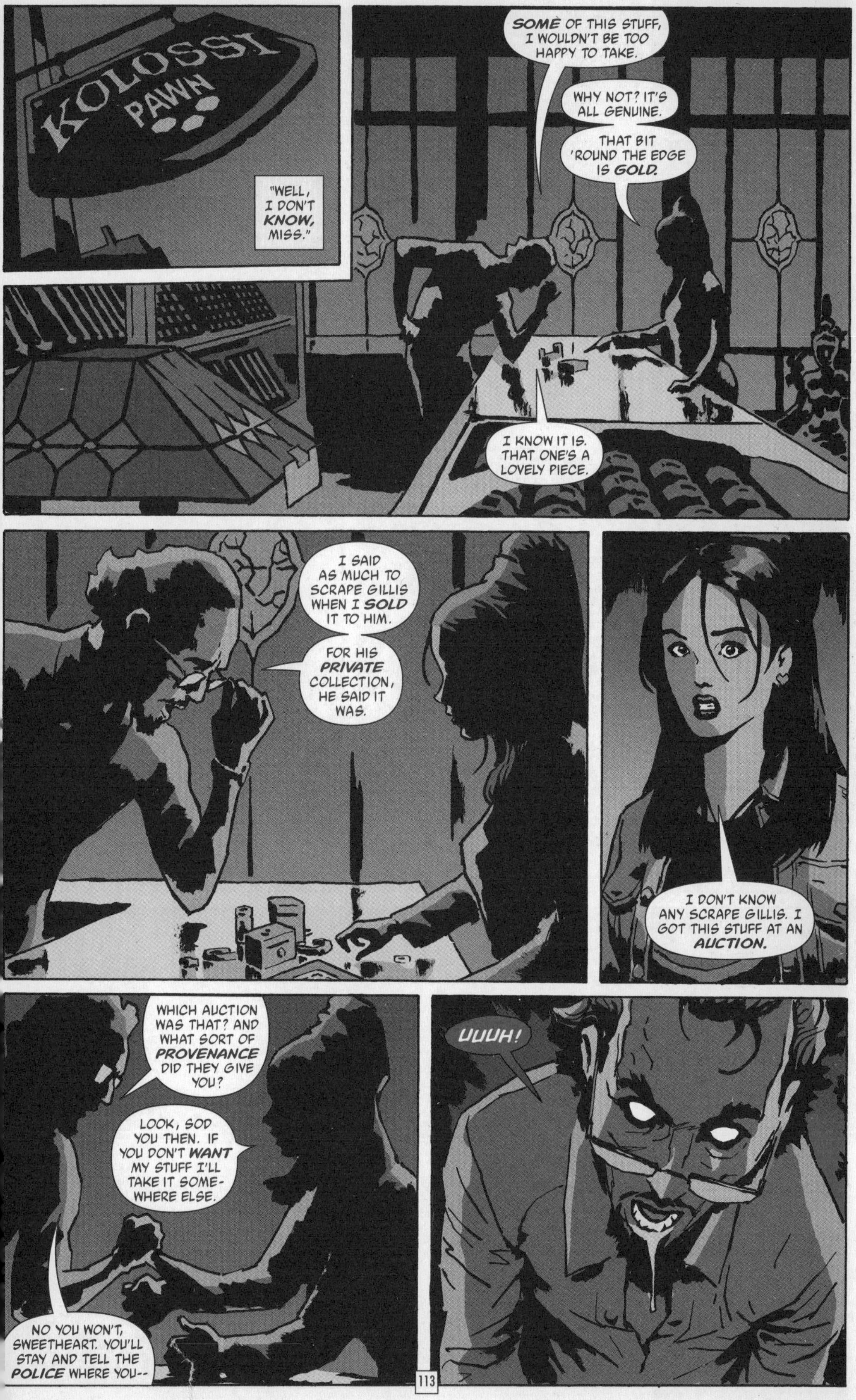

KOLOSSI PAWN
"WELL, I DON'T KNOW, MISS."
SOME OF THIS STUFF, I WOULDN'T BE TOO HAPPY TO TAKE.
WHY NOT? IT'S ALL GENUINE.
THAT BIT 'ROUND THE EDGE IS GOLD.
I KNOW IT IS. THAT ONE'S A LOVELY PIECE.
I SAID AS MUCH TO SCRAPE GILLIS WHEN I SOLD IT TO HIM.
FOR HIS PRIVATE COLLECTION, HE SAID IT WAS.
I DON'T KNOW ANY SCRAPE GILLIS. I GOT THIS STUFF AT AN AUCTION.
WHICH AUCTION WAS THAT? AND WHAT SORT OF PROVENANCE DID THEY GIVE YOU?
LOOK, SOD YOU THEN. IF YOU DON'T WANT MY STUFF I'LL TAKE IT SOME-WHERE ELSE.
NO YOU WON'T, SWEETHEART. YOU'LL STAY AND TELL THE POLICE WHERE YOU--
UUUH!

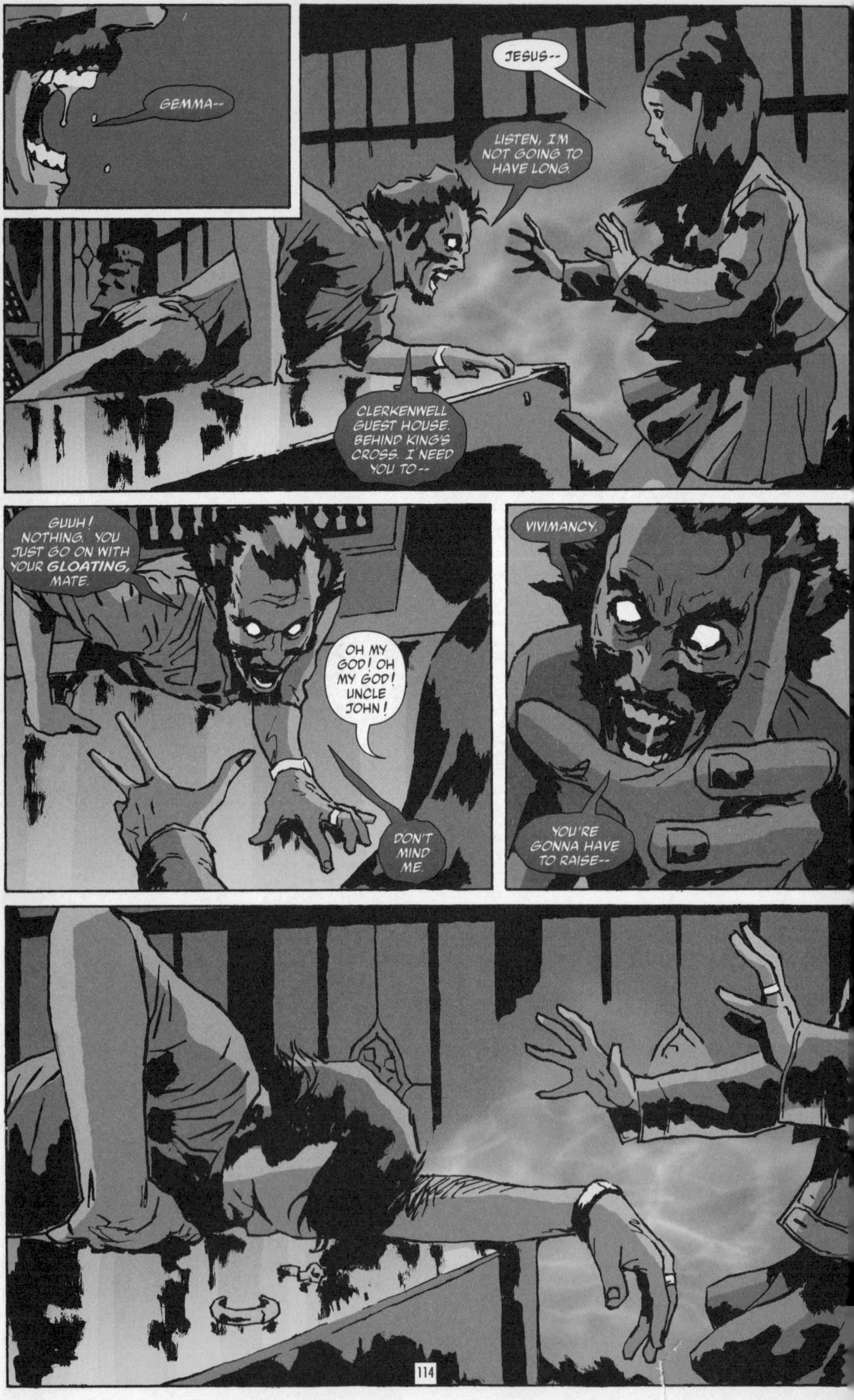
GEMMA--
JESUS--
LISTEN, I'M NOT GOING TO HAVE LONG.
CLERKENWELL GUEST HOUSE. BEHIND KING'S CROSS. I NEED YOU TO--
GUUH! NOTHING. YOU JUST GO ON WITH YOUR **GLOATING,** MATE.
OH MY GOD! OH MY GOD! UNCLE JOHN!
DON'T MIND ME.
VIVIMANCY.
YOU'RE GONNA HAVE TO RAISE--

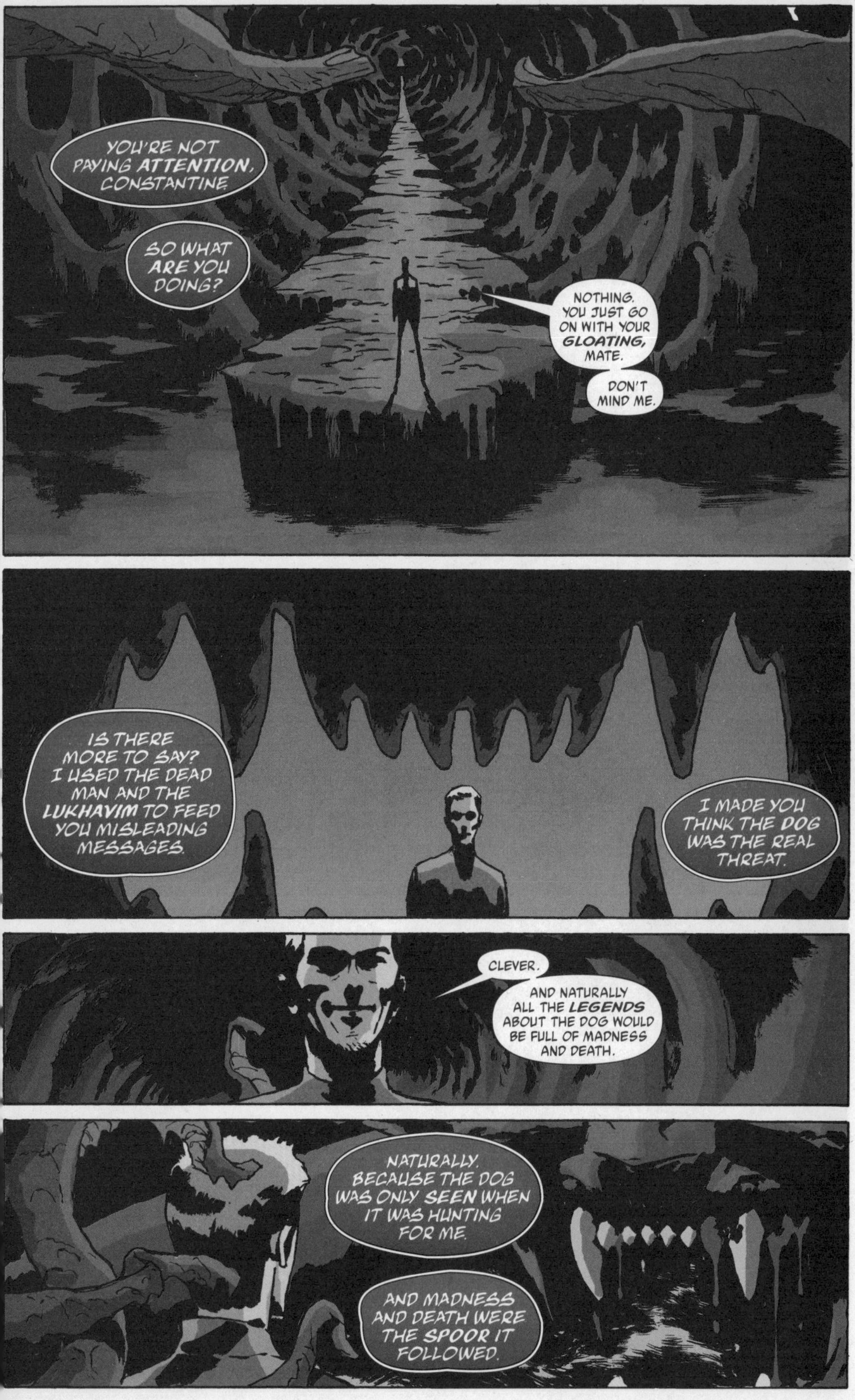
YOU'RE NOT PAYING ATTENTION, CONSTANTINE.
SO WHAT ARE YOU DOING?
NOTHING. YOU JUST GO ON WITH YOUR GLOATING, MATE.
DON'T MIND ME.
IS THERE MORE TO SAY? I USED THE DEAD MAN AND THE LUKHAVIM TO FEED YOU MISLEADING MESSAGES.
I MADE YOU THINK THE DOG WAS THE REAL THREAT.
CLEVER.
AND NATURALLY ALL THE LEGENDS ABOUT THE DOG WOULD BE FULL OF MADNESS AND DEATH.
NATURALLY. BECAUSE THE DOG WAS ONLY SEEN WHEN IT WAS HUNTING FOR ME.
AND MADNESS AND DEATH WERE THE SPOOR IT FOLLOWED.

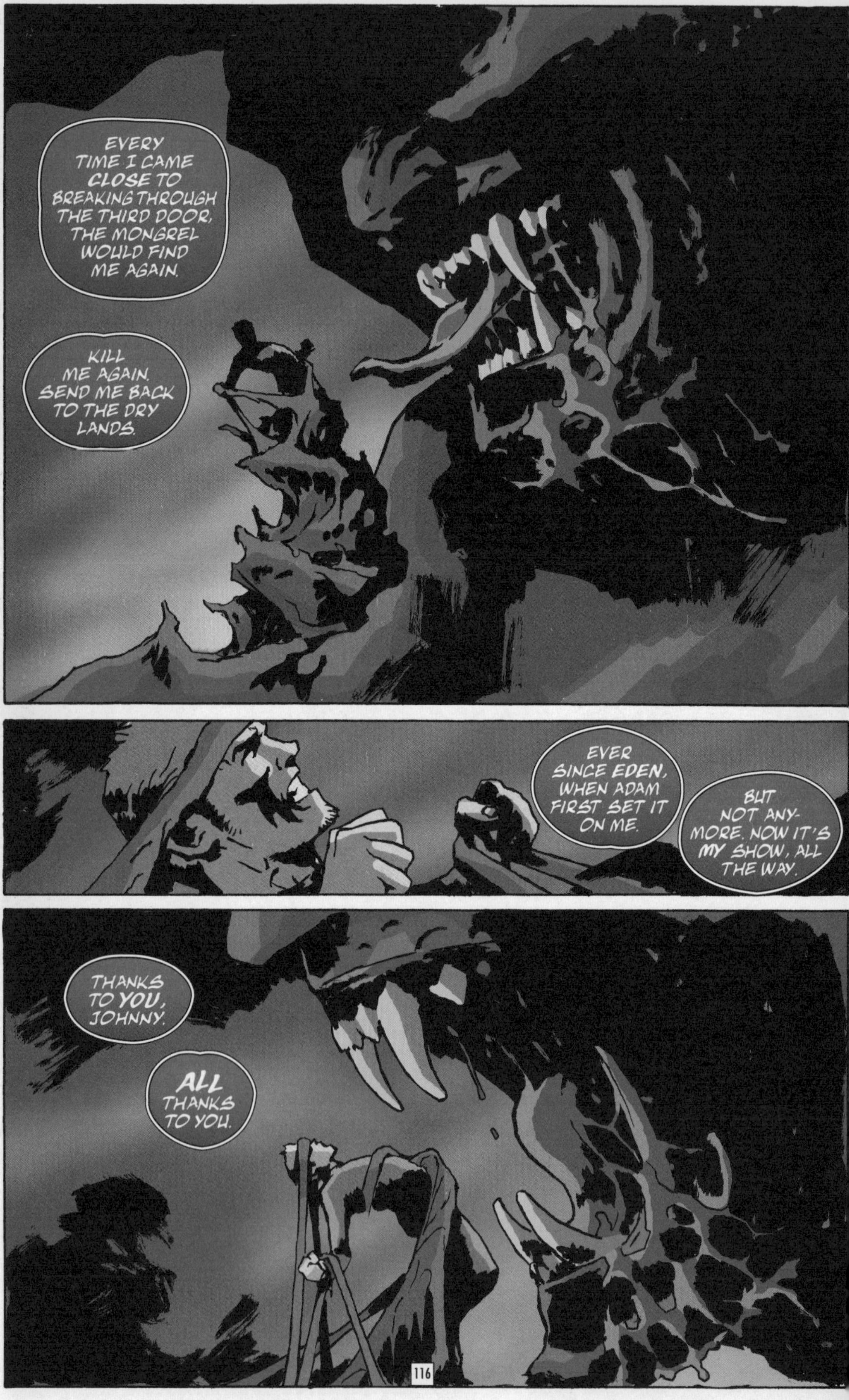
EVERY TIME I CAME CLOSE TO BREAKING THROUGH THE THIRD DOOR, THE MONGREL WOULD FIND ME AGAIN.
KILL ME AGAIN. SEND ME BACK TO THE DRY LANDS.
EVER SINCE EDEN, WHEN ADAM FIRST SET IT ON ME.
BUT NOT ANY-MORE. NOW IT'S MY SHOW, ALL THE WAY.
THANKS TO YOU, JOHNNY.
ALL THANKS TO YOU.

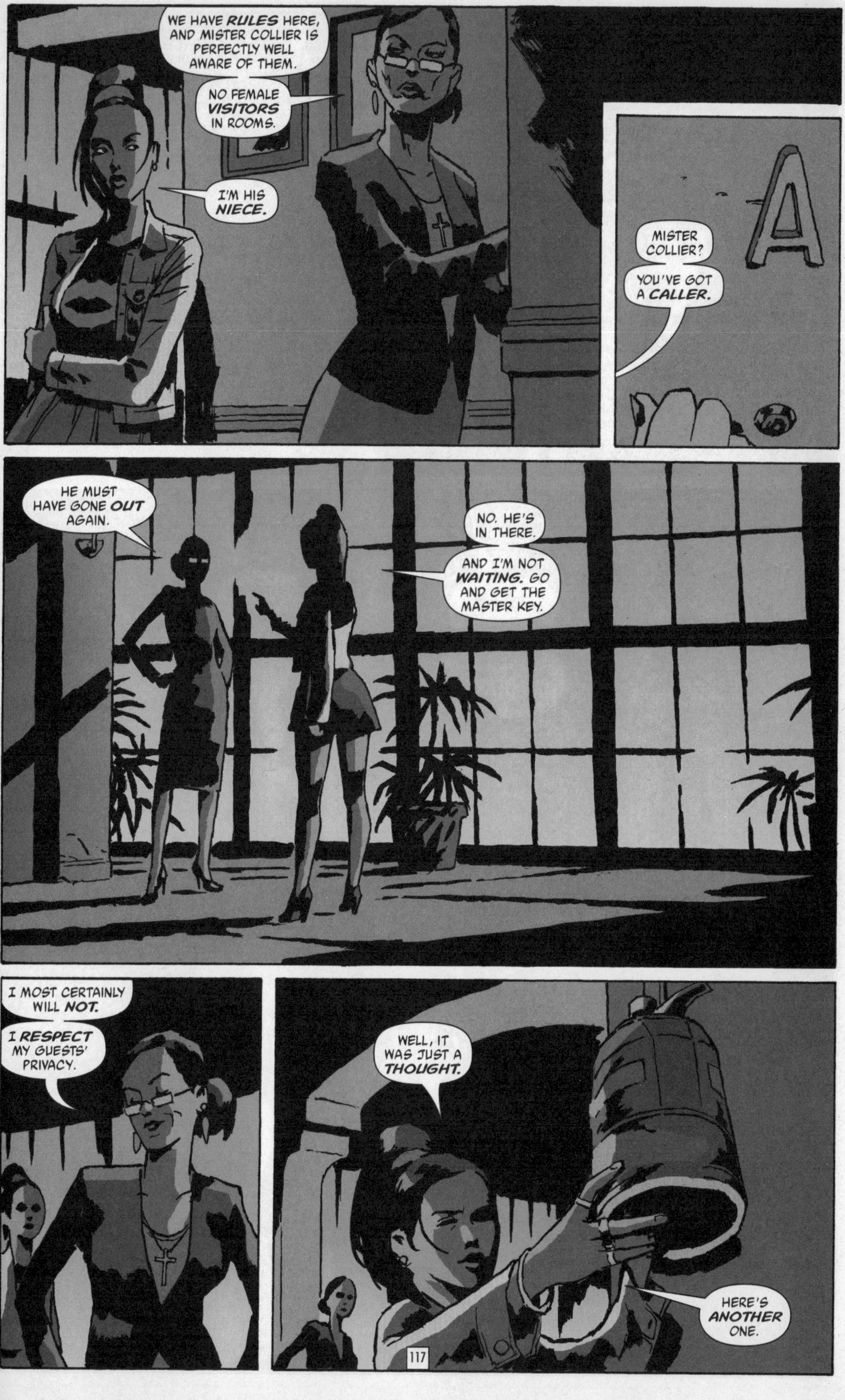
WE HAVE RULES HERE, AND MISTER COLLIER IS PERFECTLY WELL AWARE OF THEM.
NO FEMALE VISITORS IN ROOMS.
I'M HIS NIECE.
MISTER COLLIER?
YOU'VE GOT A CALLER.
HE MUST HAVE GONE OUT AGAIN.
NO. HE'S IN THERE.
AND I'M NOT WAITING. GO AND GET THE MASTER KEY.
I MOST CERTAINLY WILL NOT.
I RESPECT MY GUESTS' PRIVACY.
WELL, IT WAS JUST A THOUGHT.
HERE'S ANOTHER ONE.

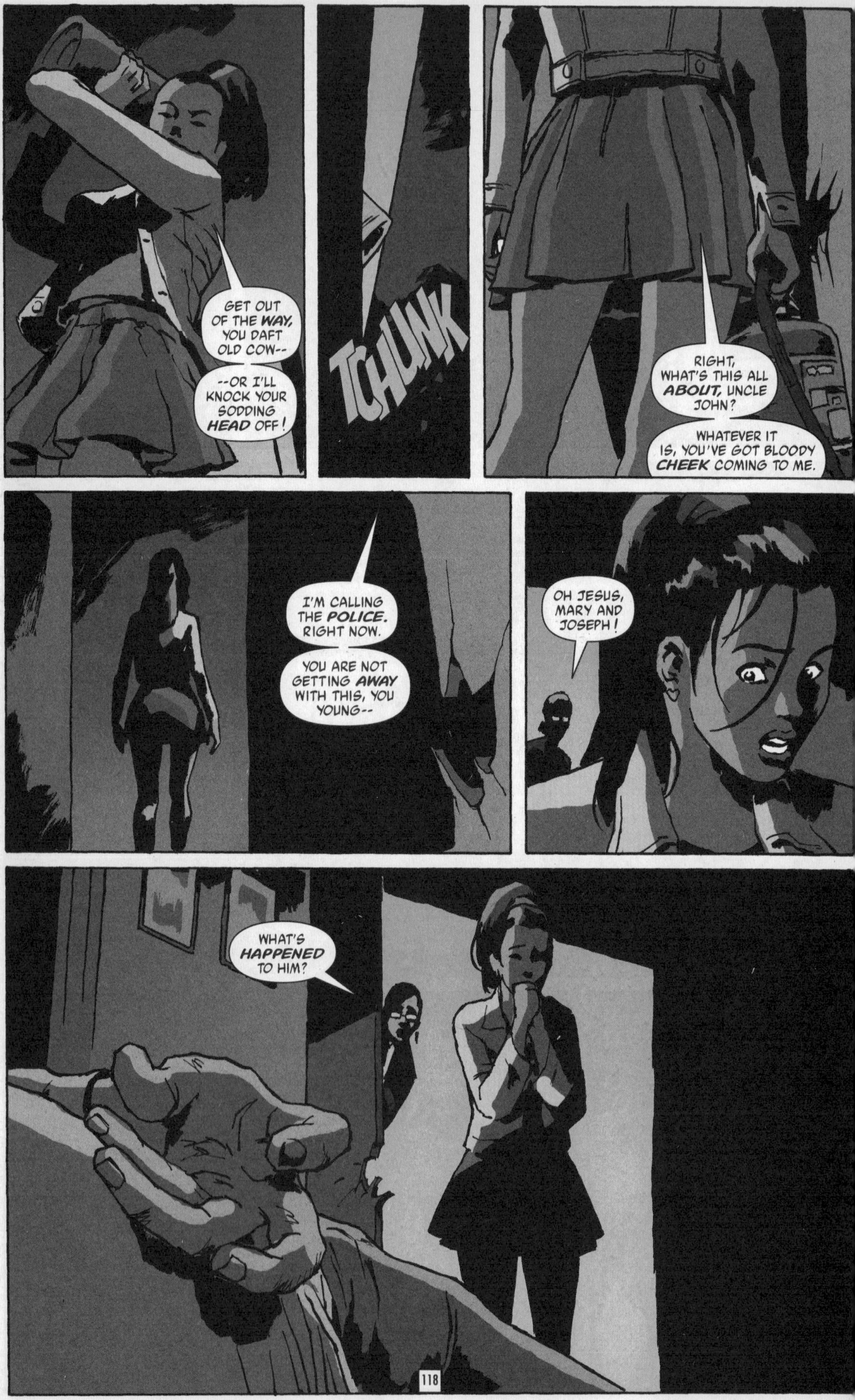

GET OUT OF THE WAY, YOU DAFT OLD COW--
--OR I'LL KNOCK YOUR SODDING HEAD OFF!
TCHUNK
RIGHT, WHAT'S THIS ALL ABOUT, UNCLE JOHN?
WHATEVER IT IS, YOU'VE GOT BLOODY CHEEK COMING TO ME.
I'M CALLING THE POLICE. RIGHT NOW.
YOU ARE NOT GETTING AWAY WITH THIS, YOU YOUNG--
OH JESUS, MARY AND JOSEPH!
WHAT'S HAPPENED TO HIM?

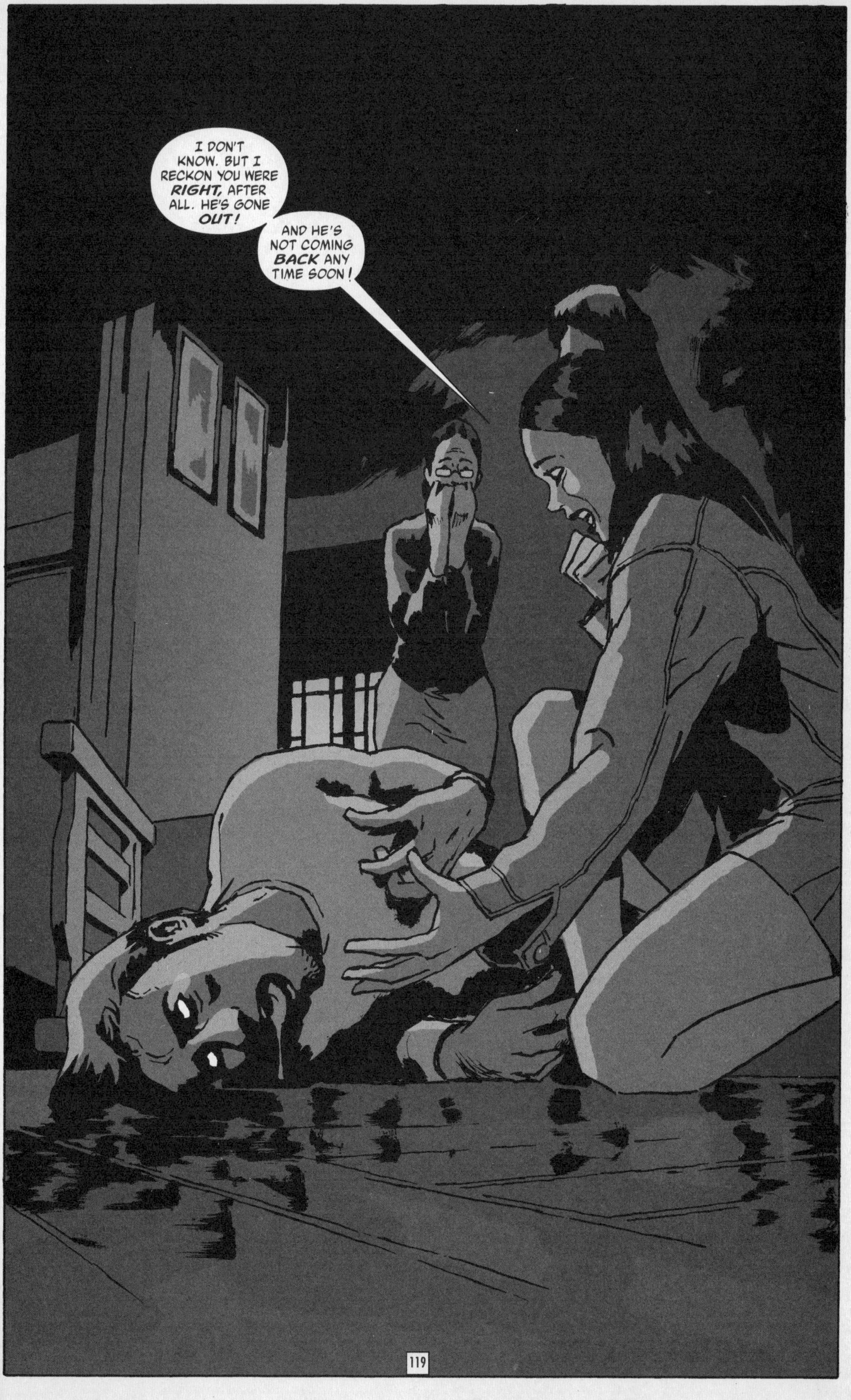
I DON'T KNOW. BUT I RECKON YOU WERE **RIGHT,** AFTER ALL. HE'S GONE **OUT!**
AND HE'S NOT COMING **BACK** ANY TIME SOON!

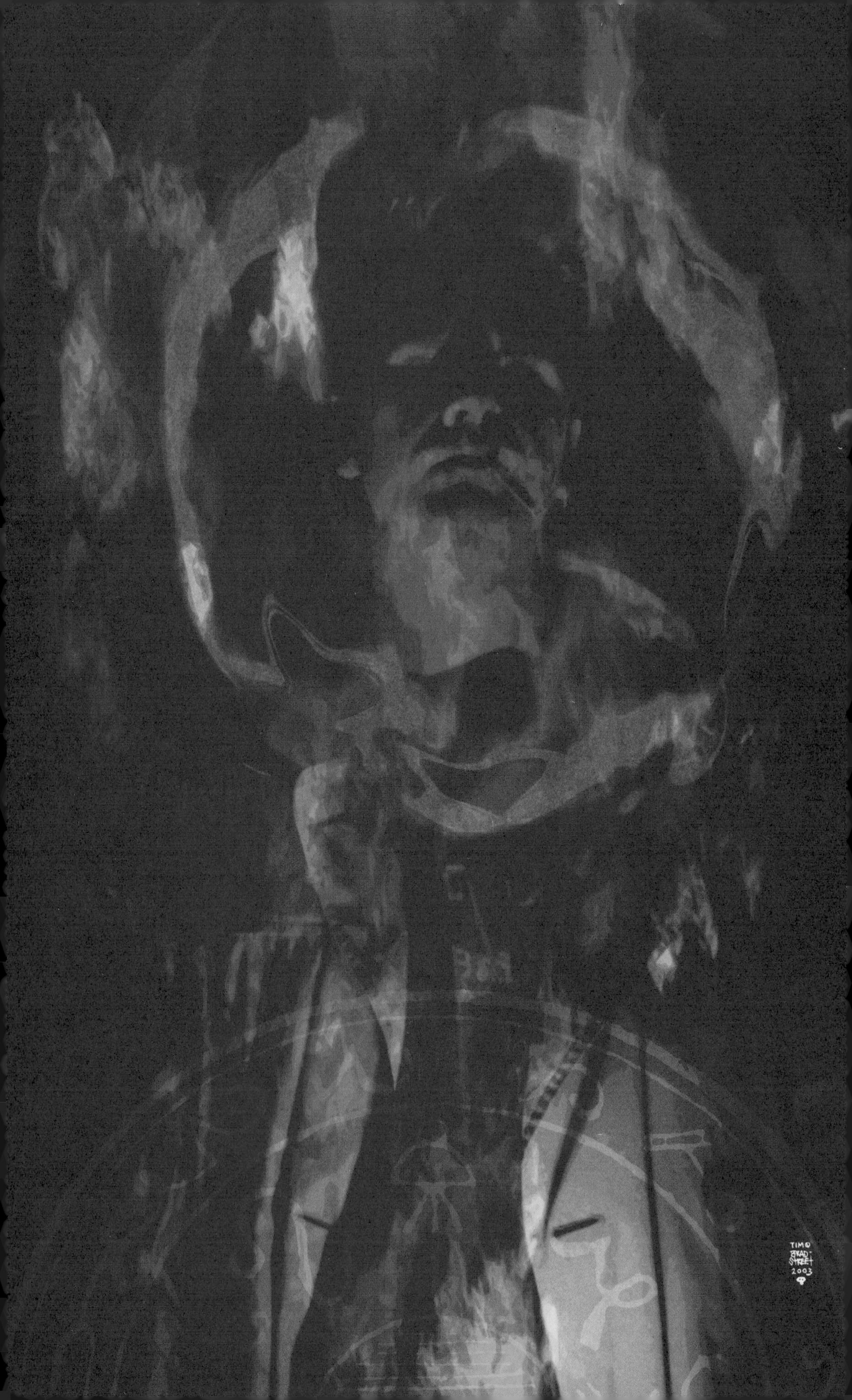
TIMO
BRAD-
STREET
2003

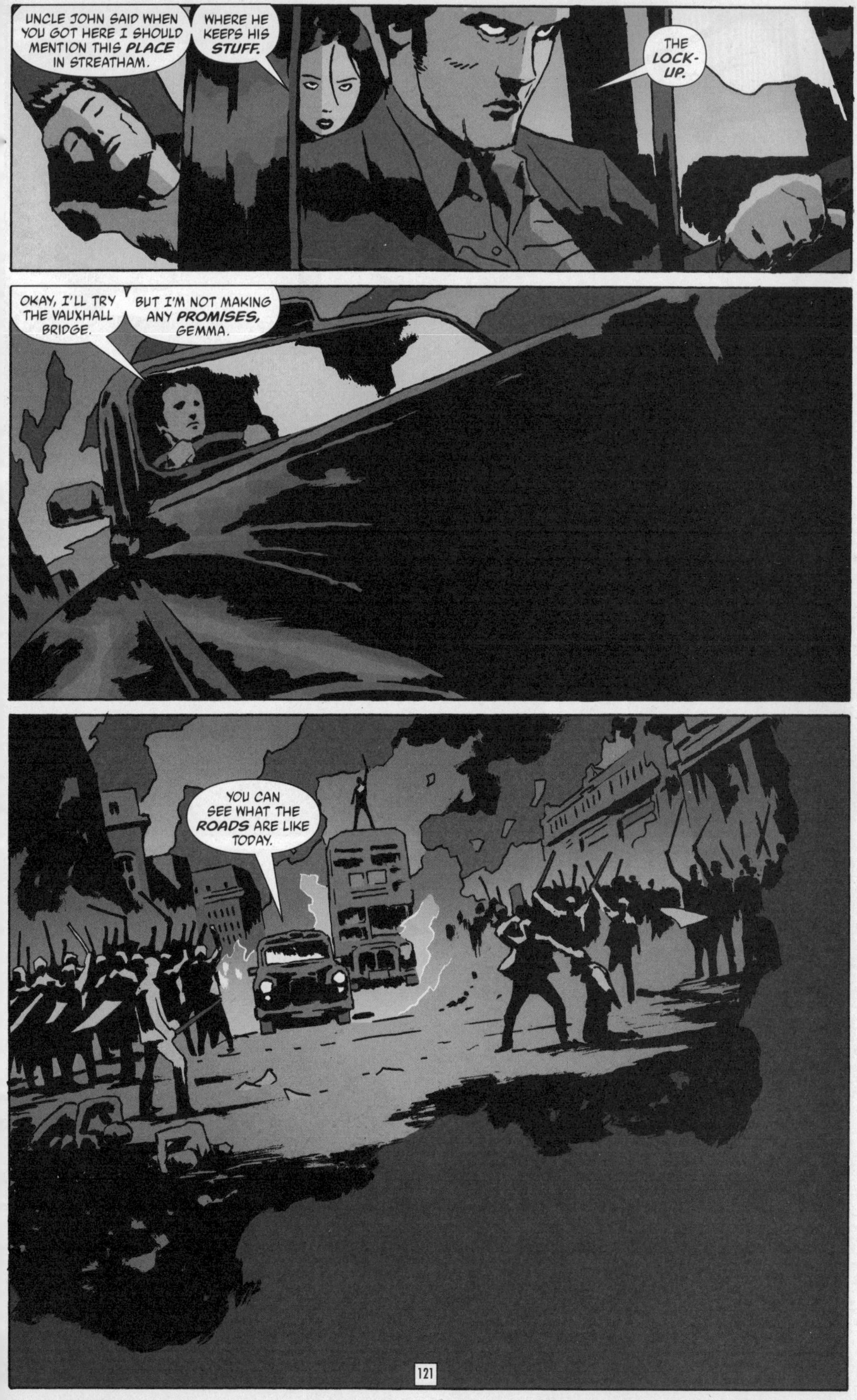
UNCLE JOHN SAID WHEN YOU GOT HERE I SHOULD MENTION THIS PLACE IN STREATHAM.
WHERE HE KEEPS HIS STUFF.
THE LOCK-UP.
OKAY, I'LL TRY THE VAUXHALL BRIDGE.
BUT I'M NOT MAKING ANY PROMISES, GEMMA.
YOU CAN SEE WHAT THE ROADS ARE LIKE TODAY.

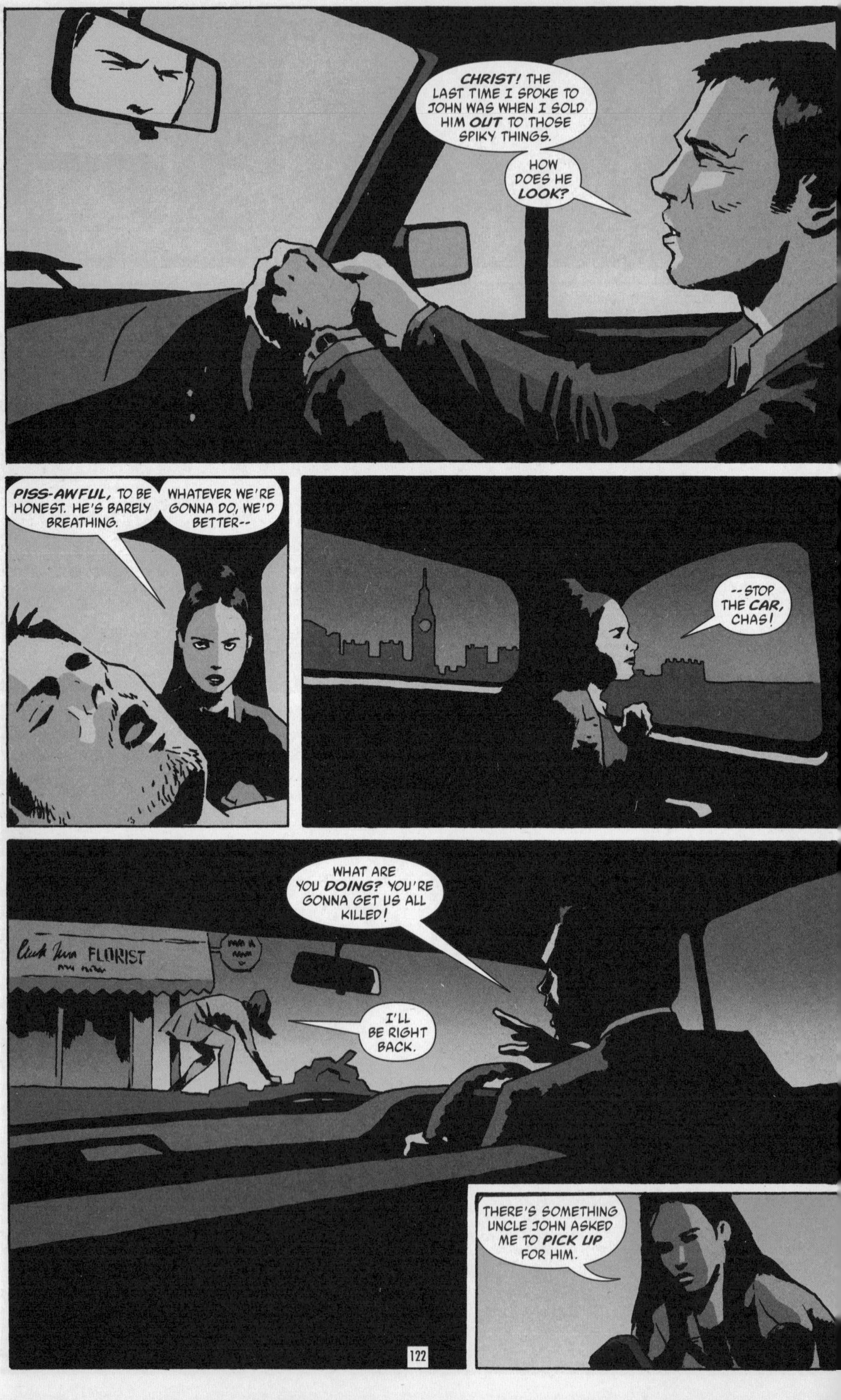

CHRIST! THE LAST TIME I SPOKE TO JOHN WAS WHEN I SOLD HIM OUT TO THOSE SPIKY THINGS.
HOW DOES HE LOOK?
PISS-AWFUL, TO BE HONEST. HE'S BARELY BREATHING.
WHATEVER WE'RE GONNA DO, WE'D BETTER--
--STOP THE CAR, CHAS!
FLORIST
WHAT ARE YOU DOING? YOU'RE GONNA GET US ALL KILLED!
I'LL BE RIGHT BACK.
THERE'S SOMETHING UNCLE JOHN ASKED ME TO PICK UP FOR HIM.

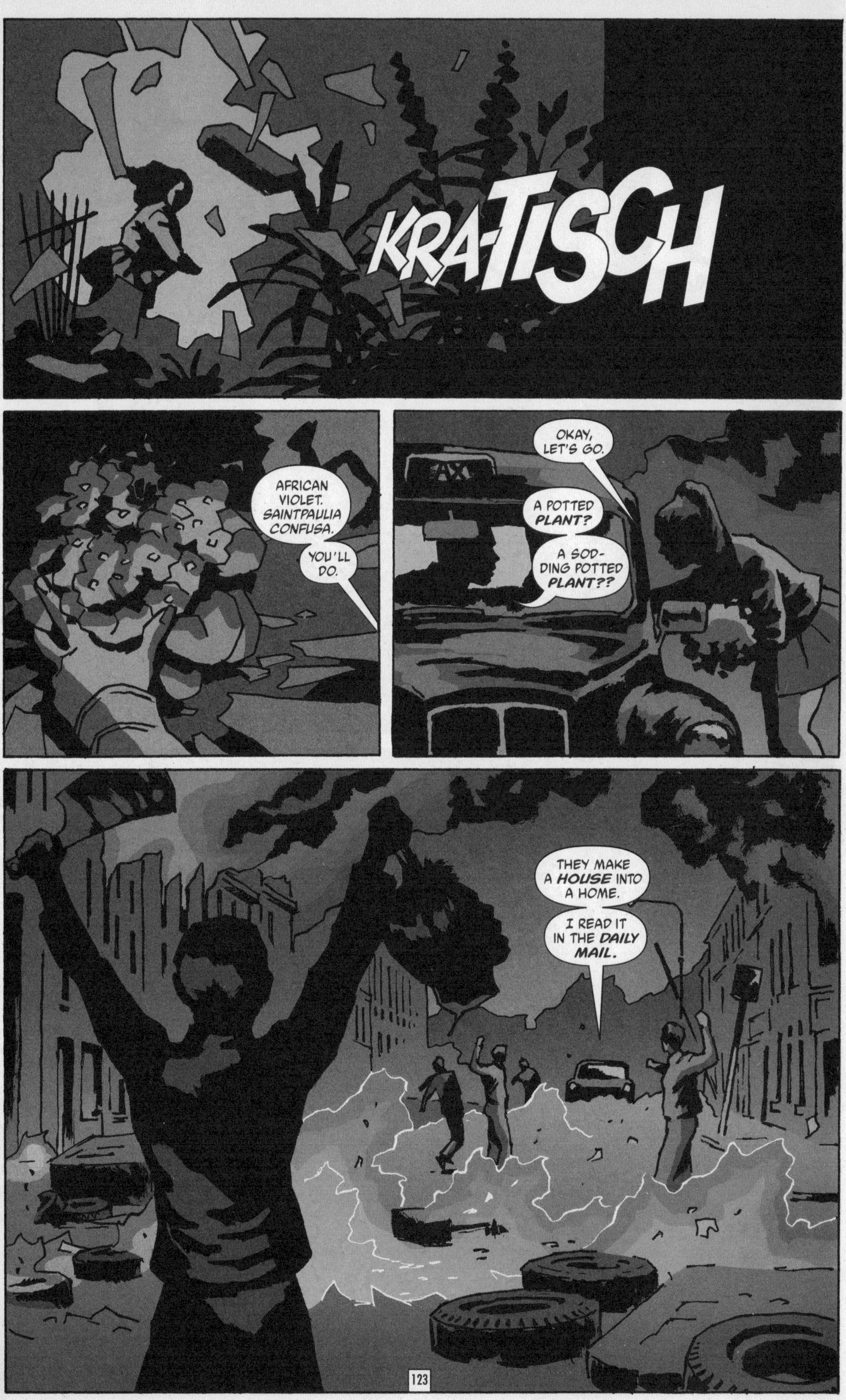
KRA-TISCH
AFRICAN VIOLET. SAINTPAULIA CONFUSA.
YOU'LL DO.
OKAY, LET'S GO.
A POTTED PLANT?
A SODDING POTTED PLANT??
THEY MAKE A HOUSE INTO A HOME.
I READ IT IN THE DAILY MAIL.

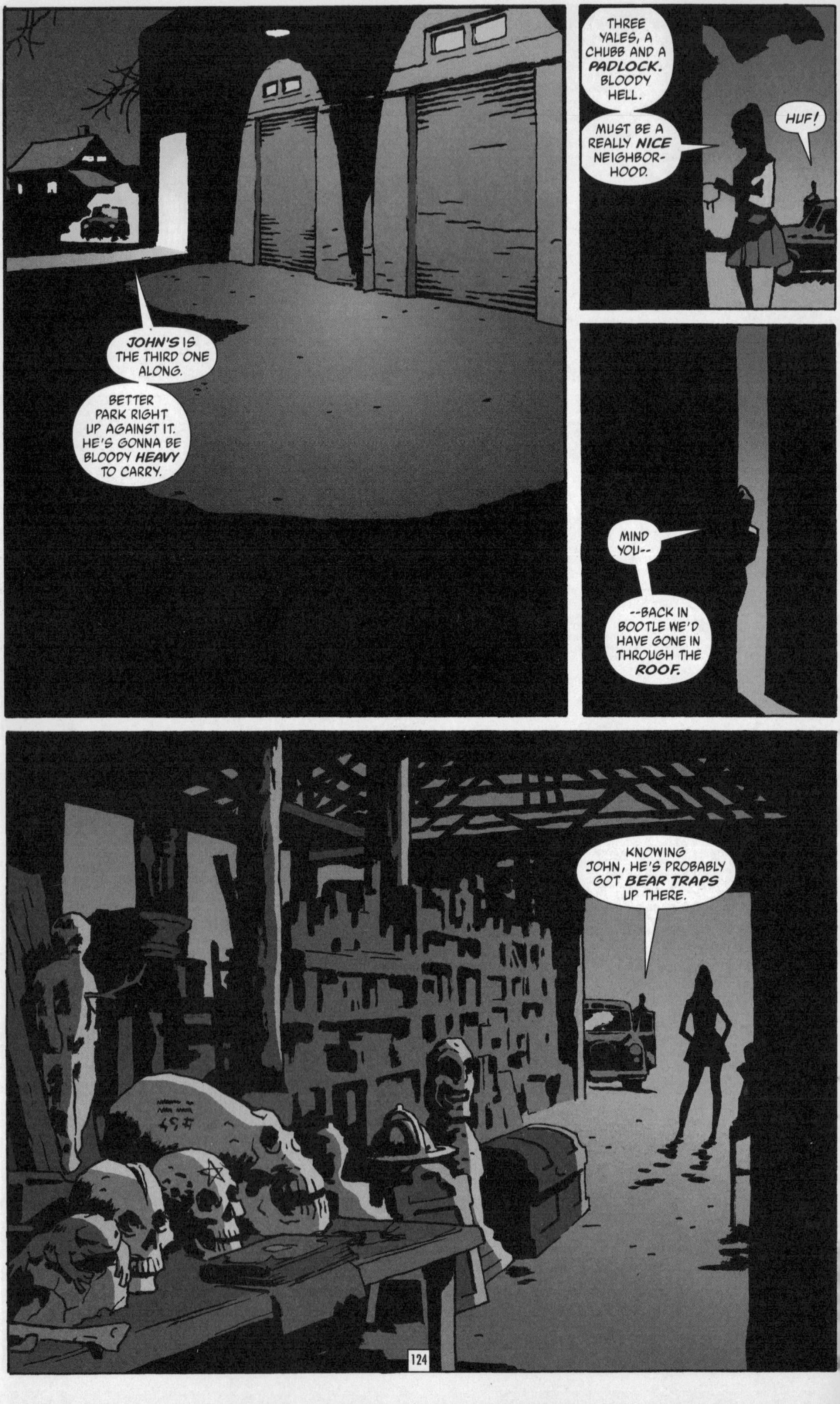
JOHN'S IS THE THIRD ONE ALONG.
BETTER PARK RIGHT UP AGAINST IT. HE'S GONNA BE BLOODY HEAVY TO CARRY.
THREE YALES, A CHUBB AND A PADLOCK. BLOODY HELL.
MUST BE A REALLY NICE NEIGHBOR-HOOD.
HUF!
MIND YOU--
--BACK IN BOOTLE WE'D HAVE GONE IN THROUGH THE ROOF.
KNOWING JOHN, HE'S PROBABLY GOT BEAR TRAPS UP THERE.

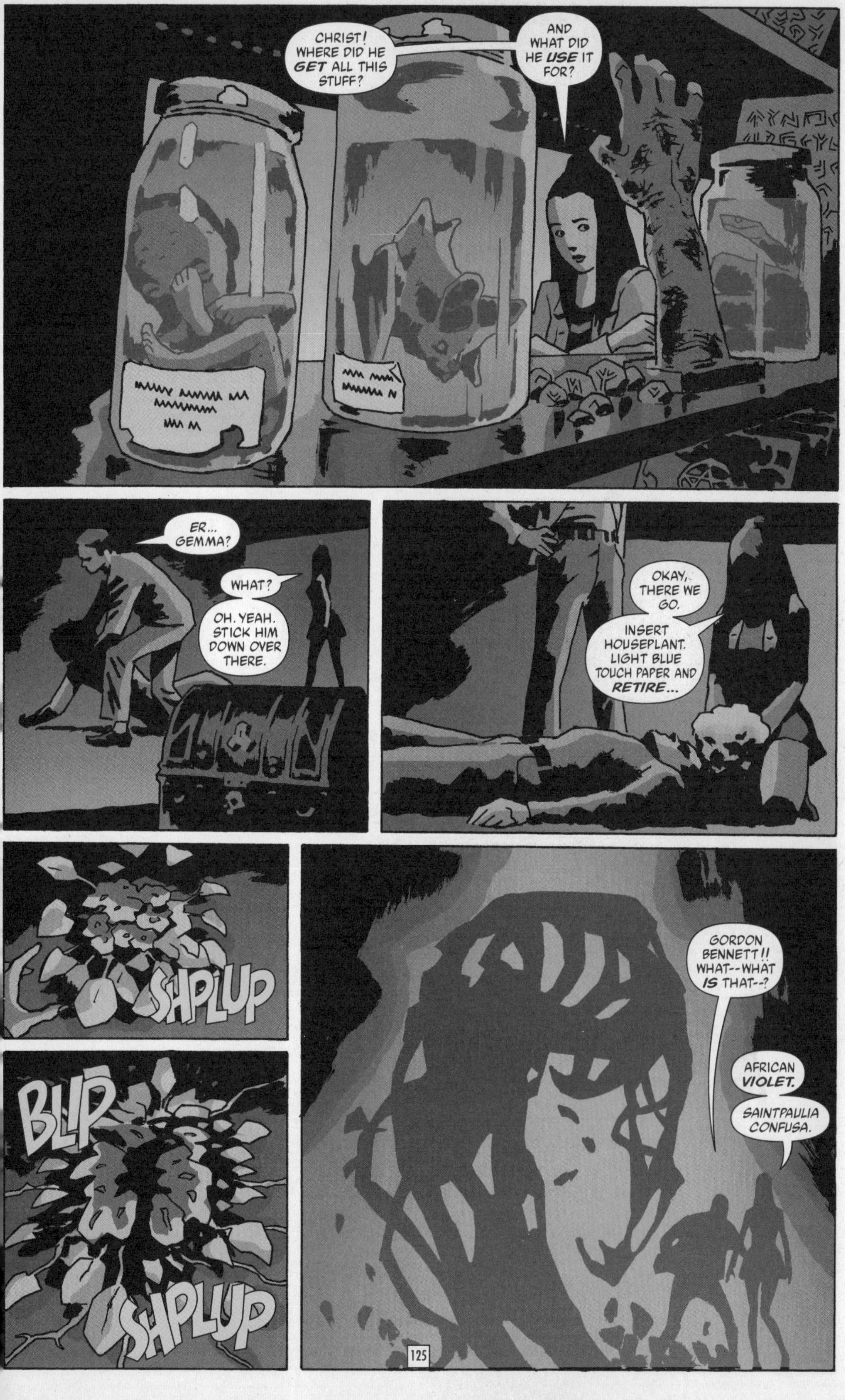
CHRIST! WHERE DID HE GET ALL THIS STUFF?
AND WHAT DID HE USE IT FOR?
ER... GEMMA?
WHAT?
OH. YEAH. STICK HIM DOWN OVER THERE.
OKAY, THERE WE GO.
INSERT HOUSEPLANT. LIGHT BLUE TOUCH PAPER AND RETIRE...
SHPLUP
BLIP
SHPLUP
GORDON BENNETT!! WHAT--WHAT IS THAT--?
AFRICAN VIOLET.
SAINTPAULIA CONFUSA.

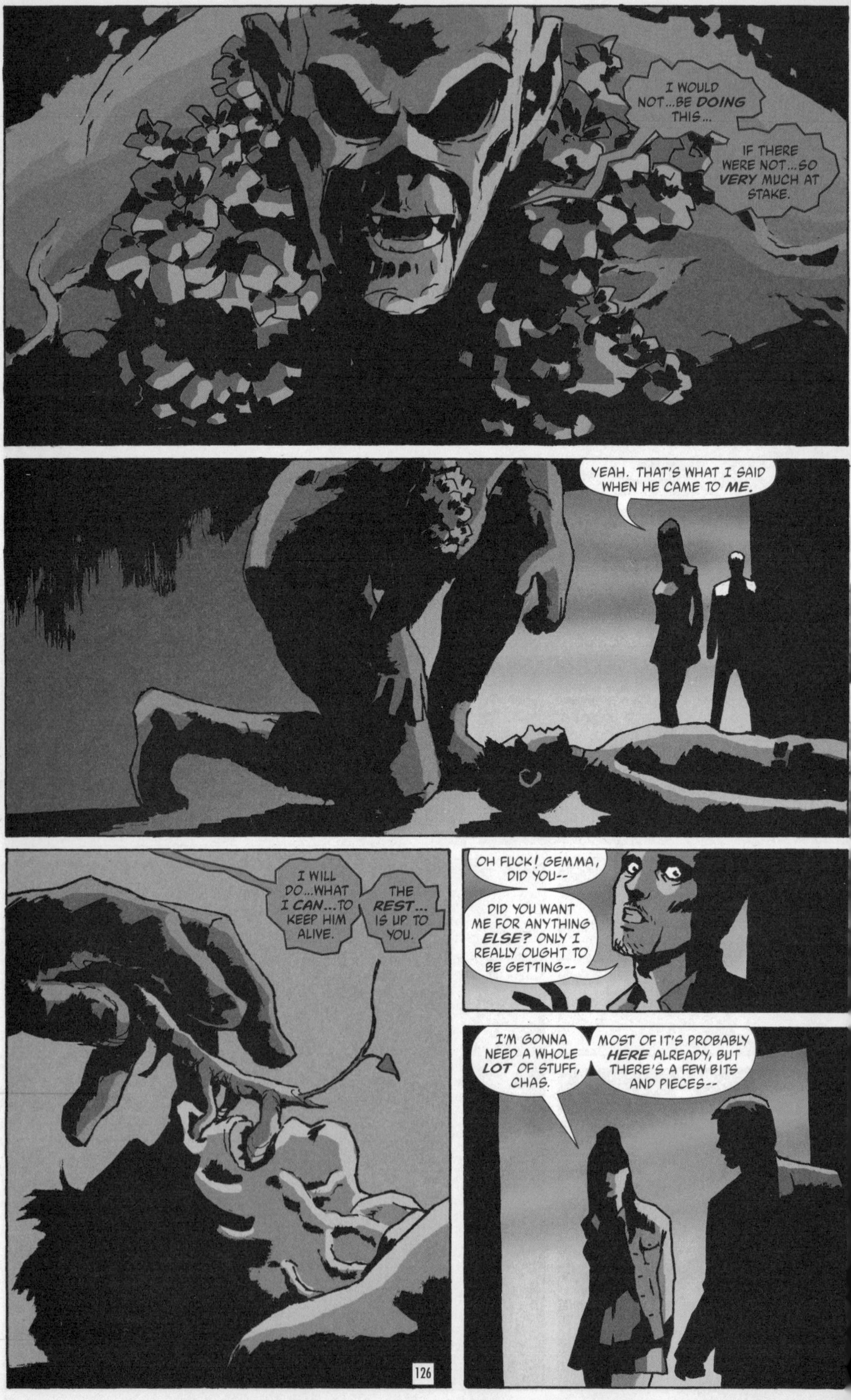
I WOULD NOT...BE DOING THIS...
IF THERE WERE NOT...SO VERY MUCH AT STAKE.
YEAH. THAT'S WHAT I SAID WHEN HE CAME TO ME.
I WILL DO...WHAT I CAN...TO KEEP HIM ALIVE.
THE REST... IS UP TO YOU.
OH FUCK! GEMMA, DID YOU--
DID YOU WANT ME FOR ANYTHING ELSE? ONLY I REALLY OUGHT TO BE GETTING--
I'M GONNA NEED A WHOLE LOT OF STUFF, CHAS.
MOST OF IT'S PROBABLY HERE ALREADY, BUT THERE'S A FEW BITS AND PIECES--

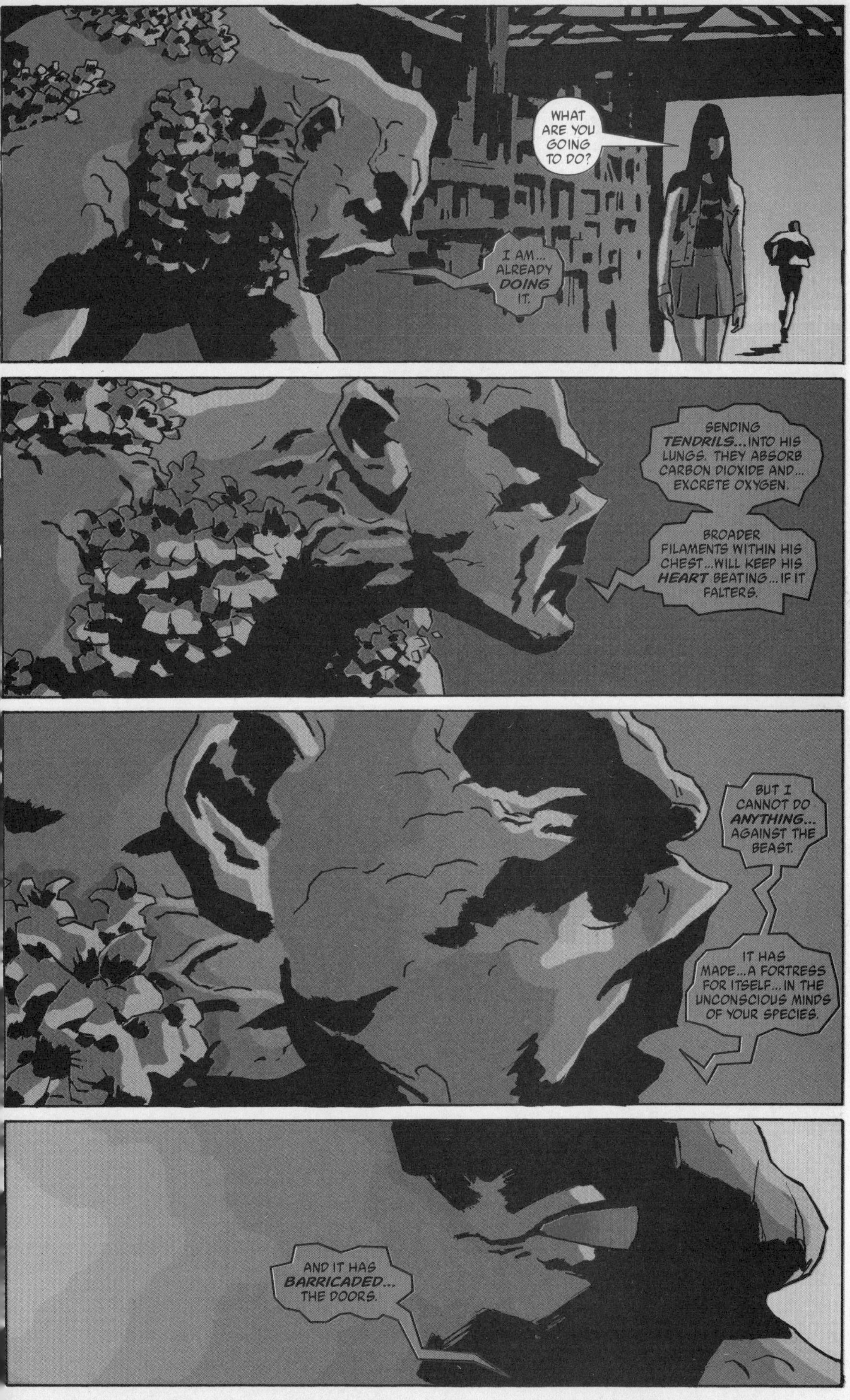
WHAT ARE YOU GOING TO DO?
I AM... ALREADY DOING IT.
SENDING TENDRILS... INTO HIS LUNGS. THEY ABSORB CARBON DIOXIDE AND... EXCRETE OXYGEN.
BROADER FILAMENTS WITHIN HIS CHEST...WILL KEEP HIS HEART BEATING... IF IT FALTERS.
BUT I CANNOT DO ANYTHING... AGAINST THE BEAST.
IT HAS MADE...A FORTRESS FOR ITSELF... IN THE UNCONSCIOUS MINDS OF YOUR SPECIES.
AND IT HAS BARRICADED... THE DOORS.

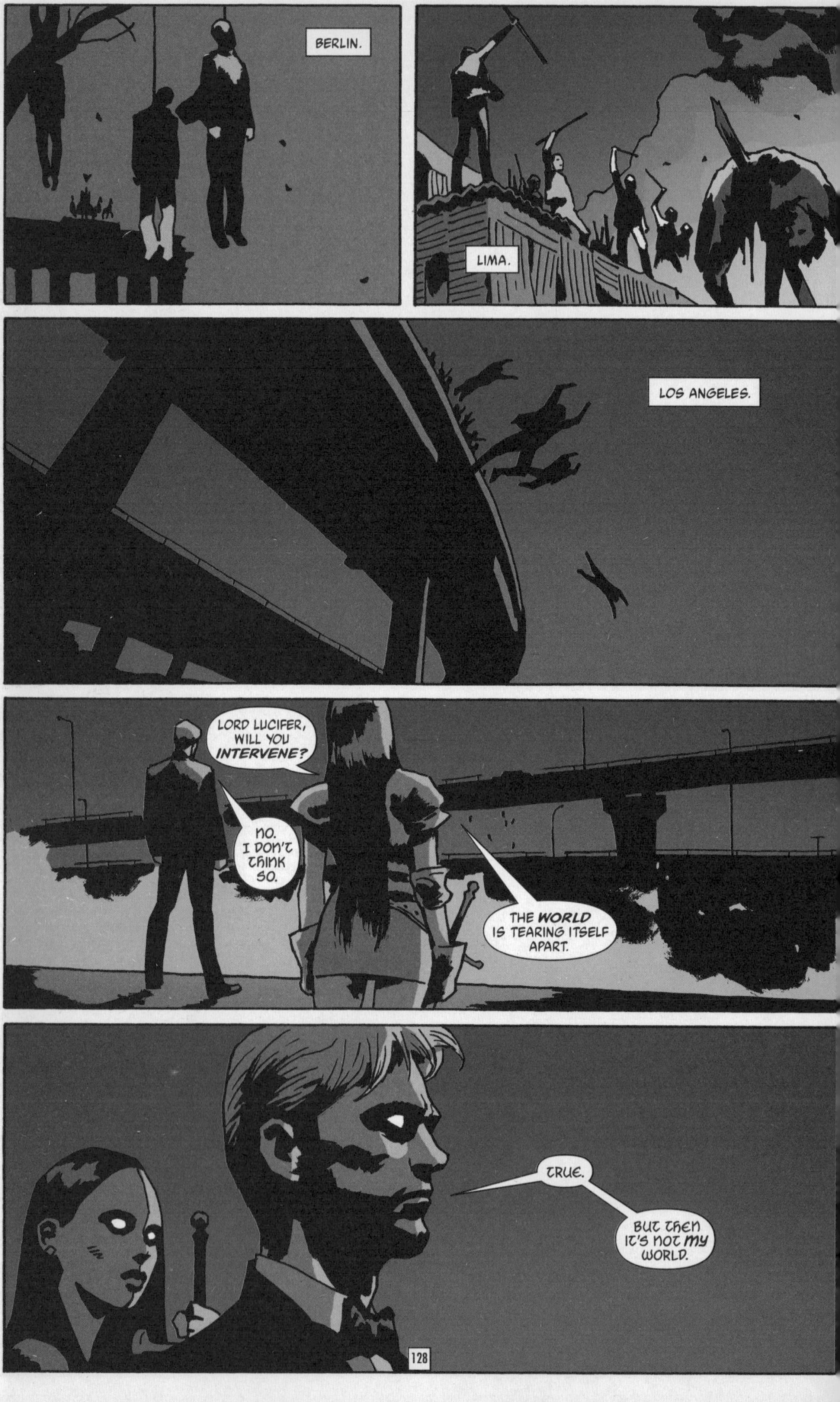
BERLIN.
LIMA.
LOS ANGELES.
LORD LUCIFER, WILL YOU INTERVENE?
NO. I DON'T THINK SO.
THE WORLD IS TEARING ITSELF APART.
TRUE.
BUT THEN IT'S NOT MY WORLD.

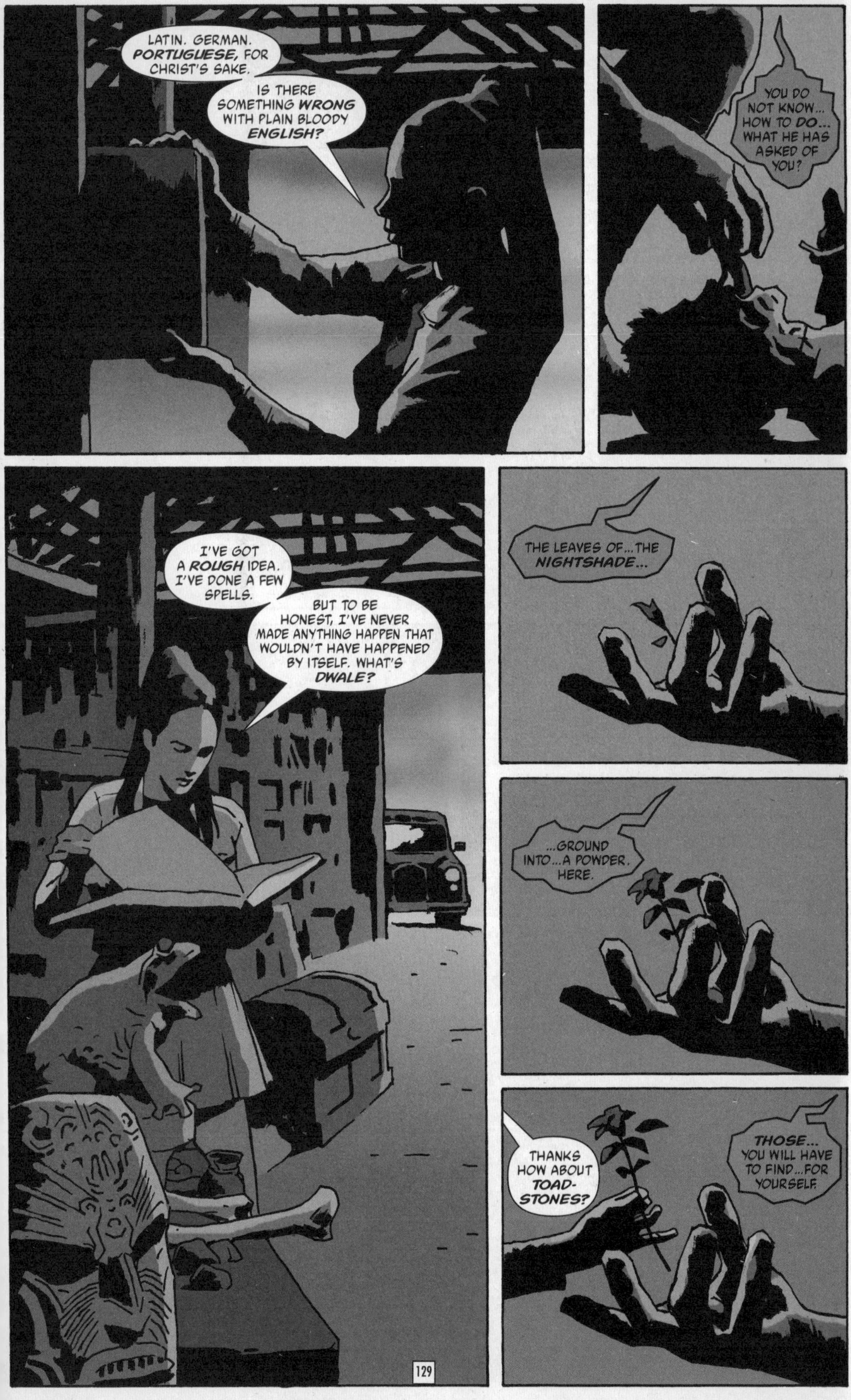
LATIN. GERMAN. PORTUGUESE, FOR CHRIST'S SAKE.
IS THERE SOMETHING WRONG WITH PLAIN BLOODY ENGLISH?
YOU DO NOT KNOW... HOW TO DO... WHAT HE HAS ASKED OF YOU?
I'VE GOT A ROUGH IDEA. I'VE DONE A FEW SPELLS.
BUT TO BE HONEST, I'VE NEVER MADE ANYTHING HAPPEN THAT WOULDN'T HAVE HAPPENED BY ITSELF. WHAT'S DWALE?
THE LEAVES OF...THE NIGHTSHADE...
...GROUND INTO...A POWDER. HERE.
THANKS HOW ABOUT TOAD-STONES?
THOSE... YOU WILL HAVE TO FIND...FOR YOURSELF.

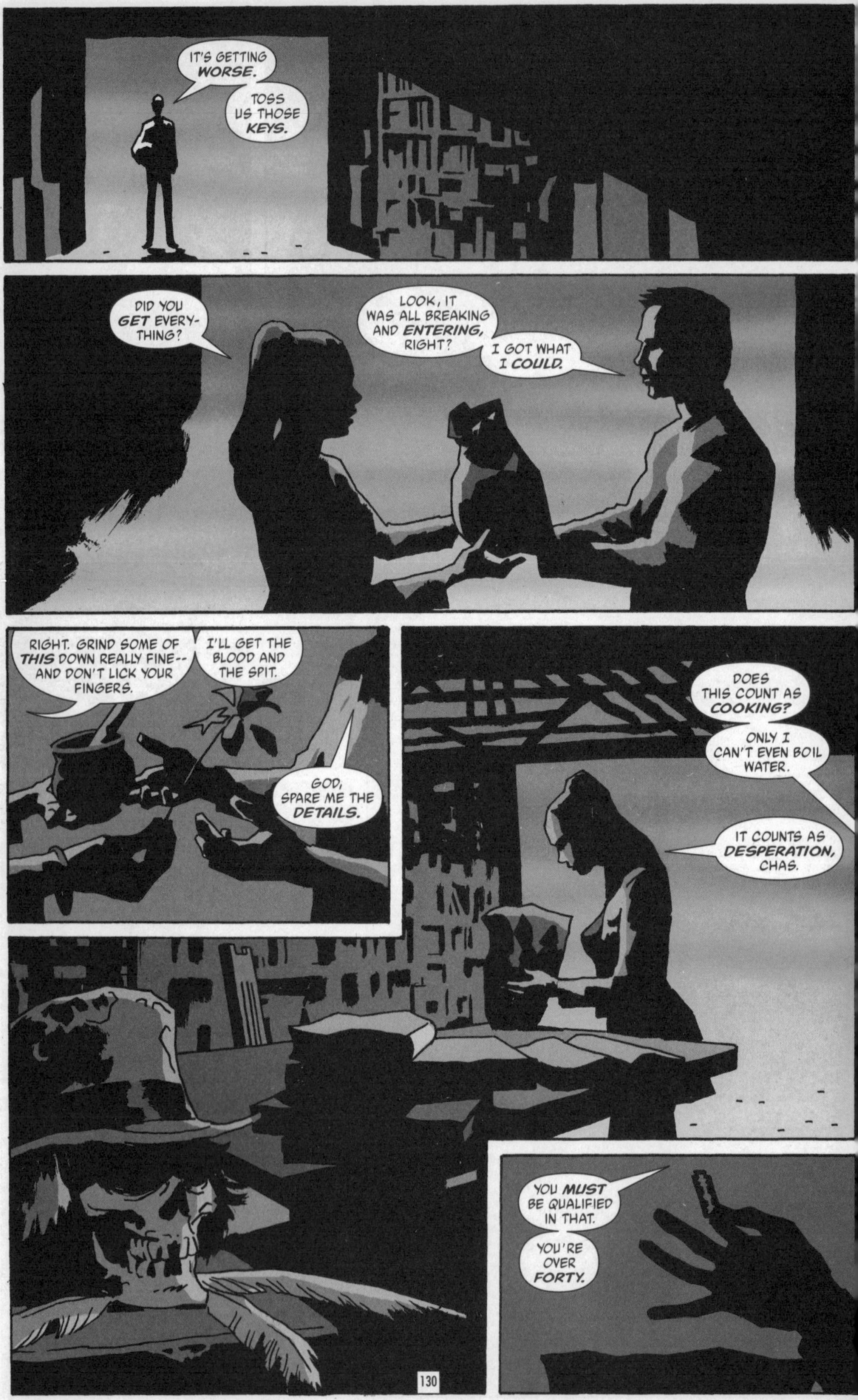
IT'S GETTING **WORSE.**
TOSS US THOSE **KEYS.**
DID YOU **GET** EVERY-THING?
LOOK, IT WAS ALL BREAKING AND **ENTERING,** RIGHT?
I GOT WHAT **I COULD.**
RIGHT. GRIND SOME OF **THIS** DOWN REALLY FINE-- AND DON'T LICK YOUR FINGERS.
I'LL GET THE BLOOD AND THE SPIT.
GOD, SPARE ME THE **DETAILS.**
DOES THIS COUNT AS **COOKING?**
ONLY I CAN'T EVEN BOIL WATER.
IT COUNTS AS **DESPERATION,** CHAS.
YOU **MUST** BE QUALIFIED IN THAT.
YOU'RE OVER **FORTY.**

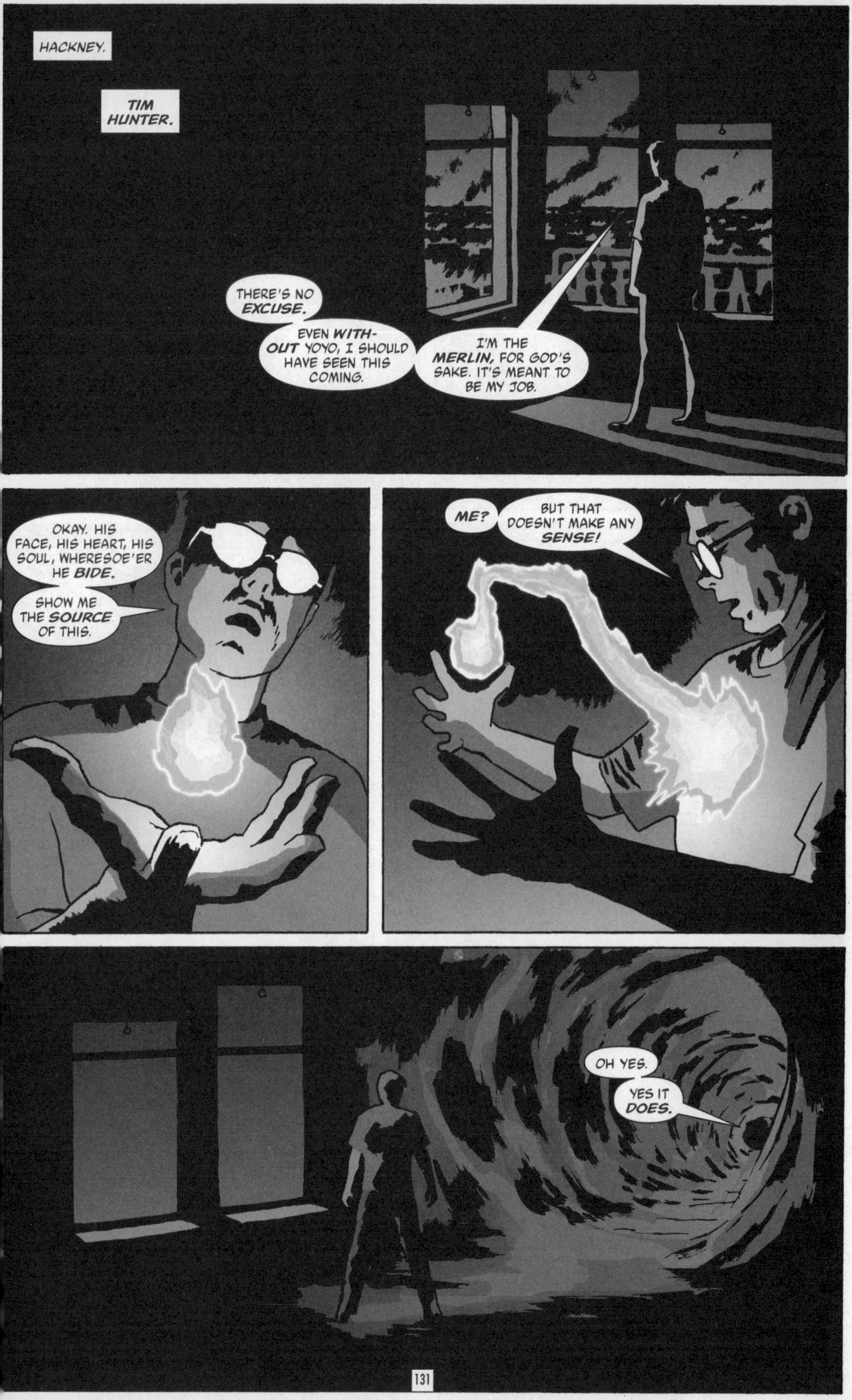
HACKNEY.
TIM HUNTER.
THERE'S NO EXCUSE.
EVEN WITHOUT YOYO, I SHOULD HAVE SEEN THIS COMING.
I'M THE MERLIN, FOR GOD'S SAKE. IT'S MEANT TO BE MY JOB.
OKAY. HIS FACE, HIS HEART, HIS SOUL, WHERESOE'ER HE BIDE.
SHOW ME THE SOURCE OF THIS.
ME?
BUT THAT DOESN'T MAKE ANY SENSE!
OH YES.
YES IT DOES.

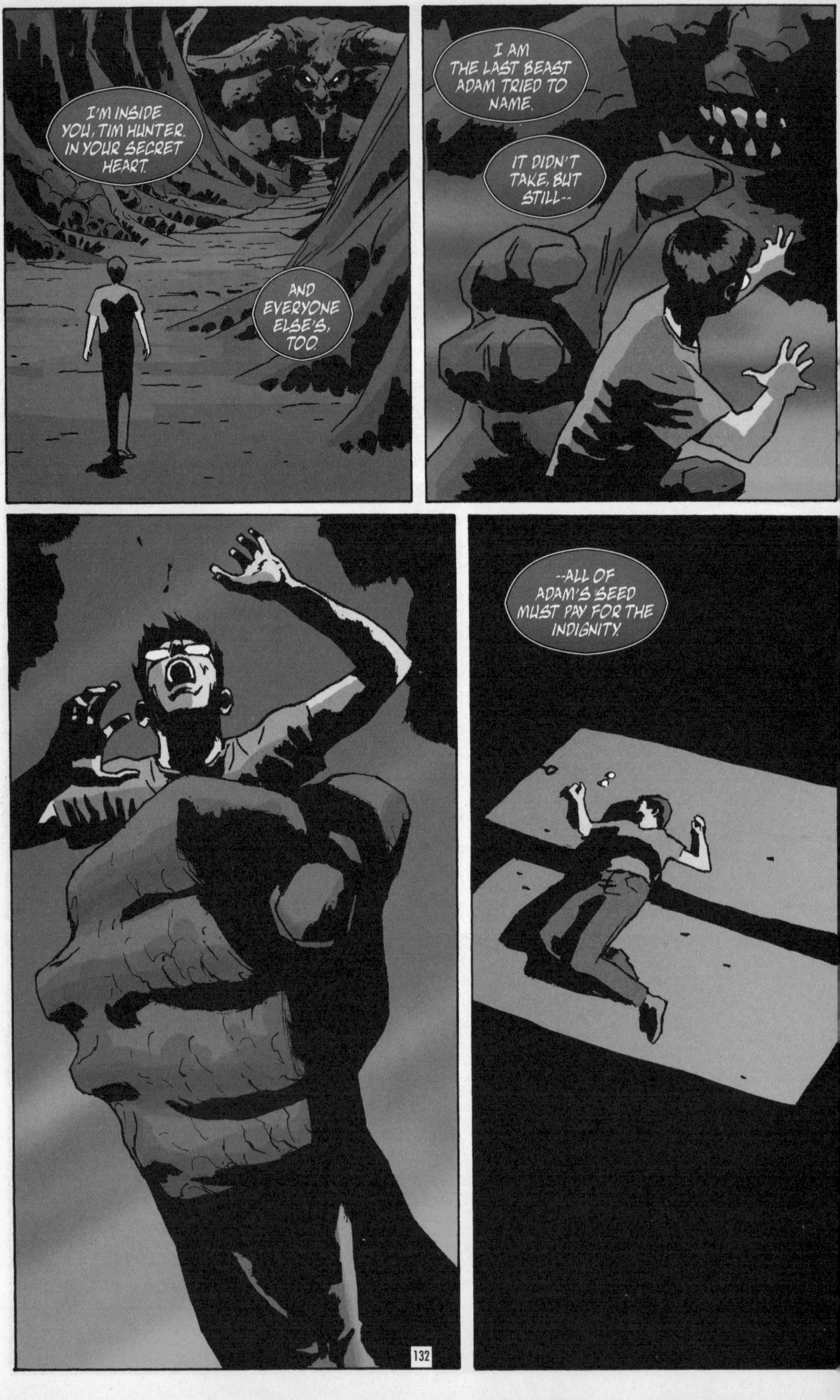
I'M INSIDE YOU, TIM HUNTER. IN YOUR SECRET HEART.
AND EVERYONE ELSE'S, TOO.
I AM THE LAST BEAST ADAM TRIED TO NAME.
IT DIDN'T TAKE, BUT STILL--
--ALL OF ADAM'S SEED MUST PAY FOR THE INDIGNITY.

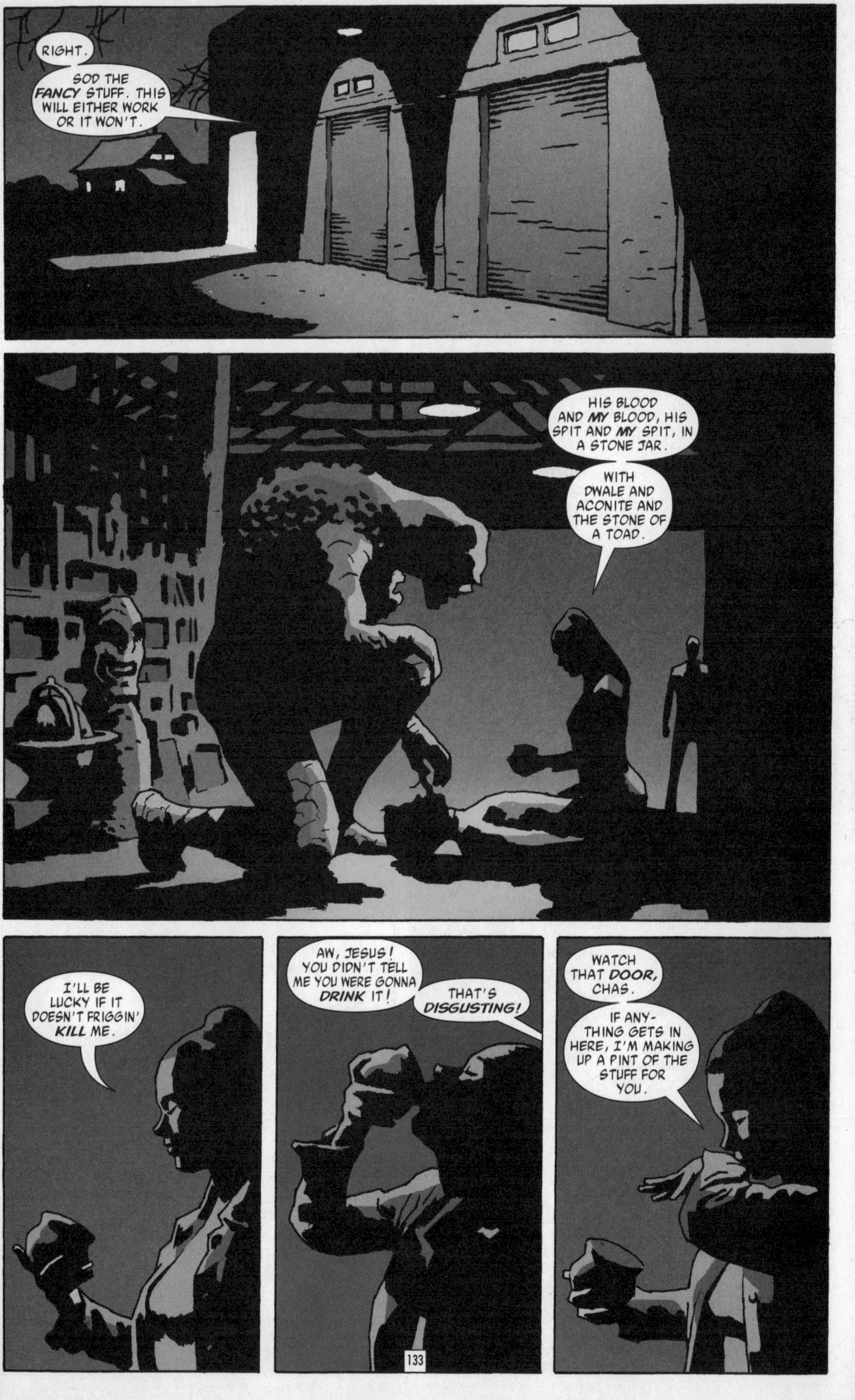

RIGHT.
SOD THE FANCY STUFF. THIS WILL EITHER WORK OR IT WON'T.
HIS BLOOD AND MY BLOOD, HIS SPIT AND MY SPIT, IN A STONE JAR.
WITH DWALE AND ACONITE AND THE STONE OF A TOAD.
I'LL BE LUCKY IF IT DOESN'T FRIGGIN' KILL ME.
AW, JESUS! YOU DIDN'T TELL ME YOU WERE GONNA DRINK IT!
THAT'S DISGUSTING!
WATCH THAT DOOR, CHAS.
IF ANY-THING GETS IN HERE, I'M MAKING UP A PINT OF THE STUFF FOR YOU.

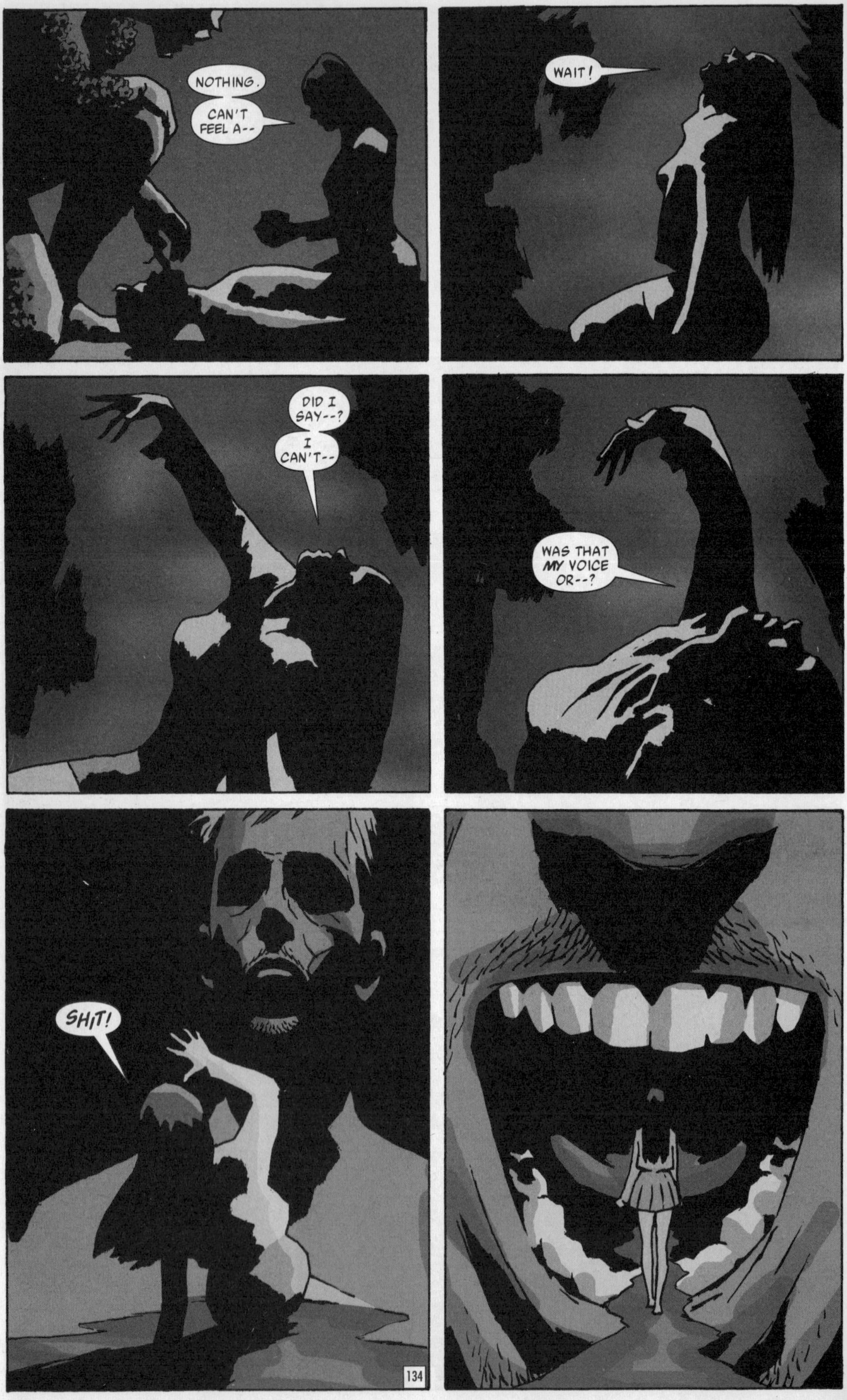
NOTHING.
CAN'T FEEL A--
WAIT!
DID I SAY--?
I CAN'T--
WAS THAT MY VOICE OR--?
SHIT!

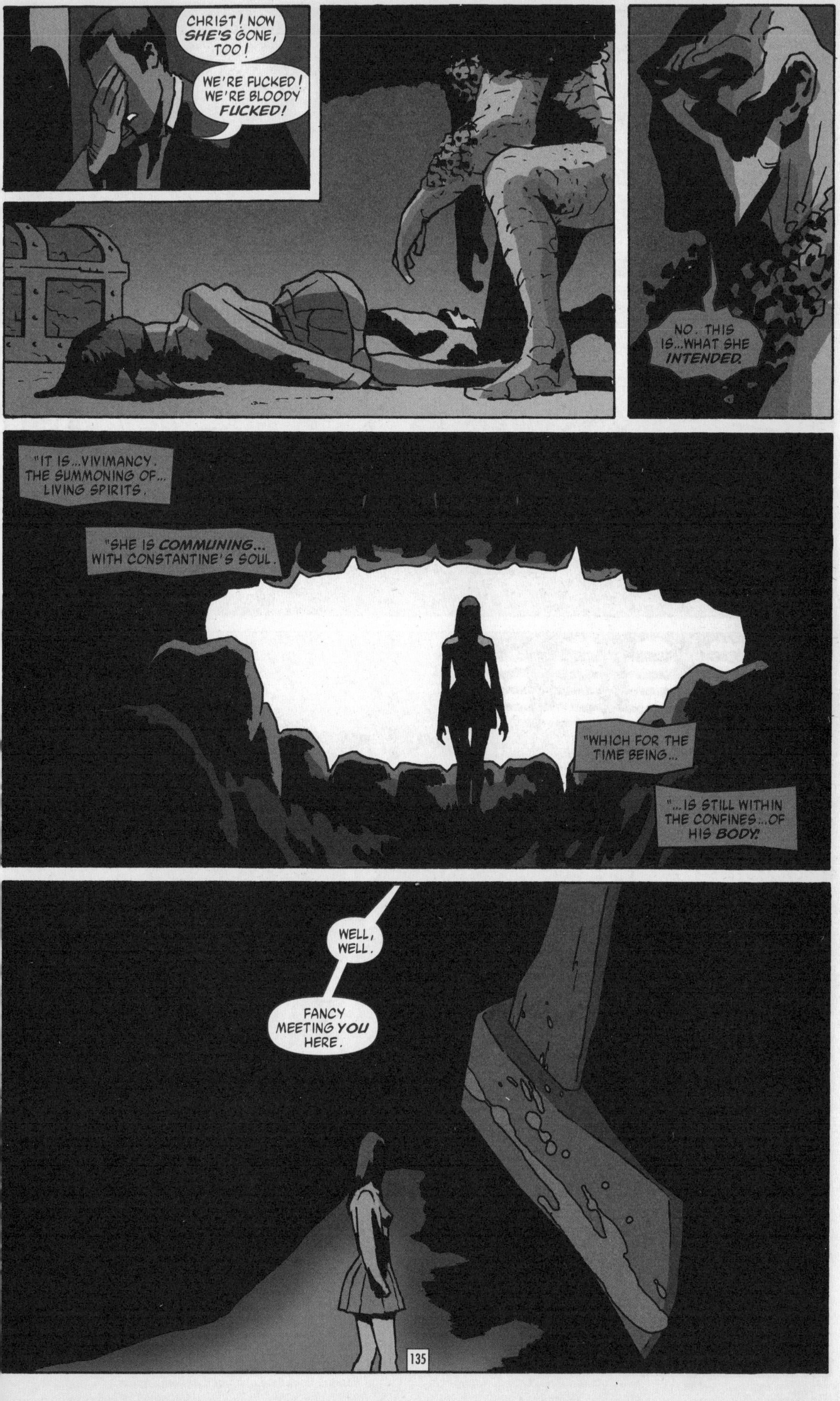

CHRIST! NOW SHE'S GONE, TOO!
WE'RE FUCKED! WE'RE BLOODY FUCKED!
NO. THIS IS...WHAT SHE INTENDED.
"IT IS...VIVIMANCY. THE SUMMONING OF... LIVING SPIRITS.
"SHE IS COMMUNING... WITH CONSTANTINE'S SOUL.
"WHICH FOR THE TIME BEING...
"...IS STILL WITHIN THE CONFINES...OF HIS BODY!
WELL, WELL.
FANCY MEETING YOU HERE.

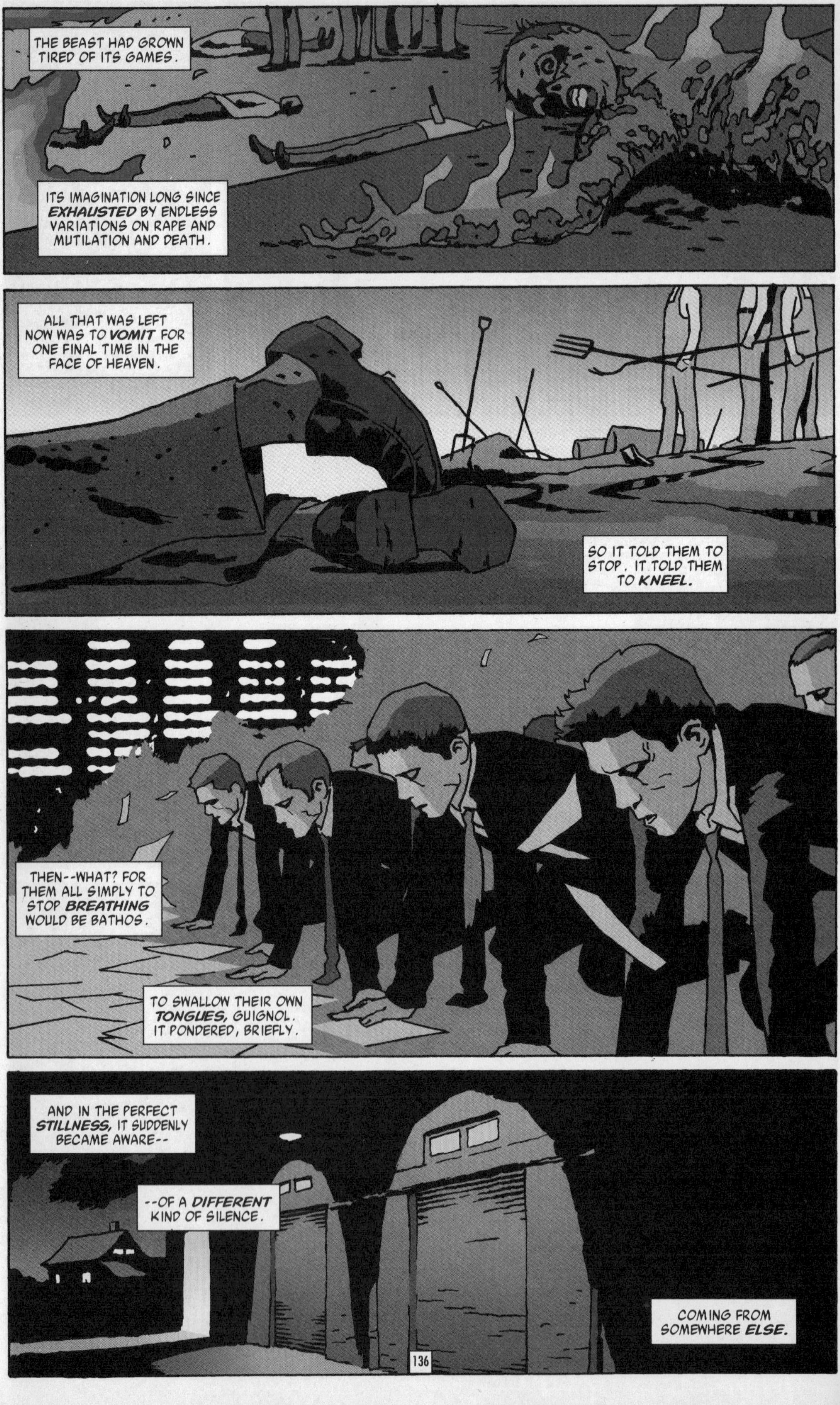
THE BEAST HAD GROWN TIRED OF ITS GAMES.
ITS IMAGINATION LONG SINCE EXHAUSTED BY ENDLESS VARIATIONS ON RAPE AND MUTILATION AND DEATH.
ALL THAT WAS LEFT NOW WAS TO VOMIT FOR ONE FINAL TIME IN THE FACE OF HEAVEN.
SO IT TOLD THEM TO STOP. IT TOLD THEM TO KNEEL.
THEN--WHAT? FOR THEM ALL SIMPLY TO STOP BREATHING WOULD BE BATHOS.
TO SWALLOW THEIR OWN TONGUES, GUIGNOL. IT PONDERED, BRIEFLY.
AND IN THE PERFECT STILLNESS, IT SUDDENLY BECAME AWARE--
--OF A DIFFERENT KIND OF SILENCE.
COMING FROM SOMEWHERE ELSE.

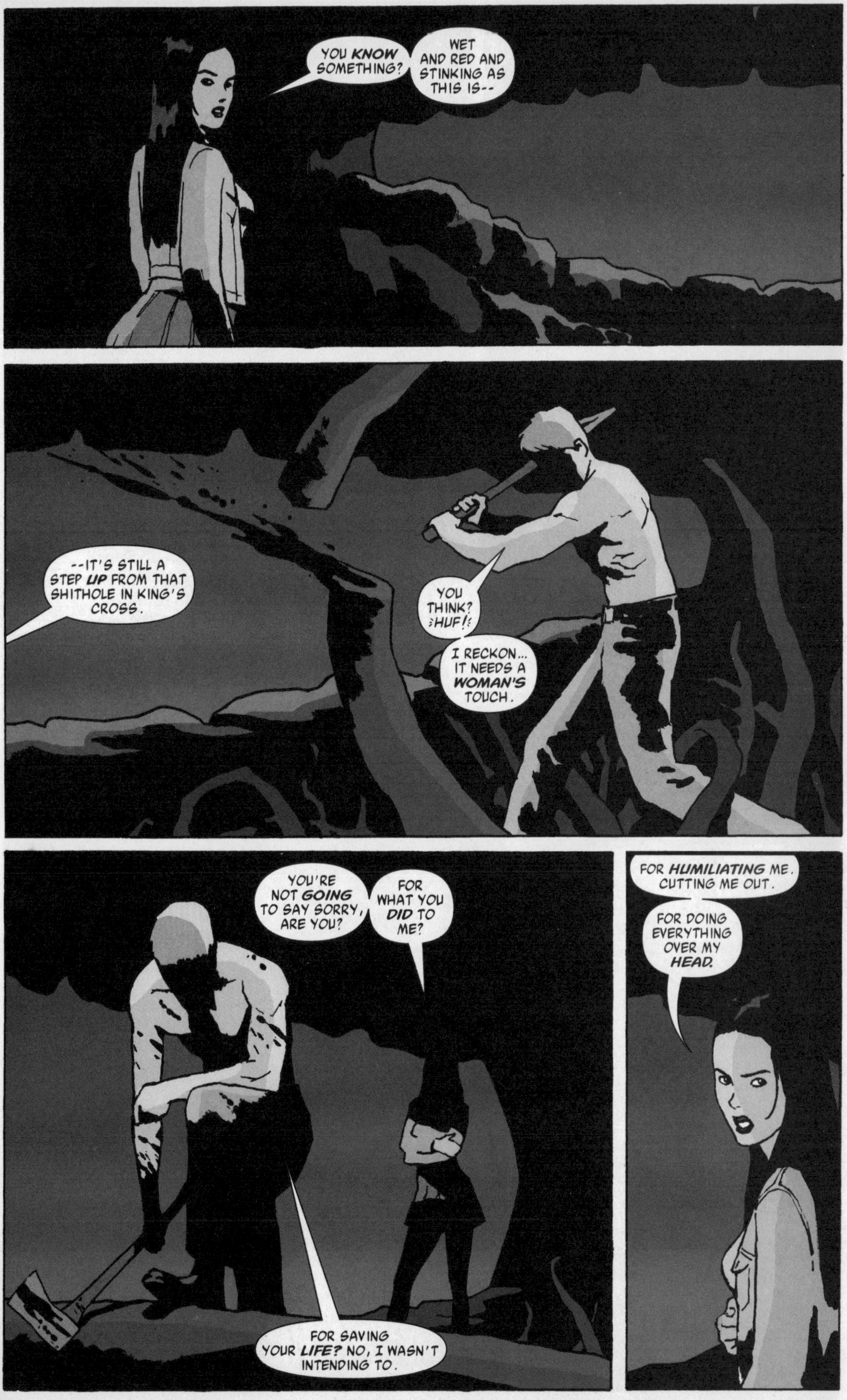
YOU KNOW SOMETHING?
WET AND RED AND STINKING AS THIS IS--
--IT'S STILL A STEP UP FROM THAT SHITHOLE IN KING'S CROSS.
YOU THINK? HUF!
I RECKON... IT NEEDS A WOMAN'S TOUCH.
YOU'RE NOT GOING TO SAY SORRY, ARE YOU?
FOR WHAT YOU DID TO ME?
FOR SAVING YOUR LIFE? NO, I WASN'T INTENDING TO.
FOR HUMILIATING ME. CUTTING ME OUT.
FOR DOING EVERYTHING OVER MY HEAD.

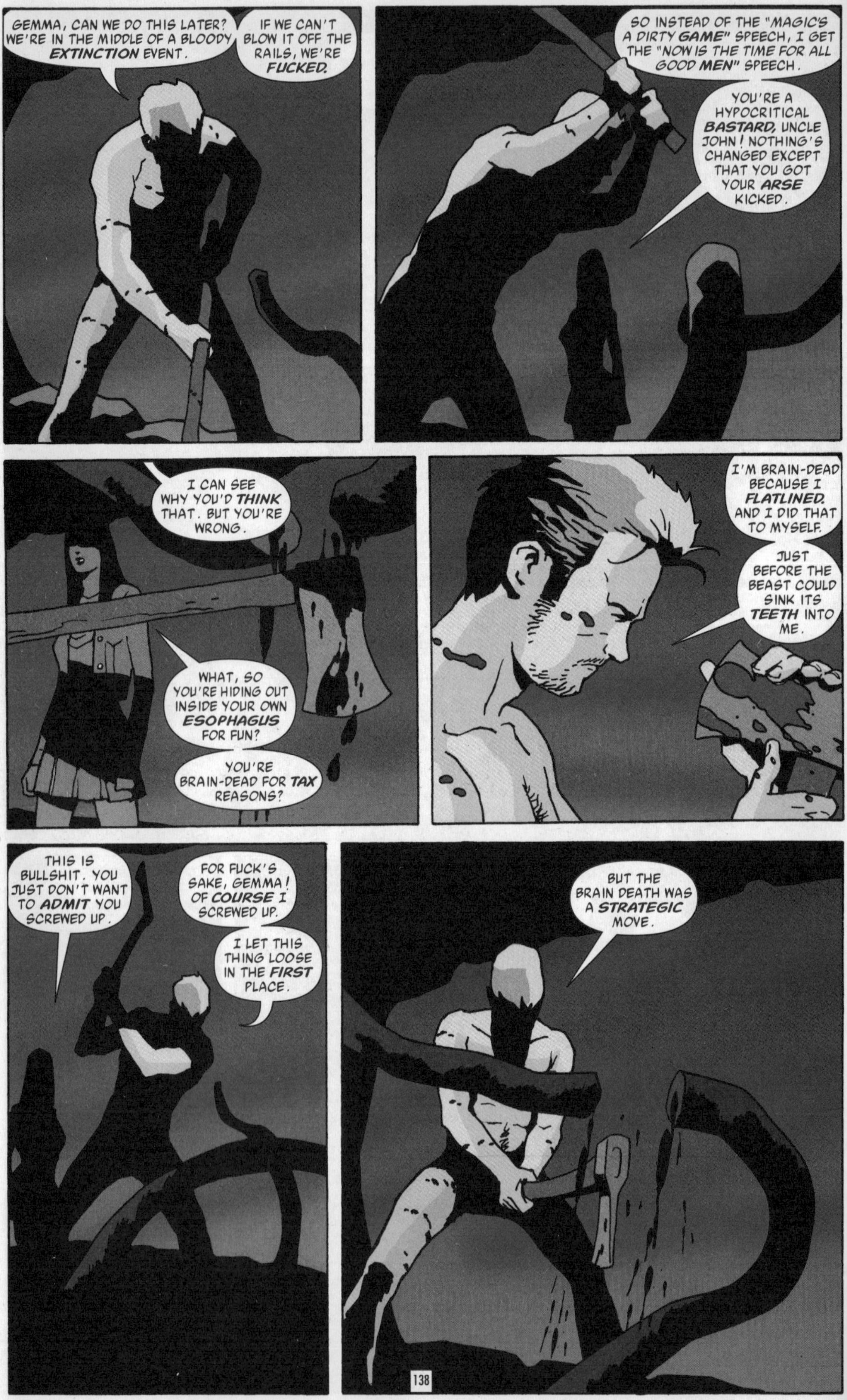
GEMMA, CAN WE DO THIS LATER? WE'RE IN THE MIDDLE OF A BLOODY EXTINCTION EVENT.
IF WE CAN'T BLOW IT OFF THE RAILS, WE'RE FUCKED.
SO INSTEAD OF THE "MAGIC'S A DIRTY GAME" SPEECH, I GET THE "NOW IS THE TIME FOR ALL GOOD MEN" SPEECH.
YOU'RE A HYPOCRITICAL BASTARD, UNCLE JOHN! NOTHING'S CHANGED EXCEPT THAT YOU GOT YOUR ARSE KICKED.
I CAN SEE WHY YOU'D THINK THAT. BUT YOU'RE WRONG.
WHAT, SO YOU'RE HIDING OUT INSIDE YOUR OWN ESOPHAGUS FOR FUN?
YOU'RE BRAIN-DEAD FOR TAX REASONS?
I'M BRAIN-DEAD BECAUSE I FLATLINED. AND I DID THAT TO MYSELF.
JUST BEFORE THE BEAST COULD SINK ITS TEETH INTO ME.
THIS IS BULLSHIT. YOU JUST DON'T WANT TO ADMIT YOU SCREWED UP.
FOR FUCK'S SAKE, GEMMA! OF COURSE I SCREWED UP.
I LET THIS THING LOOSE IN THE FIRST PLACE.
BUT THE BRAIN DEATH WAS A STRATEGIC MOVE.

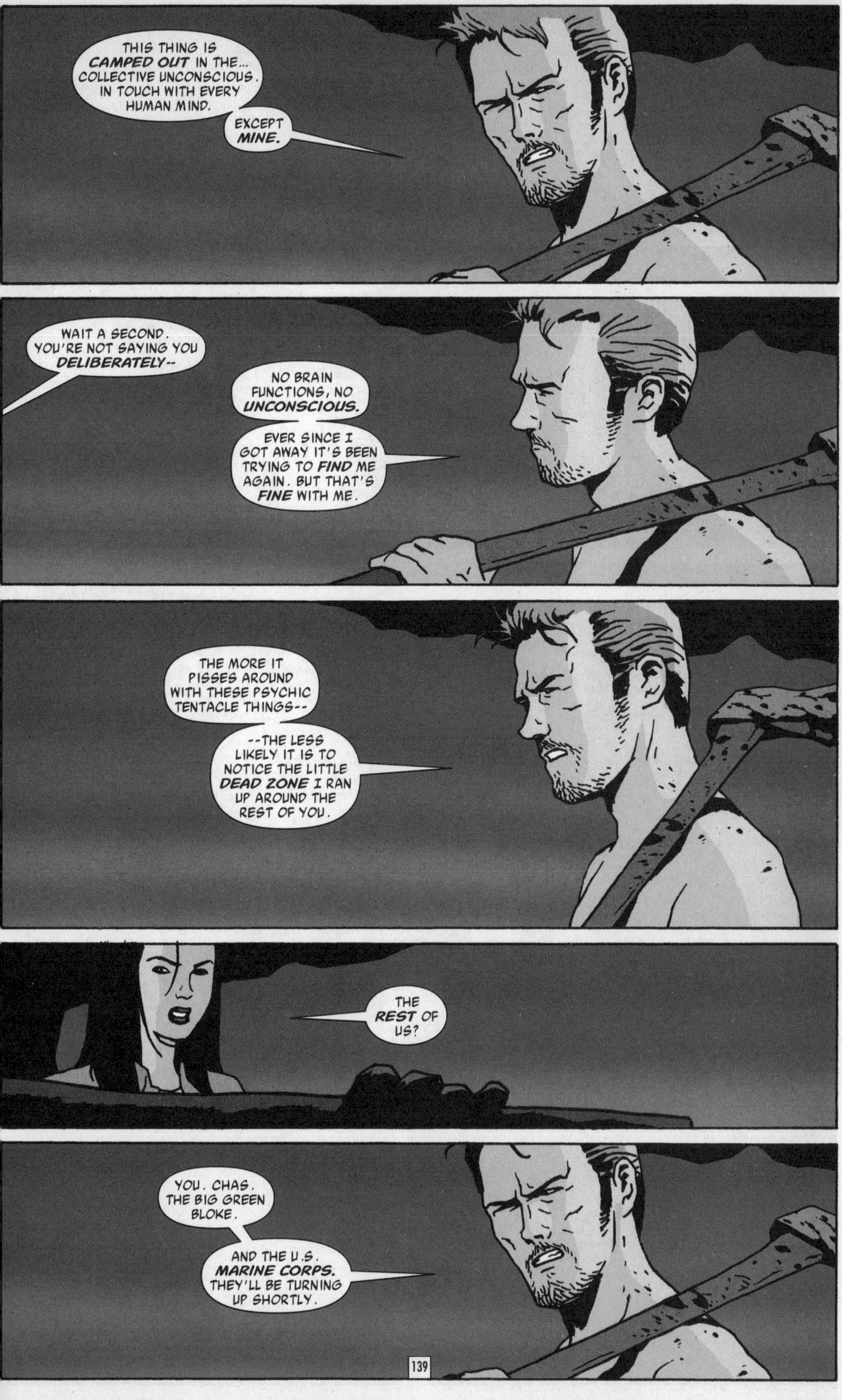
THIS THING IS CAMPED OUT IN THE... COLLECTIVE UNCONSCIOUS. IN TOUCH WITH EVERY HUMAN MIND.
EXCEPT MINE.
WAIT A SECOND. YOU'RE NOT SAYING YOU DELIBERATELY--
NO BRAIN FUNCTIONS, NO UNCONSCIOUS.
EVER SINCE I GOT AWAY IT'S BEEN TRYING TO FIND ME AGAIN. BUT THAT'S FINE WITH ME.
THE MORE IT PISSES AROUND WITH THESE PSYCHIC TENTACLE THINGS--
--THE LESS LIKELY IT IS TO NOTICE THE LITTLE DEAD ZONE I RAN UP AROUND THE REST OF YOU.
THE REST OF US?
YOU. CHAS. THE BIG GREEN BLOKE.
AND THE U.S. MARINE CORPS. THEY'LL BE TURNING UP SHORTLY.

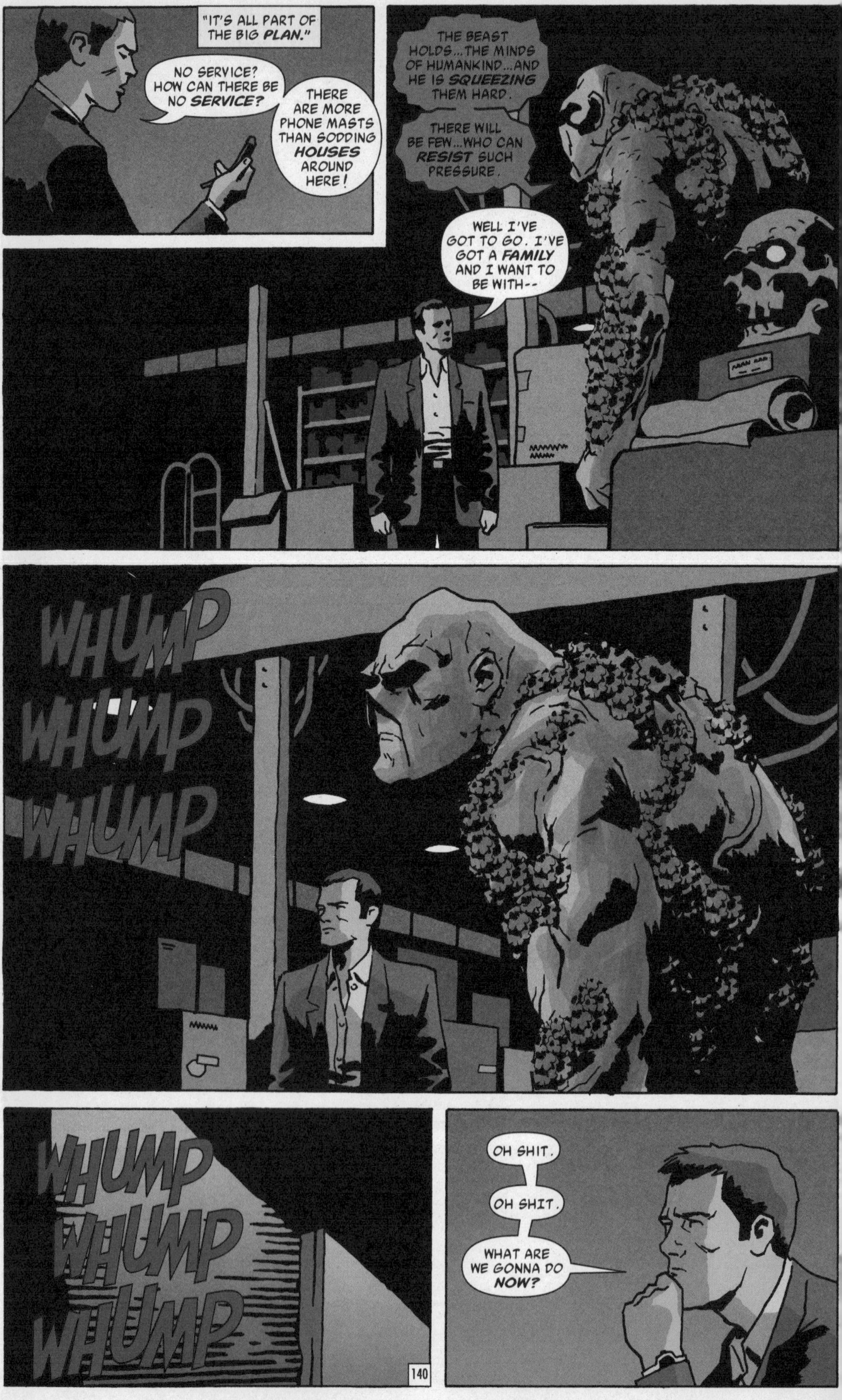
"IT'S ALL PART OF THE BIG PLAN."
NO SERVICE? HOW CAN THERE BE NO SERVICE?
THERE ARE MORE PHONE MASTS THAN SODDING HOUSES AROUND HERE!
THE BEAST HOLDS...THE MINDS OF HUMANKIND...AND HE IS SQUEEZING THEM HARD.
THERE WILL BE FEW...WHO CAN RESIST SUCH PRESSURE.
WELL I'VE GOT TO GO. I'VE GOT A FAMILY AND I WANT TO BE WITH--
WHUMP
WHUMP
WHUMP
WHUMP
WHUMP
WHUMP
OH SHIT.
OH SHIT.
WHAT ARE WE GONNA DO NOW?

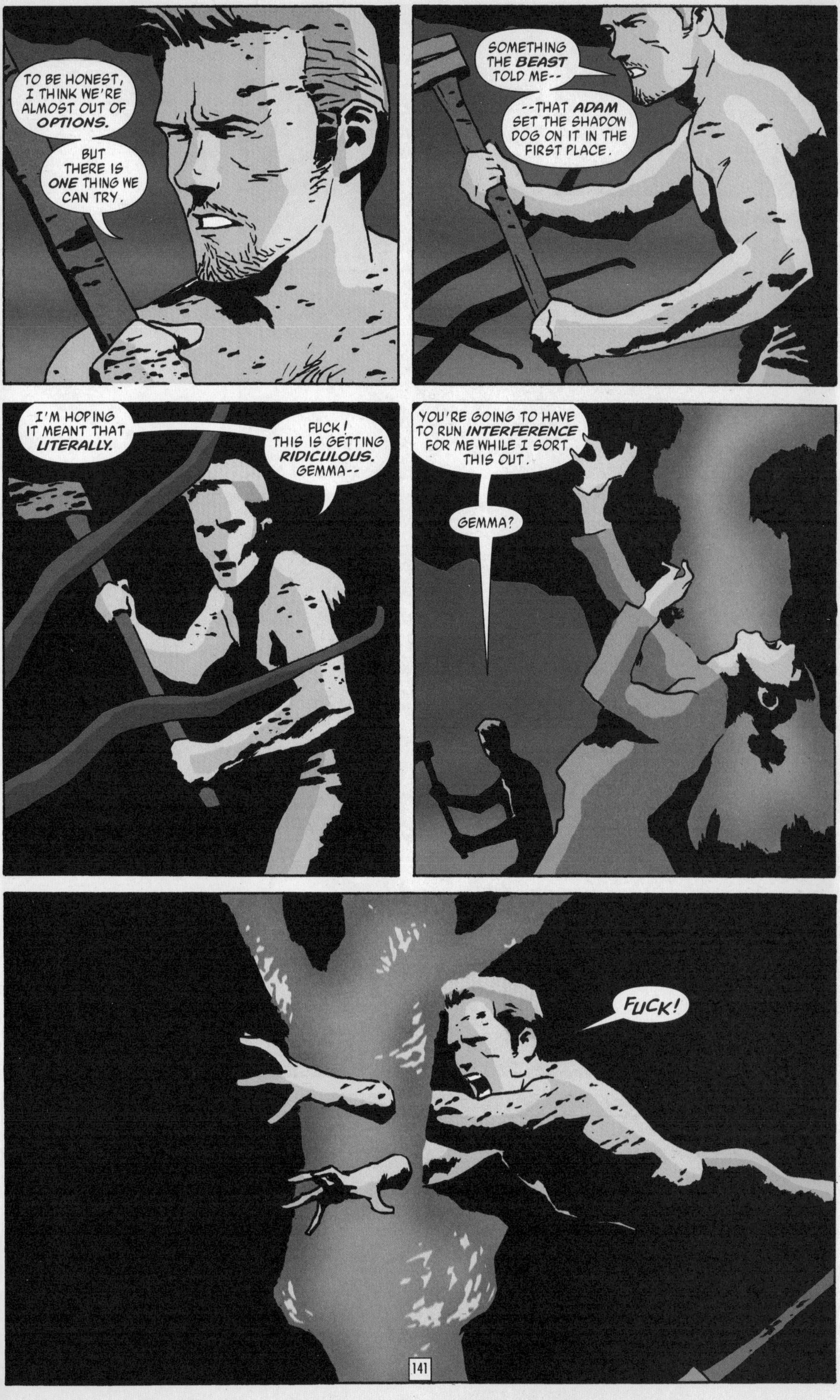
TO BE HONEST, I THINK WE'RE ALMOST OUT OF OPTIONS.
BUT THERE IS ONE THING WE CAN TRY.
SOMETHING THE BEAST TOLD ME--
--THAT ADAM SET THE SHADOW DOG ON IT IN THE FIRST PLACE.
I'M HOPING IT MEANT THAT LITERALLY.
FUCK! THIS IS GETTING RIDICULOUS. GEMMA--
YOU'RE GOING TO HAVE TO RUN INTERFERENCE FOR ME WHILE I SORT THIS OUT.
GEMMA?
FUCK!

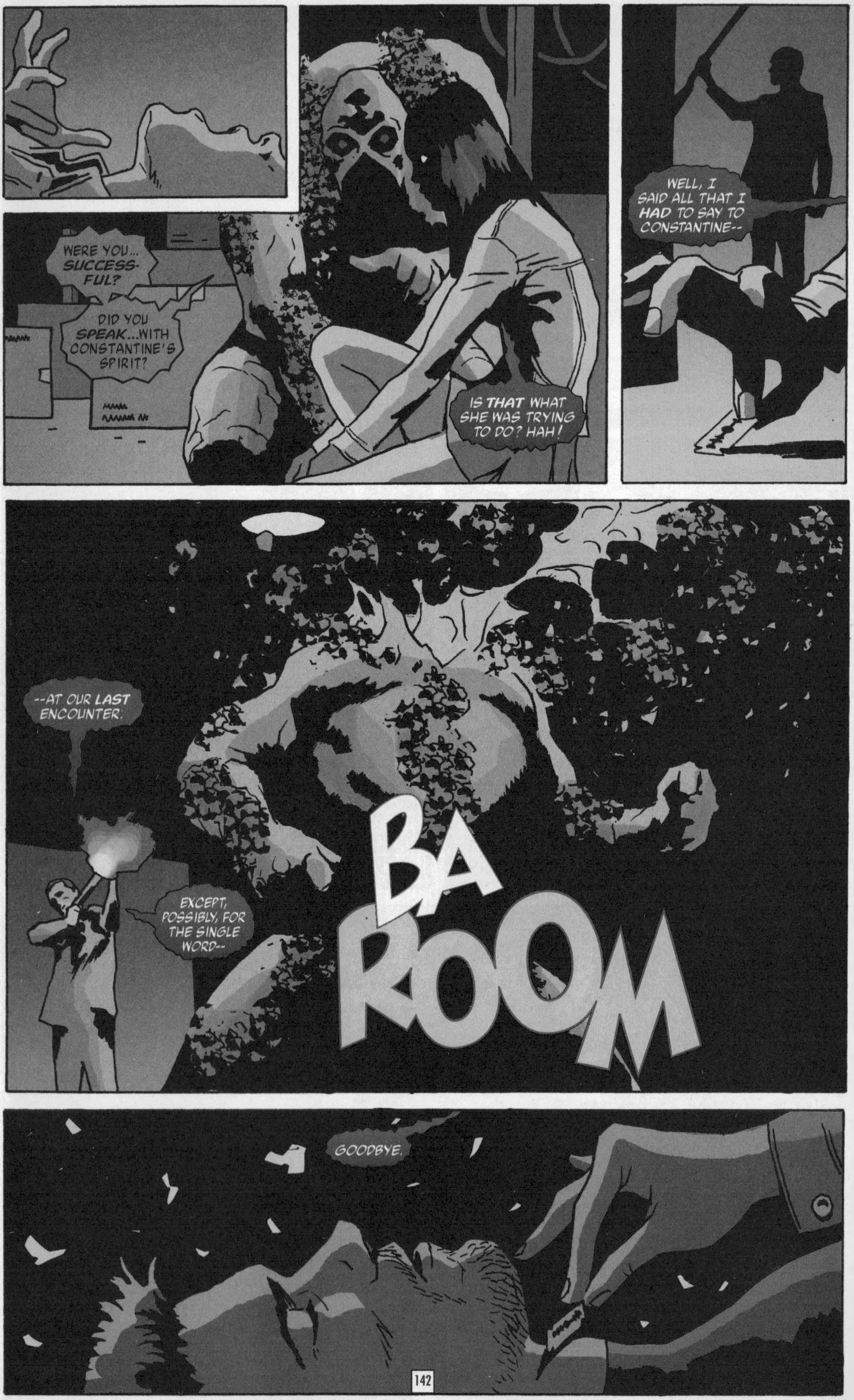
WERE YOU... SUCCESS-FUL?
DID YOU SPEAK...WITH CONSTANTINE'S SPIRIT?
IS THAT WHAT SHE WAS TRYING TO DO? HAH!
WELL, I SAID ALL THAT I HAD TO SAY TO CONSTANTINE--
--AT OUR LAST ENCOUNTER.
EXCEPT, POSSIBLY, FOR THE SINGLE WORD--
BA ROOM
GOODBYE.

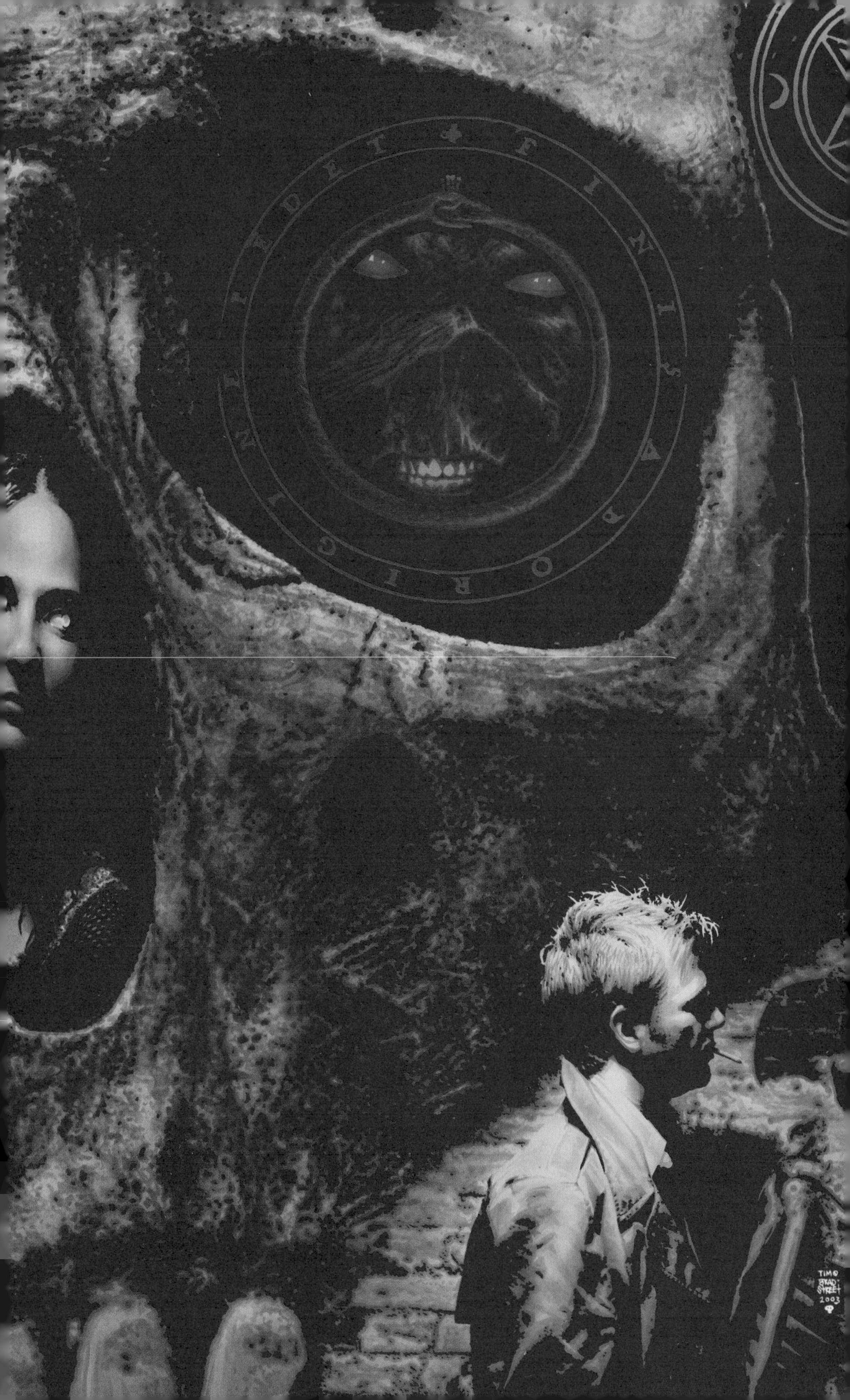
FINIS AB ORIGINE PEDET
TIMO BRADSTREET 2003

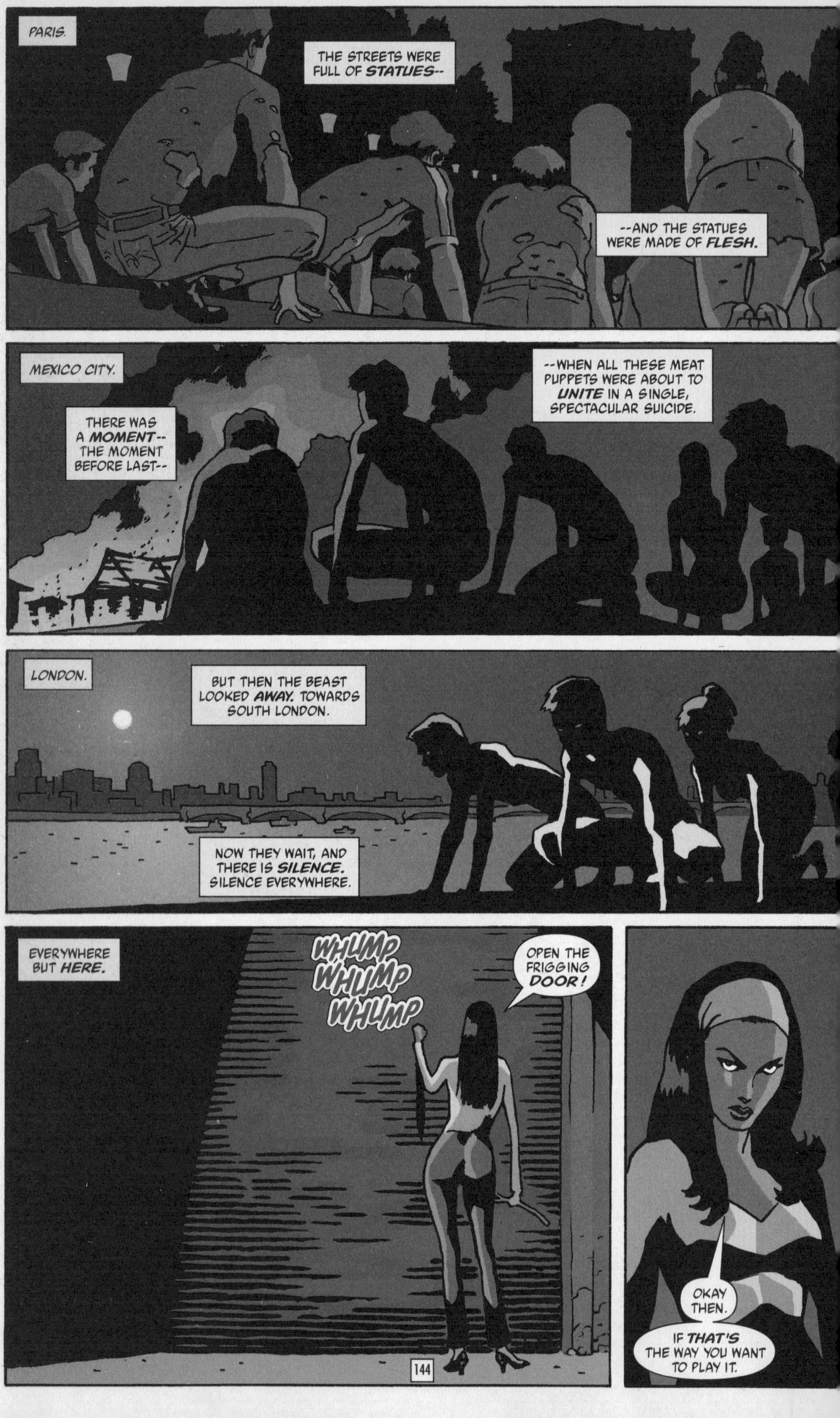
PARIS.
THE STREETS WERE FULL OF STATUES--
--AND THE STATUES WERE MADE OF FLESH.
MEXICO CITY.
THERE WAS A MOMENT-- THE MOMENT BEFORE LAST--
--WHEN ALL THESE MEAT PUPPETS WERE ABOUT TO UNITE IN A SINGLE, SPECTACULAR SUICIDE.
LONDON.
BUT THEN THE BEAST LOOKED AWAY. TOWARDS SOUTH LONDON.
NOW THEY WAIT, AND THERE IS SILENCE. SILENCE EVERYWHERE.
EVERYWHERE BUT HERE.
WHUMP WHUMP WHUMP
OPEN THE FRIGGING DOOR!
OKAY THEN.
IF THAT'S THE WAY YOU WANT TO PLAY IT.

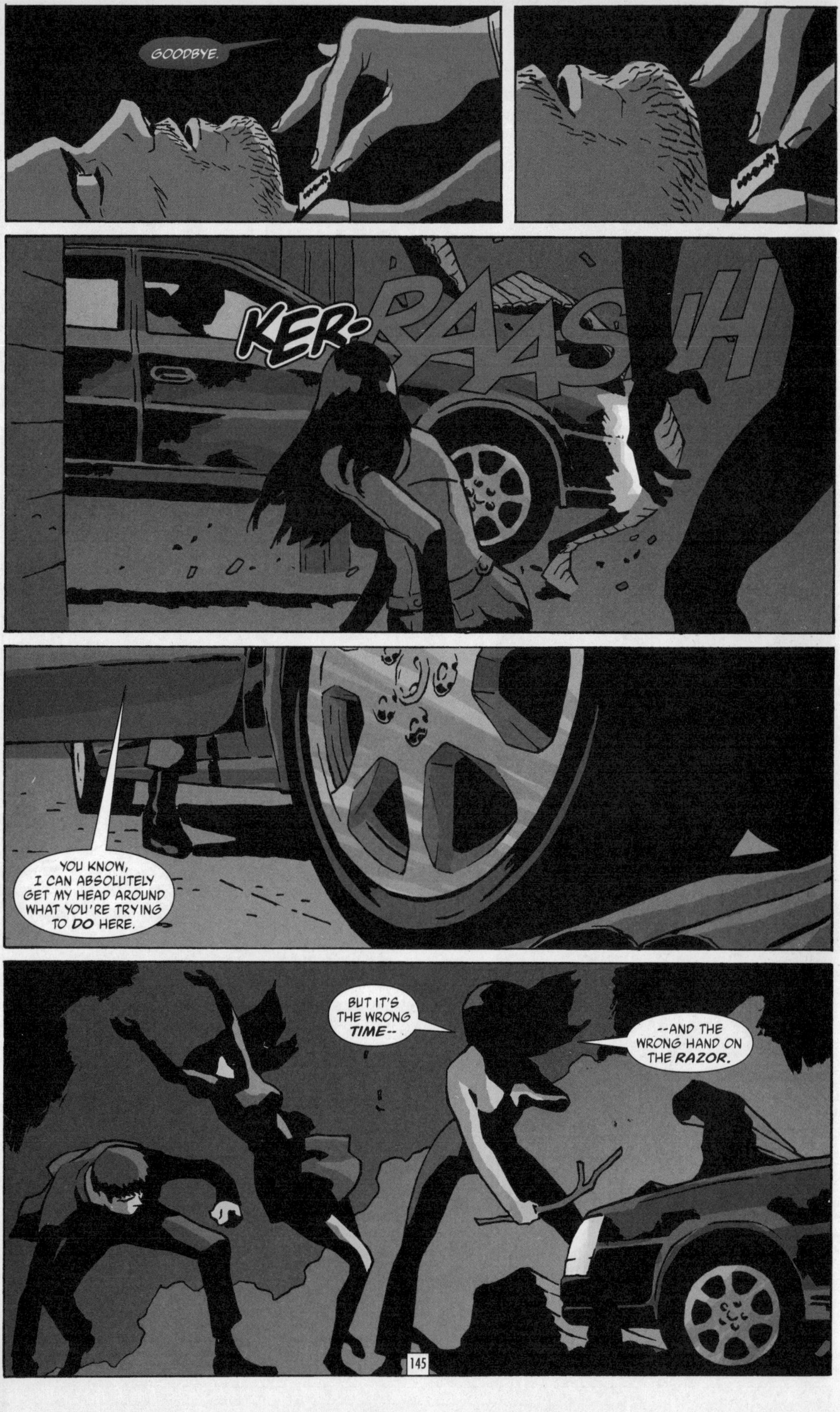
GOODBYE.
KER-RAASHH
YOU KNOW, I CAN ABSOLUTELY GET MY HEAD AROUND WHAT YOU'RE TRYING TO **DO** HERE.
BUT IT'S THE WRONG **TIME**--
--AND THE WRONG HAND ON THE **RAZOR**.

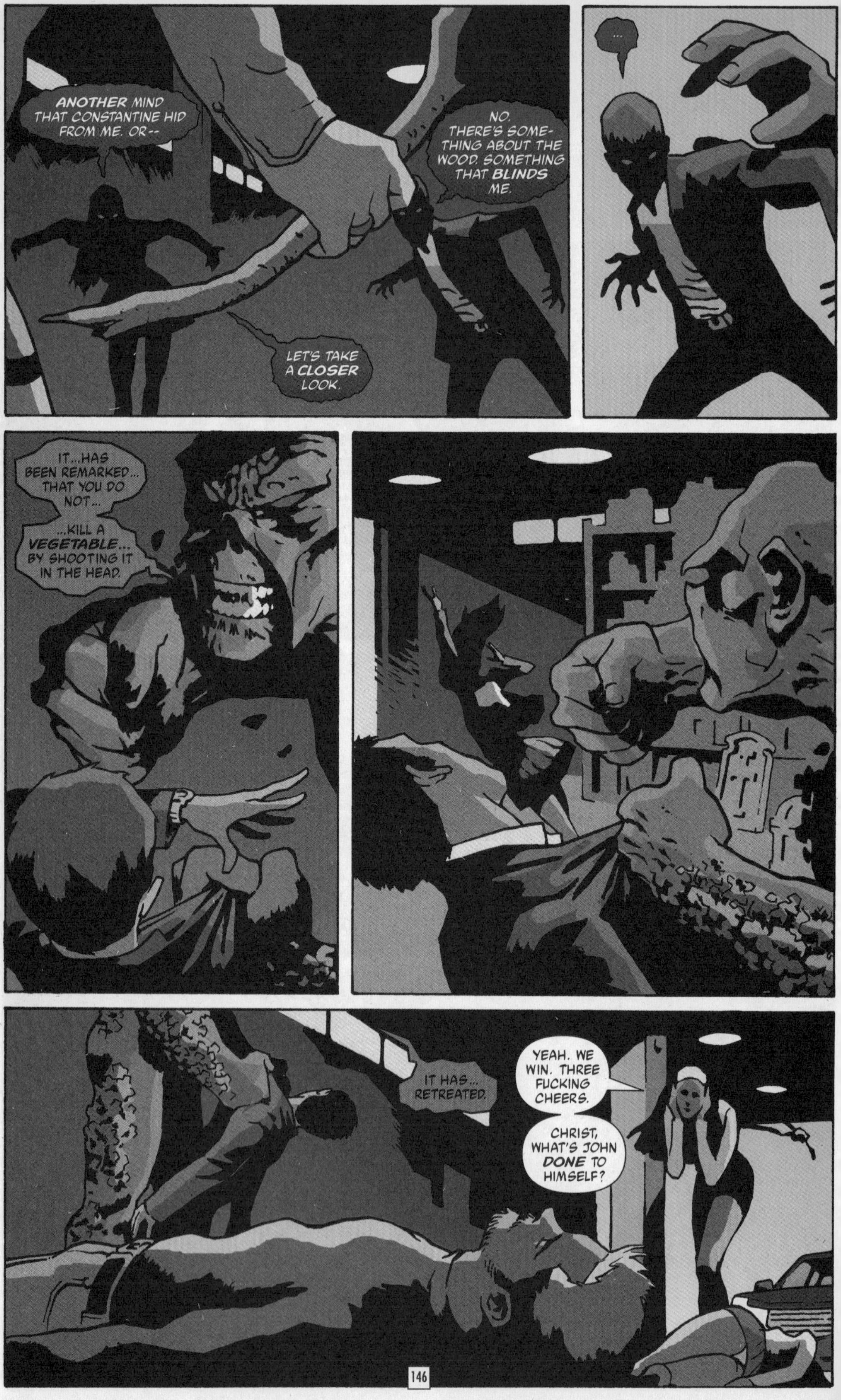

ANOTHER MIND THAT CONSTANTINE HID FROM ME. OR--
NO. THERE'S SOMETHING ABOUT THE WOOD. SOMETHING THAT BLINDS ME.
LET'S TAKE A CLOSER LOOK.
...
IT...HAS BEEN REMARKED... THAT YOU DO NOT...
...KILL A VEGETABLE... BY SHOOTING IT IN THE HEAD.
IT HAS... RETREATED.
YEAH. WE WIN. THREE FUCKING CHEERS.
CHRIST, WHAT'S JOHN DONE TO HIMSELF?

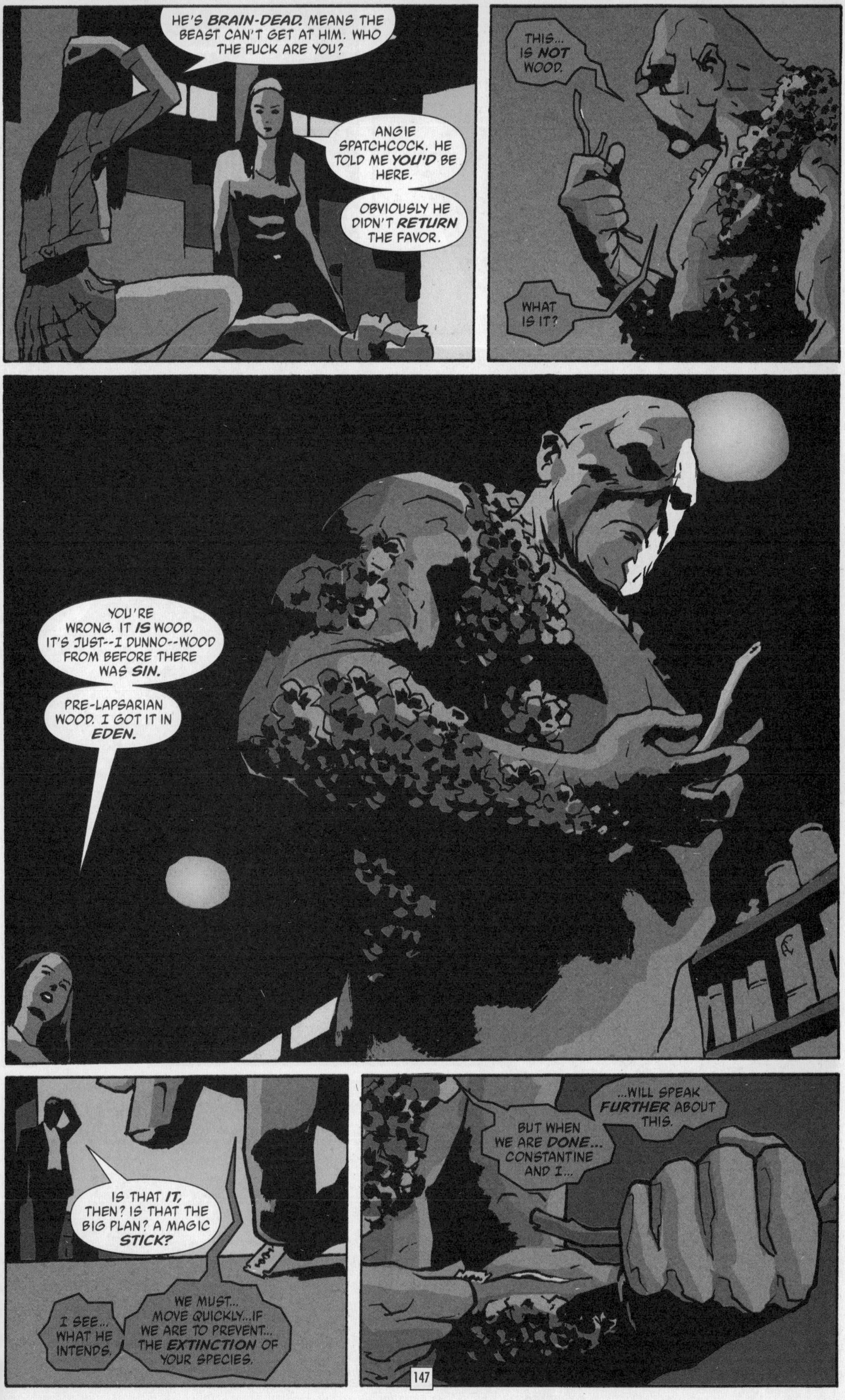
HE'S BRAIN-DEAD. MEANS THE BEAST CAN'T GET AT HIM. WHO THE FUCK ARE YOU?
ANGIE SPATCHCOCK. HE TOLD ME YOU'D BE HERE.
OBVIOUSLY HE DIDN'T RETURN THE FAVOR.
THIS... IS NOT WOOD.
WHAT IS IT?
YOU'RE WRONG. IT IS WOOD. IT'S JUST--I DUNNO--WOOD FROM BEFORE THERE WAS SIN.
PRE-LAPSARIAN WOOD. I GOT IT IN EDEN.
IS THAT IT, THEN? IS THAT THE BIG PLAN? A MAGIC STICK?
I SEE... WHAT HE INTENDS.
WE MUST... MOVE QUICKLY...IF WE ARE TO PREVENT... THE EXTINCTION OF YOUR SPECIES.
BUT WHEN WE ARE DONE... CONSTANTINE AND I...
...WILL SPEAK FURTHER ABOUT THIS.

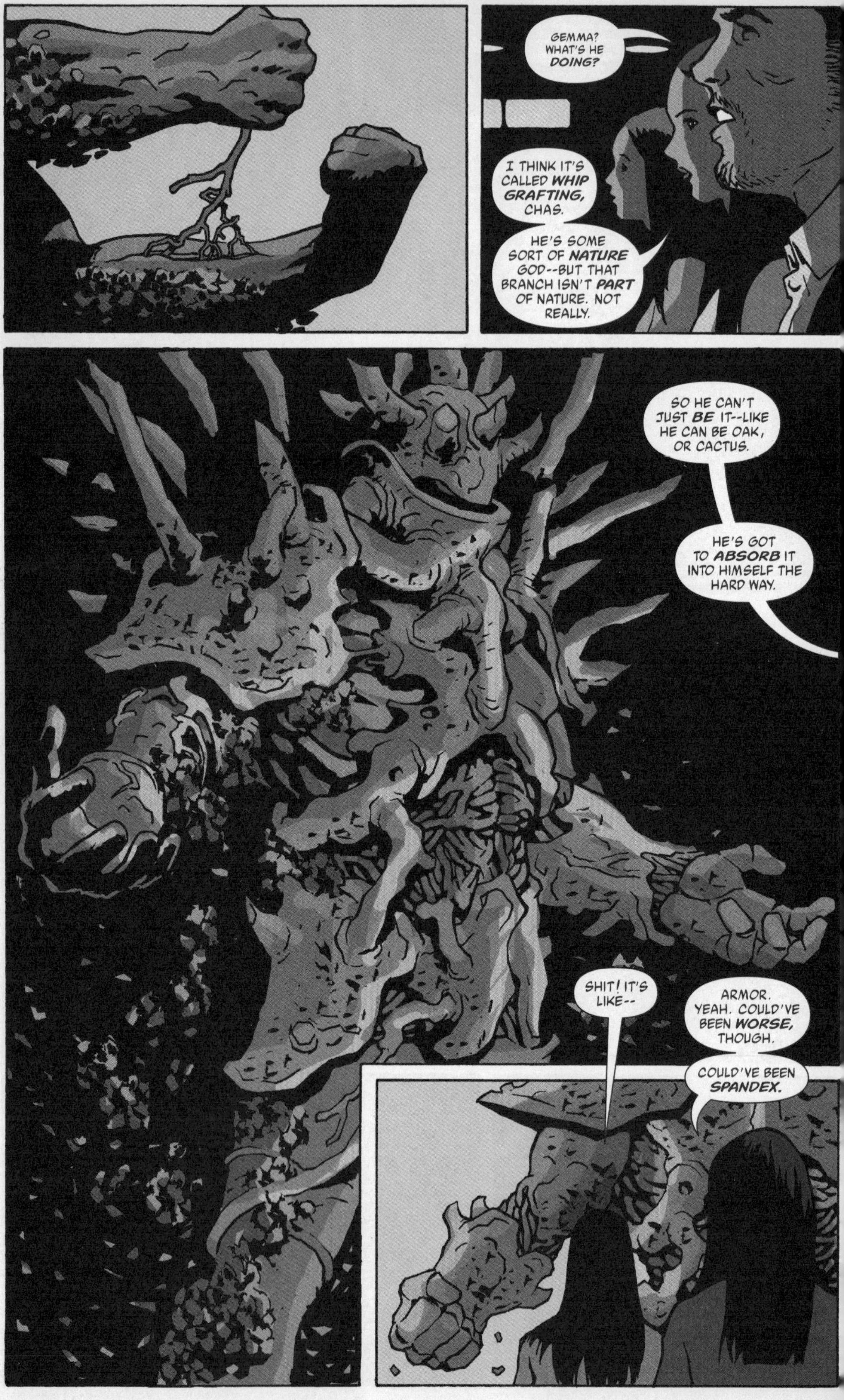
GEMMA? WHAT'S HE DOING?
I THINK IT'S CALLED WHIP GRAFTING, CHAS.
HE'S SOME SORT OF NATURE GOD--BUT THAT BRANCH ISN'T PART OF NATURE. NOT REALLY.
SO HE CAN'T JUST BE IT--LIKE HE CAN BE OAK, OR CACTUS.
HE'S GOT TO ABSORB IT INTO HIMSELF THE HARD WAY.
SHIT! IT'S LIKE--
ARMOR. YEAH. COULD'VE BEEN WORSE, THOUGH.
COULD'VE BEEN SPANDEX.

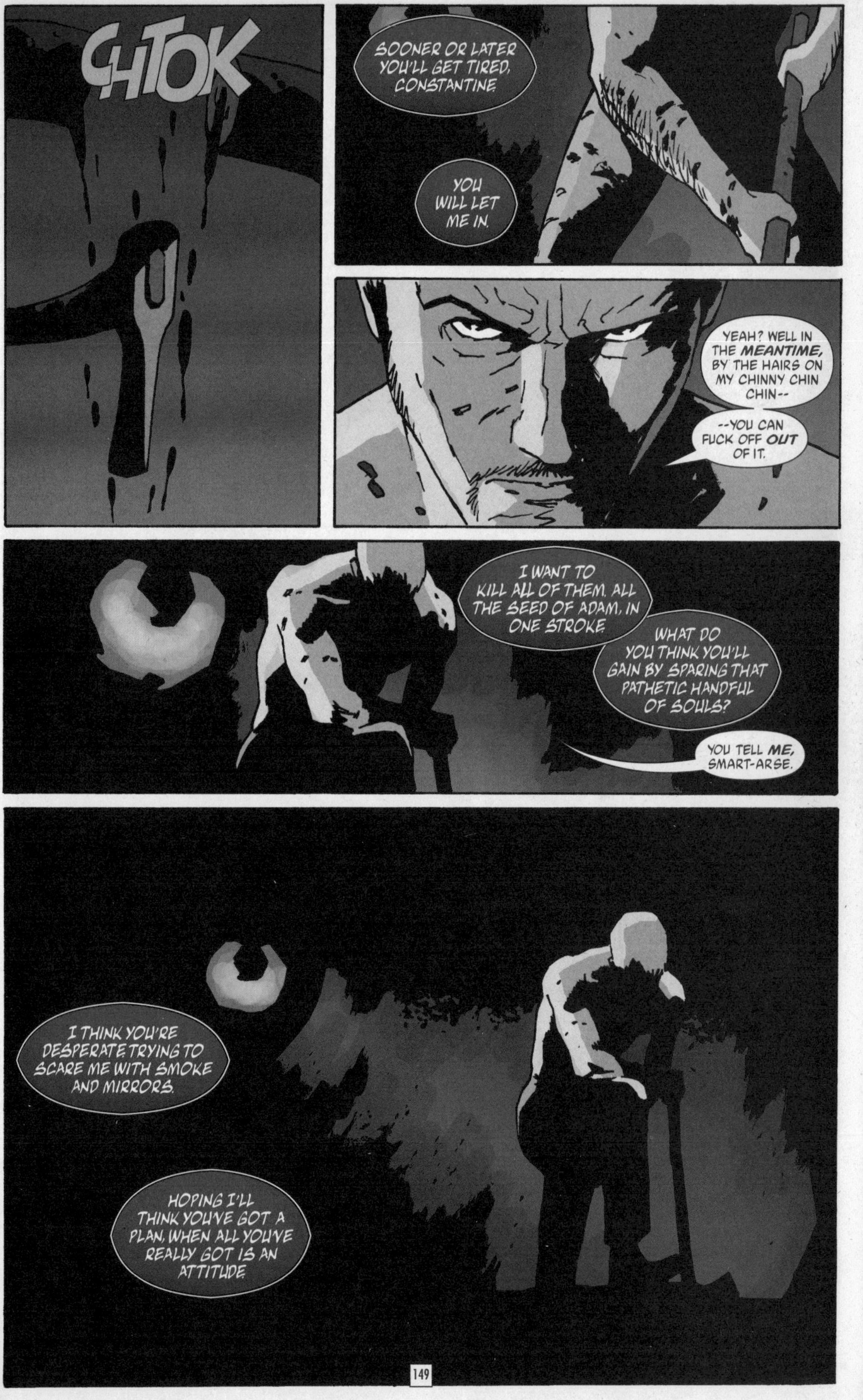
CHTOK
SOONER OR LATER YOU'LL GET TIRED, CONSTANTINE.
YOU WILL LET ME IN.
YEAH? WELL IN THE **MEANTIME,** BY THE HAIRS ON MY CHINNY CHIN CHIN--
--YOU CAN FUCK OFF **OUT** OF IT.
I WANT TO KILL ALL OF THEM. ALL THE SEED OF ADAM, IN ONE STROKE.
WHAT DO YOU THINK YOU'LL GAIN BY SPARING THAT PATHETIC HANDFUL OF SOULS?
YOU TELL **ME,** SMART-ARSE.
I THINK YOU'RE DESPERATE. TRYING TO SCARE ME WITH SMOKE AND MIRRORS.
HOPING I'LL THINK YOU'VE GOT A PLAN, WHEN ALL YOU'VE REALLY GOT IS AN ATTITUDE.

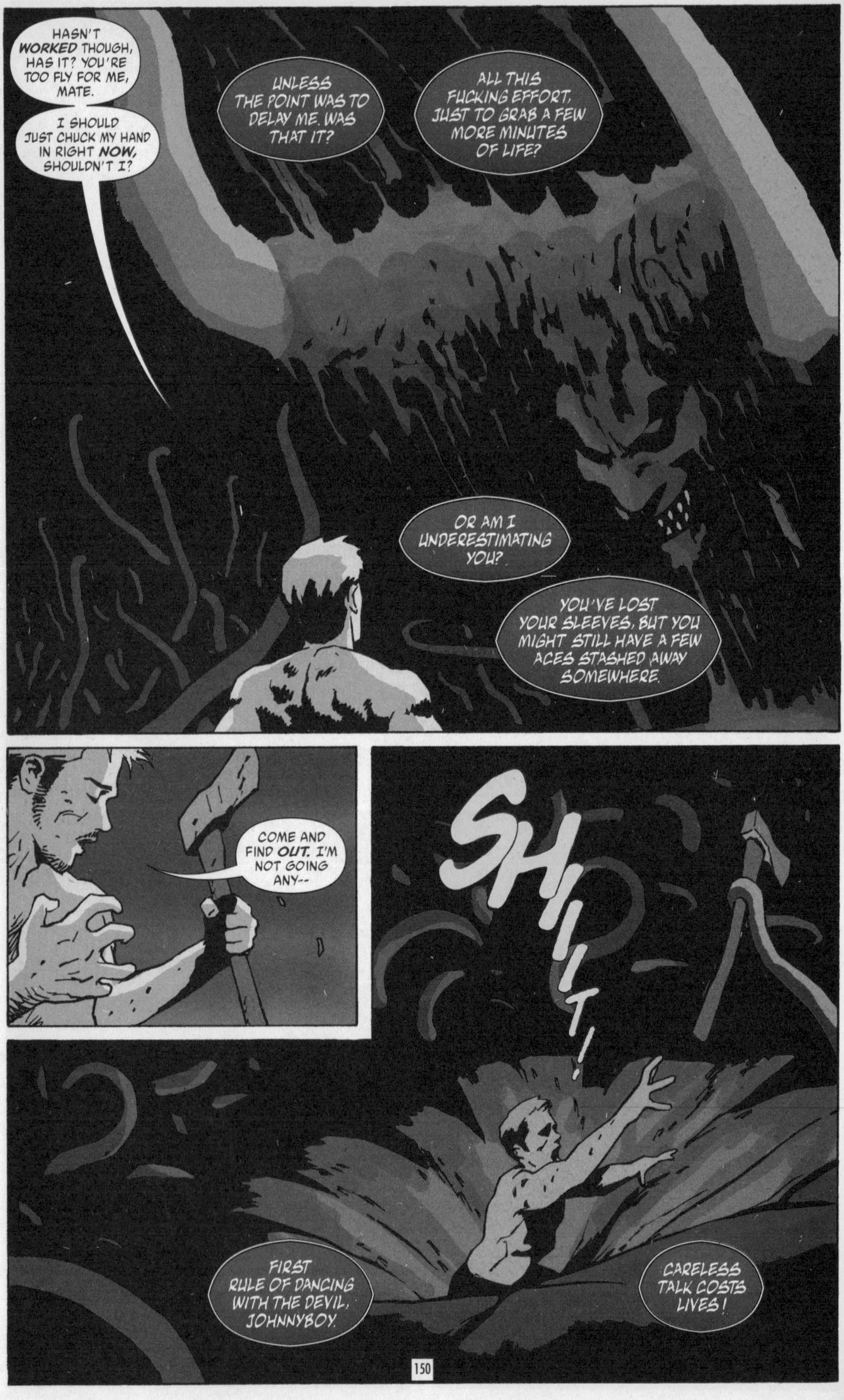
HASN'T WORKED THOUGH, HAS IT? YOU'RE TOO FLY FOR ME, MATE.
I SHOULD JUST CHUCK MY HAND IN RIGHT NOW, SHOULDN'T I?
UNLESS THE POINT WAS TO DELAY ME. WAS THAT IT?
ALL THIS FUCKING EFFORT, JUST TO GRAB A FEW MORE MINUTES OF LIFE?
OR AM I UNDERESTIMATING YOU?
YOU'VE LOST YOUR SLEEVES, BUT YOU MIGHT STILL HAVE A FEW ACES STASHED AWAY SOMEWHERE.
COME AND FIND OUT. I'M NOT GOING ANY--
SHIIIT!
FIRST RULE OF DANCING WITH THE DEVIL, JOHNNYBOY.
CARELESS TALK COSTS LIVES!

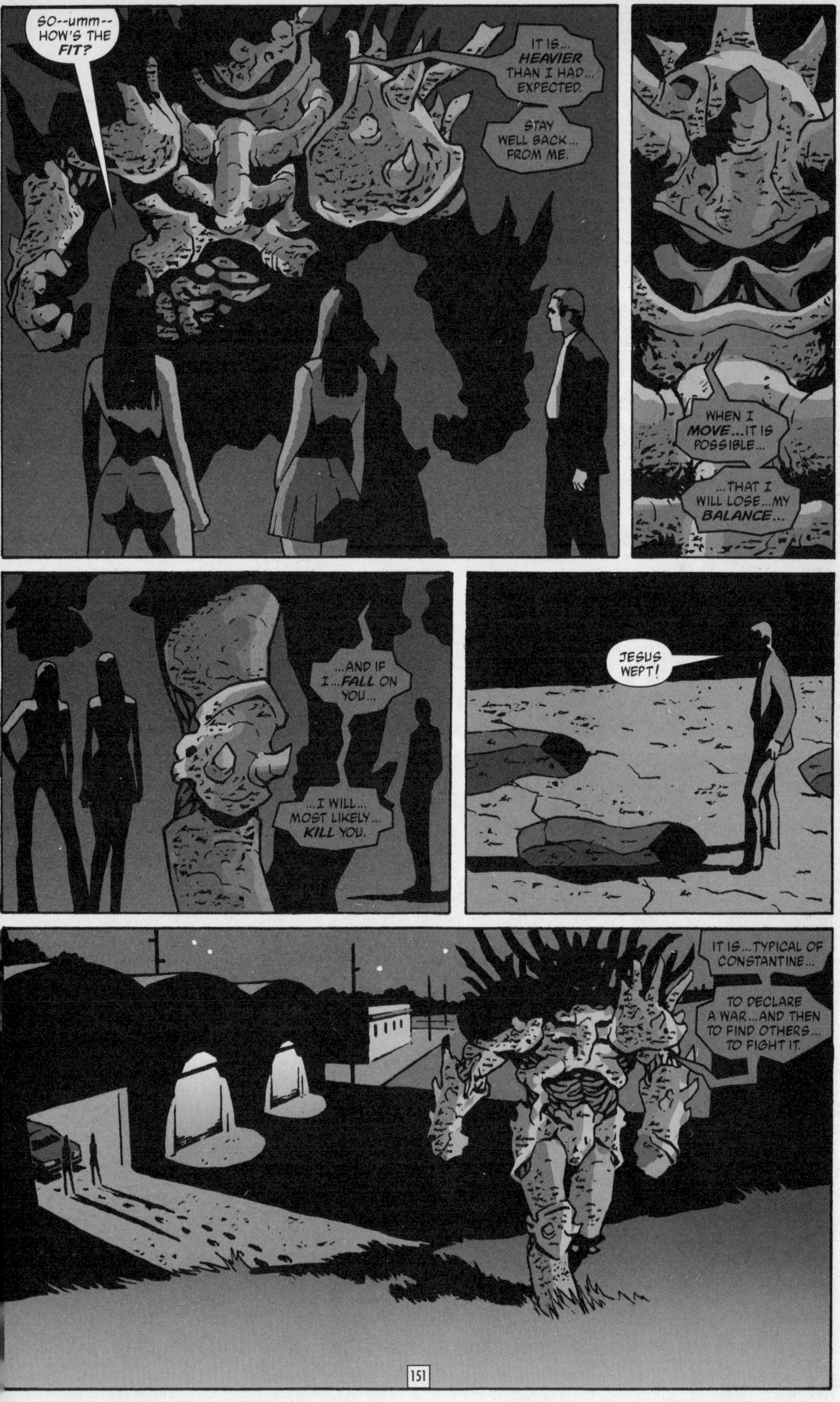
SO--umm--HOW'S THE FIT?
IT IS... HEAVIER THAN I HAD... EXPECTED.
STAY WELL BACK... FROM ME.
WHEN I MOVE...IT IS POSSIBLE...
...THAT I WILL LOSE...MY BALANCE...
...AND IF I...FALL ON YOU...
...I WILL... MOST LIKELY... KILL YOU.
JESUS WEPT!
IT IS...TYPICAL OF CONSTANTINE...
TO DECLARE A WAR...AND THEN TO FIND OTHERS... TO FIGHT IT.

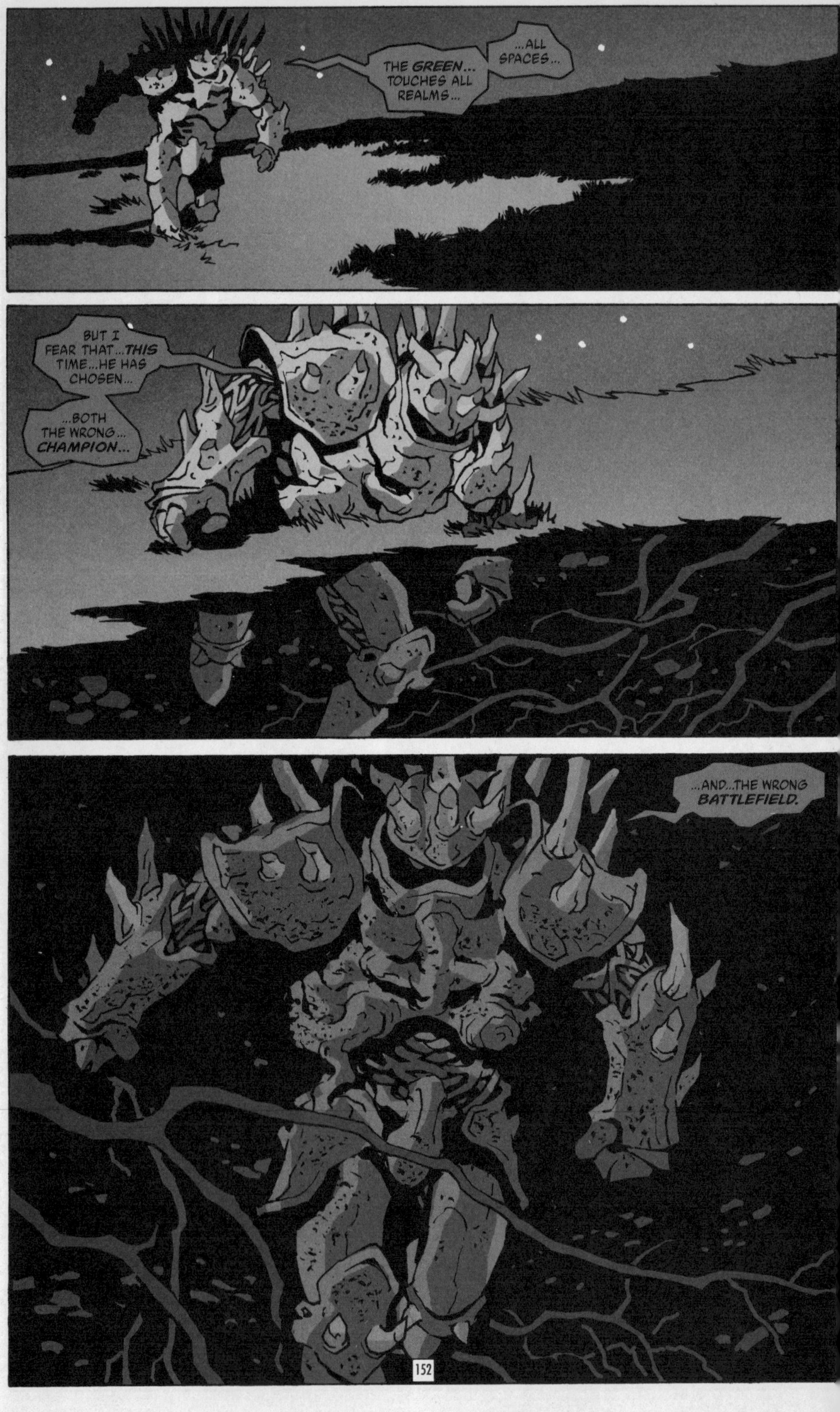
THE GREEN... TOUCHES ALL REALMS...
...ALL SPACES...
BUT I FEAR THAT...THIS TIME...HE HAS CHOSEN...
...BOTH THE WRONG... CHAMPION...
...AND...THE WRONG BATTLEFIELD.

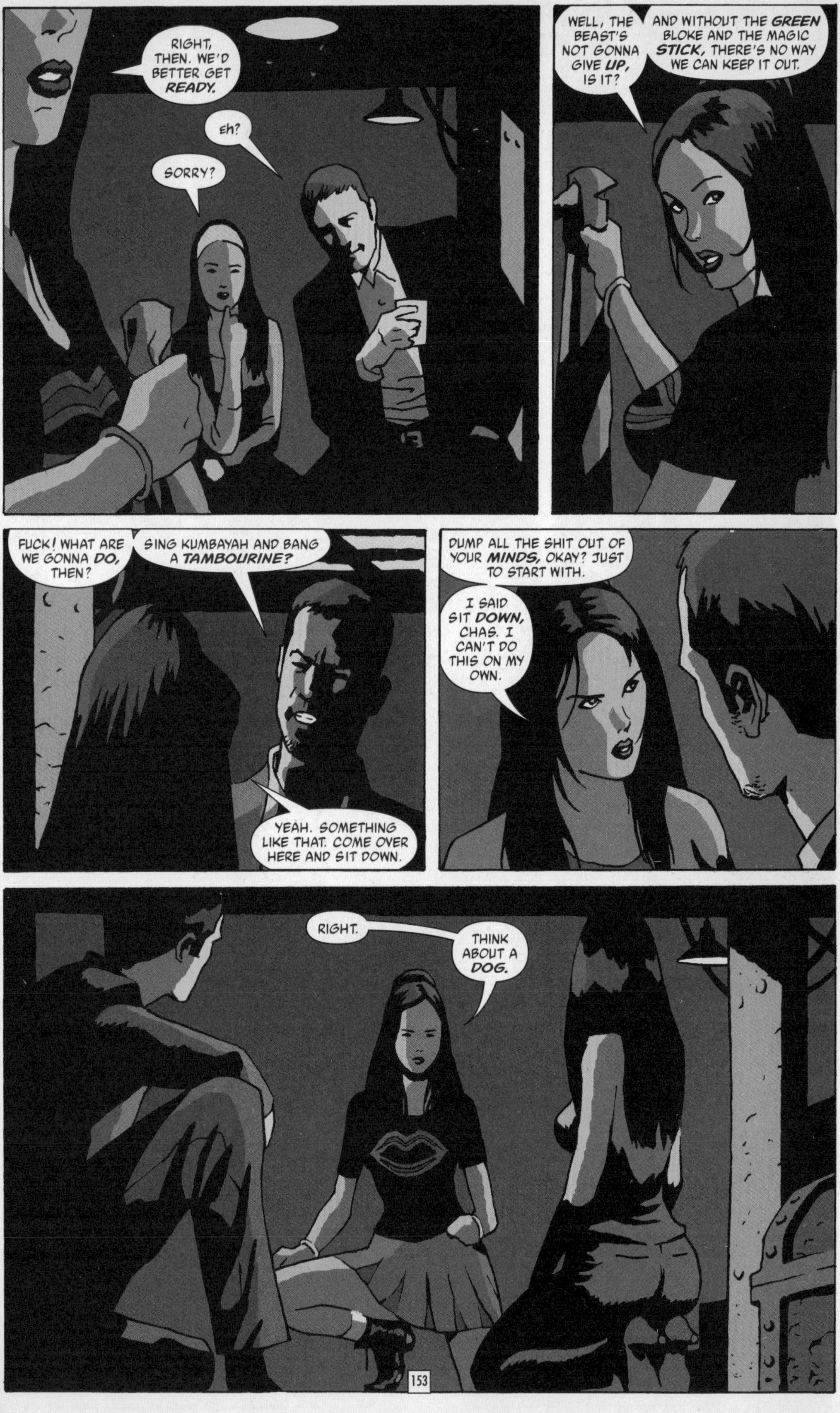
RIGHT, THEN. WE'D BETTER GET READY.
EH?
SORRY?
WELL, THE BEAST'S NOT GONNA GIVE UP, IS IT?
AND WITHOUT THE GREEN BLOKE AND THE MAGIC STICK, THERE'S NO WAY WE CAN KEEP IT OUT.
FUCK! WHAT ARE WE GONNA DO, THEN?
SING KUMBAYAH AND BANG A TAMBOURINE?
YEAH. SOMETHING LIKE THAT. COME OVER HERE AND SIT DOWN.
DUMP ALL THE SHIT OUT OF YOUR MINDS, OKAY? JUST TO START WITH.
I SAID SIT DOWN, CHAS. I CAN'T DO THIS ON MY OWN.
RIGHT.
THINK ABOUT A DOG.

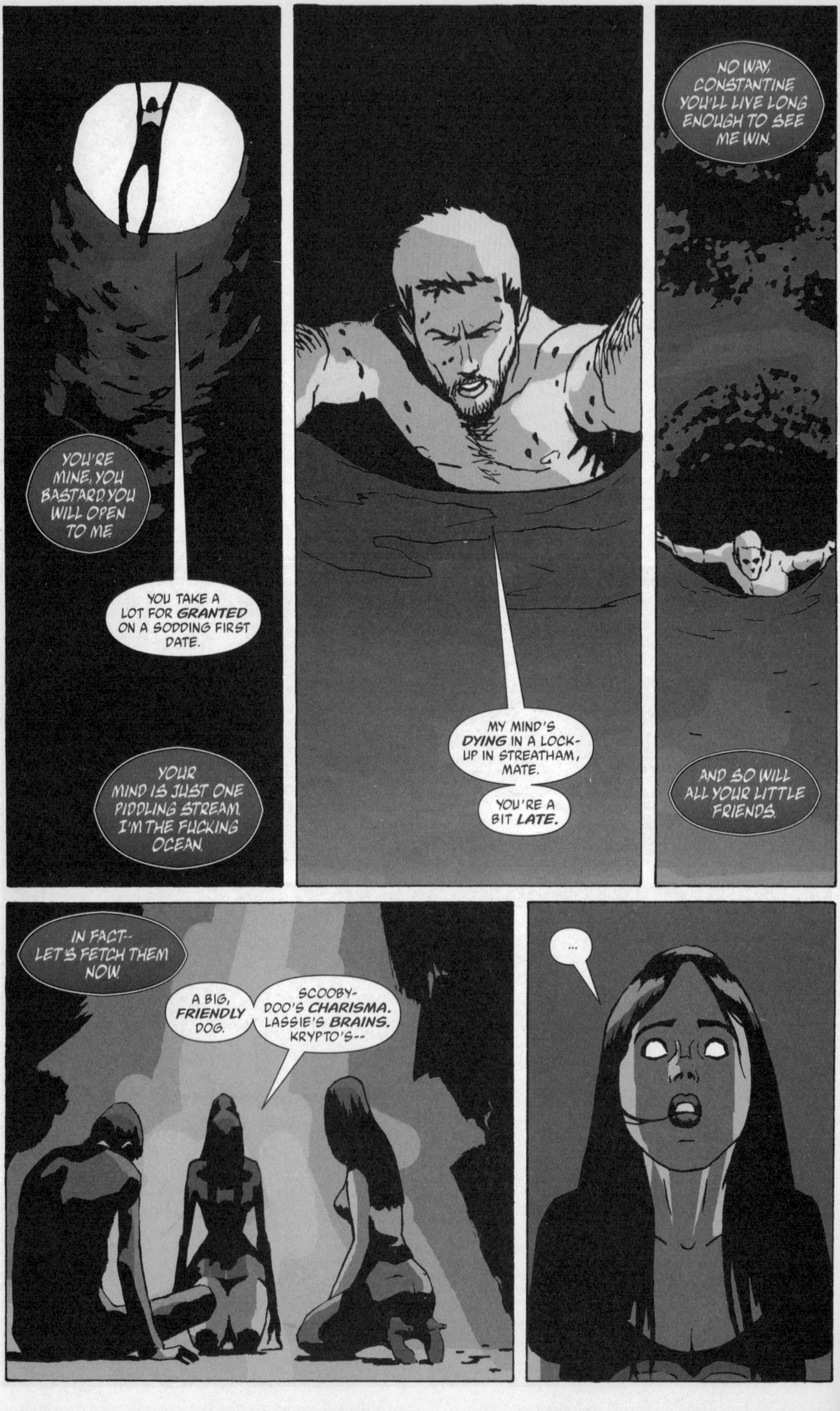

YOU'RE MINE, YOU BASTARD. YOU WILL OPEN TO ME.
YOU TAKE A LOT FOR GRANTED ON A SODDING FIRST DATE.
YOUR MIND IS JUST ONE PIDDLING STREAM. I'M THE FUCKING OCEAN.
MY MIND'S DYING IN A LOCK-UP IN STREATHAM, MATE.
YOU'RE A BIT LATE.
NO WAY, CONSTANTINE. YOU'LL LIVE LONG ENOUGH TO SEE ME WIN.
AND SO WILL ALL YOUR LITTLE FRIENDS.
IN FACT-- LET'S FETCH THEM NOW.
A BIG, FRIENDLY DOG.
SCOOBY-DOO'S CHARISMA. LASSIE'S BRAINS. KRYPTO'S--
...

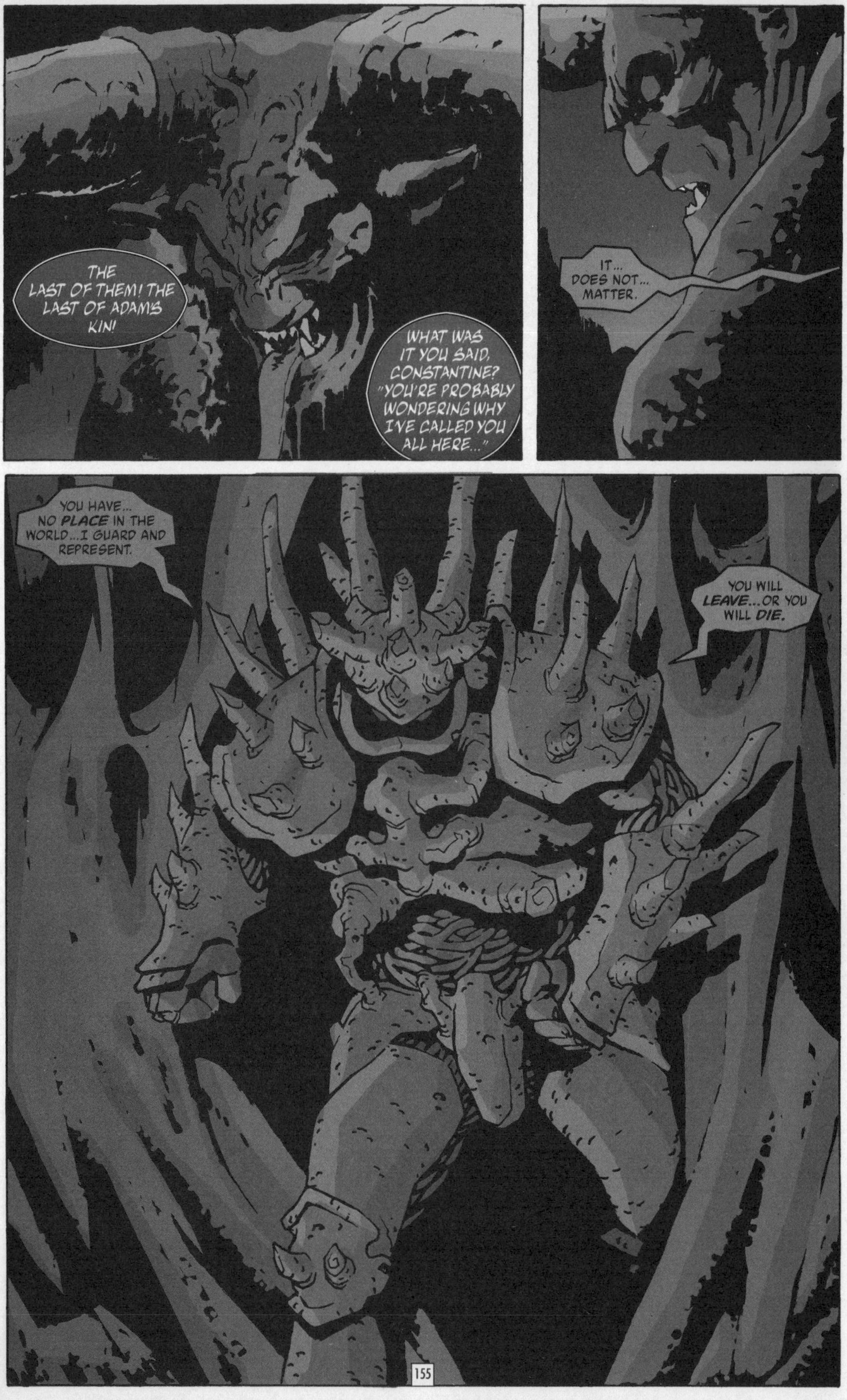
THE LAST OF THEM! THE LAST OF ADAM'S KIN!
WHAT WAS IT YOU SAID, CONSTANTINE? "YOU'RE PROBABLY WONDERING WHY I'VE CALLED YOU ALL HERE..."
IT... DOES NOT... MATTER.
YOU HAVE... NO PLACE IN THE WORLD...I GUARD AND REPRESENT.
YOU WILL LEAVE...OR YOU WILL DIE.

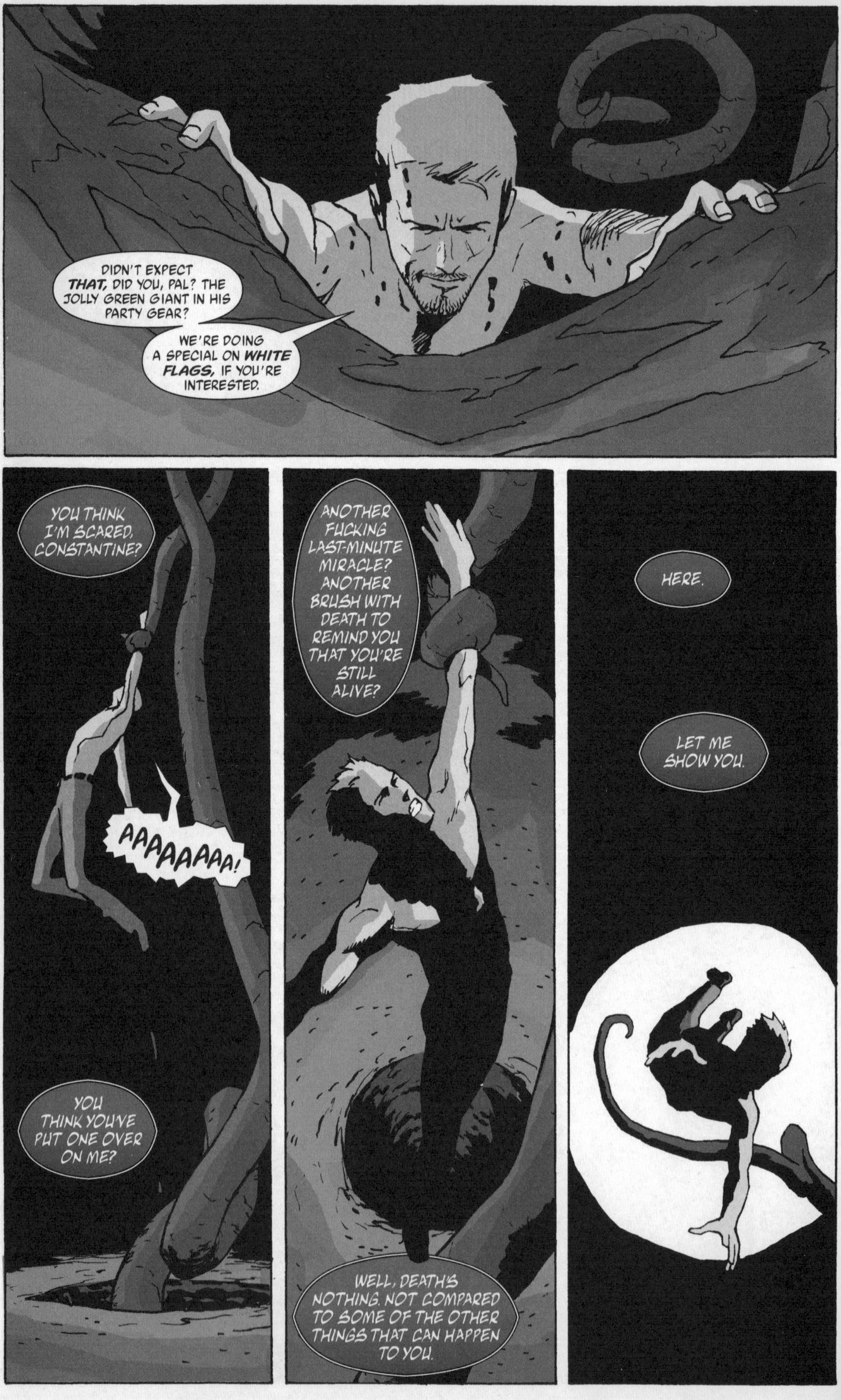
DIDN'T EXPECT THAT, DID YOU, PAL? THE JOLLY GREEN GIANT IN HIS PARTY GEAR?
WE'RE DOING A SPECIAL ON WHITE FLAGS, IF YOU'RE INTERESTED.
YOU THINK I'M SCARED, CONSTANTINE?
AAAAAAAA!
YOU THINK YOU'VE PUT ONE OVER ON ME?
ANOTHER FUCKING LAST-MINUTE MIRACLE? ANOTHER BRUSH WITH DEATH TO REMIND YOU THAT YOU'RE STILL ALIVE?
WELL, DEATH'S NOTHING. NOT COMPARED TO SOME OF THE OTHER THINGS THAT CAN HAPPEN TO YOU.
HERE.
LET ME SHOW YOU.

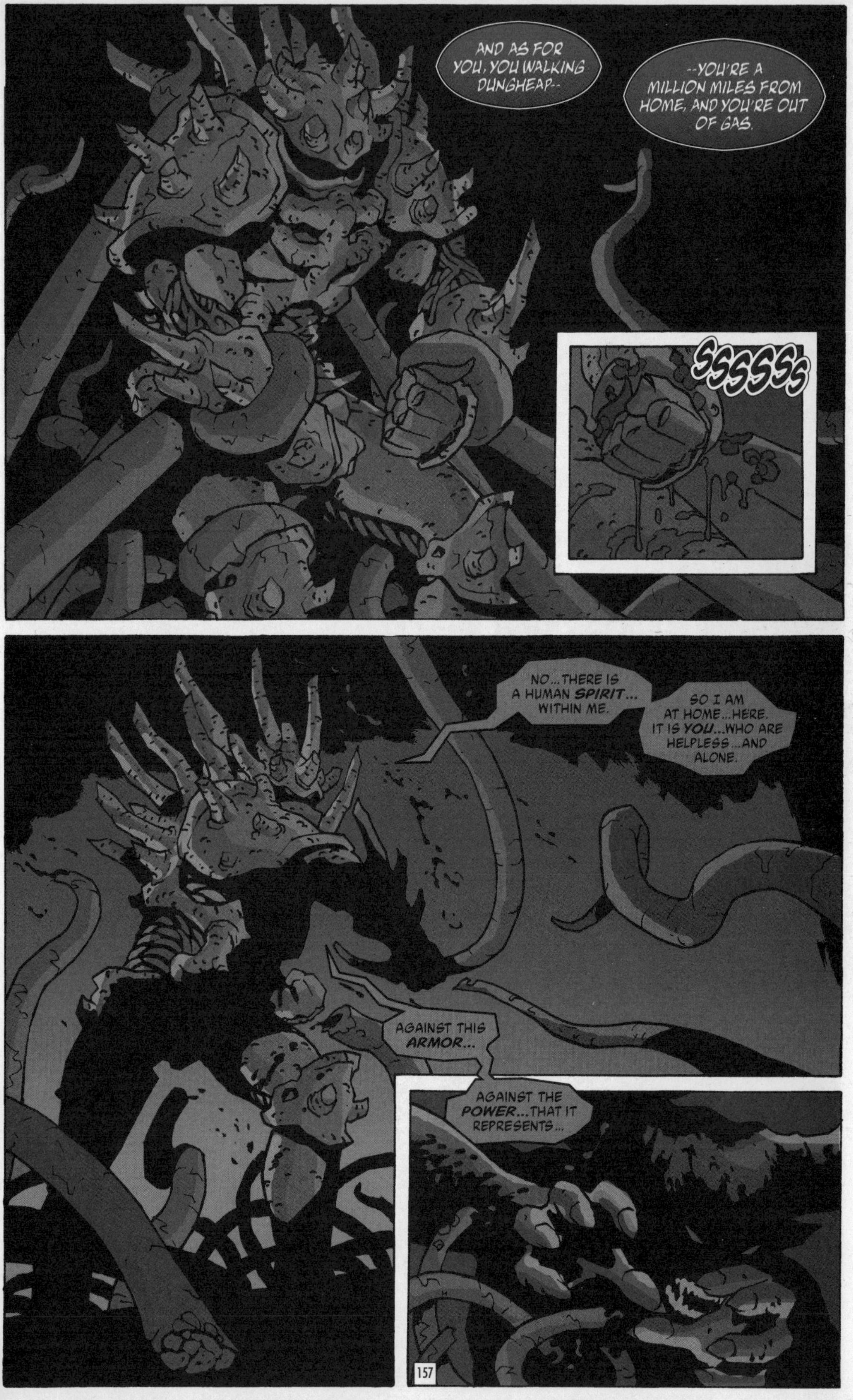
AND AS FOR YOU, YOU WALKING DUNGHEAP--
--YOU'RE A MILLION MILES FROM HOME, AND YOU'RE OUT OF GAS.
SSSSSs
NO...THERE IS A HUMAN SPIRIT... WITHIN ME.
SO I AM AT HOME...HERE. IT IS YOU...WHO ARE HELPLESS...AND ALONE.
AGAINST THIS ARMOR...
AGAINST THE POWER...THAT IT REPRESENTS...

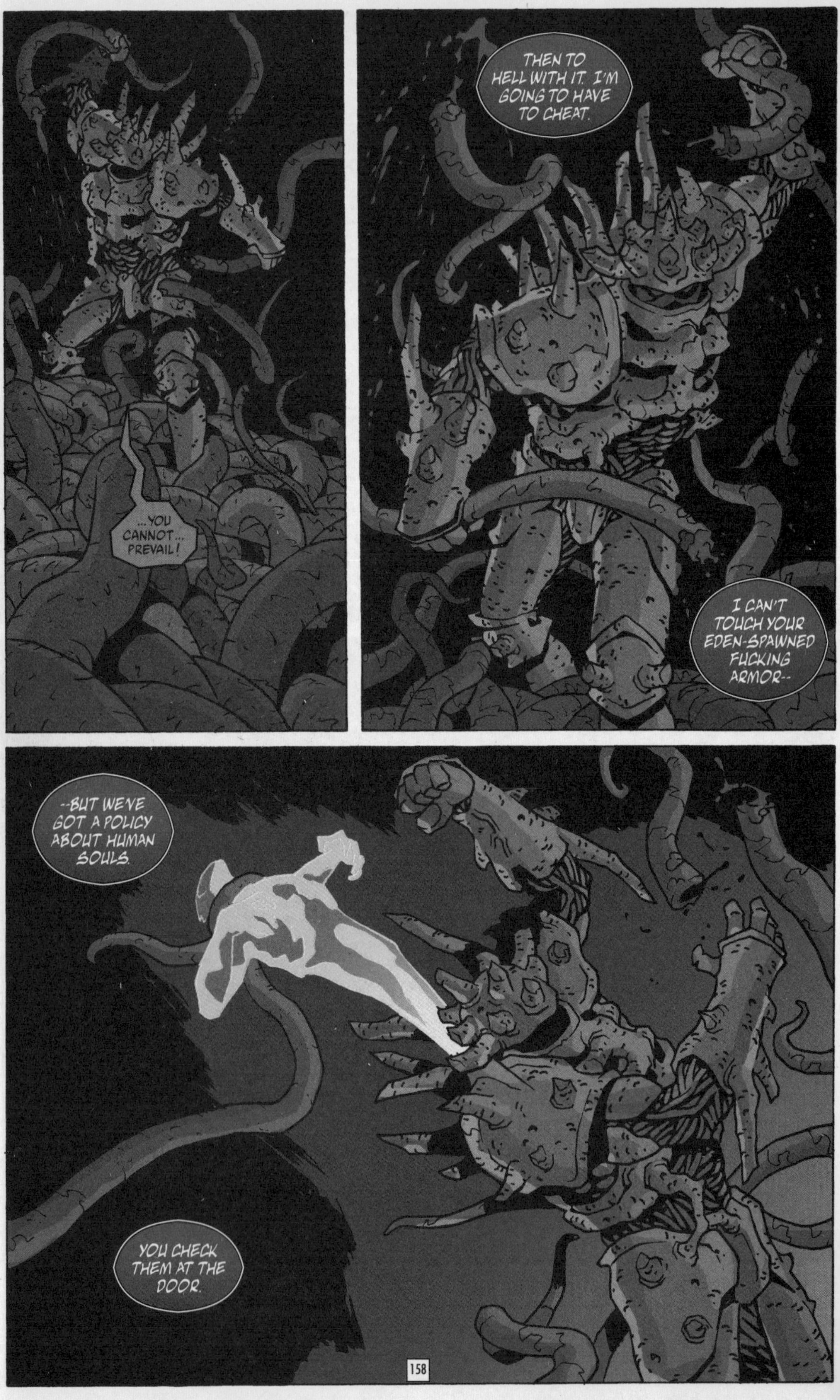
...YOU CANNOT... PREVAIL!
THEN TO HELL WITH IT. I'M GOING TO HAVE TO CHEAT.
I CAN'T TOUCH YOUR EDEN-SPAWNED FUCKING ARMOR--
--BUT WE'VE GOT A POLICY ABOUT HUMAN SOULS.
YOU CHECK THEM AT THE DOOR.

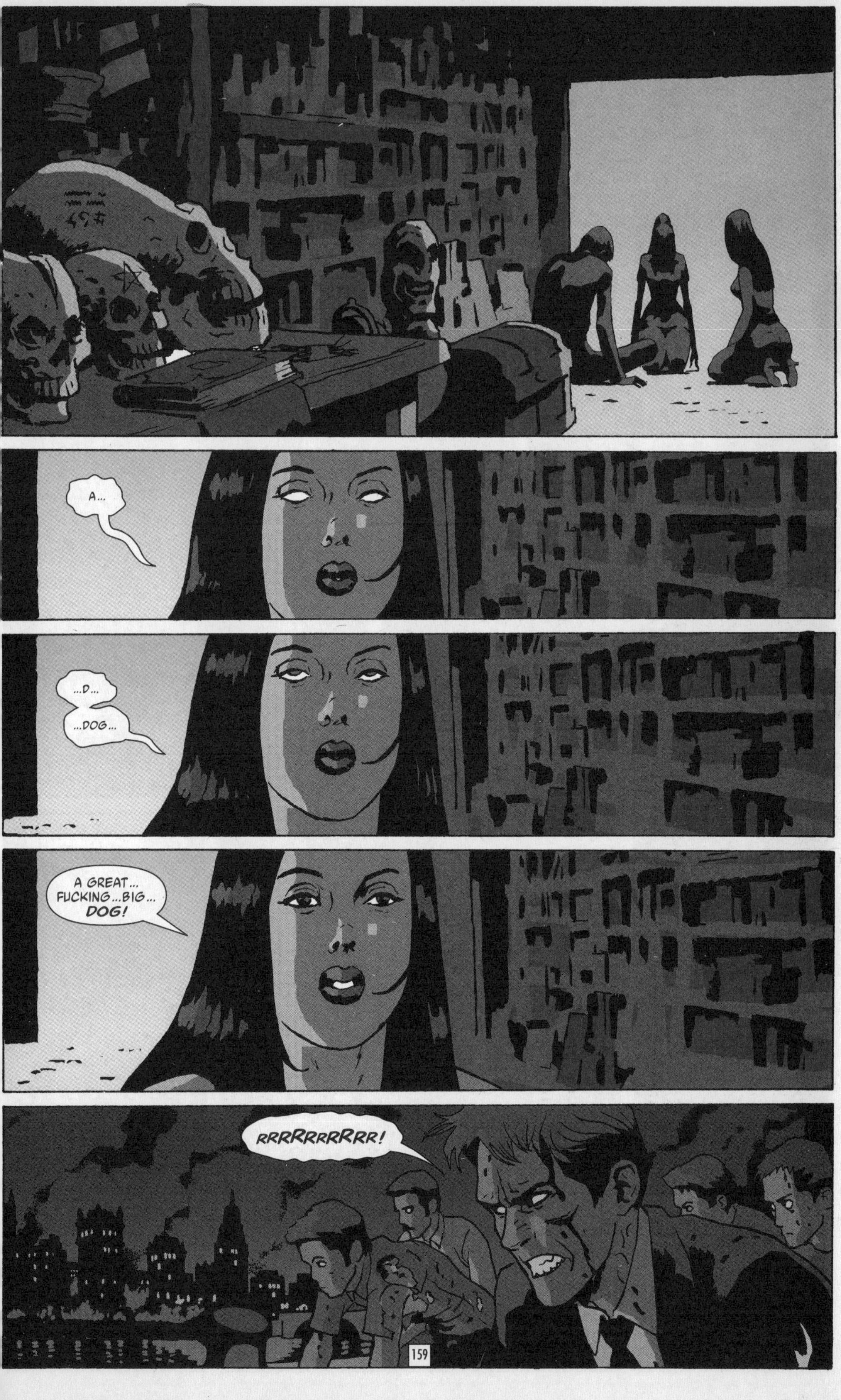

A...
...D...
...DOG...
A GREAT... FUCKING...BIG... DOG!
RRRRRRRRRR!

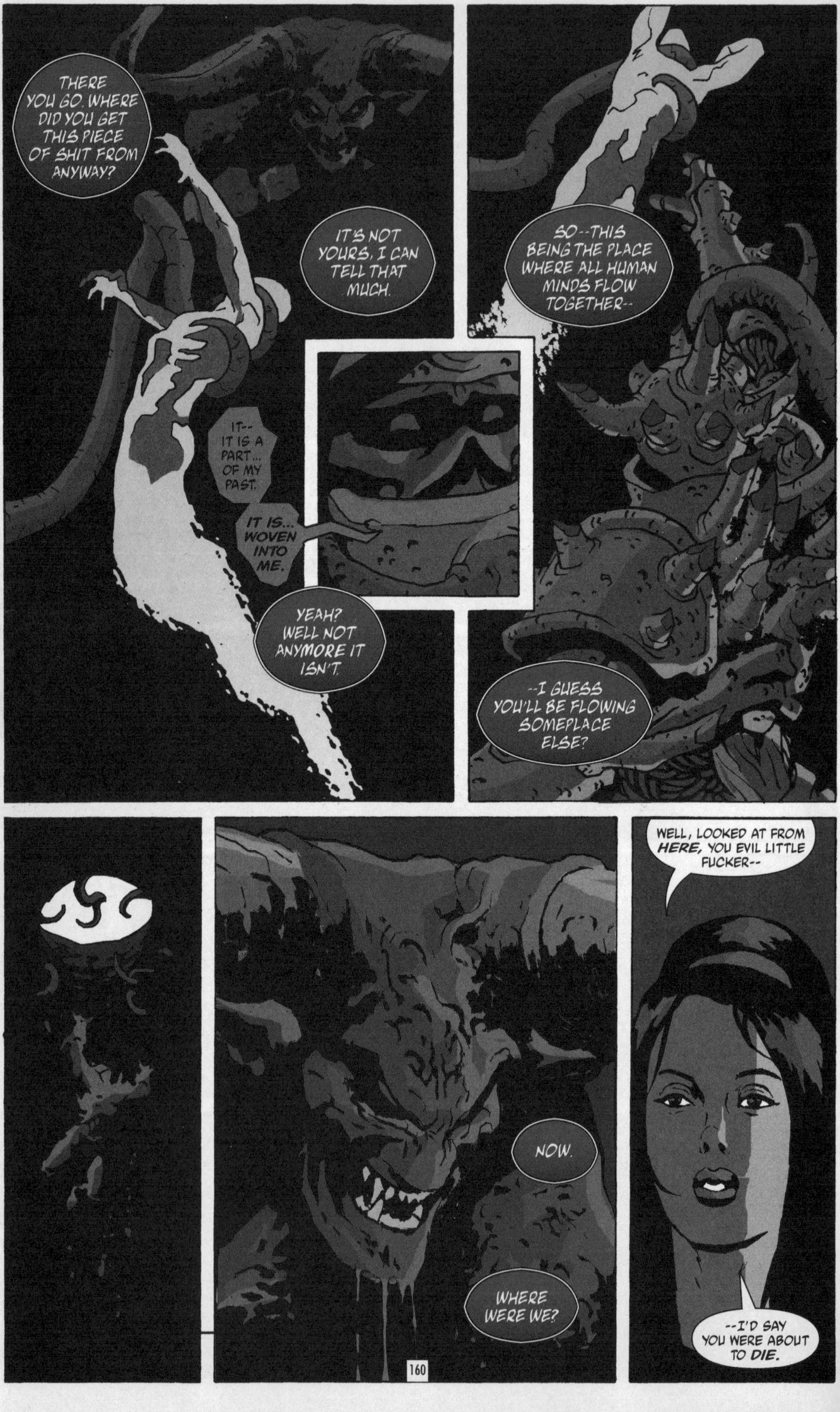
THERE YOU GO. WHERE DID YOU GET THIS PIECE OF SHIT FROM ANYWAY?
IT'S NOT YOURS, I CAN TELL THAT MUCH.
IT-- IT IS A PART... OF MY PAST.
IT IS... WOVEN INTO ME.
YEAH? WELL NOT ANYMORE IT ISN'T.
SO--THIS BEING THE PLACE WHERE ALL HUMAN MINDS FLOW TOGETHER--
--I GUESS YOU'LL BE FLOWING SOMEPLACE ELSE?
NOW.
WHERE WERE WE?
WELL, LOOKED AT FROM HERE, YOU EVIL LITTLE FUCKER--
--I'D SAY YOU WERE ABOUT TO DIE.

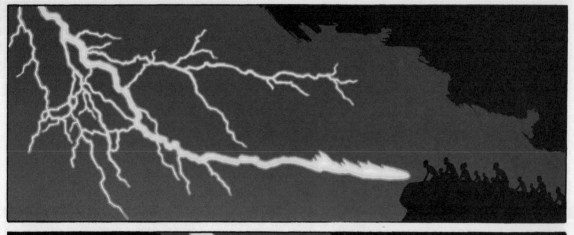

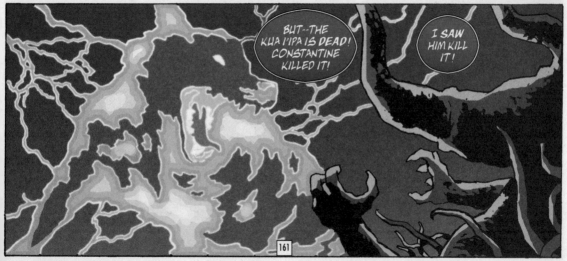

BUT--THE KUA I'IPA IS DEAD! CONSTANTINE KILLED IT!

I SAW HIM KILL IT!

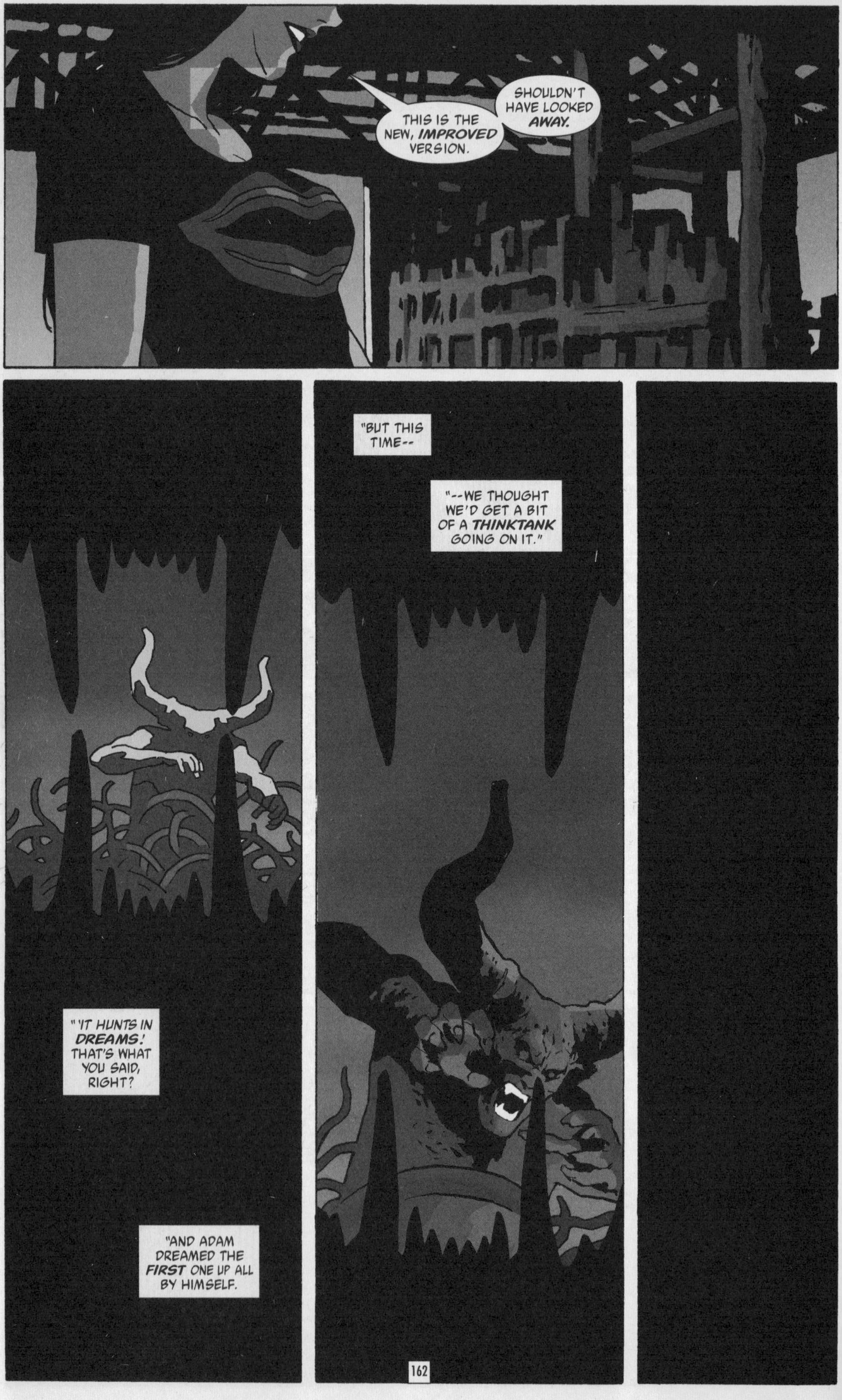
THIS IS THE NEW, IMPROVED VERSION.
SHOULDN'T HAVE LOOKED AWAY.
"'IT HUNTS IN DREAMS.' THAT'S WHAT YOU SAID, RIGHT?
"AND ADAM DREAMED THE FIRST ONE UP ALL BY HIMSELF.
"BUT THIS TIME--
"--WE THOUGHT WE'D GET A BIT OF A THINKTANK GOING ON IT."

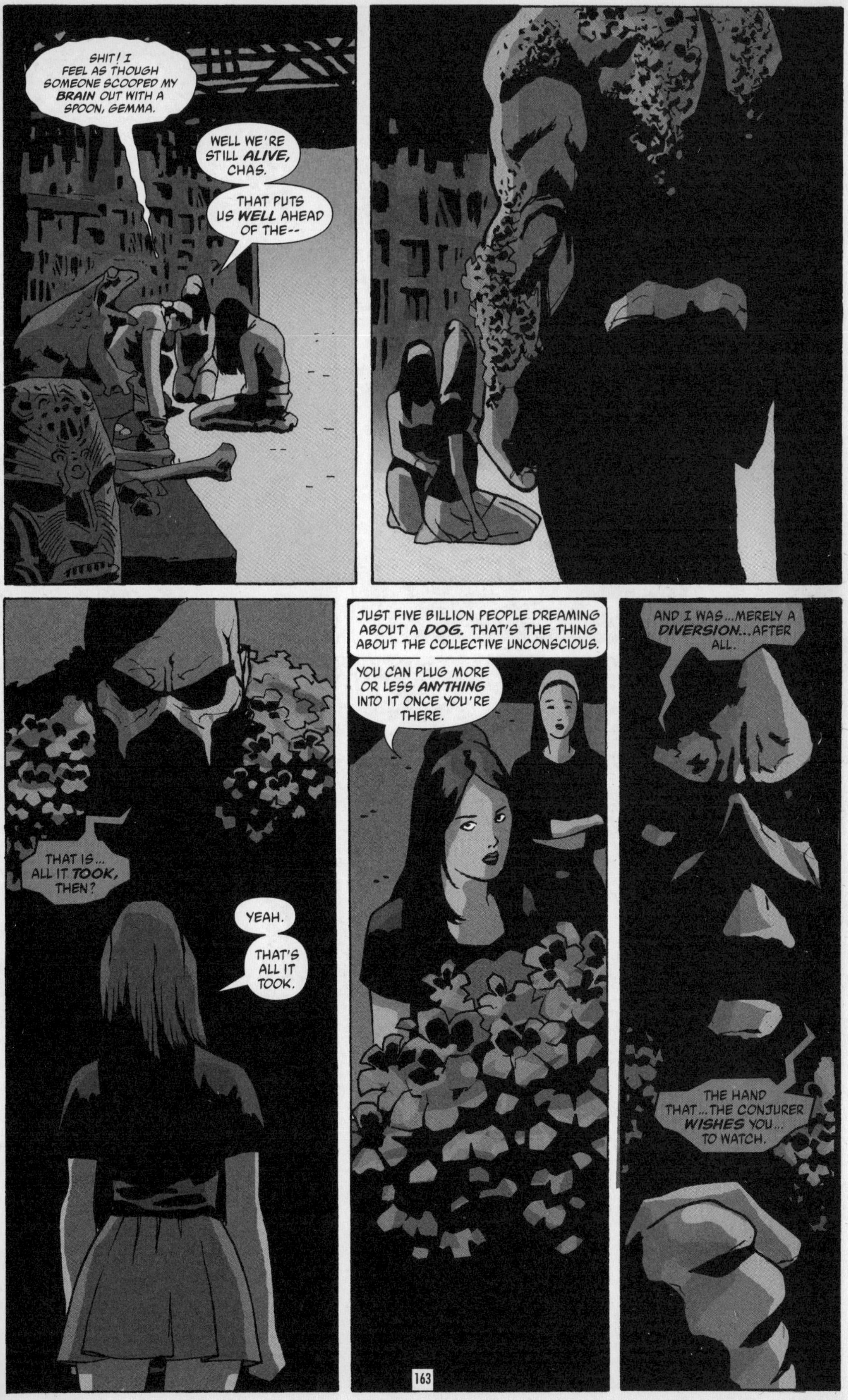

SHIT! I FEEL AS THOUGH SOMEONE SCOOPED MY **BRAIN** OUT WITH A SPOON, GEMMA.
WELL WE'RE STILL **ALIVE,** CHAS.
THAT PUTS US **WELL** AHEAD OF THE--
THAT IS... ALL IT **TOOK,** THEN?
YEAH.
THAT'S ALL IT TOOK.
JUST FIVE BILLION PEOPLE DREAMING ABOUT A **DOG.** THAT'S THE THING ABOUT THE COLLECTIVE UNCONSCIOUS.
YOU CAN PLUG MORE OR LESS **ANYTHING** INTO IT ONCE YOU'RE THERE.
AND I WAS...MERELY A **DIVERSION...** AFTER ALL.
THE HAND THAT...THE CONJURER **WISHES** YOU... TO WATCH.

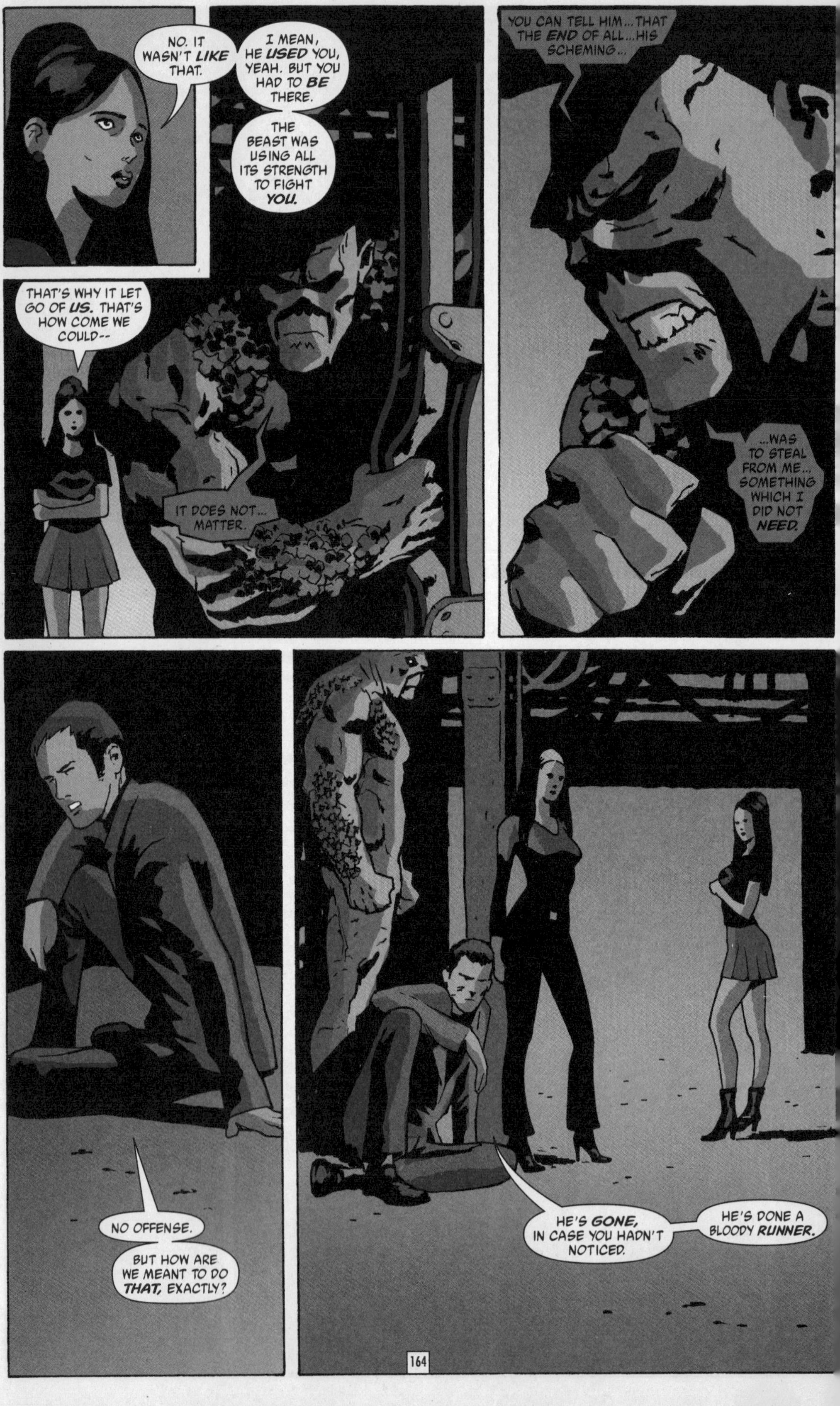
NO. IT WASN'T LIKE THAT.
I MEAN, HE USED YOU, YEAH. BUT YOU HAD TO BE THERE.
THE BEAST WAS USING ALL ITS STRENGTH TO FIGHT YOU.
YOU CAN TELL HIM...THAT THE END OF ALL...HIS SCHEMING...
THAT'S WHY IT LET GO OF US. THAT'S HOW COME WE COULD--
IT DOES NOT... MATTER.
...WAS TO STEAL FROM ME... SOMETHING WHICH I DID NOT NEED.
NO OFFENSE.
BUT HOW ARE WE MEANT TO DO THAT, EXACTLY?
HE'S GONE, IN CASE YOU HADN'T NOTICED.
HE'S DONE A BLOODY RUNNER.

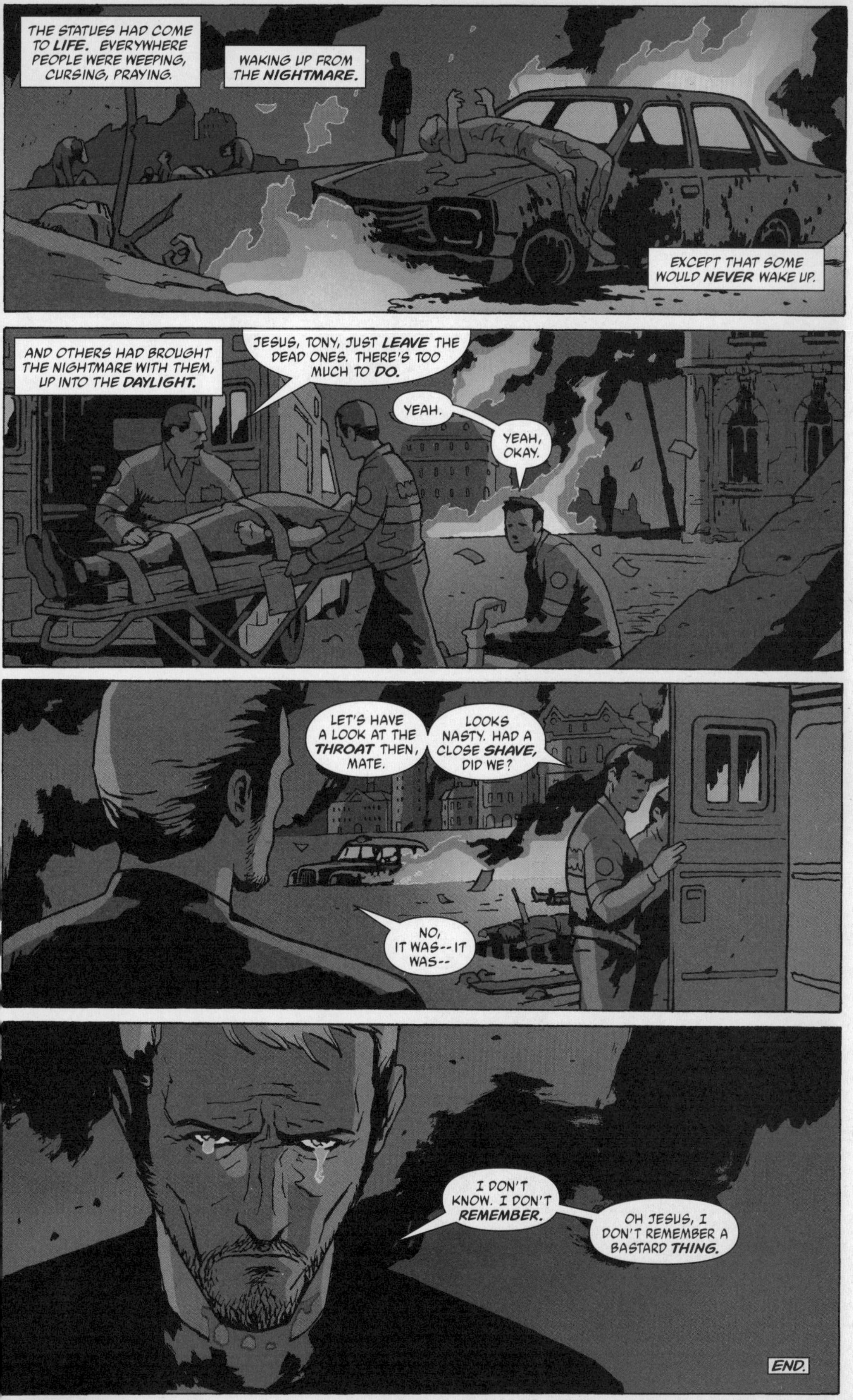
THE STATUES HAD COME TO LIFE. EVERYWHERE PEOPLE WERE WEEPING, CURSING, PRAYING.
WAKING UP FROM THE NIGHTMARE.
EXCEPT THAT SOME WOULD NEVER WAKE UP.
AND OTHERS HAD BROUGHT THE NIGHTMARE WITH THEM, UP INTO THE DAYLIGHT.
JESUS, TONY, JUST LEAVE THE DEAD ONES. THERE'S TOO MUCH TO DO.
YEAH.
YEAH, OKAY.
LET'S HAVE A LOOK AT THE THROAT THEN, MATE.
LOOKS NASTY. HAD A CLOSE SHAVE, DID WE?
NO, IT WAS-- IT WAS--
I DON'T KNOW. I DON'T REMEMBER.
OH JESUS, I DON'T REMEMBER A BASTARD THING.
END.

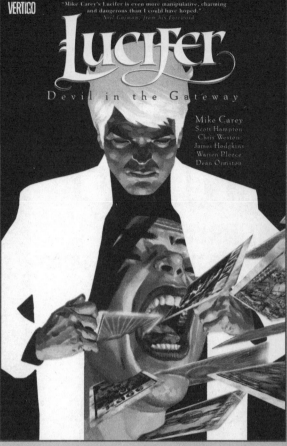

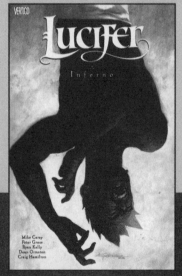

REIMAGINED BY REVOLUTIONARY COMICS WRITER ALAN MOORE, THIS CLASSIC GOTHIC NIGHTMARE BLOSSOMS INTO A MASTERPIECE OF LYRICAL FANTASY, TELLING THE HORRIFYING YET POIGNANT STORY OF A MAN REBORN AS THE LIVING AVATAR OF ALL THE GREEN LIFE ON EARTH.

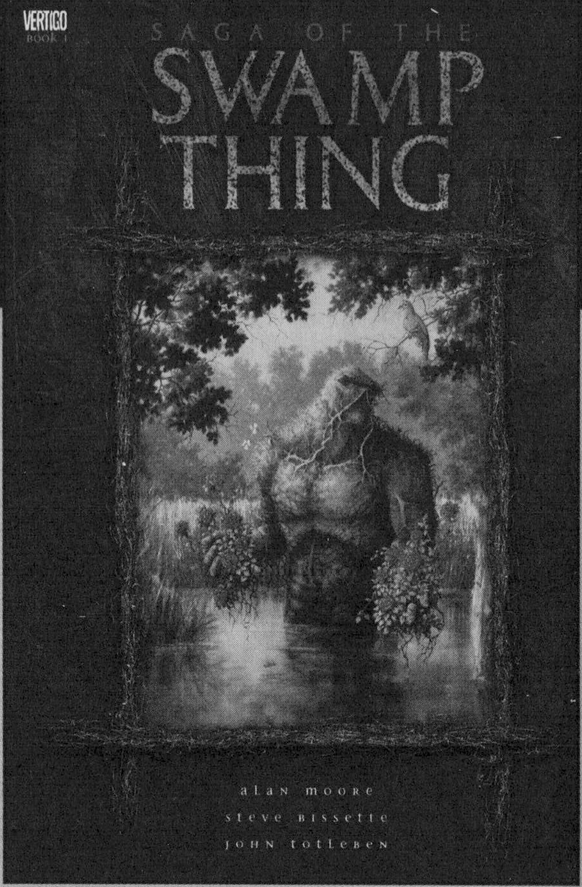
VERTIGO
BOOK 1
SAGA OF THE
SWAMP THING
alan moore
steve bissette
john totleben

SWAMP THING

VOLUME 1:
SAGA OF THE SWAMP THING

ALSO AVAILABLE:
VOL. 2: LOVE & DEATH
VOL. 3: THE CURSE
VOL. 4: A MURDER OF CROWS
VOL. 5: EARTH TO EARTH
VOL. 6: REUNION
VOL. 7: REGENESIS
VOL. 8: SPONTANEOUS GENERATION

SWAMP THING: DARK GENESIS
SWAMP THING: BAD SEED
SWAMP THING: LOVE IN VAIN
SWAMP THING: HEALING THE BREACH

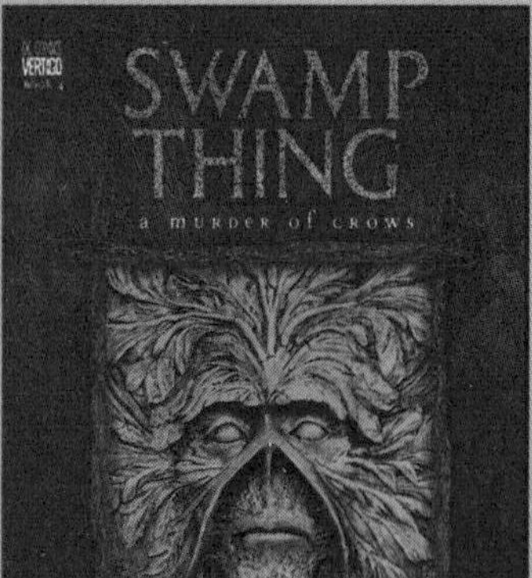
SWAMP THING
a murder of crows

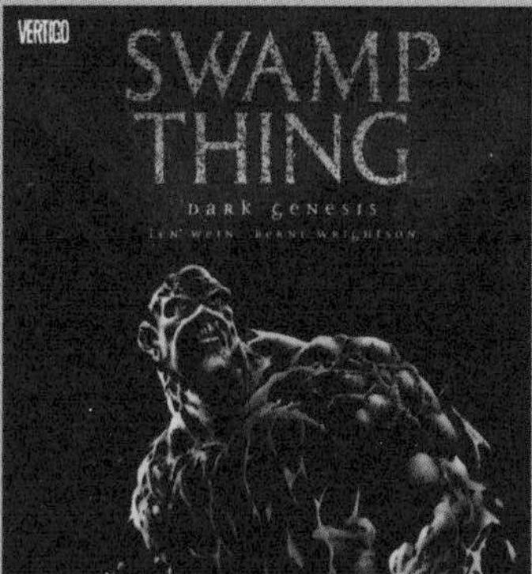
VERTIGO
SWAMP THING
dark genesis

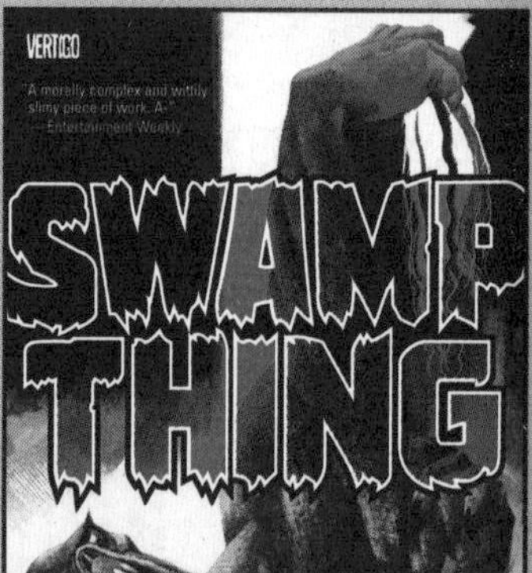
VERTIGO
"A morally complex and wittily slimy piece of work. A-" —Entertainment Weekly
SWAMP THING
BAD SEED
ANDY DIGGLE • ENRIQUE BRECCIA

ALL TITLES ARE SUGGESTED FOR MATURE READERS.

SEARCH THE GRAPHIC NOVELS SECTION OF
www.VERTIGOCOMICS.com
FOR ART AND INFORMATION ON ALL OF OUR BOOKS!